Environmental Economics and Policy

Environmental Economics and Policy is a best-selling text for environmental economics courses. Offering a policy-oriented approach, it introduces economic theory, empirical fieldwork, and case studies that show how underlying economic principles provided the foundation for environmental policies.

Key features include:

- Introductions to the theory and method of environmental economics, including externalities, benefit-cost analysis, valuation methods, and ecosystem goods and services.
- Extensive coverage of the major issues including climate change mitigation and adaptation, air and water pollution, and environmental justice.
- Boxed "Examples" and "Debates" throughout the text, which highlight global examples and major talking points.

This text will be of use to undergraduate students of economics. Students will leave the course with a global perspective of how environmental economics has played and can continue to play a role in promoting fair and efficient environmental management.

The text is fully supported with end-of-chapter summaries, discussion questions, and self-test exercises in the book. Additional online resources include references, as well as PowerPoint slides for each chapter.

Lynne Lewis is Elmer W. Campbell Professor of Economics at Bates College, Maine, USA.

Tom Tietenberg is the Mitchell Family Professor of Economics, Emeritus, at Colby College, Maine, USA.

"The authors transform masterfully the leading-edge of environmental economics research into language that is accessible, insightful, and relevant to a broad audience. The book is an essential resource for all undergraduate environmental economics and environmental policy courses."

Assistant Professor Jacob Hochard, Department of Economics, East Carolina University

"Lewis and Tietenberg provide a highly relevant and up-to-date economics-based framework for evaluating environmental problems and policy solutions. In examining the most critical environmental issues of the day, the authors embrace a wide range of disciplinary perspectives. This book is perfect for undergraduate economics students or graduate policy students."

Professor Sarah L. Stafford, Chair of the Department of Economics, William & Mary

Brief Contents

Contents

Figures

Tables

Preface

A glance at any newspaper will confirm that environmental economics is now a major player in environmental policy. Concepts such as cap-and-trade, renewable portfolio standards, block pricing, renewable energy credits, carbon trading, the commons, congestion pricing, corporate average fuel economy standards, strategic petroleum reserves, payments for ecosystem services, and sustainable development have moved from the textbook to the legislative hearing room. As the large number of current examples in *Environmental Economics and Policy* demonstrates, not only are ideas that were once restricted to academic discussions now part of the policy mix, but they are making a significant difference as well.

An overview of the book

Environmental Economics and Policy attempts to bring those who are beginning the study of environmental economics close to the frontiers of knowledge. Although the book is designed to be accessible to students who have completed a two-semester introductory course in economics or a one-semester introductory microeconomics course, it can be used in upper-level undergraduate courses as well as lower-level environmental studies, environmental management, or environmental policy graduate courses.

The structure and topical coverage of this book facilitates its use in a variety of contexts. For a survey course in environmental economics, all chapters are appropriate. This surplus material provides flexibility for the instructor to choose those topics that best fit his or her course design. In this book, we examine many of these newly popular market mechanisms within the context of both theory and practice. Environmental economics is a rapidly growing and changing field as many environmental issues become global in nature. In this text, we tackle some of the complex issues that face our globe and explore both the nature of the problems and how economics can provide potential solutions.

This book has a strong policy orientation. Although a great deal of theory and empirical evidence is discussed, their inclusion is motivated by the desire to increase understanding of intriguing market situations and policy problems. This explicit integration of research and policy within each chapter avoids a problem frequently encountered in applied economics textbooks – that is, in such texts the theory developed in earlier chapters is often only loosely connected to the rest of the book.

This is an economics book, but it goes beyond economics. Insights from the natural and physical sciences, literature, political science, and other disciplines are scattered liberally throughout the text. In some cases, these references raise outstanding issues that economic analysis can help resolve, while in other cases they affect the structure of the economic analysis or provide a contrasting point of view. They play an important role in overcoming the tendency to accept the material uncritically at a superficial level by highlighting those characteristics that make the economics approach unique.

Reflecting this new role of environmental economics in policy, a number of journals are now devoted either exclusively or mostly to the topics covered in this book. One journal, *Ecological Economics,* is dedicated to bringing economists and ecologists closer together in a common search for appropriate solutions for environmental challenges. Interested readers can also find advanced work in the field in *Land Economics*, *Journal of Environmental Economics and Management*, *Review of Environmental Economics and Policy*, *Environmental and Resource Economics*, *International Review of Environmental and National Resource Economics*, *Environment and Development Economics*, *Resource and Energy Economics*, and *Natural Resources Journal*, among others.

A discussion list that involves material covered by this book is ResEcon. It is an academically inclined list focusing on problems related to environmental management.

A very useful blog that deals with issues in environmental economics and their relationship to policy is located at www.env-econ.net.

Services on the Internet change so rapidly that some of this information may become obsolete. Please visit the online resources for this text at www.routledge.com/9781138587595 to find a reference document which contains all references cited in this book.

Acknowledgements

The most rewarding part of writing this book is that we have met so many thoughtful people. We very much appreciate the faculty and students who pointed out areas of particular strength or areas where coverage could be expanded. Their support has been gratifying and energizing. One can begin to understand the magnitude of our debt to our colleagues by glancing at the several hundred names in the lists of references. Because their research contributions make this an exciting field, full of insights worthy of being shared, our task was easier and a lot more fun than it might otherwise have been.

Working with Routledge has been a delightful experience. Our commissioning editor, Andy Humphries, has been continually helpful since the initiation of this edition. We would also like to acknowledge Kate Fornadel, project manager, as well as Dana Richards (copyeditor), Jac Nelson (indexer), Gareth Toye (cover designer). Thanks to you all!

Lynne's most helpful research assistant for this edition was Benjamin Skiest.

Working with all of the fine young scholars who have assisted with this text over the years has made it all the more obvious why teaching is the world's most satisfying profession.

Finally, Lynne would like to express her gratitude to Jack for his unwavering support, patience, and generosity. Tom would like to express publicly his deep appreciation to his wife, Gretchen, his daughter Heidi, and his son Eric for their love and support. Thank you.

Lynne Lewis
Tom Tietenberg

Section I

Economic analysis
Options and applications

Chapter 1

The role of economics in formulating and implementing policy

From the arch of the bridge to which his guide has carried him, Dante now sees the Diviners . . . coming slowly along the bottom of the fourth Chasm. By help of their incantations and evil agents, they had endeavored to pry into the future which belongs to the almighty alone, and now their faces are painfully twisted the contrary way; and being unable to look before them, they are forced to walk backwards.

– Dante Alighieri, *Divine Comedy: The Inferno*, translated by Carlyle (1867)

Introduction

As the scale of economic activity has proceeded steadily upward, the scope of environmental problems triggered by that activity has transcended both geographic and generational boundaries. Scientists now believe that environmental problems such as climate change, ozone depletion, water scarcity and the loss of biodiversity, to mention only a few, present significant future challenges to our institutions.

Our market system is one of those institutions. In some ways the market system is remarkably resilient in how it responds to challenges. Prices react to scarcity, for example. These reactions provide incentives not only for the wise use of current resources but also for promoting innovations that can broaden the menu of future options.

Yet, as we shall also see, market outcomes may not always be consistent with effectively managing these challenges; even worse they may actually intensify them. The key, of course, is to be able to discern the circumstances that give rise to the desirable outcome from the circumstances that give rise to intensifying the threats.

The role of economics

How this generation and those that follow respond to these environmental challenges will depend largely on the behavior of humans acting individually or collectively. Economic analysis provides an incredibly useful set of tools for anyone interested in understanding the role of human behavior, particularly in the face of challenges such as these. In many cases, this analysis identifies the sources of the market system's resilience. In others, it provides a basis not only for identifying the circumstances where markets fail, but also for clarifying how and why that specific set of circumstances supports degradation. This understanding can then be used as the basis for complementary policies that restore a sense of harmony in the relationship between the economy and the environment for those cases where the market would fall short.

Over the years, two different, but related, economic approaches have been devised to address the challenges the future holds. Debate 1.1 explores the similarities and the differences of ecological economics and environmental economics and what they both can bring to the table.

DEBATE 1.1

Ecological economics versus environmental economics

Over several decades or so, the community of scholars dealing with the role of the economy and the environment has settled into two camps: ecological economics (www.isecoeco.org/) and environmental economics (www.aere.org/ or www.eaere.org/). Although they share many similarities, ecological economics is consciously more methodologically pluralist, whereas environmental economics is based solidly on the standard paradigm of neoclassical economics. While neoclassical economics emphasizes maximizing human welfare and using economic incentives to modify destructive human behavior, ecological economics uses a variety of methodologies, including neoclassical economics, depending upon the purpose of the investigation.

While some observers see the two approaches as competitive (presenting an "either–or" choice), others, including the authors of this text, see them as complementary. Complementarity, of course, does not mean full acceptance. Significant differences exist not only between these two fields, but also within them over such topics as the valuation of environmental resources, the impact of trade on the environment, and the appropriate means for evaluating policy strategies for long-duration problems such as climate change. These differences arise not only over methodologies but also over the values that are brought to bear on the analysis.

This book draws from both fields. Although the basic foundation for the analysis is environmental economics, the chapters draw heavily from ecological economics to critique that view when it is controversial and to complement it with useful insights drawn from outside the neoclassical paradigm, when appropriate. Pragmatism is the reigning criterion. If a particular approach or study helps us to understand environmental problems and their resolution, it has been included in the text regardless of which field it came from.

The use of models

All of the topics covered in this book will be examined as part of the general focus on satisfying human wants and needs in light of limited environmental and natural resources. Because this subject is complex, it is better understood when broken into manageable portions. Once we master the components in individual chapters, we will be able to coalesce the individual insights into a more complete picture in the concluding chapter.

In economics, as in most other disciplines, we use models to investigate complex subjects such as relationships between the economy and the environment. Models are simplified characterizations of reality. Consider a familiar analog. Maps, by design, leave out much detail. They are, nonetheless, useful guides to reality. By showing how various locations relate to each other, maps give an overall perspective. Although they cannot capture all of the unique details that characterize particular locations, maps highlight those characteristics that are crucial for the purpose at hand.

The models in this text are similar. Through simplification, less detail is considered so that the main concepts and the relationships among them become more obvious.

Fortunately, models allow us to study rigorously issues that are interrelated and global in scale. Unfortunately, due to their selectivity, models may yield conclusions that are dead wrong. Details that are omitted may turn out, in retrospect, to be crucial in understanding a particular dimension. Therefore, models are useful abstractions, but the conclusions they yield depend on the structure of the model. As you shall see as you proceed though this book, change that structure and you are likely to change the conclusions. As a result, as a guide to real outcomes models should always be viewed with some caution, but also welcomed for the insights they provide that might be overlooked if the models were not part of the investigation process.

Most people's views of the world are based on models, although frequently the assumptions and relationships involved may be implicit, perhaps even subconscious. In economic theory, the models are explicit; objectives, relationships, and assumptions are clearly specified so that the reader understands exactly how the conclusions are derived. The models are transparent.

The validity and reliability of economic models are tested by examining the degree to which they can explain actual behavior in markets or other settings. An empirical field known as *econometrics* uses statistical techniques, primarily regression analysis, to derive key economic functions. These data-derived functions, such as cost curves or demand functions, can then be used for such diverse purposes as testing hypotheses about the effects of various water policies or forecasting future prices of solar panels.

Examining human behavior in a non-laboratory setting, however, poses special challenges because it is nearly impossible to control completely for all the various factors that influence an outcome beyond those of primary interest. The search for more control over the circumstances that provide the data we use to understand human behavior has given rise to the use of another complementary analytical approach – *experimental economics* (see Example 1.1). Together, econometrics and experimental economics can provide different lenses to help us understand human behavior and its impact on the world around us.

EXAMPLE 1.1

Experimental economics: studying human behavior in a laboratory

The appeal of experimental economics is based upon its ability to study human behavior in a more controlled setting. During the mid-twentieth century economists began to design controlled laboratory experiments with human subjects. The experimental designs mimic decision situations in a variety of settings. Paid participants are informed of the rules of the experiment and asked to make choices. By varying the treatments faced by participants in these controlled settings experimenters can study how the treatments affect both choices and collective outcomes.

Consider one policy example of how these methods have been used in resource policy. (Cummings et al., 2004). In April 2000, the Georgia legislature passed The Flint River Drought Protection Act, which required the state to hold an auction in drought years to pay some farmers to suspend irrigation. The purpose was to use a market mechanism to identify those farmers who could forego irrigation at the lowest cost and to fairly compensate them for their reduction in water use. With time running short to implement this act, state policy makers relied upon laboratory experiments designed by a team of economists that used local farmers as participants. The results were used to inform the process of choosing the specific auction design that was used to fulfill the requirements of this act.

To the extent that the results of experiments have proved to be replicable, they have created a deeper understanding about the effectiveness of markets, policies, and institutions. The large and growing literature on experimental economics has already shed light on such widely divergent topics as the effectiveness of alternative policies for controlling pollution and allocating water, how uncertainty affects choices, and how the nature of cooperative agreements affects the sustainability of shared natural resources.

While experiments have the advantage of being able to control the decision-making environment, the artificiality of the laboratory setting raises questions about the degree to which the results from laboratories can shed light on actual human behavior outside the lab. While the degree of artificiality can be controlled by careful research design, it cannot be completely eliminated. Over the years, however, this approach has provided valuable information that can complement what we have learned from observed behavior using econometrics.

Sources: Cummings, R. G., & Taylor, L. O. (2001/2002). Experimental economics in natural resource and environmental management. In H. Folmer and T. Tietenberg (Eds.), The *International Yearbook of Environmental and Natural Resource Economics*. Cheltenham, U.K.: Edward Elgar, 123–149; Smith, V. L. (1998). Experimental methods in economics. In J. Eatwell, M. Murray, & P. Newman (Eds.), *The New Palgrave Dictionary of Economics, Volume 2*. London: The Macmillan Press, 241–249; Cummings, Ronald G., Holt, Charles A., & Laury, Susan K. (2004). Using laboratory experiments for policymaking: An example from the Georgia irrigation reduction auction. *Journal of Policy Analysis and Management*, 23(2), 341–363.

Historically economic analysis has relied on models based upon the assumption that humans are rational, meaning that they fully understand the details of the choices they face and they make choices by maximizing the benefits they would receive from their choice. This maximization might take the form of profit-maximization for businesses or utility maximization for individuals.

In 1955 the Nobel Memorial Prize in Economic Sciences went to Prof. Herbert Simon. One of the major aspects of his work was the concept of "bounded rationality." This concept recognized that human rationality was in fact bounded in practice in the sense that many decisions we make are so complex and involve so many factors that it is reasonable in many circumstances for us to use rules of thumb (or heuristics) rather than full optimization to make our decisions.

Subsequently a psychologist, Daniel Kahneman, working with another psychologist Amos Tversky, began exploring and explaining the heuristics that humans actually use make economic decisions in practice. Their work found that humans did indeed frequently use heuristics in decision making and that the resulting decisions did not always maximize outcomes for them. The insights emerging from this research, as well as the subsequent research it spawned, have created an entire new subfield in economics, now known as *behavioral economics*.

This subfield has had a profound impact on environmental economics as well as other branches of economics. Behavioral economics has provided a deeper understanding of the cognitive mechanisms at the core of individual decision making. This deeper understanding can pave (and has paved) the way for more effective design, implementation and evaluation of policies to improve environmental management. A report[1] by the Organization of Economic Cooperation and Development (OECD) found that these behavioral insights have been successfully applied to a wide array of environmental management challenges: energy, water and food consumption, transport, waste management, compliance with environmental regulation and participation in voluntary schemes.

The road ahead

Not only does environmental economics provide a firm basis for understanding the behavioral sources of environmental problems, but it also provides a firm foundation for crafting specific solutions to those problems. In subsequent chapters, for example, you will be exposed to how economic analysis can be (and has been) used to forge solutions to such diverse areas as climate change, biodiversity loss, and water scarcity. Many of the solutions arising from this analysis are quite novel.

In the following chapters you will study the rich and rewarding field of environmental economics in the context of what it can add to the search for ways of improving environmental policy. The menu of topics is broad and varied. Economics provides a powerful analytical framework for examining the relationships between the environment, on one hand, and the economic and political systems, on the other. The study of economics can assist in identifying circumstances that give rise to environmental problems, in discovering causes of these problems, and in devising solutions.

In Chapter 2 we lay the groundwork by identifying the most important sources of market failure in the relationship between the environment and the economy. We start by defining and explaining the criteria for determining failure (cost-effectiveness and efficiency) and using these criteria to identify the specific circumstances that give rise to these failures and how these circumstances give rise to the challenges that face us.

In Chapter 3 we show how the information in Chapter 2 can be used to design economic policy instruments to correct the failures. These instruments tend to have some unique, desirable characteristics that in many circumstances make them an attractive component of an environmental policy mix. They are, for example, commonly the most cost-effective policy options. Additionally many of these instruments collect revenue while addressing the challenge. This revenue can be used to make sure the policies are fair, and/or to increase the political likelihood that these policies can be enacted into law.

Chapter 4 considers the range of economic decision-making metrics that guide governmental policy choices and Chapter 5 discusses how key inputs to these metrics are monetized via the relatively new field of environmental valuation. This approach is used in government decision making in such widely diverse fields as calculating the court-imposed monetary damages owed by a company responsible for an oil spill that ruined a marine ecosystem to designating critical habitat under the Endangered Species Act.

Chapters 6–14 apply these techniques to specific areas of environmental management and policy. Chapter 6 focuses specifically on how ecosystems and the services they provide to humans can be protected. Chapter 7 tackles the especially difficult problem of managing commercially valuable ecosystems such as fisheries. Chapters 8–11 tackle one of the main challenges we shall face over the next decades – climate change.

Chapter 8 sets the stage by characterizing the state of the climate science as it defines the nature of the challenges we face and our understanding of the economic aspects of such fundamental questions as how much action should we be taking now? What is the best ways to manage the challenges given the uncertainty associated with forecasting both the timing and intensity of possible future outcomes? Chapter 9 goes into some detail about one major component of managing climate challenges – energy policy. Chapter 10 deals examines both the potential and the current experience with the main complementary emissions reduction approach currently being used in climate policy – carbon pricing. Chapter 11 considers the role of adaptation as both a complement to and substitute for the two approaches discussed in the two previous chapters.

Chapters 12–14 cover, respectively transportation policy and both the congestion and air pollution problems associated with this sector, managing water quality and quantity and the management of toxic substances and hazardous waste in an environmentally just way.

Chapter 15 looks back to draw upon some the key insights flowing from the individual chapters to integrate them into an overarching view of the existing and potential future role for economics in helping to craft effective responses to the challenges we face.

Market forces are extremely powerful. Attempts to solve environmental problems that ignore these forces run a high risk of failure. Where normal market forces are compatible with efficient and sustainable outcomes, those outcomes can be supported and reinforced. Where normal market forces prove inefficient and/or unsustainable, they can be channeled into new directions that restore compatibility between outcomes and objectives. Environmental economics provides a specific set of directions for how this compatibility between goals and outcomes can be achieved.

The overarching questions

In the search for ways of managing these threats we naturally turn to the main institutions we have for responding – the market and the government. It will probably not come as a surprise that in these times of political fragmentation the politics of defining an implementing an effective harmonization of these two approaches has become increasingly complicated.

The political right sees the market as our main or even only ally in creating solutions, while the government is viewed as an unreliable potential ally at best and as an institution that could intensify damages at worst. In this camp the market is seen as more flexible and better able to respond quickly than a government. Further governments are seen as slowing down innovation and frequently revealing inept administration, resulting in choices that not only cost more than necessary, but also ultimately may not stand the test of time.

The political left on the other hand is generally suspicious of the market and many times prefers to replace market decisions with government decisions. For example, they see the production flowing from the market as a crucial source of the pollution and see explicit market choices as unnecessarily intensifying the rise of these emissions. Democratic governments, however, are seen by the left as having both the power and the will to not only specify the desired outcomes but also to mandate the paths for reaching them in an efficient and equitable manner.

In reality managing these environmental threats is not likely to be an either-or choice. Management strategies are likely to involve some combination of market and government decisions. What does the evidence say about the possibilities?

In the chapters that follow we will examine the possibilities though the lenses of economic theory, empirical research, and close observation of the successes and failures of programs inspired by economics that are already being tried around the world. This examination will include some guiding questions:

- What does the theory and evidence suggest about the most promising respective roles for government and market? Could the market manage these threats on its own? Why or why not? Could the government manage these threats on its own? Why or why not?
- What are potentially promising avenues for the government to work with market in jointly meeting these challenges? What, for example, is the case for market-based policy instruments in government choices? What specific roles are appropriate for the executive, legislative, and judicial branches of government?
- Many environmental problems are characterized by a considerable degree of uncertainty about the severity of the problem and the relative effectiveness of potential solutions. Can our economic and political institutions respond to this uncertainty in reasonable ways or does uncertainty become a paralyzing force?
- Can the economic and political systems work together to eradicate poverty and social injustice while meeting the environmental challenges we face? Or does meeting those challenges inevitably conflict with the desire to treat all people, especially the most vulnerable, with fairness? Can short- and long-term goals be harmonized?
- Many early programs are underway to meet these environmental challenges. What can be learned from these about what is working and what is not working as well as the circumstances that gave rise to each of these outcomes?

The rest of this book uses economic analysis and evidence to suggest answers to these complex questions.

Discussion questions

1 In his book *The Ultimate Resource*, economist Julian Simon makes the point that calling the resource base "finite" is misleading. To illustrate this point, he uses a yardstick, with its one-inch markings, as an analogy. The distance between two markings is finite – one inch – but an infinite number of points is contained within that finite space. Therefore, in one sense, what lies between the markings is finite, while in another, equally meaningful sense, it is infinite. Is the concept of a finite resource base useful or not? Why or why not?

2 How compelling do you find the evidence on impending environmental challenges we face? Which evidence do you find the most compelling? Least compelling?

3 In his book *Thank you for Being Late: An Optimist's Guide to Thriving in the Age of Accelerations,* Thomas L. Friedman documents how the digital revolution is fundamentally changing life as we have known it. How do you think it will change the relationship between humans and the environment? Is this likely to be a force for renewed harmony or intensified disruption? Why? Do you have any specific examples to share that illustrate one outcome or the other?

Self-test exercise

1 Does the normal reaction of the price system to a resource shortage intensify the problem or alleviate it? Why?

Note

1 OECD. (2017). *Tackling Environmental Problems with the Help of Behavioural Insights*. Paris: OECD Publishing. https://doi.org/10.1787/9789264273887-en. See www.globalchange.gov/climate-change

Further reading

Batabyal, A. A., & Nijkamp, P. (2011). Introduction to research tools in natural resource and environmental economics. In A. A. Batabyal & P. Nijkamp (Eds.), *Research Tools in Natural Resource and Environmental Economics*. Hackensack, NJ: World Scientific Publishing, 3–26. An introduction to the most frequently used theoretical, empirical, experimental, and interdisciplinary research tools in natural resource and environmental economics.

Carlsson, F., & Johansson-Stenman, O. (2012). Behavioral economics and environmental policy. *Annual Review of Resource Economics*, 4, 75–99. A survey that concludes that behavioral economics has a lot to offer environmental economics. In particular it concludes some normative policy recommendations have to be modified, but the most fundamental policy recommendations in environmental economics generally prevail and are sometimes even reinforced through behavioral economics insights.

Delbeke, J., Klaassen, G., van Ierland, T., & Zapfel, P. (2009). The role of environmental economics in recent policy making at the European Commission. *Review of Environmental Economics and Policy*, 4, 24–43. This article examines how environmental economics has been used at the European Commission in climate change, energy, and air pollution policy.

Managi, S. (Ed.). (2015). *The Routledge Handbook of Environmental Economics in Asia*. New York: Routledge. An edited collection of essays that illustrates how the principles and methods of environmental economics can be applied to specific environmental and natural resource issues in Asia.

Noussair, C. N., & van Soest, D. P. (2014). Economic experiments and environmental policy. *Annual Review of Resource Economics*, 6, 319–337. This survey reviews the literature addressing whether government intervention is always necessary to protect the environment and whether it is always effective in doing so, and discusses the use of experimental laboratories to test market-based approaches to environmental policy.

Spash, C. (2017). *The Routledge Handbook of Ecological Economics*. New York: Routledge. Edited by a leading figure in the field, this handbook provides a current guide to the literature on ecological economics in an informative and easily accessible form.

Stavins, R. N. (Ed.). (2019). *Economics of the Environment: Selected Readings*, 7th ed. Cheltenham, UK: Edward Elgar Publishing Ltd. A compendium of significant articles in environmental economics, together with an original introductory chapter by the highly respected editor.

Additional references and other historically significant references are available on this book's eResource page: www.routledge.com/9781138587595

Chapter 2

The economic approach

Property rights, externalities, and environmental problems

> The charming landscape which I saw this morning, is indubitably made up of some twenty or thirty farms. Miller owns this field, Locke that, and Manning the woodland beyond. But none of them owns the landscape. There is a property in the horizon which no man has but he whose eye can integrate all the parts, that is, the poet. This is the best part of these men's farms, yet to this their land deeds give them no title.
>
> – Ralph Waldo Emerson, *Nature* (1836)

Introduction

Before examining specific environmental problems and the policy responses to them, it is important that we develop and clarify the economic approach, so that we have some sense of the forest before examining each of the trees. By having a feel for the conceptual framework, it becomes easier not only to deal with individual cases but also, perhaps more importantly, to see how they fit into a comprehensive approach.

In this chapter, we develop the general conceptual framework used in economics to approach environmental problems. We begin by examining the relationship between human actions, as manifested through the economic system, and the environmental consequences of those actions. We can then establish criteria for judging the desirability of the outcomes of this relationship. These criteria provide a basis for identifying the nature and severity of environmental problems, and a foundation for designing effective policies to deal with them.

Throughout this chapter, the economic point of view is contrasted with alternative points of view. These contrasts bring the economic approach into sharper focus and stimulate deeper and more critical thinking about all possible approaches.

The economic approach

Two different types of economic analysis can be applied to increase our understanding of the relationship between the economic system and the environment: *Positive* economics attempts to describe *what is, what was,* or *what will be. Normative* economics, by contrast, deals with what *ought to be.* Disagreements within positive economics can usually be resolved by an appeal to the facts. Normative disagreements, however, involve value judgments.

Both branches are useful. Suppose, for example, we want to investigate the relationship between trade and the environment. Positive economics could be used to describe the kinds of impacts trade would have on the economy and the environment. It could not, however, provide any guidance on the question of whether trade was desirable. That judgment would have to come from normative economics, a topic we explore in the next section.

The fact that positive analysis does not, by itself, determine the desirability of some policy action does not mean that it is not useful in the policy process. Example 2.1 provides one example of the kinds of economic impact analyses that are used in the policy process.

EXAMPLE 2.1

Economic impacts of reducing hazardous pollutant emissions from iron and steel foundries

The U.S. Environmental Protection Agency (EPA) was tasked with developing a "maximum achievable control technology standard" to reduce emissions of hazardous air pollutants from iron and steel foundries. As part of the rule-making process, the EPA conducted an *ex ante* economic impact analysis to assess the potential economic impacts of the proposed rule.

If implemented, the rule would require some iron and steel foundries to implement pollution control methods that would increase the production costs at affected facilities. One interesting question addressed by the analysis is how large those impacts would be.

The impact analysis estimated annual costs for existing sources to be $21.73 million. These cost increases were projected to result in small increases in output prices. Specifically, prices were projected to increase by only 0.1 percent for iron castings and 0.05 percent for steel castings. The impacts of these price increases were expected to be experienced largely by iron foundries using cupola furnaces as well as consumers of iron foundry products. Unaffected domestic foundries and foreign producers of coke were actually projected to earn slightly higher profits as a result of the rule.

This analysis helped in two ways. First, by showing that the impacts fell under the $100 million threshold that mandates review by the Office of Management and Budget, the analysis eliminated the need for a much more time- and resource-consuming analysis. Second, showing how small the expected impacts would be served to lower the opposition that might have arisen from unfounded fears of much more severe impacts.

Sources: Office of Air Quality Planning and Standards, United States Environmental Protection Agency; (November 2002). *Economic Impact Analysis of Proposed Iron and Steel Foundries*. NESHAP; Final Report. National Emissions Standards for Hazardous Air Pollutants for Iron and Steel Foundries; (April 17, 2007). Proposed Rule. *Federal Register,* 72(73), 19150–19164.

One context for this analysis arises when the policy question involves simply comparing one defined policy option to another. For example should a specific set of congestion charges be imposed on all vehicles entering New York City during periods when the roadways are congested?

A rather different context for normative economics can arise when the possibilities are more open-ended. For example, we might ask, to what degree should we control emissions of greenhouse gases (which contribute to climate change) and how fast should we increase the degree of control? Or we might ask, how much forest of various types should be preserved rather than harvested? Answering these questions requires us to consider the entire range of possible outcomes and to select the best or optimal one. Although that is a much more difficult question to answer than one that asks us only to compare two predefined alternatives, the basic normative analysis framework is the same in both cases.

Environmental problems and economic efficiency

Static efficiency

The chief normative economic criterion for choosing among various outcomes occurring at the same point in time is called *static efficiency*, or merely *efficiency*. An allocation of resources is said to satisfy the static efficiency criterion if the economic surplus derived from those resources is maximized by that allocation. Economic surplus, in turn, is the sum of consumer's surplus and producer's surplus. This is equivalent to maximizing the net benefits (benefits minus costs) from possible allocations of these resources.

Consumer surplus is the value that consumers receive from an allocation minus what it costs them to obtain it. Consumer surplus is measured as the area under the demand curve minus the consumer's cost. This is the shaded triangle in Figure 2.1. The cost to the consumer is the area under

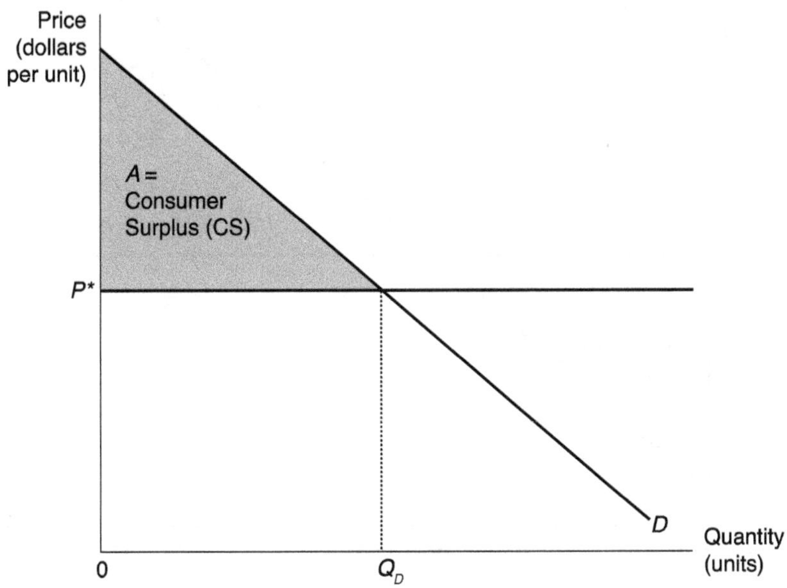

Figure 2.1 The Consumer's Choice

the price line, bounded from the left by the vertical axis and the right by the quantity of the good. This rectangle, which captures price times quantity, represents consumer expenditure on this quantity of the good.

Why is this area above the price line thought of as a surplus? For each quantity purchased, the corresponding point on the market demand curve represents the amount of money some person would have been willing to pay for the last unit of the good. The *total willingness to pay* for some quantity of this good – say, three units – is the sum of the willingness to pay for each of the three units. Thus, the total willingness to pay for three units would be measured by the sum of the willingness to pay for the first, second, and third units, respectively. It is now a simple extension to note that the total willingness to pay is the area under the continuous market demand curve to the left of the allocation in question. For example, in Figure 2.1 the total willingness to pay for Q_D units of the commodity is the total area under the demand curve up to Q_D. Thus it is the shaded triangle of consumer surplus plus the rectangle of cost. Total willingness to pay is the concept we shall use to define the total value a consumer would receive from the amount of the good they take delivery of. Thus, total value the consumer would receive is equal to the area under the market demand curve from the origin to the allocation of interest. Consumer surplus is thus the excess of total willingness to pay over the (lower) actual expenditure.

Meanwhile, sellers face a similar choice (see Figure 2.2). Given price P^*, the seller maximizes his or her own producer surplus by choosing to sell Q_S units. The *producer surplus* is designated by the shaded area *B*, the area under the price line that lies above the marginal cost curve (supply Curve S), bounded from the left by the vertical axis and the right by the quantity of the good. To calculate producer or consumer surplus, notice that as long as the functions are linear (as they are in the figures), each area is represented as a right triangle. Remember that the area of a right triangle is calculated as 1/2 × the base of the triangle × the height of the triangle. Using this formula, try calculating these areas in the first self-test exercise at the end of this chapter.

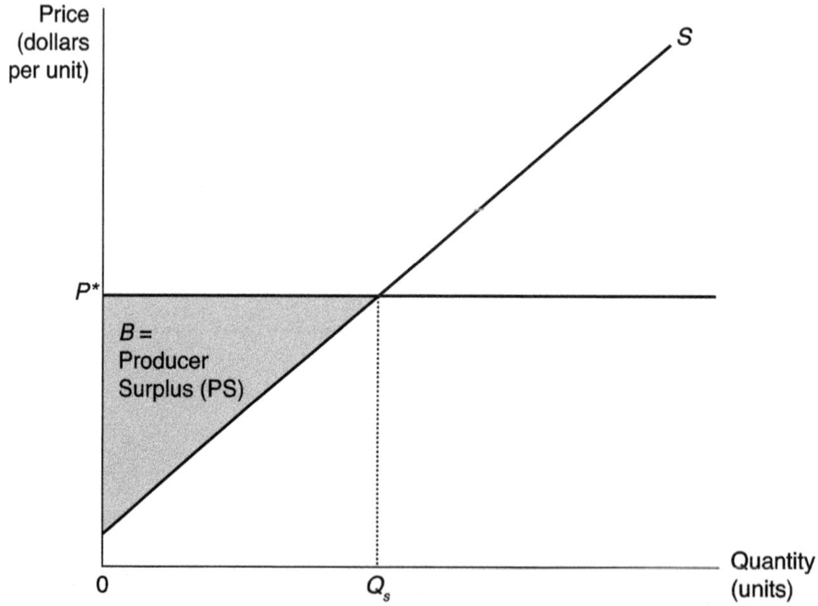

Figure 2.2 The Producer's Choice

Property rights

Property rights and efficient market allocations

The manner in which producers and consumers use environmental resources depends on the property rights governing those resources. In economics, *property rights* refer to a bundle of entitlements defining the owner's rights, privileges, and limitations for use of the resource. By examining such entitlements and how they affect human behavior, we will better understand how environmental problems arise from government and market allocations.

These property rights can be vested either with individuals, groups or with the state. How can we tell when the pursuit of profits is consistent with efficiency and when it is not?

Efficient property rights structures

Let's begin by describing the structure of property rights that could produce efficient allocations in a well-functioning market economy. An efficient structure has three main characteristics:

1 *Exclusivity* – All benefits and costs accrued as a result of owning and using the resources should accrue to the owner, and only to the owner, either directly or indirectly by sale to others.
2 *Transferability* – All property rights should be transferable from one owner to another in a voluntary exchange.
3 *Enforceability* – Property rights should be secure from involuntary seizure or encroachment by others.

An owner of a resource with a well-defined property right (one exhibiting these three characteristics) has a powerful incentive to use that resource efficiently because a decline in the value of that resource represents a personal loss. Farmers who own the land have an incentive to fertilize and irrigate it because the resulting increased production raises their income. Similarly, they have an incentive to rotate crops when that raises the productivity of their land.

When well-defined property rights are exchanged, as in a market economy, this exchange facilitates efficiency. We can illustrate this point by examining the incentives consumers and producers face when a well-defined system of property rights is in place. Because the seller has the right to prevent the consumer from consuming the product in the absence of payment, the consumer must pay to receive the product. Given a market price, the consumer decides how much to purchase by choosing the amount that maximizes his or her individual consumer surplus.

Is this allocation efficient? According to our definition of static efficiency, it is clear the answer is yes. The economic surplus is maximized by the market allocation and, as seen in Figure 2.3, it is equal to the sum of consumer and producer surpluses (areas $A + B$). Thus, we have not only established a procedure for measuring efficiency, but also a means of describing how the surplus is distributed between consumers and producers.

This distinction is crucially significant. Efficiency is *not* achieved because consumers and producers are seeking efficiency. They aren't! In a system with well-defined property rights and competitive markets in which to sell those rights, producers try to maximize their surplus and consumers try to maximize their surplus. The price system, then, induces those self-interested parties to make choices that also turn out to be efficient from the point of view of society as a whole. It channels the energy motivated by self-interest into socially productive paths.

Familiarity may have dulled our appreciation, but it is noteworthy that in these circumstances a system designed to produce a harmonious and congenial outcome could function effectively while

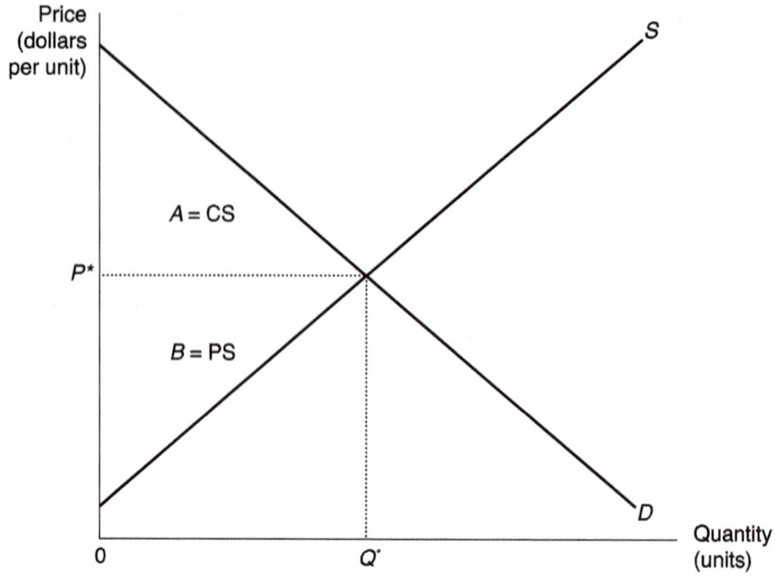

Figure 2.3 Market Equilibrium

allowing consumers and producers so much individual freedom in making choices. This is truly a remarkable accomplishment.

Producer's surplus, scarcity rent, and long-run competitive equilibrium

Since the area under the price line is total revenue, and the area under the marginal cost (or supply) curve is total variable cost, producer's surplus is related to profits. In the short run when some costs are fixed, producer's surplus is equal to profits plus fixed cost. In the long run when all costs are variable, producer's surplus is equal to profits plus rent, the return to scarce inputs owned by the producer. As long as new firms can enter into profitable industries without raising the prices of purchased inputs, long-run profits and rent will equal zero.

Scarcity rent

Most natural resource industries, however, give rise to a form of rent, which is not eliminated by competition, even with free entry. This producer's surplus, which persists in long-run competitive equilibrium, is called *scarcity rent.*

David Ricardo was the first economist to recognize the existence of scarcity rent. Ricardo suggested that the price of land was determined by the least fertile marginal unit of land. Since the price had to be sufficiently high to allow the poorer land to be brought into production, other, more fertile land could be farmed at an economic profit. Competition could not erode that profit because the amount of high-quality land was limited and lower prices would serve only to reduce the supply of land below demand. The only way to expand production would be to bring additional, less fertile land (costlier to farm) into production; consequently, additional production does not lower price, as it does in a constant-cost industry.

Externalities as a source of market failure

The concept introduced

Exclusivity is one of the chief characteristics of an efficient property rights structure. This characteristic is frequently violated in practice. One broad class of violations occurs when an agent making a decision does not bear all of the consequences of his or her action.

Suppose two firms are located by a river. The first produces steel, while the second, somewhat downstream, operates a resort hotel. Both use the river, although in different ways. The steel firm uses it as a receptacle for its waste, while the hotel uses it to attract customers seeking water recreation. If these two facilities have different owners, an efficient use of the water is not likely to result. Because the steel plant does not bear the cost of reduced business at the resort resulting from waste being dumped into the river, it is not likely to be very sensitive to that cost in its decision making. As a result, it could be expected to dump too much waste into the river, and an efficient allocation of the river would not be attained.

This concept that explains this set of circumstances is called an externality. An *externality* exists whenever the welfare of some agent, either a firm or household, depends not only on his or her activities, but also on activities under the control of some other agent. In our example, the increased waste in the river imposed an external cost on the resort, a cost the steel firm could not be counted upon to consider appropriately in deciding the amount of waste to dump.

The effect of this external cost on the steel industry is illustrated in Figure 2.4, which shows the market for steel. Steel production inevitably involves producing pollution as well as steel. The demand for steel is shown by the demand curve *D*, and the private marginal cost of producing the steel (exclusive of pollution control and damage) is depicted as *MCp*. Because society considers both the cost of

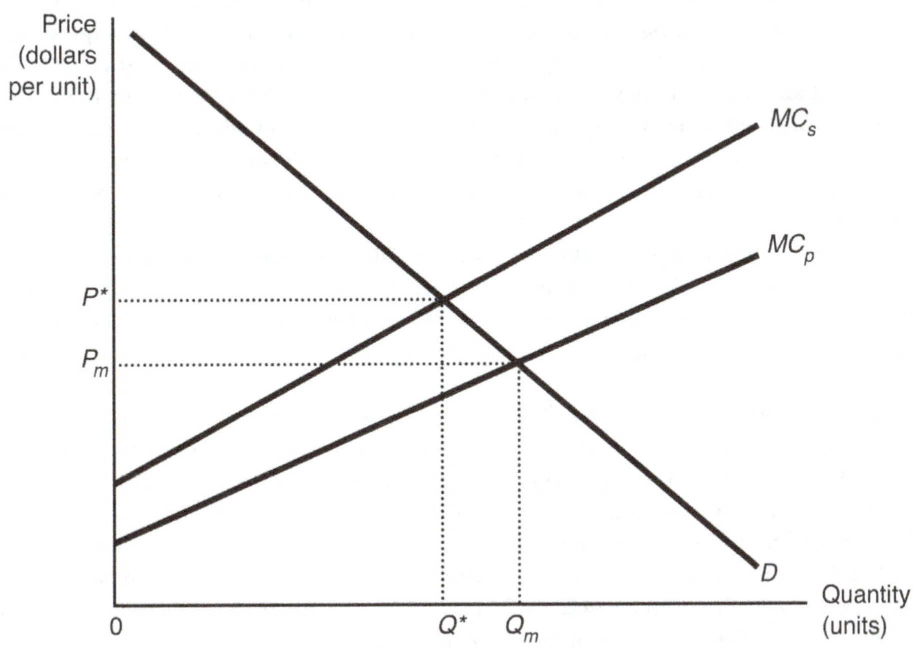

Figure 2.4 The Market for Steel

pollution and the cost of producing the steel, the social marginal cost function (*MCs*) adds both of these external costs to the private costs.

If the steel industry faced no outside control on its emission levels, it would seek to produce Q_m. That choice, in a competitive setting, would maximize its private producer surplus. But that is clearly not efficient, since the net benefit is maximized at Q^*, not Q_m. Can you see the amount of net benefits lost via this inefficiency? This loss in efficiency is called a deadweight loss. A deadweight loss arises whenever marginal social costs are not equal to marginal social benefits. Notice that in this case, marginal social costs are higher than marginal benefits at the market allocation.

With the help of Figure 2.4, we can draw a number of conclusions about market allocations of commodities causing pollution externalities:

1 The output of the commodity is too large.
2 Too much pollution is produced.
3 The prices of products whose production was responsible for the pollution are too low.
4 As long as the costs remain external, no incentives to search for ways to yield less pollution per unit of output are introduced by the market.
5 Recycling and reuse of the polluting substances are discouraged because release into the environment is so inefficiently cheap.

The effects of a market imperfection for one commodity end up affecting the demands for raw materials, labor, and so on. The ultimate effects are felt through the entire economy.

Types of externalities

External effects, or externalities, can be positive or negative. Historically, the terms *external cost* (*external diseconomy*) and *external benefit* (*external economy*) have been used to refer, respectively, to circumstances in which the affected party is damaged by or benefits from the externality. Clearly, the water pollution example represents an external cost. External benefits are not hard to find, however. As noted in the opening quote to this chapter, private individuals who preserve a particularly scenic area provide an external benefit to all who pass. Generally, when external benefits are present, the market will undersupply the resources (preserved lands in this case) providing the external benefits.

One other distinction is important. One class of externalities, known as *pecuniary externalities*, does not present the same kinds of problems as pollution does. Pecuniary externalities arise when the external effect is transmitted through altered prices. Suppose that a new firm moves into an area and drives up the rental price of land. That increase creates a negative effect on all those paying rent and, therefore, is an external diseconomy.

This pecuniary diseconomy, however, does not cause a market failure because the resulting higher rents are reflecting the true scarcity of land. The land market provides a mechanism by which the parties can bid for land; the resulting prices reflect the value of the land in its various uses. Without pecuniary externalities, the price signals would fail to sustain an efficient allocation.

The pollution example is *not* a pecuniary externality because the effect is not transmitted through prices. In this example, prices do not adjust to reflect the increasing waste load. The damage to the water resource is not reflected in the steel firm's costs. An essential feedback mechanism that is present for pecuniary externalities is not present for the pollution case.

The externalities concept is a broad one, covering a multitude of sources of market failure (Example 2.2 illustrates one). The next step is to investigate some specific environmental circumstances that can give rise to externalities.

EXAMPLE 2.2

Shrimp farming externalities in Thailand

In the Tha Po village on the coast of Surat Thani Province in Thailand, more than half of the 1,100 hectares of mangrove swamps have been cleared for commercial shrimp farms. Although harvesting shrimp is a lucrative undertaking, mangroves also serve as nurseries for fish and as barriers for storms and soil erosion. Following the destruction of the local mangroves, Tha Po villagers experienced a decline in fish catch and suffered storm damage and water pollution. Can market forces be trusted to strike the efficient balance between preservation and development for the remaining mangroves?

Calculations by economists Sathirathai and Barbier (2001) demonstrated that the value of the ecological services that would be lost from further destruction of the mangrove swamps exceeded the value of the shrimp farms that would take their place. Preservation of the remaining mangrove swamps would be the efficient choice.

Would a potential shrimp-farming entrepreneur make the efficient choice? Unfortunately, the answer is no. This study estimated the economic value of mangroves in terms of local use of forest resources, offshore fishery linkages, and coastal protection to be in the range of $27,264–$35,921 per hectare. In contrast, the economic returns to shrimp farming, once they are corrected for input subsidies and for the costs of water pollution, are only $194–$209 per hectare. However, as shrimp farmers are heavily subsidized *and do not have to consider the external costs of pollution*, their financial returns are typically $7,706.95–$8,336.47 per hectare. In the absence of some sort of external control imposed by collective action, converting mangroves to shrimp farming would be the normal, if inefficient, result. The externalities associated with the ecological services provided by the mangroves support a biased decision that results in fewer social net benefits, but greater private net benefits.

Sources: Sathirathai, S., & Barbier, E. B. (April 2001). Valuing mangrove conservation in southern Thailand. *Contemporary Economic Policy*, 19(2). 109–122; Barbier, E. B., & Cox, M.(2004). An economic analysis of shrimp farm expansion and mangrove conversion in Thailand. *Land Economics*, 80(3), 389–407.

Perverse incentives arising from some property right structures

Private property is, of course, not the only possible way of defining entitlements to resource use. Other possibilities include:

- state-property regimes (the government owns and controls the property);
- common-property regimes (the property is jointly owned and managed by a specified group of co-owners); and
- *res nullius* regimes, or open-access regimes (in which no one owns or exercises control over the resources).

All of these create rather different incentives for resource use.

State-property regimes exist to varying degrees in virtually all countries of the world. Parks and public forests, for example, are frequently owned and managed by the government in capitalist as well as in socialist nations. Problems with both efficiency and sustainability can arise in state-property regimes when the incentives of bureaucrats, who implement and/or make the rules for resource use, diverge from collective interests.

Common-property resources are those shared resources that are managed in common rather than privately. Entitlements to use common-property resources may be formal, protected by specific legal rules, or they may be informal, protected by tradition or custom. Common-property regimes exhibit varying degrees of efficiency and sustainability, depending on the rules that emerge from collective decision making. While some very successful examples of common-property regimes exist, unsuccessful examples are even more common.

One successful example of a common-property regime involves the system of allocating grazing rights in Switzerland. Although agricultural land is normally treated as private property, in Switzerland grazing rights on the Alpine meadows have been treated as common property for centuries. Overgrazing is protected by specific rules, enacted by an association of users, which limit the amount of livestock permitted on the meadow. The families included on the membership list of the association have been stable over time as rights and responsibilities have passed from generation to generation. This stability has apparently facilitated reciprocity and trust, thereby providing a foundation for continued compliance with the rules that support an efficient and sustainable outcome.

Unfortunately, that kind of stability may be the exception rather than the rule, particularly in the face of heavy population pressure. The more common situation can be illustrated by the experience of Mawelle, a small fishing village in Sri Lanka.[1] Initially, a complicated but effective rotating system of fishing rights was devised by villagers to ensure equitable access to the best spots and best times while protecting the fish stocks. Over time, population pressure and the infusion of outsiders raised demand and undermined the collective cohesion sufficiently that the traditional rules became unenforceable, producing overexploitation of the resource and lower incomes for all the participants.

Res nullius property resources, the main focus of this section, can be exploited on a first-come, first-served basis because no individual or group has the legal power to restrict access. *Open-access resources,* as we shall henceforth call them, have given rise to what has become known popularly as the "tragedy of the commons."

The problems created by open-access resources can be illustrated by recalling the fate of the American bison. Bison are an example of "common-pool" resources. *Common-pool resources* are shared resources characterized by nonexclusivity and divisibility. *Nonexclusivity* implies that resources can be exploited by anyone, while *divisibility* means that the capture of part of the resource by one group subtracts it from the amount available to the other groups. (Note the contrast between common-pool resources and public goods, the subject of the next section.) In the early history of the United States, bison were plentiful; unrestricted hunting access was not a problem. Indigenous or more recent immigrant frontier people who needed hides or meat could easily get whatever they needed; the aggressiveness of any one hunter did not affect the time and effort expended by other hunters. In the absence of scarcity, efficiency was not threatened by open access.

As the years slipped by, however, the demand for bison increased and scarcity became a factor. As the number of hunters increased, eventually every additional unit of hunting activity increased the amount of time and effort required to produce an additional yield of bison.

Consider graphically how various property rights structures (and the resulting level of harvest) affect the scarcity rent (in this case, equivalent to the economic surplus received by consumers and producers), where the amount of rent is measured as the difference between the revenues received from the harvest minus the costs associated with producing that harvest. Figure 2.5 compares the revenue and costs for various levels of harvest. In the top panel the revenue is calculated by multiplying, for each

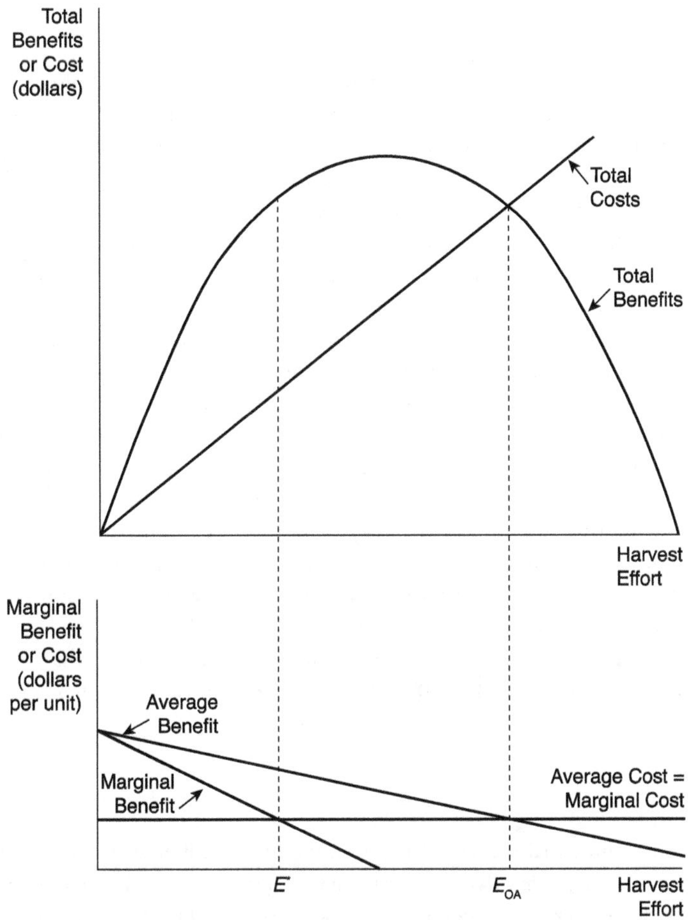

Figure 2.5 Bison Harvesting

level of hunting activity, the (assumed constant) price of bison by the amount harvested. The upward sloping total cost curve simply reflects that fact that increases in harvest effort result in higher total costs. (Marginal cost is assumed to be constant for this example.)

In terms of the top panel of Figure 2.5, the total surplus associated with any level of effort is measured as the vertical difference between the total revenue (benefits) curve and the total cost curve for that level of harvest.

In the bottom panel the marginal revenue curve is downward sloping (despite the constant price) because as the amount of hunting effort increases, the resulting bison population size decreases. Smaller populations support smaller harvests per unit of effort expended.

The efficient level of hunting activity in this model (E^*) maximizes the surplus. This can be seen graphically in two different ways. First, E^* maximizes the vertical difference between the total cost and total benefit (top panel). Second, in the bottom panel E^* is the level where the marginal revenue, which records the addition to the surplus from an additional unit of effort, crosses the marginal cost curve, which measures the reduction in the surplus due to the additional cost of expending that last unit of effort. These two panels are simply two different (mathematically equivalent) ways to demonstrate the same outcome. (The curves in the bottom panel are derived from the curves in the top panel.)

With all hunters having completely unrestricted access to the bison, the resulting allocation would not be efficient. No individual hunter would have an incentive to protect scarcity rent by restricting his/her hunting effort. Individual hunters, under this "open access" scenario (without exclusive rights), would exploit the resource until their total benefit equaled total cost, implying a level of effort equal to (EOA). Excessive exploitation of the herd occurs because individual hunters cannot appropriate the scarcity rent; therefore, they ignore it. One of the losses from further exploitation that could be avoided by exclusive owners – the loss of scarcity rent due to overexploitation – is not part of the decision-making process of open-access hunters.

Two characteristics of this formulation of the open-access allocation are worth noting: (1) in the presence of sufficient demand, unrestricted access will cause resources to be overexploited; (2) the scarcity rent is dissipated – no one is able to appropriate the rent, so it is lost.

Why does this happen? Unlimited access destroys the incentive to conserve. A hunter who can preclude others from hunting his stock has an incentive to keep the herd at an efficient level. This restraint results in lower costs in the form of less time and effort expended to produce a given yield of bison. On the other hand, a hunter exploiting an open-access resource would not have an incentive to conserve because the potential additional economic surplus derived from self-restraint would, to some extent, be captured by other hunters who simply kept harvesting. Thus, unrestricted access to scarce resources promotes an inefficient allocation. As a result of excessive harvest and the loss of habitat as land was converted to farm and pasture, the Great Plains bison herds nearly became extinct (Lueck, 2002). Many fisheries provide another example of open-access resources.

Public goods

Public goods, defined as those that exhibit both consumption indivisibilities and nonexcludability, present a particularly complex category of environmental resources. *Nonexcludability* refers to a circumstance where, once the resource is provided, even those who fail to pay for it cannot be excluded from enjoying the benefits it confers. Consumption is said to be *indivisible* when one person's consumption of a good does not diminish the amount available for others. Several common environmental resources are public goods, including not only the "charming landscape" referred to by Emerson, but also clean air and biological diversity.[2]

Biological diversity includes two related concepts: (1) the amount of genetic variability among individuals within a single species, and (2) the number of species within a community of organisms. *Genetic diversity*, critical to species survival in the natural world, has also proved to be important in the development of new crops and livestock. It enhances the opportunities for crossbreeding and, thus, the development of superior strains. The availability of different strains was the key, for example, in developing new, disease-resistant barley.

Because of the interdependence of species within ecological communities, any particular species may have a value to the community far beyond its intrinsic value. Certain species contribute balance and stability to their ecological communities by providing food sources or holding the population of the species in check.

The richness of diversity within and among species has provided new sources of food, energy, industrial chemicals, raw materials, and medicines. Yet, considerable evidence suggests that biological diversity is decreasing. Biodiversity is a valuable ecosystem service.

Can we rely solely on the private sector to produce the efficient amount of public goods, such as biological diversity? Unfortunately, the answer is no. Suppose that in response to diminishing ecological diversity we decide to take up a collection to provide some means of preserving endangered species.

Would the collection yield sufficient revenue to pay for an efficient level of ecological diversity? The general answer is no. Let's see why.

In Figure 2.6, individual demand curves for preserving biodiversity have been presented for two consumers, A and B. The market demand curve is represented by the vertical summation of the two individual demand curves. A vertical summation is necessary because everyone can simultaneously

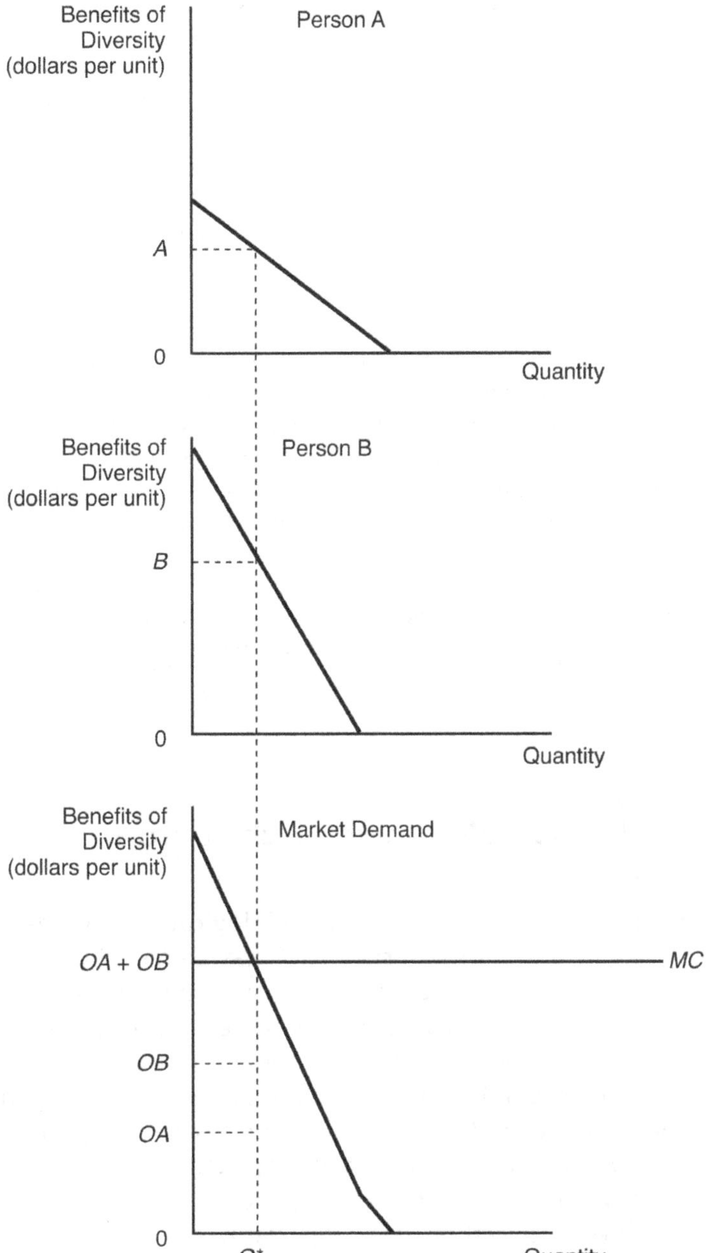

Figure 2.6 Efficient Provision of Public Goods

consume the same amount of biological diversity. We are, therefore, able to determine the market demand by finding the sum of the amounts of money they would be willing to pay for that level of diversity.

What is the efficient level of diversity? It can be determined by a direct application of our definition of efficiency. The efficient allocation maximizes economic surplus, which is represented geometrically by the portion of the area under the market demand curve that lies above the constant marginal cost curve. The allocation that maximizes economic surplus is Q^*, the allocation where the demand curve crosses the marginal cost curve.

Why would a competitive market not be expected to supply the efficient level of this good? Since the two consumers have very different marginal willingness to pay from the efficient allocation of this good (*OA* versus *OB*), the efficient pricing system would require charging a different price to each consumer. Person *A* would pay *OA* and person *B* would pay *OB*. (Remember consumers tend to choose the level of the good that equates their marginal willingness to pay to the price they face.) Yet the producer would have no basis for figuring out how to differentiate the prices. In the absence of excludability, consumers are not likely to willingly reveal the strength of their preference for this commodity. All consumers have an incentive to understate the strength of their preferences to try to shift more of the cost burden to the other consumers.

Therefore, inefficiency results because each person is able to become a *free rider* on the other's contribution. A *free rider* is someone who derives the value from a commodity without paying an efficient amount for its supply. Because of the consumption indivisibility and nonexcludability properties of the public good, consumers receive the value of any diversity purchased by other people. When this happens it tends to diminish incentives to contribute, and the contributions are not sufficiently large to finance the efficient amount of the public good; it would be undersupplied. (In Chapter 9 we shall use the lens provided by game theory to show how the free rider effect helps to shape climate policy.)

The privately supplied amount may not be zero, however. Some diversity would be privately supplied. Indeed, as suggested by Example 2.3, although inefficiently low, the privately supplied amount may be considerable.

EXAMPLE 2.3

Public goods privately provided: the nature conservancy

Can the demand for a public good such as biological diversity be observed in practice? Would the market respond to that demand? Apparently so, according to the existence of an organization called the Nature Conservancy.

The Nature Conservancy was born of an older organization called the Ecologist Union on September 11, 1950, for the purpose of establishing natural area reserves to aid in the preservation of areas, objects, and fauna and flora that have scientific, educational, or aesthetic significance. This organization purchases, or accepts as donations, land that has some unique ecological or aesthetic significance, to keep it from being used for other purposes. In so doing it preserves many species by preserving the habitat.

From humble beginnings, the Nature Conservancy has, as of 2017, been responsible for the preservation of 119 million acres of forests, marshes, prairies, mounds, and islands around the world. Additionally, the Nature Conservancy has protected 5,000 miles of rivers and operates over 100 marine conservation projects. These areas serve as home to rare and endangered species of wildlife and plants. The Conservancy owns and manages the largest privately owned nature preserve system in the world.

This approach has considerable merit. A private organization can move more rapidly than the public sector. Because it has a limited budget, the Nature Conservancy sets priorities and concentrates on acquiring the most ecologically unique areas. Yet the theory of public goods reminds us that if this were to be the sole approach to the preservation of biological diversity, it would preserve a smaller-than-efficient amount.

Source: The Nature Conservancy, www.nature.org/en-us/about-us/who-we-are/accountability/

Imperfect market structures

Environmental problems also occur when one of the participants in an exchange of property rights is able to exercise an inordinate amount of power over the outcome. This can occur, for example, when a product is sold by a single seller, or *monopoly*.

It is easy to show that monopolies violate our definition of *efficiency* in the goods market (see Figure 2.7). According to our definition of *static efficiency*, the efficient allocation would result when *OB*

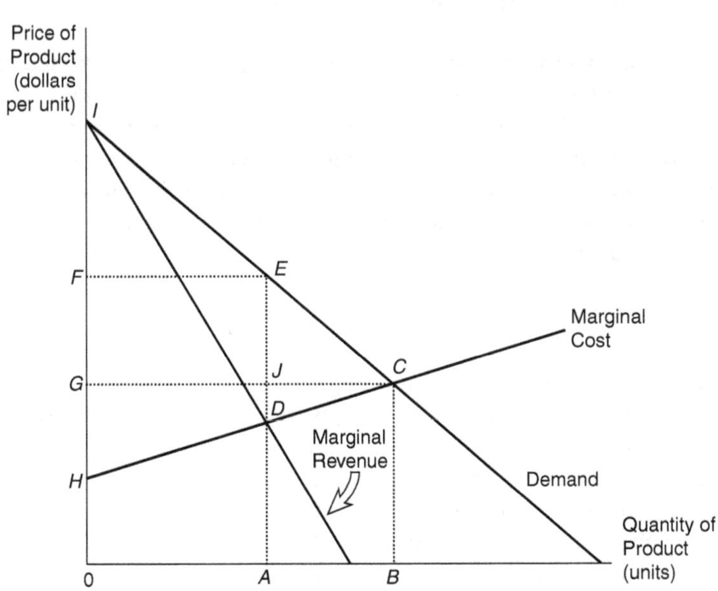

Figure 2.7 Monopoly and Inefficiency

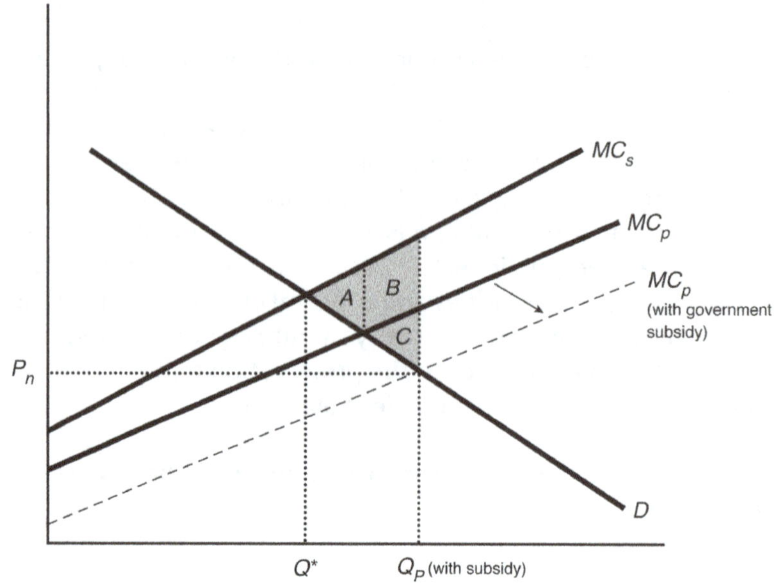

Figure 2.8 The Market for Steel Revisited

is supplied. This would yield consumer surplus represented by triangle *IGC and* producer surplus denoted by triangle *GCH*. The monopoly, however, would produce and sell *OA*, where marginal revenue equals marginal cost, and would charge price *OF*. At this point, although the producer's surplus (*HFED*) is maximized, the sum of consumer and producer surplus is clearly not, because this choice causes society to lose economic surplus equal to triangle *EDO*.[3] Monopolies supply an inefficiently small amount of the good.

Imperfect markets clearly play some role in environmental problems. For example, the major oil-exporting countries have formed a cartel, resulting in higher-than-normal prices and lower-than-normal production. A *cartel* is a collusive agreement among producers to restrict production and raise prices. This collusive agreement allows the group to act as a monopolist. The inefficiency in the goods market would normally be offset to some degree by an associated reduction in social costs. The reduction in the combustion of oil would result in lower levels of pollution and, hence, the social cost associated with that pollution.

Asymmetric information

When all parties to a specific situation or transaction have access to the same amount of information about that situation, the information is said to be symmetrically distributed. If, however, one or more parties have more information than the others, the information distribution is said to be asymmetric.

Asymmetric information creates problems for the market when it results in a decision maker knowing too little to make an efficient choice. Suppose, for example, a consumer preferred organic food, but didn't know what food choices were truly organic. Since it would be relatively easy for producers to claim their produce was organically grown even if it wasn't, consumers who could not accurately distinguish truly organic produce from its fraudulent substitute would tend to be unwilling to pay a higher price for organic produce. As a result, both the profits and the output of organic farmers would be inefficiently low. If consumers do not have full information, negative externalities may result.

(We shall encounter asymmetric information problems in several chapters, including energy, pollution control, and ecosystem services.)

Government failure

Market processes are not the only sources of inefficiency. Political processes are fully as culpable. Corruption is one obvious source, but political choices may also be thwarted by something as simple as inadequate information. As we shall see sometimes the amount and type of information needed to put a solution in place will differ greatly depending upon the type of solution. As will become clear in the chapters that follow, some environmental problems have arisen from a failure of political, rather than economic, institutions. To complete our study of the ability of institutions to allocate environmental resources, we must understand this source of inefficiency as well.

Government failure shares with market failure the characteristic that improper incentives are the root of the problem. Special interest groups use the political process to engage in what has become known as *rent seeking*. Rent seeking is the use of resources in lobbying and other activities directed at securing legislation that results in more profitable outcomes for those funding this activity.

Rent seeking can take several forms. It can involve lobbying to try to affect legislation or regulatory activities. It can involve information (or sometimes disinformation) campaigns designed to convert the public (especially voters) to their point of view. It can use campaign financing to gain access to decision makers and/or to influence political appointments.

The most successful of these campaigns can even result in "regulatory capture." Regulatory capture is a form of government failure that occurs when a regulatory agency advances the special interests of the industry or sector it is charged with overseeing instead of the public interest. This can occur either due the power of the regulated community on the regulatory process or to political appointees who are appointed to "stack the deck" in terms of favorable treatment of the regulated community.

Successful rent-seeking activity will typically increase the net benefits going to the special interest group, but it will also frequently lower the surplus to society as a whole. In these instances, it is a classic case of the aggressive pursuit of a larger slice of the pie leading to a smaller pie.

Why don't the losers rise up to protect their interests? One main reason is voter ignorance. It is economically rational for voters to remain at least partially ignorant on many issues simply because of the high cost of keeping fully informed on the huge number of issues that arise and the low probability that any single vote will be decisive. In addition, it is difficult for diffuse groups of individuals, each of whom is affected only to a small degree, to organize a coherent, unified opposition. Successful opposition is, in a sense, a public good, with its attendant tendency for free riding. Opposition to special interests would normally be underfunded, especially when the opposition is dispersed and the special interests are concentrated.

The favorable treatment that results from rent seeking can take many forms. Producers can seek protection from competitive pressures brought by imports or can seek price floors to hold prices above their efficient levels or can seek lower levels of enforcement and/or oversight. Consumer groups can seek price ceilings on goods or special subsidies to transfer part of their costs to the general body of taxpayers.

Rent seeking is not the only source of inefficient government policy. Sometimes governments act without full information and establish policies that are ultimately very inefficient. For example, some time ago, one technological strategy chosen by the government to control motor vehicle pollution involved adding a chemical substance (MTBE) to gasoline. Designed to promote cleaner combustion, this additive turned out to create a substantial water pollution problem and was subsequently banned.

Governments may also pursue social policy objectives that have the side effect of causing an environmental inefficiency. For example, looking back at Figure 2.4, suppose that the government, when

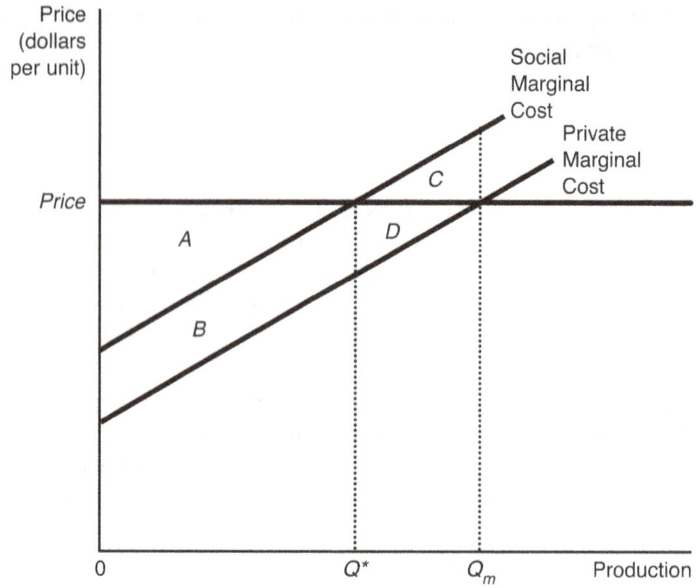

Figure 2.9 Efficient Output with Pollution Damage

pressured by lobbyists, decides to subsidize the production of steel. Figure 2.9 illustrates the outcome. The private marginal cost curve shifts down and to the right causing a further increase in production, lower prices, and even more pollution produced. Thus, the subsidy moves us even further away from where surplus is maximized at $Q^\star$. The shaded triangle A shows the deadweight loss (inefficiency) without the subsidy. With the subsidy, the deadweight loss grows to areas $A + B + C$. This social policy has the side effect of increasing an environmental inefficiency.

In another historical example in 1974–75 the legislative desire to hold down natural gas prices for consumers led to subsequent shortages. These examples provide a direct challenge to the presumption that more direct intervention by the government automatically leads to either greater efficiency or greater sustainability.

These cases illustrate the general economic premise that environmental problems arise because of a divergence between individual and collective objectives. This is a powerful explanatory device because not only does it suggest why these problems arise, but it also suggests how they might be resolved – by realigning individual incentives to make them compatible with collective objectives. As self-evident as this approach may be, it is controversial when people disagree about whether the problem is our improper values or the improper translation of our quite proper values into action.

Economists have always been reluctant to argue that values of consumers are warped, because that would necessitate dictating the "correct" set of values. Both capitalism and democracy are based on the presumption that the majority knows what it is doing, whether it is casting ballots for representatives or dollar votes for goods and services. Do you find that presumption reasonable or not? If you do not find it reasonable where does your finding lead you in terms of defining the role of markets and government actions in meeting the future environmental challenges we face?

This analysis suggests that both governments and markets can fail to deliver efficient environmental management in certain circumstances. In the next chapter we examine the degree to which these institutional deficiencies can be overcome, paying particular attention to the choice of policy instruments.

Summary

How producers and consumers use the resources making up the environmental asset depends on the nature of the entitlements embodied in the property rights governing resource use. When property rights systems are exclusive, transferable, and enforceable, the owner of a resource has a powerful incentive to use that resource efficiently, since the failure to do so results in a personal loss.

The economic system will not always sustain efficient allocations, however. Specific circumstances that could lead to inefficient allocations include externalities, improperly defined property rights systems (such as open-access resources and public goods), imperfect markets for trading the property rights to the resources (monopoly), and asymmetric information. When these circumstances arise, market allocations typically do not maximize the surplus.

Due to rent-seeking behavior by special interest groups or the less-than-perfect implementation of efficient plans, the political system can produce inefficiencies as well. Voter ignorance on many issues, coupled with the public-good nature of any results of political activity, tends to create a situation in which maximizing an individual's private surplus (through lobbying, for example) can be at the expense of a lower economic surplus for all consumers and producers.

The efficiency criterion can be used to assist in the identification of circumstances in which our political and economic institutions lead us astray. It can also assist in the search for remedies by facilitating the design of regulatory, judicial, or legislative solutions.

Discussion questions

1 In a well-known legal case, *Miller v. Schoene* (287 U.S. 272), a classic conflict of property rights was featured. Red cedar trees, used only for ornamental purposes, carried a disease that could destroy apple orchards within a radius of two miles. There was no known way of curing the disease except by destroying the cedar trees or by ensuring that apple orchards were at least two miles away from the cedar trees. Apply the Coase theorem to this situation. Does it make any difference to the outcome whether the cedar tree owners are entitled to retain their trees or the apple growers are entitled to be free of them? Why or why not?

2 In primitive societies, the entitlements to use land were frequently possessory rights rather than ownership rights. Those on the land could use it as they wished, but they could not transfer it to anyone else. One could acquire a new plot by simply occupying and using it, leaving the old plot available for someone else. Would this type of entitlement system cause more or less incentive to conserve the land than an ownership entitlement? Why? Would a possessory entitlement system be more efficient in a modern society or a primitive society? Why?

3 In this chapter we have discussed how markets work. Recently some new markets have emerged that focus on sharing of durable goods among a wider circle of users. Examples include Airbnb and Uber. The rise of these sharing markets may well have an impact on the relationship between the economy and the environment.

   a What are the market niches these firms have found? How is Airbnb different from Hilton? How is Uber different from Hertz or Yellow Cab? Is this a matter mainly of a different type of supply or is the demand side affected as well?
   b Why now? Markets for personal transportation and temporary housing have been around for a long time. How can these new companies find profitable opportunities in markets that have existed for some time? Is it evidence that the markets are not competitive? Or have the new opportunities been created by some changes in market conditions?
   c Are these new sharing markets likely on balance to be good for or harmful to the environment? Why?

Self-test exercises

1 Suppose the market demand function (expressed in dollars) for a normal product is $P = 80 - q$, and the marginal cost (in dollars) of producing it is $MC = 1q$, where P is the price of the product and q is the quantity demanded and/or supplied.

a How much would be supplied by a competitive market?
b Compute the consumer surplus and producer surplus. Show that their sum is maximized.
c Compute the consumer surplus and the producer surplus assuming this same product was supplied by a monopoly. (*Hint:* The marginal revenue curve has twice the slope of the demand curve.)
d Using b. and c., note that when this market is controlled by a monopoly, producer surplus is larger, consumer surplus is smaller, and the sum of the two surpluses is smaller than when the market is controlled by competitive industry.

2 Label each of the following propositions as descriptive or normative and defend your choice:

a Energy efficiency programs have created jobs.
b Money spent on protecting endangered species is wasted.
c Fisheries must be privatized to survive.
d Raising transport costs lower suburban land values.
e Birth control programs are counterproductive.

3 Identify whether each of the following resource categories is a public good, a common- pool resource, or neither and defend your answer:

a A pod of whales in the ocean to whale hunters.
b A pod of whales in the ocean to whale watchers.
c The benefits from reductions of greenhouse gas emissions.
d Water from a town well that excludes nonresidents.
e Bottled water.

Note

1 Ostrom, Elinor. (1990). *Governing the Commons: The Evolution of Institutions for Collective Action.* Cambridge, UK: Cambridge University Press, Chapter 5.

Further reading

Lueck, D. (2002). The extermination and conservation of the American bison. *Journal of Legal Studies*, 31(S2), s609–s652. A fascinating look at the role property rights played in the fate of the American bison.

Mason, C. F. (2012). The economics of eco-labeling: Theory and empirical implications. *International Review of Environmental and Resource Economics*, 6, 341–372. A survey of the growing literature on eco-labeling.

Ostrom, E. (1992). *Crafting Institutions for Self-Governing Irrigation Systems.* San Francisco, CA: ICS Press. A classic book by a Nobel Prize laureate that demonstrates that in favorable circumstances common-pool problems can sometimes be solved by voluntary organizations, rather than by a coercive state; among the cases considered are communal tenure in meadows and forests, irrigation communities, and fisheries.

Ostrom, E., Dietz, T., Dolsak, N., Stern, P., Stonich, S., & Weber, E. U. (Eds.). (2002). *The Drama of the Commons*. Washington, DC: National Academy Press. A compilation of articles and papers on common-pool resources.

Stavins, R. (2012). *The Economics of the Environment: Selected Readings*, 6th ed. New York: W. W. Norton and Company. A carefully selected collection of readings that would complement this text.

Additional references and other historically significant references are available on this book's eResource page: www.routledge.com/9781138587595

Chapter 3

The role of policy instrument choice in efficient environmental management

In the last chapter we examined the sources of market and government failure. In this chapter we examine the extent to which market and government deficiencies can be overcome through the careful design of policy. We will pay particular attention to the available types of policy instruments and how they differ in terms of the ease of design and how well they succeed in promoting efficiency.

The changing role for government over time

While the economic approach suggests that in the absence of regulatory capture government action could well be used to restore efficiency, it also suggests that inefficiency is not a sufficient condition to justify government intervention. Any corrective mechanism involves transaction costs. If these transaction costs are high enough, and the surplus to be derived from correcting the inefficiency is small enough, then it is best simply to live with the inefficiency.

Over time, however, the scale of economic activity and the resulting impact on the environment have increased. For example, cities have experienced increasing severe problems from air and water pollutants because the increase in the sheer number of emitters and their clustering have increased the amount of emissions per unit volume of air or water. As a result, pollutant concentrations have caused perceptible problems with human health, vegetation growth, and aesthetics.

Additionally, as incomes have risen, the demand for leisure activities has also risen. Many of these leisure activities, such as canoeing and backpacking, take place in unique, pristine environmental areas. With the number of these areas declining as a result of conversion to other uses, the value of remaining undeveloped areas has increased. Thus, the values derived from protecting some areas have risen over time until they have exceeded the transaction costs of protecting them from pollution and/or development.

Can government respond efficiently or will rent seeking prevent efficient political solutions? We devote much of this book to pinning down the answer to that question.

The choice of policy instruments

As we have seen in previous chapters the market plays a large role in resource allocation in modern society, but it is not always an efficient allocator. When this happens, the government usually gets involved. Government intervention can either replace market decisions with government decisions or it can use policy instruments to nudge the market back onto an efficient and/or fair course.

In the former case replacement may be necessary when the efficient or fair strategy is simply to prohibit a market outcome that would otherwise take place. This is currently the case with some toxic substances. See Example 3.1.

EXAMPLE 3.1

The arduous path to managing toxic risk: Bisphenol A

One example of a potentially toxic substance that has been working its way through the government regulatory bureaucracy is Bisphenol A (BPA). The food industry was using more than 6 billion pounds of BPA every year to make the resins that line food cans and the polycarbonate plastics used to make baby bottles and many other products. The Centers for Disease Control and Prevention (CDC) says that 95 percent of us carry measurable amounts of BPA in our blood.

In April 2008, the National Toxicology Program (NTP) at the National Institutes of Health (NIH) expressed some concern that exposure to BPA during pregnancy and childhood could impact the developing breast and prostate, hasten puberty, and affect behavior in American children. Not long after those concerns were expressed, the Canadian government moved to ban polycarbonate infant bottles containing BPA, the most popular type of bottle on the market.

Despite the absence of any such ruling from the U.S. government, after the Canadian move the U.S. market reacted. Major BPA manufacturers, including Playtex, which makes bottles and cups, and Nalgene, which makes portable water bottles, announced a shift to BPA-free products. Major retailers, including Walmart and Toys "R" Us, announced they would quickly phase out BPA-containing baby bottles. Furthermore since 2009 13 states and the District of Columbia enacted further restrictions.

In January 2010, the U.S. Food and Drug Administration (FDA), which had previously found BPA to be safe, announced:

> On the basis of results from recent studies using novel approaches to test for subtle effects, both the National Toxicology Program at the National Institutes of Health and FDA have some concern about the potential effects of BPA on the brain, behavior, and prostate gland in fetuses, infants, and young children.

In July 2012, the agency announced that it would no longer allow BPA in baby bottles and children's drinking cups. The agency did not restrict its use in other consumer products.

How this risk was handled in the United States is especially noteworthy in that both the market and the states reacted before federal regulation was in place, but the federal government did ultimately follow their lead.

Sources: The National Institutes of Health website: www.niehs.nih.gov/health/topics/agents/sya-bpa/ (accessed December 5, 2016); Food and Drug Administration website: www.fda.gov/NewsEvents/PublicHealthFocus/ucm064437.htm (accessed May 23, 2013); Environmental Working Group website: www.ewg.org/bpa/ (accessed December 5, 2016).

Why would consumers ever buy a product when its benefits are lower than its cost? One possibility occurs when the health risks associated with use of the product are not known or are insufficiently known to potential buyers. In that case this product might seem (incorrectly) to be a good buy. To eliminate inefficient choices, which are clear to the government after completing its research, the product might be banned.

Why not let companies produce the product and rely on courts to force the manufacturers to pay the damages? Wouldn't this provide an incentive for manufacturers to exercise care lest they get sued? Further isn't it true that when damages are paid, the health care costs that were previously externalized to the uninformed customer would be internalized to the manufacturer? And once they are internalized wouldn't the producer discover that producing this product would no longer be profitable?

That part of the story is accurate, but it is also incomplete and therefore misleading. Legal remedies have certain deficiencies that limit their usefulness in setting like this. Many people could already have been needlessly damaged by the time this remedy was applied. Even if the suit were ultimately successful in holding manufacturers responsible, the suit would typically not be filed, much less resolved, until many years after the product became available and caused considerable damage. Further, judicial proceedings are typically expensive as well as slow. The alternative, prohibition, would prevent people from getting hurt and eliminate the need for any legal proceedings.

In other types of cases, however, nudging the market rather than replacing it may be called for. The market can be a very powerful force. It is a useful force to have on the side of efficiency and fairness, if that can be achieved. When it deviates from an efficient, fair path, sometime it is possible to rectify that market failure by using economic policy instruments to nudge the market onto the right path rather than simply to substitute government action for market action.

What types of economic instruments are available to fulfil this function? How does each type of instrument work? What types of circumstances lead to a policy preference for one type of instrument over another? What are some examples of circumstances where each type of instrument is currently being used in environmental policy? By answering the questions in this chapter, we will set the stage for showing in more detail in subsequent chapters a host of circumstances where these instruments have been used.

The starting point for applying most of these instruments is to identify the nature of the market failure that causes the market to go astray. Let's start with the market failure that is associated with pollution control to illustrate the basic logic of the analysis, leaving the details of other types of market failure to later chapters where the specific policy context is clear.

Most commonly the market failure associated with pollution involves an externality. When a firm can pass some of its costs onto others, this externality can lead these costs to be either totally ignored or diminished. Externalities are actually very common in environmental management. For example, fossil fuel consumers emit carbon into the atmosphere whenever they heat their homes or drive cars that use these fuels. As we shall see in Chapter 8, these emissions impose potentially huge costs on others in the form of ocean acidification, which harms coral reefs and shell fish, and more intense storms, which damage property and endanger life itself, among other effects. Further these costs may even be borne by people who may live in different parts of the country or even different parts of the world. As a consequence, when homeowners or businesses choose the type of fuel they will use, the amount of carbon that is emitted to the air by each fuel is not likely to play much, if any, role in that decision. The most likely outcome is that they will choose the cheapest fuel to them, not the fuel imposing a much larger cost to everyone. Market choices in this case are biased against low- or no-carbon fuels.

The role of policy instruments: defining the objectives

Once the nature of the market failure has been identified, the next step is to identify the policy objective. Economists use two related types of policy objectives: efficiency and cost-effectiveness. In the last chapter we defined efficiency as the allocation of resources that maximizes net benefits and cost-effectiveness as the allocation of resources that minimizes the cost of reaching a specific environmental target. In this chapter it will be useful to derive mathematically equivalent versions of these concepts in terms of the marginal conditions that are consistent with these definitions.

Efficiency

In our discussion of policy instruments a concept called the first equimarginal principle, will prove helpful.

> First Equimarginal Principle (the "Efficiency Equimarginal Principle"): Social net benefits are maximized when the social marginal benefits from an allocation equal the social marginal costs.

In pollution control the benefits are the reduced damages resulting from the emissions reduction so the principle can be rephrased as efficiency is achieved when the marginal cost of control is equal to the marginal damage that would be suffered if that unit was not controlled.

To examine the efficient allocation graphically, we need to know something about how control costs vary with the degree of control and how the damages vary with the amount of pollution emitted. Though our knowledge in these areas is less than complete, economists normally agree on the general shapes of these relationships. To understand this point see Figure 3.1.

Generally, the marginal damage caused by a unit of pollution increases with the amount emitted. When small amounts of the pollutant are emitted, the incremental damage is quite small. However, when large amounts are emitted, the marginal unit can cause significantly more damage. It is not hard to understand why. Small amounts of pollution are more easily diluted in the environment, and the body can tolerate small quantities of substances. However, as the cumulative amount in the atmosphere increases, dilution is less effective and the body is less tolerant.

Marginal control costs commonly increase with the amount controlled. Suppose a source of pollution tries to cut down on its particulate emissions by purchasing an electrostatic precipitator that captures 80 percent of the particulates as they flow past in the stack. If the source wants further control, it can purchase another precipitator and place it in the stack above the first one. This second precipitator captures 80 percent of the remaining 20 percent, or 16 percent of the uncontrolled emissions. Thus, the first precipitator would achieve an 80 percent reduction from uncontrolled emissions, while the second precipitator, which costs the same as the first, would achieve only a further 16 percent reduction (80 percent of the remaining 20 percent). Obviously, each unit of emissions reduction achieved by the second precipitator costs more than the reduction achieved by the first.

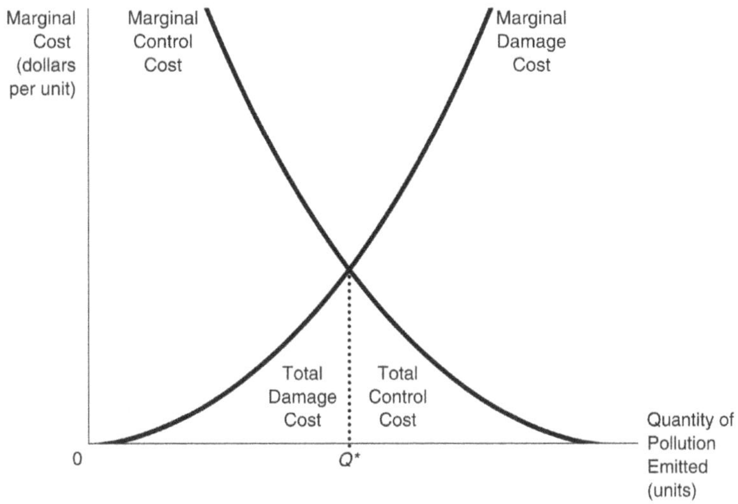

Figure 3.1 The Efficient Level of a Quantity Control

In Figure 3.1 we use these two pieces of information on the shapes of the relevant curves to graphically illustrate the efficient allocation. A movement from right to left refers to greater control and less pollution emitted. The efficient allocation is represented by $Q^\star$, the point at which the damage caused by the marginal unit of pollution is exactly equal to the marginal cost of avoiding it.

How do we know that is the efficient outcome? Greater degrees of control (points to the left of $Q^\star$) are inefficient because the further increase in avoidance costs would exceed the reduction in damage costs. Hence, total costs would rise. Similarly, levels of control lower than $Q^\star$ would result in a lower cost of control but the increase in damage costs would be even larger than the savings in control cost, yielding another increase in total cost. Increasing or decreasing the amount controlled causes an increase in total costs. Hence, $Q^\star$ must be efficient.

While in this diagram (and in many policy contexts) the optimal level of pollution is not zero, in some circumstances the optimal level of pollution *may* be zero, or close to it. The diagram can help us understand the circumstances that could give rise to this outcome. This situation occurs when the damage caused by even the first unit of pollution is so severe that it is higher than the marginal cost of controlling it. This would be reflected in Figure 3.1 as a leftward shift of the damage cost curve of sufficient magnitude that its intersection with the vertical axis would lie above the point where the marginal cost curve intersects the vertical axis. This circumstance characterizes the treatment of highly dangerous radioactive pollutants such as plutonium.

Cost-effectiveness

Whereas the efficiency objective seeks to balance the cost of policy action with the costs of inaction, cost effectiveness focuses on keeping the control costs as low as possible for achieving a particular policy target.

Consider a simple example. Assume that two emissions sources are currently emitting 15 units each for a total 30 units. Assume further that the control authority determines that the environment can assimilate 15 units in total, so that a reduction of 15 units is necessary. How should this 15-unit reduction be allocated between the two sources in order to minimize the total cost of the reduction?

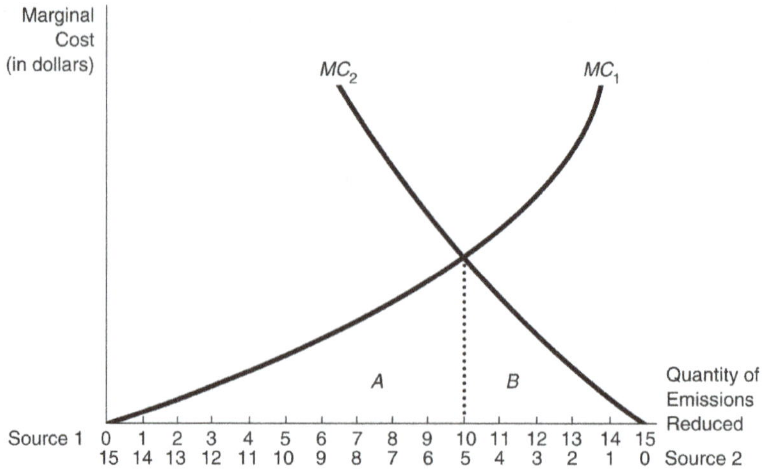

Figure 3.2 Cost-Effective Allocation of Pollution Control

We can demonstrate the answer with the aid of Figure 3.2 which is drawn by measuring the marginal cost of control for the first source from the left-hand axis (MC_1) and the marginal cost of control for the second source from the right-hand axis (MC_2). Note that a total 15-unit reduction is achieved for every point on this graph; each point represents some different combination of reduction by the two sources that sums to 15. Drawn in this manner, the diagram represents all possible allocations of the 15-unit reduction between the two sources. The left-hand axis, for example, represents an allocation of the entire reduction to the second source, while the right-hand axis represents a situation in which the first source bears the entire responsibility. All points in between represent different degrees of shared responsibility. What allocation minimizes the cost of control?

In the cost-effective allocation, the first source cleans up ten units, while the second source cleans up five units. The total variable cost of control for this particular assignment of the responsibility for the reduction is represented by area *A* plus area *B*. Area *A* is the cost of control for the first source; area *B* is the cost of control for the second. Any other allocation would result in a higher total control cost. (Convince yourself that this is true.)

Figure 3.2 also demonstrates the cost-effectiveness equimarginal principle.

> Second Equimarginal Principle (the Cost-Effectiveness Equimarginal Principle): The minimum cost of achieving an environmental target will have been achieved when the marginal costs of the emissions reductions from all possible sources of reduction are equal.

This is demonstrated by the fact that the marginal cost curves intersect at the cost-effective allocation.

When market failures cause the market to deviate from either or both of these objectives, what policy instruments can be used to restore efficiency and/or cost-effectiveness?

Categories of policy instruments

Historically the government has relied mainly on quantity-based policy instruments such as standards or prohibitions, but more recently a host of new types of instruments have been playing a larger role.

Traditional policy instruments

Environmental regulation could require the installation of particular pollution control equipment (as when catalytic converters were required on automobiles), or deny the use of a particular production ingredient (as when lead was removed from gasoline). In other words, they can regulate outputs, inputs, production processes, emissions, and even the location of production in their attempt to produce an efficient outcome.

On the whole, however, environmental authorities have for some time relied mainly on a defining a set of enforceable emissions standards (or maximum permissible emission levels) to control pollution. One possibility that was described in the introduction to this chapter is just simply to prohibit any emissions of a particularly dangerous substance. This is used for some radioactive substances and some toxic substances.

For more conventional pollutants two rather different kinds of standards are commonly employed: (1) air or water quality standards and (2) emission standards (air) and effluent standards (water). Air and water quality standards are targeted at setting maximum acceptable threshold pollution concentrations in the ambient environment. Historically standards designed to protect human health, for example, have been established based upon analysis to detect the lowest levels at which some harm to humans appears. The standards are set below this level with a margin of safety. The emissions or effluent standards are imposed on individual pollution sources and they control what is discharged into the environment in terms of both the amount and composition of the discharges.

These quantity-based policy instruments have played an important role in many environmental policies for good reasons. First this approach accords well with common sense – if a market produces too much pollution it seems reasonable to contain that excess by setting an enforceable maximum level. Second the harm from pollution is directly related to ambient concentrations and ambient concentrations are related to the amounts being injected into the air or water.

On the other hand over time some weaknesses of this approach have become clear. The concept of a safe pollution concentration threshold turns out to have been undermined as instrumentation has become able to detect much smaller concentrations and our epidemiology research had found that some harm occurs at much lower levels than previously thought. The existence of a safe threshold has come into question. As a practical matter the unreliability of the safe threshold concept as a basis for setting standards requires the introduction of some new basis.

Additionally notice that this quantity-based approach pays no attention to the costs of reaching the standard. Suppose as a standard is tightened a point is reached where any further reduction of harm is trivially small, but the cost of reaching that point is very large. Shouldn't that matter?

Why not simply use the efficiency principle to set these standards? While identifying the efficient level of standards can be easily defined in principle, they are not so easy to implement in practice. For the emission or effluent standards the discharge should be reduced to that level where the marginal cost of reducing the last unit was equal to the reduction of the marginal damage it would have caused. Monetizing the marginal damage is difficult enough, but the environmental manager normally knows very little about the control costs associated with hundreds of thousands emitters. Different firms use different processes with different costs of controlling those processes.

How can environmental authorities allocate pollution control responsibility in a reasonable manner when the information burdens are apparently so unrealistically large? The answer is provided by some newer types of policy instruments that are designed to nudge the economy back onto an efficient or cost-effective path. These are collectively known as economic or market-based instruments.

Market-based policy instruments

Although the potential list of market-based policy instruments is quite large, we shall limit our focus here to three main categories: (1) Price mechanisms (such as per unit taxes or subsides), (2) Mixed price and quantity mechanisms (e.g., cap-and-trade) and (3) Information strategies (e.g., labeling or mandatory disclosure regulations).

Price mechanisms

A common price mechanism involves putting a per unit tax or fee on emissions. An *emissions or effluent charge* is a fee, collected by the government, levied on each unit of pollutant emitted into the air or water. The total payment any source would be assessed would be the fee per unit of discharge times the amount discharged into the air or water. Emissions or effluent charges reduce pollution because paying the fees costs the firm money. To save money, the source seeks ways to reduce the amount of emissions subject to the fee.

How much pollution control would the firm choose? A profit-maximizing firm would control, rather than emit, pollution whenever it proved cheaper to do so. We can illustrate the firm's decision with Figure 3.3. In this figure the level of uncontrolled emissions is 15 units and the emissions charge is *T*. Thus, if the firm were to decide against controlling any emissions, it would have to pay *T* times 15, represented by area *0TBC*.

Is this the best the firm can do? Obviously not, since it can control some pollution at a lower cost than paying the emissions charge. The firm would lower its costs by reducing its emissions until the marginal cost of reduction is equal to the emissions charge. After that point it is cheaper for the firm to pay the tax since the marginal cost curve rises above the tax. To be specific the firm would minimize its cost by choosing to clean up ten units of pollution and to emit five units. At this allocation the firm would pay control costs equal to area *0AD* and total emissions charge payments equal to area *ABCD* for a total cost of *0ABC*. This is clearly less than 0*TBC*, the amount the firm would pay if it chose not to clean up any pollution.

Let's carry this one step further. Suppose that we had two emitters with the control costs depicted in Figure 3.2. Suppose further that we levied a per unit emissions charge of T on both sources discussed in Figure 3.4. Each source would then control its emissions until its marginal control cost equaled the emissions charge. (Faced with an emissions charge T, the second source would clean up five units.) Since they both face the same emissions charge, they will *independently* choose levels of control consistent with equal marginal control costs. This is precisely the condition that yields a cost-minimizing allocation.

This is a remarkable finding. We have shown that as long as the control authority imposes the same emissions charge on all sources, the resulting incentives are *automatically* compatible with minimizing

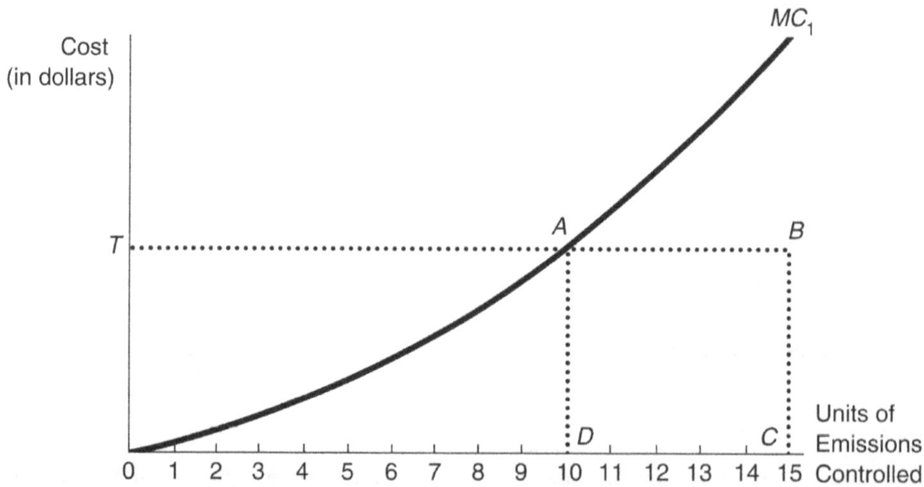

Figure 3.3 Cost-Minimizing Control of Pollution with an Emissions Charge

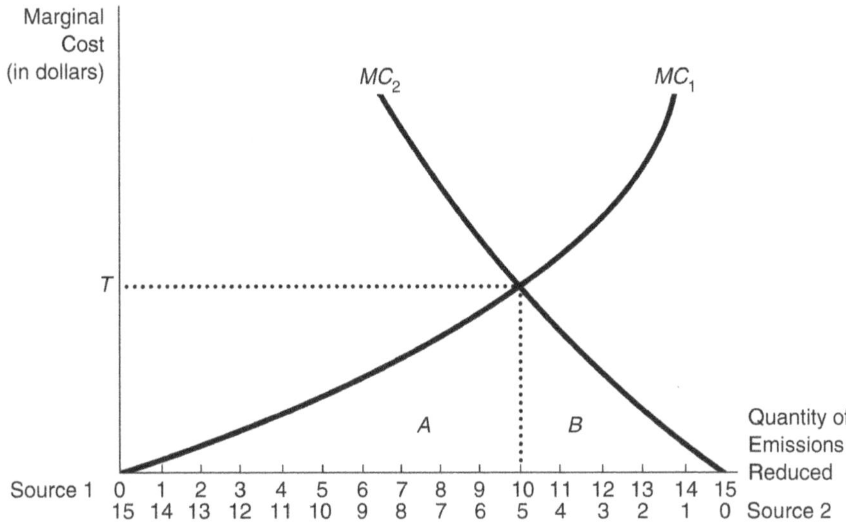

Figure 3.4 Imposing the Same Emissions Fee on Two Firms

the costs of achieving the chosen level of control (15 units in this case). This is true in spite of the fact that the control authority may not have any knowledge of each firm's control costs. The environmental manager can make profit-maximizing work for them.

However, we have not yet dealt with the issue of how the appropriate level of the emissions charge would be determined. Each level of a charge will result in *some* level of emissions reduction and that level would have been reached cost effectively, but it may not be the "right" level as set by the target. How high should the charge be set to ensure that the resulting emissions reduction is the *desired* level of emissions reduction?

Without having the requisite information on control costs, the control authority cannot normally establish the correct tax rate on the first try. It is possible, however, to develop an iterative, trial-and-error process to find the appropriate charge rate. This process is initiated by choosing a "best guess" charge rate (based upon the best available evidence) and observing the amount of reduction that occurs once that charge is imposed. If the observed reduction is larger than desired, it means the charge is higher than necessary; if the reduction is smaller, the charge is too low. The charge can then be adjusted in the desired direction. The new reduction that results from the adjusted charge can then be observed and compared with the desired reduction. Further adjustments in the charge can be made as needed. This process can be repeated until the actual and desired reductions are equal. At that point the correct emissions charge would have been found in the sense that it not only has achieved the desired emissions reduction target, but the final allocation of control responsibility among sources is cost-effective.

The advantages of this approach do not stop there. These charges also stimulate the development of newer, cheaper means of controlling emissions, as well as promoting technological progress. This is illustrated in Figure 3.5.

The reason for this is rather straightforward. With an emissions charge system, the firm is given an incentive to adopt cheaper new emissions-reduction technologies. As long as the firm can reduce its pollution at a marginal cost lower than *T*, it pays to adopt the new technology. In Figure 3.5, MC^0 represents the MC before the new technology is adopted and MC^1 is the new lower marginal cost with the adoption of the new technology. The firm saves *A* and *B* by adopting the new technology and voluntarily increases its emissions reduction from Q^0 to Q^1.

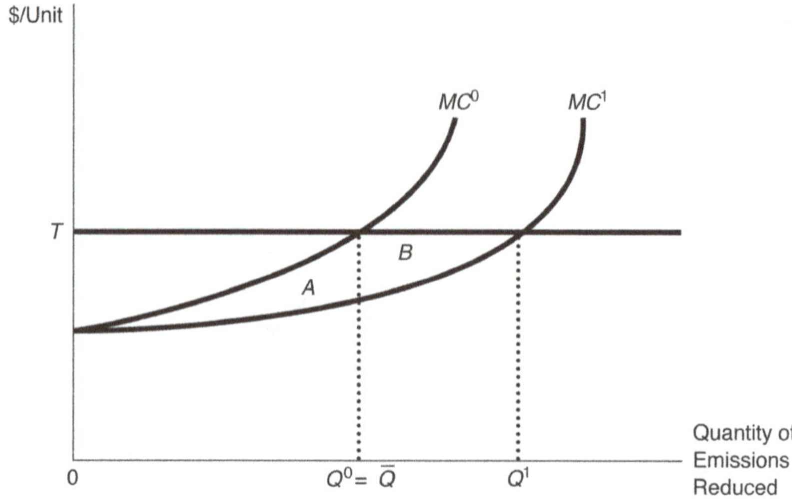

Figure 3.5 The Effect of Technological Progress

And finally a putting a price on pollution raises revenue. This turns out to be a significant aspect of this approach because how the revenue is used can help to promote fairness in the policy and to increase political support for it. We will explore the revenue using options and their consequences in subsequent chapters, but just to give you a flavor of the possibilities, consider how the revenue was used by Sweden when it sought to craft a charge to control nitrogen oxide emissions in the face of possible widespread opposition (see Example 3.2).

EXAMPLE 3.2

The Swedish nitrogen oxide charge

One of the dilemmas facing those who wish to use charges to control pollution is that the amounts of revenue extracted from those emitters subject to the tax can be considerable and that additional expense (over and above the cost of controlling the emissions) can produce a lot of political resistance to the policy. This resistance can be lowered if the revenue is rebated to those who pay it. However if all firms know they are getting their money back, the economic incentive to limit emissions is lost. Is it possible to design a system of rebates that will promote political feasibility without undermining abatement incentives?

The Swedish nitrogen oxide charge was designed specifically to resolve this dilemma. It was first imposed in 1992 on large energy sources. Some 120 heating plants and industrial facilities with about 180 boilers were subject to the tax.

It was intended from the beginning to have a significant emission-reduction incentive effect, but it was not designed to raise revenue for the government. Although the charge rate was high by international standards (thereby producing an effective economic incentive), the revenue from this tax was rebated to the emitting sources (thereby lowering resistance to the policy by the regulated sources).

It is the form of this rebate that makes this an interesting scheme. While the tax is collected on the basis of emissions, it is rebated on the basis of energy production. In effect, this system rewards plants that emit little nitrogen oxide per unit of energy and penalizes plants that emit more per unit of energy. Designed in this way it provides incentives to reduce emissions per unit of energy produced.

As expected, emissions per unit of energy produced fell rather dramatically. Over the period from 1992 to 2007, the plants were able to reduce the amount of emissions per unit of input energy by 67 percent. According to one study (OECD, 2010) there were three main explanations for this:

- Cumulative energy output produced by the plants increased by 74 percent over the period. The expansion in output mostly took place in plants that were relatively emission-efficient.
- Regulated plants invested in NOx mitigation and were therefore able to produce more energy output with fewer emissions.
- Innovations in mitigation technology made it possible to reach even lower emission intensity levels for the same output level.

Sources: Organization for Economic Co-operation and Development. (2013). The Swedish tax on nitrogen oxide emissions: Lessons in environmental policy reform. OECD Environment Policy Paper No. 2; OECD. (2010). Innovation Impacts of the Swedish NOx Charge. Paris: OECD. Available at www.oecd.org/greengrowth/consumption-innovation/43211635.pdf.

Pricing pollution has become a major alternative to traditional regulation and nowhere is that clearer than in the policy discussions about how to manage the threats posed by climate change. Carbon pricing is probably now a familiar phrase to most readers of this book. Many countries of the world such as Sweden, Switzerland, Finland, Norway, Denmark, France, Ireland and the Canadian Province of British Columbia, among others already have imposed carbon taxes. Upcoming chapters will cover this use of pricing in more detail.

Mixed price and quantity mechanisms

Is it possible for the control authority to find the cost-minimizing allocation without going through a trial-and-error process? It is possible if the environmental authority switches to a mixed system of prices and quantities. Suppose cap-and-trade (a form of emissions trading) is the chosen policy. Under this system, all sources face a *collective* limit on their emissions (the cap). Suppose for the sake of argument that the cap is 100,000 tons of the emissions each year. Once the magnitude of the cap is chosen the environmental authority next creates 100,000 allowances with each allowance authorizing 1 ton of emissions. These allowances are then auctioned off to the highest bidder. At the end of the control period each firm has to buy (and surrender to the environmental authority) enough allowances to cover their actual emissions during that control period. Any emissions by a source in excess of those allowed by its allowance surrender at the end of the year would cause the source to face severe monetary sanctions.

Why this system automatically leads to a cost-effective allocation can be seen in Figure 3.6. This figure treats the same set of circumstances as in Figure 3.2. Remember that these allowances are normally purchased via the auction before the control period ends, which means they may not perfectly anticipate what they will need when it is time to settle up with the government. Suppose that the first source purchased seven allowances (each corresponds to one emission unit). Because it has 15 units of uncontrolled emissions, this would mean it must control eight units. Similarly, suppose that the second source purchased the remaining eight allowances. It would have to clean up seven units. These allowances are fully tradable at any time during the control period. Notice that both firms have an incentive to trade. The marginal cost of control for the second source (*C*) is substantially higher than that for the first (*A*). The second source could lower its cost if it could buy an additional allowance from the first source at a price lower than *C*. Meanwhile, the first source would be better off if it could sell an allowance for a price higher than *A*. Because *C* is greater than *A*, grounds for trade certainly exist

Allowance trading would take place until the first source had only five allowances left (and controlled ten units), while the second source had ten allowances (and controlled five units). At this point, the allowance price would equal B, because that is the marginal value of that allowance to both sources, and neither source would have any incentive to trade further. The allowance market would be in equilibrium.

Notice that the market equilibrium for an emissions allowance system is the cost-effective allocation! Simply by issuing the appropriate number of allowances (15) and letting the market do the rest, the control authority can achieve a cost-effective allocation without having even the slightest

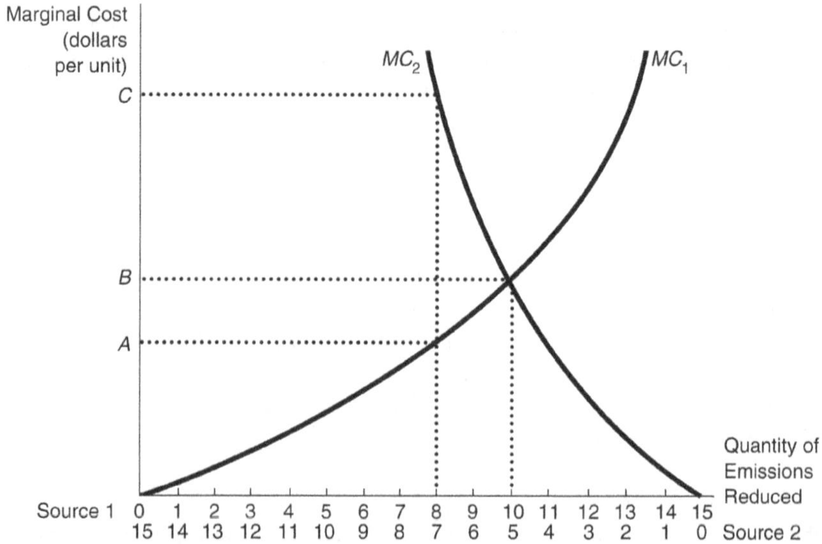

Figure 3.6 Cost-Effectiveness and Emissions Trading

knowledge about control costs. This system allows the government to meet its policy objective, while allowing greater flexibility in how that objective is met.

This intriguing idea of using tradable permits to combine a collective maximum limit (a cap) on the use of a particular environmental resource with allowing the market to allocate the authorizations consistent with that cap to individual users is not only being used in controlling the threats posed by carbon and other types of pollution, but it also is being used in such widely varying policy areas as the efficient management of fisheries (individual transferable quotas), promoting renewable energy (renewable energy credits), protecting wetlands banking), removing impediments to efficient land use control tradable development rights) to mention a few. In upcoming chapters we shall examine several operational applications and their consequences.

Disclosure strategies

Our final category is quite a different animal from the two market-based strategies previously discussed. The market depends on decentralized decision making to do its job of procuring efficient outcomes. Both consumers and producers have roles to play. If they are going to play that role effectively, they must be fully informed about the consequences of various choices. The first phase of pollution control involved applying traditional quantity-based remedies such as emissions standards. Over time however, it became clear that these traditional regulatory approaches to pollution control were excessively costly in some circumstances and incapable of achieving the stipulated goals in others. In response to these deficiencies in the second phase the use of market-based approaches such as cap-and trade, and emission charges have become much more common. In some instances they have substituted for traditional remedies, but in most cases, they have complemented them. In general these approaches have added flexibility and improved cost-effectiveness to the control of pollution.

Dealing with asymmetric information

Even the addition of these two types of market-based approaches, has not, however, fully solved the problems. In the industrialized countries the system remains over burdened by the sheer number of substances to be controlled. Neither staffs nor budgets are adequate for the task of regulating all of the potentially harmful substances which are emitted by firms and households.

In many of the developing countries the regulatory infrastructure is commonly insufficiently developed and/or subject to corruption. In either case it is incapable of adequately handling the burden of designing, implementing, monitoring and enforcing an effective pollution control system.

Phase three in the evolution of pollution control policy involves investment in the provision of information. This increasing role for disclosure strategies seems to emanate not only from the increasing perceived need for more regulatory tools, but also from the falling cost of information collection, aggregation and dissemination. Rising benefits and falling costs imply that however inefficient their use may have been perceived to be in the past, changed circumstances merit another look.

The disclosure strategies considered in this book involve public and/or private attempts to increase the availability of information on pollution and other threats to workers, consumers, shareholders and the public at large. Provision of greater information may either complement or replace traditional regulation strategies. And in so doing they interact in sometimes complex ways with traditional standard setting and enforcement strategies. Whether they complement phase one and two strategies or substitute for them, they involve a rather different role for government – one which seems to offer the possibility of fulfilling the large and growing need for control despite limited budgets and staffs.

Legislation and/or regulation can also help to resolve the asymmetric information problem. Because the fundamental problem is that one or more of the parties do not have sufficient crucial, trustworthy information, the obvious solution involves providing that information. How should that information be provided?

Labeling is one attempt to provide more information to consumers. Examples of labeling for food products include notifying consumers about products containing genetically modified organisms, and identifying organically grown crops and fair trade products.

A recent source of encouragement for organic farms has been the demonstrated willingness of consumers to pay a premium for organically grown fruits and vegetables. To allow consumers to discern which products are truly organic, growers need a reliable certification process. Additionally, fear of lost access to important foreign markets, such as the European Union, led to an industry-wide push in the United States for *mandatory* labeling standards that would provide the foundation for a national uniform seal. (*Voluntary* U.S. certification programs had proved insufficient to assure access to European markets, since they were highly variable by state.)

In response to these pressures, the Organic Foods Production Act (OFPA) was enacted in the 1990 Farm Bill. Title 21 of that law states the following objectives:

> (1) to establish national standards governing the marketing of certain agricultural products as organically produced; (2) to assure consumers that organically produced products meet a consistent standard; and (3) to facilitate interstate commerce in fresh and processed food that is organically produced.

The USDA National Organic Program, established as part of this Act, is responsible for a mandatory certification program for organic production. The Act also established the National Organic Standards Board (NOSB) and charged it with defining the "organic" standards. The new rules, which took effect in October 2002, require certification by the USDA for labeling. Foods labeled as "100 percent organic" must contain only organic ingredients. Foods labeled as "organic" must contain at least 95 percent organic agricultural ingredients, excluding water and salt. Products labeled as "Made with Organic Ingredients" must contain at least 70 percent organic agricultural ingredients. Certification allows socially conscious consumers to make a difference.

Disclosure strategies take many different forms and comprehensive treatment in a chapter like this is clearly impossible. Perhaps the easiest way to reveal their nature is through a couple of specific policy examples here and a more comprehensive treatment in upcoming chapters.

The Toxic Release Inventory (TRI) was enacted by the U.S. Congress in January 1986 as a part of the Environmental Protection and Community Right to Know Act (EPCRA). EPCRA was enacted partially in response to two incidents. In 1984, methyl isocyanate killed thousands of people in Bhopal, India. A chemical release at a sister plant in West Virginia happened soon after. The public's (workers' and community members') demand for information about toxic chemicals was the impetus for EPCRA. Together with the Pollution Prevention Act (PPA) of 1990, it mandates the collection of data on toxic chemicals that are treated on-site, recycled, and combusted for energy recovery. The TRI is a publicly available database designed to provide information to the public on releases of toxic substances into the environment. Most of the substances involved are not themselves subject to release standards.

TRI states that firms that *use* 10,000 or more pounds of a listed chemical in a given calendar year or firms that *import, process, or manufacture* 25,000 or more pounds of a listed chemical must file a report on each of the chemicals in existence within the plant if they also have ten or more full-time employees. Approximately 650 chemicals are covered in the TRI. Most recently the TRI has been expanded to include lower reporting thresholds for certain persistent bioaccumulative toxic (PBT) chemicals. PBT chemicals are pollutants that can accumulate in body tissue. PBT chemicals include mercury, pesticides, and dioxins.

Reporting of emissions or use of listed chemicals is accomplished annually. (For the data, see www.epa.gov/tri/tridata/index.htm.) The reports include such information as the name of the company, the name of the parent company if it exists, the toxic released and frequency of release, and the medium in which the chemical is released. Data by state are also available and all data are available to the public. Firms must also separately report emissions to their state and local authorities as well as to fire and emergency officials.

Several other countries now use similar reporting mechanisms, known as Pollutant Release and Transfer Registers (PRTR). All have slight variations on the TRI. In Japan, the PRTR includes data on diffuse sources (e.g., automobiles). The Canadian PRTR, called the National Pollutant Release Inventory (NPRI), also collects data on the number of employees at each facility. The Mexican PRTR is voluntary and so data are limited.

Has the existence of the TRI reduced toxic emissions into the environment? EPA's annual reports reveal that substantial reductions have occurred. Although careful examination of the filings found that some of these reductions merely reflect a change in definition, other reductions have been found to be genuine. Apparently, the reported magnitude of the reductions is likely to be overstated, but real reductions have occurred. Among the chemicals that are reported to TRI, about 180 are known or suspected carcinogens. In 2011, the EPA reported that the air releases of these carcinogens decreased by 50 percent between 2003 and 2011.

Proposition 65, the *Safe Drinking Water and Toxic Enforcement Act of 1986*, was established in the state of California by popular vote in November 1986, following the inception of the Toxic Release Inventory by the EPA. Proposition 65 is intended to protect California citizens and the state's drinking water sources from toxic chemicals. Proposition 65 requires companies producing, using, or transporting one or more of the listed chemicals to notify those who are potentially impacted. Chemicals are listed as carcinogenic or as causing reproductive harm. When their use or potential exposure levels exceed "safe harbor numbers" established by a group of approved scientists, the impacted people must be notified. The "safe harbor" threshold is uniquely determined for each chemical and depends upon its intrinsic potency or the potency of a released mixture. Proposition 65 also requires the governor of California to publish, at least annually, a list of chemicals known to the state to cause cancer or reproductive toxicity.

The program involves three forms of notification: (1) warning labels must be placed on all products that will cause adverse health effects when used for a prolonged period of time; (2) a company whose toxic emissions to air, ground, or water exceed levels deemed safe for prolonged exposure must provide public notification; and (3) workers must be warned of the potential danger if toxic chemicals defined by Proposition 65 are used in manufacturing a product or are created as a by-product of manufacturing.

Only companies with ten or more full-time workers are required to notify people of exposure. Nonprofit organizations like hospitals, recycling plants, and government organizations, which account for over 65 percent of California's pollution, are not required to comply with Proposition 65.

Under the proposition, private citizens, other industry members, and environmental groups can sue companies that fail to notify people of exposure appropriately. Plaintiffs who make a successful legal claim can keep a substantial portion of the settlement; this encourages private enforcement of the law and reduces the need for government monitoring. Industry members also have a strong incentive to monitor each other, so that one company does not cheat and look greener than its rivals.

Did this program change behavior? At least in controlling exposure to lead, it clearly did (see Example 3.3).

EXAMPLE 3.3

Regulating through mandatory disclosure: the case of lead

Rechtschaffen (1999) describes a particularly interesting case study involving how Proposition 65 produced a major reduction in the amount of lead exposure by promoting new technologies, production-process changes, and pollution-prevention measures. He even goes so far as to suggest that Proposition 65 seemed even more effective than federal law in addressing certain lead hazards from drinking water, consumer products, and other sources.

Rechtschaffen identifies several characteristics about Proposition 65 that explain its relative success. We mention two here.

First, despite periodic calls for such an integrated strategy, no coordinated federal approach to controlling lead hazards had emerged. Rather, lead exposures were regulated by an array of agencies acting under a multitude of regulatory authorities. In contrast, the Proposition 65 warning requirement applies without limitation to *any* exposure to a listed chemical unless the exposure falls under the safe harbor standard, regardless of its source. Thus, the coverage of circumstances leading to lead exposure is very high and the standards requiring disclosure are universally applied.

Second, unlike federal law, Proposition 65 is self-executing. Once a chemical is listed by the state as causing cancer or reproductive harm, Proposition 65 applies. This contrasts with federal statutes, where private activity causing lead exposures is permitted until and unless the government sets a restrictive standard. Whereas under the federal approach fighting the establishment of a restrictive standard made economic sense (by delaying the date when the provisions would apply), under Proposition 65 exactly the opposite incentives prevail. In the latter case, since the provisions took effect soon after enactment, the only refuge from the statute rested on the existence of a safe harbor standard that could insulate small exposures from the statute's warning requirements. For Proposition 65, at least some subset of firms had an incentive to make sure the safe harbor standard was in place; delay in implementing the standard was costly, not beneficial.

Source: Rechtschaffen, C. (1999). How to reduce lead exposure with one simple statute: The experience with Proposition 65. *Environmental Law Reporter*, *29*, 10581–10591.

As we shall see in upcoming chapters information approaches are being applied across a much larger scope of environmental management issues than pollution control in general and toxic substances regulation in particular (see Example 3.4).

EXAMPLE 3.4

HELIX: improving incentives in the residential energy market

Heating, cooling, and lighting of residences is a major source of carbon emissions. With full information we would expect homeowners to do a good job in reducing energy waste (and the associated carbon emissions) in their homes not only because reducing waste would save them money now, but an energy efficient house would claim a higher price at the time of sale.

Unfortunately the residential market does a very poor job of sharing information to potential buyers on how energy efficient any home is. The primary barrier to widespread access to energy information for homes on the market has been the absence of any system in place to transmit this data directly from sellers trying to market homes to the real estate listings buyers use to compare the available choices. More transparent data on energy use would increase the incentives for homeowners to invest in energy efficiency since those investments would make their house worth more to potential buyers.

To respond to this information deficiency various stakeholders formed the HELIX (*Home Energy Labeling Information eXchange*) team in 2016 with the assistance of a U.S. DOE State Energy Program grant hosted by Vermont. This project, which focuses on the six New England states and New York, is designed to develop a database capable of automatically populating real estate listings (whether they are accessed through local Multiple Listing Services (MLS) or portals like Trulia and Zillow) with home energy information that is available and approved by the seller. Future plans will include information on solar investments as well. To what degree might the information HELIX provides increase residential investments in more efficient heating, cooling and lighting devices, saving both energy and carbon emissions? Stay tuned.

Source: HELIX website, https://neep.org/home-energy-labeling-information-exchange-helix?utm_source=NEEP+Master+List&utm_campaign=5ed0bdc45d-EM%26VFallMeeting_COPY_01&utm_medium=email&utm_term=0_d09b004d10–5ed0bdc45d-224810349

Thanks to behavioral economics we now also know that how the information is framed matters in how effective it is. One classic example involves using information to encourage homeowners to use electricity more efficiently (see Example 3.5).

EXAMPLE 3.5

How the information is framed can improve energy conservation

One detailed case study found that by providing feedback to customers on home electricity and natural gas usage with a focus on peer comparisons, utilities could reduce energy consumption at a low cost. This study used data from two large-scale, random-assignment field experiments involving two large power companies in partnership with a private company, Opower. Opower randomly assigned a subset of these households to periodically receive mailed "home energy reports" comparing their energy usage to that of nearby neighbors in similarly sized houses. The first experiment involved electricity supplied by the Sacramento Municipal Utility District [SMUD]) while the second involved electricity and natural gas (Puget Sound Energy [PSE]). Relative to the control (no peer reports) these experiments found a reduction in energy consumption of 1.2 percent (PSE) to 2.1 percent (SMUD) with the decrease sustained over time (seven months [PSE] and 12 months [SMUD]).

Source: Ayres, Ian, Sophie Raseman and Alice Shih (2013) "Evidence from Two Large Field Experiments that Peer Comparison Feedback Can Reduce Residential Energy" *Journal of Law, Economics, & Organization*, Volume 29, Issue 5, 992–1022, https://doi.org/10.1093/jleo/ews020

Summary

In this chapter we developed the conceptual framework needed to evaluate the role of various possible policy instruments in efficient and cost-effective environmental management.

While markets are powerful means for allocating resources they are far from infallible. In our society government typically plays a role when market fail to produce efficient or cost-effective outcomes. The government can either replace market actions (substituting government outcomes for market outcomes) or it can work to correct the incentives that led the market astray.

Leaving a more comprehensive discussion to upcoming chapters, we focused on four types of policy instruments in the context of managing pollution control as a means of illustrating how these various approaches work.

Since pollution is a classic externality, markets will generally produce more than the efficient amount of both fund pollutants and stock pollutants. For both types of pollutants, this will imply higher-than-efficient damages and lower-than-efficient control costs. For stock pollutants, an excessive amount of pollution would accumulate in the environment, imposing a detrimental externality on future generations as well as on current generations.

The market would not provide any automatic ameliorating response to the accumulation of pollution as it would in the case of natural resource scarcity. Firms attempting to unilaterally control their pollution could be placed at a competitive disadvantage. Hence, the case for some sort of government intervention is particularly strong for pollution control.

Using the concepts of efficiency and cost-effectiveness we derived the incentives that arise from each these instruments and the resulting resource outcomes from those faced with those incentives. We then compared these to the conditions required for either efficient or cost-effective outcomes and noted some rather remarkable differences among the traditional instruments and the market-based instruments.

First the traditional regulatory preference for quantity-based instruments is with "appropriate design" perfectly capable of sustaining both efficiency and cost-effective outcomes in principle, but in actual administrative practice the amount of information required to implement that "appropriate design" can prove to be a considerable barrier.

That is not true for either the market-based pricing or mixed price-and-quantity strategies. Uniform emissions charges or an allowance system focused purely on emissions could be used to attain the cost-effective allocation, even when the control authority has no information whatsoever on either control costs or damage costs. Uniform emissions standards would not, except by coincidence, be cost-effective. In addition, either emissions trading or charges would provide more incentives for technological progress in pollution control than would emissions standards.

Our final market-based strategy focuses on market failures that arise from a lack of good information about the consequences of their decisions. Helping uninformed market participants to overcome information deficiencies (for example, on the health damage that can occur from exposure to toxic substances) can help to nudge the market toward more efficient or cost-effective solutions.

Finally as we will demonstrate in upcoming chapters these advantages for market-based instruments actually apply to many different areas of environmental management, one reason they are spreading to many new countries and many new types of environmental management problems.

Self-test exercises

1 Suppose the state is trying to decide how many miles of a very scenic river it should preserve. There are 100 people in the community, each of whom has an identical inverse demand function given by $P = 10 - 1.0q$, where q is the number of miles preserved and P is the per-mile price he or she is willing to pay for q miles of preserved river. (a) If the marginal cost of preservation is \$500 per mile, how many miles would be preserved in an efficient allocation? (b) How large is the economic surplus?

2 Suppose you were asked to comment on a proposed policy to control oil spills. Since the average cost of an oil spill has been computed as \$*X*, the proposed policy would require any firm responsible for a spill immediately to pay the government \$*X*. Is this likely to result in the efficient amount of precaution against oil spills? Why or why not?

3 "In environmental liability cases, courts have some discretion regarding the magnitude of compensation polluters should be forced to pay for the environmental incidents they cause. In general, however, the larger the required payments the better." Discuss.

Further reading

Freeman, J., & Kolstad, C. D. (Eds.). (2007). *Moving to Markets: Lessons from Twenty Years of Experience*. New York: Oxford University Press. A collection of 16 essays from leading scholars exploring what lessons can be extracted from actual experience with moving to market-based environmental regulation.

Hamilton, J. T. (2005). *Regulation by Revelation: The Origins, Impacts and Politics of the Toxics Release Inventory Program*. Cambridge, UK: Cambridge University Press. An examination of one of the major examples of a disclosure strategy.

OECD. (2017a). *Policy Instruments for the Environment* (Database of quantitative and qualitative information on over 3200 policy instruments from around the world). Available at: www.oecd.org/environment/indicators-modelling-outlooks/policy-instrument-database/

OECD. (2017b). *Tackling Environmental Problems with the Help of Behavioural Insights.* Paris: OECD Publishing. http://dx.doi.org/10.1787/9789264273887-en. This report provides an up-to-date review of relevant behavioral interventions in OECD countries and beyond in a variety of environmental policy areas.

Schmalensee, R., & Stavins, R. N. (2017). The design of environmental markets: What have we learned from experience with cap and trade? *Oxford Review of Economic Policy*, 33(4), 572–588.

Sterner, T., & Muller, A. (Eds.). (2016). *Environmental Taxation in Practice*, International Library of Environmental Economics and Policy. New York: Routledge. Focusing on environmental taxation in practice this book collects key contributions on a wide range of topics, including comparisons in different countries and key aspects of implementation.

Tietenberg, T. (2006). *Emissions Trading: Principles and Practice*, 2nd ed. Washington, DC: Resources for the Future. This book considers how the use of emissions trading to control pollution has evolved, looks at how these programs have been implemented in the United States and internationally, and offers an objective evaluation of the resulting successes, failures, and lessons learned over a 25-year period.

Yokessa, M., & Marette, S. (2019). A review of eco-labels and their economic impact. *International Review of Environmental and Resource Economics*, 13, 119–163. Combines a critical literature review with discussions of empirical examples.

Chapter 4

Evaluating trade-offs

Benefit-cost analysis and other decision-making metrics

Introduction

In the last chapter we noted that economic analysis has both positive and normative dimensions. The normative dimension helps to separate the policies that make sense from those that don't. Since resources are limited, it is not possible to undertake all ventures that might appear desirable, so making choices is inevitable.

Normative analysis can be useful in public policy in several different situations. It might be used, for example, to evaluate the desirability of a proposed new pollution control regulation or a proposal to preserve an area currently scheduled for development. In these cases, the analysis helps to provide guidance on the desirability of a program before that program is put into place. In other contexts, it might be used to evaluate how an already-implemented program has worked out in practice. Here the relevant question is: Was this a wise use of resources? In this chapter, we present and demonstrate the use of several decision-making metrics that can assist us in evaluating options.

Normative criteria for decision making

Normative choices can arise in two different contexts. In the first context, we need simply to choose among options that have been predefined, while in the second we try to find the optimal choice among all the possible options.

Evaluating predefined options: benefit-cost analysis

If you were asked to evaluate the desirability of some proposed action, you would probably begin by attempting to identify both the gains and the losses from that action. If the gains exceed the losses, then it seems natural to support the action.

That simple framework provides the starting point for the normative approach to evaluating policy choices in economics. Policies typically have both benefits and costs. If the benefits exceed the costs, then the action is desirable. On the other hand, if the costs exceed the benefits, then the action is not desirable. (Comparing benefits and costs across time will be covered later in this chapter.)

We can formalize this in the following way. Let B be the benefits from a proposed action and C be the costs. Our decision rule would then be

if $B > C$, support the action.
Otherwise, oppose the action.[1]

As long as B and C are positive, a mathematically equivalent formulation would be

if $B/C > 1$, support the action.
Otherwise, oppose the action.

So far so good, but how do we measure benefits and costs? In economics, the system of measurement is anthropocentric, which simply means human centered. All benefits and costs are valued in terms of their effects (broadly defined) on humanity. As shall be pointed out later, that does *not* imply (as it might first appear) that ecosystem effects are ignored unless they *directly* affect humans. The fact that large numbers of humans contribute voluntarily to organizations that are dedicated to environmental protection provides ample evidence that humans place a value on environmental preservation that goes well beyond any direct use they might make of it. Nonetheless, the notion that humans are doing the valuing is a controversial point that will be revisited and discussed in Chapters 5 and 6, along with the specific techniques for valuing these effects.

In benefit-cost analysis, benefits are measured simply as the relevant area under the demand curve since the demand curve reflects consumers' willingness to pay. Total costs are measured by the relevant area under the marginal cost curve.

It is important to stress that environmental services have costs even though they are produced without any human input. All costs should be measured as opportunity costs. To firm up this notion of opportunity cost, consider an example. Suppose a particular stretch of river can be used either for white-water rafting or to generate electric power. Since the dam that generates the power would flood the rapids, the two uses are incompatible. The opportunity cost of producing power is the foregone net benefit that would have resulted from the whitewater rafting. The *marginal opportunity cost curve* defines the additional cost of producing another unit of electricity resulting from the associated incremental loss of net benefits due to reduced opportunities for white-water rafting.

Since net benefit is defined as the excess of benefits over costs, it follows that net benefit is equal to that portion of the area under the demand curve that lies above the supply curve.

Consider Figure 4.1, which illustrates the net benefits from preserving a stretch of river. Suppose that we are considering preserving a four-mile stretch of river and that the benefits and costs of that action are reflected in Figure 4.1. Should that stretch be preserved? Why or why not? Hold on to your answer because we will return to this example later.

Finding the optimal outcome

In the preceding section, we examined how benefit-cost analysis can be used to evaluate the desirability of specific actions. In this section, we want to examine how this approach can be used to identify "optimal," or best, approaches.

In subsequent chapters, which address individual environmental problems, the normative analysis will proceed in three steps. First, we will identify an optimal outcome. Second, we will attempt to discern the extent to which our institutions produce optimal outcomes and, where divergences occur

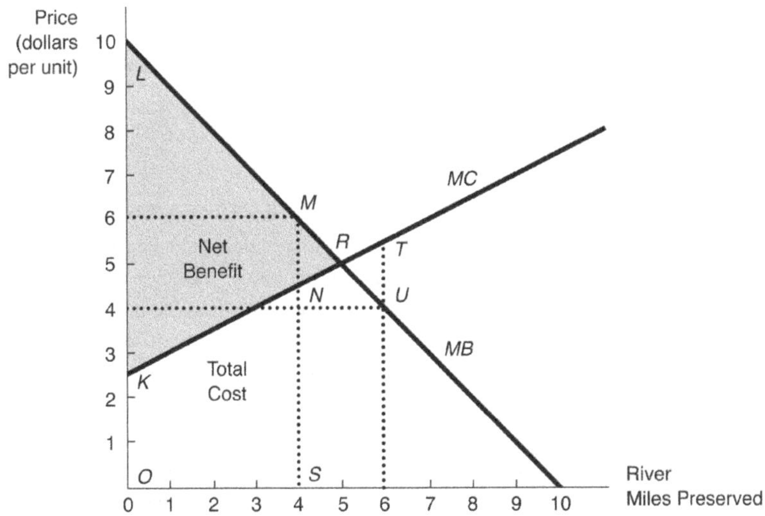

Figure 4.1 The Derivation of Net Benefits

between actual and optimal outcomes, to attempt to uncover the behavioral sources of the problems. Finally, we can use both our knowledge of the nature of the problems and their underlying behavioral causes as a basis for designing appropriate policy solutions. Although applying these three steps to each of the environmental problems must reflect the uniqueness of each situation, the overarching framework used to shape that analysis remains the same.

To provide some illustrations of how this approach is used in practice, consider two examples: one drawn from natural resource economics and another from environmental economics. These are meant to be illustrative and to convey a flavor of the argument; the details are left to upcoming chapters.

Consider the rising number of depleted ocean fisheries. Depleted fisheries, which involve fish populations that have fallen so low as to threaten their viability as commercial fisheries, not only jeopardize oceanic biodiversity, but also pose a threat to both the individuals who make their living from the sea and the communities that depend on fishing to support their local economies.

How would an economist attempt to understand and resolve this problem? The first step would involve defining the optimal stock or the optimal rate of harvest of the fishery. The second step would compare this level with the actual stock and harvest levels. Once this economic framework is applied, not only does it become clear that stocks are much lower than optimal for many fisheries, but also the reason for excessive exploitation becomes clear. Understanding the nature of the problem has led quite naturally to some solutions. Once implemented, these policies have allowed some fisheries to begin the process of renewal. The details of this analysis and the policy implications that flow from it are covered in Chapter 7.

Another problem involves greenhouse gas emissions that are contributing to climate change. As the atmospheric carbon dioxide passes threshold levels (now over 400 ppm), what can be done?

Economists start by thinking about "optimal" warming threshold (2 degrees celsius). The analysis not only reveals that current emissions levels are excessive, but also suggests some specific behavioral sources of the problem. Based upon this understanding, specific economic solutions can be identified and implemented. Communities that have adopted these measures are generally more resilient to climate change impacts.

In the rest of the book, similar analysis is applied to water pollution, climate change adaptation, and a host of other topics. In each case, the economic analysis helps to point the way toward solutions. To initiate that process, we must begin by defining "optimal."

Relating optimality to efficiency

According to the normative choice criterion introduced earlier in this chapter, desirable outcomes are those where the benefits exceed the costs. It is therefore a logical next step to suggest that optimal polices are those that maximize net benefits (benefits minus costs). The concept of *static efficiency*, or merely *efficiency*, was introduced in Chapter 2. An allocation of resources is said to satisfy the static efficiency criterion if the economic surplus from the use of those resources is maximized by that allocation. Notice that the net benefits area to be maximized in an "optimal outcome" for public policy is identical to the "economic surplus" that is maximized in an efficient allocation. Hence, efficient outcomes are also optimal outcomes.

Let's take a moment to show how this concept can be applied. Previously, we asked whether an action that preserved four miles of river was worth doing (Figure 4.1). The answer is yes because the net benefits from that action are positive. (Can you see why?)

Static efficiency, however, requires us to ask a rather different question, namely, what is the optimal (or efficient) number of miles to be preserved? We know from the definition that the optimal amount of preservation would maximize net benefits. Does preserving four miles maximize net benefits? Is it the efficient outcome?

We can answer that question by establishing whether it is possible to increase the net benefit by preserving more or less of the river. If the net benefit can be increased by preserving more miles, clearly, preserving four miles could not have maximized the net benefit and, therefore, could not have been efficient.

Consider what would happen if society were to choose to preserve five miles instead of four. Refer back to Figure 4.1. What happens to the net benefit? It increases by area *MNR*. Since we can find another allocation with greater net benefit, four miles of preservation could not have been efficient. Could five? Yes. Let's see why.

We know that five miles of preservation convey more net benefits than four. If this allocation is efficient, then it must also be true that the net benefit is smaller for levels of preservation higher than five. Notice that the additional cost of preserving the sixth unit (the area under the marginal cost curve) is larger than the additional benefit received from preserving it (the corresponding area under the demand curve). Therefore, the triangle *RTU* represents the reduction in net benefit that occurs if six miles are preserved rather than five.

Since the net benefit is reduced, both by preserving less than five miles and by preserving more than five, we conclude that five units is the preservation level that maximizes net benefit (the shaded area). Therefore, from our definition, preserving five miles constitutes an efficient or optimal allocation.[2]

One implication of this example, which will be very useful in succeeding chapters, is what we shall call the "first equimarginal principle":

> First Equimarginal Principle (the "Efficiency Equimarginal Principle"): Social net benefits are maximized when the social marginal benefits from an allocation equal the social marginal costs.

The social marginal benefit is the increase in social benefits received from supplying one more unit of the good or service, while social marginal cost is the increase in cost incurred from supplying that additional unit of the good or service.

This criterion helps to minimize wasted resources, but is it fair? The ethical basis for this criterion is derived from a concept called *Pareto optimality*, named after the Italian-born Swiss economist Vilfredo Pareto, who first proposed it around the turn of the twentieth century.

> Allocations are said to be Pareto optimal if no other feasible allocation could benefit at least one person without any deleterious effects on some other person.

Allocations that do not satisfy this definition are suboptimal. Suboptimal allocations can always be rearranged so that some people can gain net benefits without the rearrangement causing anyone else to lose net benefits. Therefore, the gainers could use a portion of their gains to compensate the losers sufficiently to ensure they were at least as well off as they were prior to the reallocation.

Efficient allocations are Pareto optimal. Since net benefits are maximized by an efficient allocation, it is not possible to increase the net benefit by rearranging the allocation. Without an increase in the net benefit, it is impossible for the gainers to compensate the losers sufficiently; the gains to the gainers would necessarily be smaller than the losses to the losers.

Inefficient allocations are judged inferior because they do not maximize the size of the pie to be distributed. By failing to maximize net benefit, they are forgoing an opportunity to make some people better off without harming others.

Comparing benefits and costs across time

The analysis we have covered so far is very useful for thinking about actions where time is not an important factor. Yet many of the decisions made now have consequences that persist well into the future. Time is a factor. Exhaustible energy resources, once used, are gone. Biological renewable resources (such as fisheries or forests) can be overharvested, leaving smaller and possibly weaker populations for future generations. Persistent pollutants can accumulate over time. How can we make choices when the benefits and costs occur at different points in time?

Incorporating time into the analysis requires an extension of the concepts we have already developed. This extension provides a way for thinking not only about the magnitude of benefits and costs, but also about their timing. In order to incorporate timing, the decision rule must provide a way to compare net benefits received in different time periods. The concept that allows this comparison is called *present value*. Before introducing this expanded decision rule, we must define present value.

Present value explicitly incorporates the time value of money. A dollar today invested at 10 percent interest yields \$1.10 a year from now (the return of the \$1 principal plus \$0.10 interest). The present value of \$1.10 received one year from now is therefore \$1, because, given \$1 now, you can turn it into \$1.10 a year from now by investing it at 10 percent interest. We can find the present value of any amount of money (X) received one year from now by computing $X/(1 + r)$, where r is the appropriate interest rate (10 percent in our preceding example).

What could your dollar earn in two years at r percent interest? Because of compound interest, the amount would be $\$1(1 + r)(1 + r) = \$1(1 + r)^2$. It follows then that the present value of X received two years from now is $X/(1 + r)^2$. The present value of X received in three years is $X/(1 + r)^3$.

By now the pattern should be clear. The present value of a *one-time* net benefit received n years from now is

$$PV[B_n] = \frac{(B-C)_n}{(1+r)^n}$$

The present value of a stream of net benefits $\{(B-C)_0, \ldots, (B-C)_n\}$ received over a period of n years is computed as

$$PV\left[(B-C)_0, \ldots, (B-C)_n\right] = \sum_{i=0}^{n} \frac{(B-C)_i}{(1+r)^i}$$

where r is the appropriate interest rate and $(B-C)_0$ is the amount of net benefits received immediately. The process of calculating the present value is called *discounting*, and the rate r is referred to as the discount rate.

The number resulting from a present-value calculation has a straightforward interpretation. Suppose you were investigating an allocation that would yield the following pattern of net benefits on the last day of each of the next five years: \$3,000, \$5,000, \$6,000, \$10,000, and \$12,000. If you use an interest rate of 6 percent ($r = 0.06$) and the preceding formula, you will discover that this stream has a present value of \$29,205.92 (see Table 4.1). Notice how each amount is discounted back the appropriate number of years to the present and then these discounted values are summed.

What does that number mean? If you put \$29,205.92 in a savings account earning 6 percent interest and wrote yourself checks, respectively, for \$3,000, \$5,000, \$6,000, \$10,000, and \$12,000 on the last day of each of the next five years, your last check would just restore the account to a \$0 balance (see Table 4.2). Thus, you should be indifferent about receiving \$29,205.92 now or in the specific five-year stream of benefits totaling \$36,000; given one, you can get the other. Hence, the method is called present value because it translates everything back to its current worth.

It is now possible to show how this analysis can be used to evaluate actions. Calculate the present value of net benefits from the action. If the present value is greater than zero, the action can be supported. Otherwise it should not.

Table 4.1 Demonstrating Present Value Calculations

Year	*1*	*2*	*3*	*4*	*5*	*Sum*
Annual Amounts	\$3,000	\$5,000	\$6,000	\$10,000	\$12,000	\$36,000
Present Value (r = 0.06)	\$2,830.19	\$4,449.98	\$5,037.72	\$7,920.94	\$8,967.10	\$29,205.92

Table 4.2 Interpreting Present Value Calculations

Year	*1*	*2*	*3*	*4*	*5*	*6*
Balance at Beginning of Year	\$29,205.92	\$27,958.28	\$24,635.77	\$20,113.92	\$11,320.75	**\$0.00**
Year-End Fund Balance before Payment (r = 0.06)	\$30,958.28	\$29,635.77	\$26,113.92	\$21,320.75	\$12,000.00	
Payment	\$3,000	\$5,000	\$6,000	\$10,000	\$12,000	

Dynamic efficiency

The static efficiency criterion is very useful for comparing resource allocations when time is not an important factor. How can we think about optimal choices when the benefits and costs occur at different points in time?

The traditional criterion used to find an optimal allocation when time is involved is called *dynamic efficiency*, a generalization of the static efficiency concept already developed. In this generalization, the present-value criterion provides a way for comparing the net benefits received in one period with the net benefits received in another.

An allocation of resources across *n* time periods satisfies the dynamic efficiency criterion if it maximizes the present value of net benefits that could be received from all the possible ways of allocating those resources over the *n* periods.

Applying the concepts

Having now spent some time developing the concepts we need, let's take a moment to examine some actual studies in which they have been used.

Pollution control

Benefit-cost analysis has been used to assess the desirability of efforts to control pollution. Pollution control certainly confers many benefits, but it also has costs. Do the benefits justify the costs? That was a question the U.S. Congress wanted answered, so in Section 812 of the Clean Air Act Amendments of 1990, it required the U.S. Environmental Protection Agency (EPA) to evaluate the benefits and costs of the U.S. air pollution control policy initially over the 1970–1990 period and subsequently over the 1990–2020 time period (see Example 4.1).

EXAMPLE 4.1

Does reducing pollution make economic sense? Evidence from the Clean Air Act

In its 1997 report to Congress, the EPA presented the results of its attempt to discover whether the Clean Air Act had produced positive net benefits over the period 1970 to 1990. The results suggested that the present value of benefits (using a discount rate of 5 percent) was $22.2 trillion, while the costs were $0.523 trillion. Performing the necessary subtraction reveals that the net benefits were therefore equal to $21.7 trillion. According to this study, U.S. air pollution control policy during this period made very good economic sense.

Soon after the period covered by this analysis, substantive changes were made in the Clean Air Act Amendments of 1990 (the details of those changes are covered in later chapters). Did those additions also make economic sense?

In August of 2010, the U.S. EPA issued a report of the benefits and costs of the Clean Air Act from 1990 to 2020. This report suggests that the costs of meeting the 1990 Clean Air Act Amendment requirements are expected to rise to approximately $65 billion per year by 2020 (2006 dollars). Almost half of the compliance costs ($28 billion) arise from pollution controls placed on cars, trucks, and buses, while another $10 billion arises from reducing air pollution from electric utilities.

These actions are estimated to cause benefits (from reduced pollution damage) to rise from roughly $800 billion in 2000 to almost $1.3 trillion in 2010, ultimately reaching approximately $2 trillion per year (2006 dollars) by 2020! For persons living in the United States, a cost of approximately $200 per person by 2020 produces approximately a $6,000 gain in benefits per person from the improvement in air quality. Many of the estimated benefits come from reduced risk of early mortality due to exposure to fine particulate matter. Table 4.3 provides a summary of the costs and benefits and includes a calculation of the benefit/cost ratio.

Table 4.3 Summary Comparison of Benefits and Costs from the Clean Air Act (1990–2020) (Estimates in Million 2006$)

	Annual Estimates			*Present Value Estimate*
	2000	*2010*	*2020*	*1990–2020*
Monetized Direct Costs:				
Low[1]				
Central	$20,000	$53,000	$65,000	$380,000
High[1]				
Monetized Direct Benefits:				
Low[2]	$90,000	$160,000	$250,000	$1,400,000
Central	$770,000	$1,300,000	$2,000,000	$12,000,000
High[2]	$2,300,000	$3,800,000	$5,700,000	$35,000,000
Net Benefits:				
Low	$70,000	$110,000	$190,000	$1,000,000
Central	$750,000	$1,200,000	$1,900,000	$12,000,000
High	$2,300,000	$3,700,000	$5,600,000	$35,000,000
Benefit/Cost Ratio:				
Low[3]	5/1	3/1	4/1	4/1
Central	39/1	25/1	31/1	32/1
High[3]	115/1	72/1	88/1	92/1

Notes:

1 The cost estimates for this analysis are based on assumptions about future changes in factors such as consumption patterns, input costs, and technological innovation. We recognize that these assumptions introduce significant uncertainty into the cost results; however, the degree of uncertainty or bias associated with many of the key factors cannot be reliably quantified. Thus, we are unable to present specific low and high cost estimates.

2 Low and high benefit estimates are based on primary results and correspond to 5th and 95th percentile results from statistical uncertainty analysis, incorporating uncertainties in physical effects and valuation steps of benefits analysis. Other significant sources of uncertainty not reflected include the value of unquantified or unmonetized benefits that are not captured in the primary estimates and uncertainties in emissions and air quality modeling.

3 The low benefit/cost ratio reflects the ratio of the low benefits estimate to the central costs estimate, while the high ratio reflects the ratio of the high benefits estimate to the central costs estimate. Because we were unable to reliably quantify the uncertainty in cost estimates, we present the low estimate as "less than X" and the high estimate as "more than Y," where X and Y are the low and high benefit/cost ratios, respectively.

Sources: U.S. Environmental Protection Agency. (1997). *The Benefits and Costs of the Clean Air Act, 1970 to 1990*. Washington, D.C.: Environmental Protection Agency, Table 18, p. 56; U.S. Environmental Protection Agency Office of Air and Radiation, *The Benefits and Costs of the Clean Air Act, 1990 to 2020 – Summary Report, 8/16/2010*. Full Report available at www.epa.gov/clean-air-act-overview/benefits-and-costs-clean-air-act-1990-2010-first-prospective-study (accessed January 14, 2018).

In responding to this congressional mandate, the EPA set out to quantify and monetize the benefits and costs of achieving the emissions reductions required by U.S. policy. Benefits quantified by this study included reduced death rates and lower incidences of chronic bronchitis, lead poisoning, strokes, respiratory diseases, and heart disease as well as the benefits of better visibility, reduced structural damages, and improved agricultural productivity.

We shall return to this study later in the book for a deeper look at how these estimates were derived, but a couple of comments are relevant now. First, despite the fact that this study did not attempt to value all pollution damage to ecosystems that was avoided by this policy, the net benefits are still strongly positive. While presumably the case for controlling pollution would have been even stronger had all such avoided damage been included, the desirability of this form of control is evident even with only a partial consideration of benefits. An inability to monetize *all* benefits and costs does not necessarily jeopardize the ability to reach sound policy conclusions.

Although these results justify the conclusion that pollution control made economic sense, they do not justify the stronger conclusion that the policy was efficient. To justify that conclusion, the study would have had to show that the present value of net benefits was maximized, not merely positive. In fact, this study did not attempt to calculate the maximum net benefits outcome, and if it had, it would have almost certainly discovered that the policy during this period was not optimal. The costs of the chosen policy approach were higher than necessary to achieve the desired emissions reductions. With an optimal policy mix, the net benefits would have been even higher.

Estimating benefits of carbon dioxide emission reductions

Benefit-cost analysis is frequently complicated by the estimation of benefits and costs that are difficult to quantify. (Chapter 5 takes up the topic of nonmarket valuation in detail.) One such value is the benefit of reductions in carbon emissions.

Executive Order 12866 requires government agencies "to assess both the costs and the benefits of an intended regulation and, recognizing that some costs and benefits are difficult to quantify, propose or adopt a regulation only upon a reasoned determination that the benefits of the intended regulation

Table 4.4 Revised Social Cost of CO_2 (2015–2050) (in 2007 Dollars per Metric Ton of CO_2)

	Discount		*Rates*	
Year	*5% Avg*	*3% Avg*	*2.5% Avg*	*3% 95th*
2015	$11	$36	$56	$105
2020	$12	$42	$62	$123
2025	$14	$46	$68	$138
2030	$16	$50	$73	$152
2035	$18	$55	$78	$168
2040	$21	$60	$84	$183
2045	$23	$64	$89	$197
2050	$26	$69	$95	$212

Source: https://19january2017snapshot.epa.gov/climatechange/social-cost-carbon_.html (accessed October 28, 2019).

justify its costs."[3] In order to include benefits from reducing carbon dioxide emission, agencies use what is called the "social cost of carbon" to reflect what those damages would have been in the absence of the reductions. The social cost of carbon is the marginal increase in the present value (in dollars) of the economic damages (e.g., sea level rise, floods, changes in agricultural productivity, and altered ecosystem services) resulting from a small increase (usually 1 metric ton) in carbon dioxide emissions. Since the social cost of carbon is a present value calculation, both the timing of the emission reduction and the discount rate play an important role.

The Interagency Working Group on Social Cost of Carbon presented the first set of estimates for the social cost of carbon in 2010. In 2013, these estimates were revised upwards with the estimate for the social cost of carbon increasing from $22 to approximately $37 per ton of carbon (using a discount rate of 3 percent). In 2016, they were revised again. Table 4.4 illustrates the 2016 revised social cost of carbon dioxide using 2.5, 3, and 5 percent discount rates for selected years. The fourth column presents the extreme case (95th percentile) using a 3 percent discount rate. Notice the importance of the discount rate in determining what value is used. (Can you explain why?)

The social cost of carbon is useful in making sure that the calculated benefits of carbon reductions reflect the reduced damages that can be expected. Example 4.2 demonstrates one way the social cost of carbon has been used in policy.

EXAMPLE 4.2

Using the social cost of carbon: the DOE microwave oven rule

In 2013, the Department of Energy (DOE) announced new rules for energy efficiency for microwave ovens in standby mode. By improving the energy efficiency of these ovens, this rule would reduce carbon emissions. In the regulatory impact analysis associated with this rule, it was necessary to value the reduced damages from this lower level of emissions. The social cost of carbon was used to provide this information.

Using the 2010 social cost of carbon (SCC) produced a present value of net benefits for the microwave oven rule over the next 30 years of $4.2 billion. Since this value is positive, it means that implementing this rule would increase efficiency.

We know that using the revised 2013 number would increase the present value of net benefits, but by how much? According to the DOE, using the 2013 instead of the 2010 social cost of carbon increases the present value of net benefits to $4.6 billion. In this case the net benefits were large enough both before and after the new SCC estimates to justify implementing the rule, but it is certainly possible that in other cases these new estimates would justify rules that prior to the change would not have been justified.

Note that microwave purchasers will bear the cost of this set of rules (as prices rise to reflect the higher production costs), but they will not receive all of the benefits (those reflecting a reduction in external costs). However, the DOE notes that due to the increased energy efficiency of the appliances subject to these rules (and the resulting lower energy costs for purchasers), the present value of savings to consumers is estimated to be $3.4 billion over the next 30 years (DOE 2013), an amount that is larger than the costs. In this case the rules represent a win for both microwave consumers and the planet.

Sources: http://energy.gov/articles/new-energy-efficiency-standards-microwave-ovens-save-consumers-energy-bills; *Technical Update of the Social Cost of Carbon for Regulatory Impact Analysis – Under Executive Order 12866*, https://obamawhitehouse.archives.gov/sites/default/files/omb/inforeg/scc-tsd-final-july-2015.pdf; Department of Energy (2013). *Energy Conservation Program: Energy Conservation Standards for Standby Mode and Off Mode for Microwave Ovens.* www.federalregister.gov/documents/2013/06/17/2013-13535/energy-conservation-program-energy-conservation-standards-for-standby-mode-and-off-mode-for

How much difference has it made in general? One study examined all economically significant federal regulations since 2008 to see what difference using a social cost of carbon would make. When they compared the ranking of the proposed policy to the status quo, they found little evidence that use of the social cost of carbon to include carbon reduction benefits into the calculation affected U.S. policy choices to date. The authors speculate that the absence of a discernible impact may be explained, in part, because U.S. regulators have succeeded in selecting the "low-hanging fruit," where the net benefits of early policies that reduce carbon are the largest and therefore most likely to pass a benefit-cost test even without using the social cost of carbon.[4]

In 2017, with the election of President Donald Trump everything changed. Soon after taking office President Trump signed an Executive Order that calls on agencies to disband the Interagency Working

Group on Social Cost of Greenhouse Gases and to withdraw the documents that are the basis for the current calculation of the social cost of carbon. That EPA website has now been removed, although scientists have preserved the material (it can be found at https://19january2017snapshot.epa.gov/climatechange/social-cost-carbon_.html).

While this order does not abandon the concept completely, it does signal a desire to use a new approach to measuring and using the concept. What will this mean for future policies? Stay tuned.

Issues in benefit estimation

The analyst charged with the responsibility for performing a benefit-cost analysis encounters many decision points requiring judgment. If we are to understand benefit-cost analysis, the nature of these judgments must be clear in our minds.

Primary versus secondary effects

Environmental projects usually trigger both primary and secondary consequences. For example, the primary effect of cleaning a lake will be an increase in recreational uses of the lake. This primary effect will cause a further ripple effect on services provided to the increased number of users of the lake. Are these secondary benefits to be counted?

The answer depends upon the employment conditions in the surrounding area. If this increase in demand results in employment of previously unused resources, such as labor, the value of the increased employment should be counted. If, on the other hand, the increase in demand is met by a shift in previously employed resources from one use to another, it is a different story. In general, secondary employment benefits should be counted in high unemployment areas or when the particular skills demanded are underemployed at the time the project is commenced. They should not be counted when the project simply results in a rearrangement of productively employed resources.

Accounting stance

The accounting stance refers to the geographic scale or scope at which the benefits are measured. Scale matters because in a benefit-cost analysis only the benefits or costs affecting that specific geographic area are counted. Suppose, for example, that the federal government picks up many of the costs, but the benefits are received by only one region. Even if the benefit-cost analysis shows this to be a great project for the region that will not necessarily be the case for the nation as a whole. Once the national costs are factored in, the national project benefits may not exceed the national project costs. Debate 4.1 examines this issue in relation to the social cost of carbon.

DEBATE 4.1

What is the proper geographic scope for the Social Cost of Carbon?

The Social Cost of Carbon is an estimate of the economic damages associated with a small increase in carbon dioxide (CO_2) emissions, conventionally 1 metric ton, in a given year. Any reduction in these damages resulting from a proposed regulation is used to estimate the climate benefits of U.S. rulemakings.

Because climate change is a global public good, the efficient damage estimate must include all damages, not just damages to the United States. Some critics argue that, because it is used in U.S. regulatory procedures, it should include only U.S. damages; otherwise it might justify regulations that impose costs on U.S. citizens for the purpose of producing benefits enjoyed by citizens of other countries who do not bear the cost.

Proponents of the global metric point out that the measure is designed to be a means of internalizing a marginal external cost and it cannot do that accurately and efficiently if it leaves out some of the costs. Calculating it only for U.S. damages would create a biased measure that would underestimate the damages and raise the possibility of biased regulatory decisions based upon it.

Furthermore, they argue that the characterization of this measure as allowing benefits created by American citizens to be enjoyed by foreign citizens is a bit misleading. These benefits do not reflect goods and services purchased by U.S. citizens that are enjoyed abroad. Rather they reflect a reduction in the damages that U.S. citizens would otherwise be imposing on others. American law typically does not allow someone to inflict damage on neighbors simply because they are on the other side of some boundary. Reducing damages imposed on others has a different moral context than spillover benefits.

Some regulatory analysts have now suggested that the "U.S.-only" measure should not replace the existing measure, but complement it. Both should be provided. What do you think?

Source: Dudley, Susan E., Fraas, Art, Gayer, Ted, Graham, John, Lutter, Randall, Shogren, Jason F., & Viscusi, W. Kip. (2016). How much will climate change rules benefit Americans? *Forbes* (February 9).

Aggregation

Related to accounting stance are challenges of aggregation. Estimates of benefits and costs must be aggregated in order to derive total benefits and total costs. How many people benefit and how many people incur costs are very important in any aggregation, but, additionally, *how* they benefit might impact that aggregation. Suppose, for example, those living closer to the project received more benefits per household than those living farther away. In this case these differences should be accounted for.

With and without principle

The "with and without" principle states that only those benefits that would result from the project should be counted, ignoring those that would have accrued anyway. Mistakenly including benefits that would have accrued anyway would overstate the benefits of the program.

Tangible versus intangible benefits

Tangible benefits are those that can reasonably be assigned a monetary value. *Intangible benefits* are those that cannot be assigned a monetary value, either because data are not available or reliable enough or because it is not clear how to measure the value even with data.[5] Quantification of intangible benefits is the primary topic of the next chapter.

How are intangible benefits to be handled? One answer is perfectly clear: they should not be ignored. To ignore intangible benefits is to bias the results. That benefits are intangible does not mean they are unimportant.

Intangible benefits should be quantified to the fullest extent possible. One frequently used technique is to conduct a sensitivity analysis of the estimated benefit values derived from less than perfectly reliable data. We can determine, for example, whether or not the outcome is sensitive, within wide ranges, to the value of this benefit. If not, then very little time has to be spent on the problem. If the outcome is sensitive, the person or persons making the decision bear the ultimate responsibility for weighing the importance of that benefit.

Approaches to cost estimation

Estimating costs is generally easier than estimating benefits, but it is not easy. One major problem for both derives from the fact that benefit-cost analysis is forward-looking and thus requires an estimate of what a particular strategy *will* cost, which is much more difficult than tracking down what an existing strategy *does* cost.

Two approaches have been developed to estimate these costs: the survey approach and the engineering approach.

The survey approach

One way to discover the costs associated with a policy is to ask those who bear the costs, and presumably know the most about them, to reveal the magnitude of the costs to policy makers. Polluters, for example, could be asked to provide control-cost estimates to regulatory bodies. The problem with this approach is the strong incentive not to be truthful. An overestimate of the costs can trigger less stringent regulation; therefore, it is financially advantageous to provide overinflated estimates.

The engineering approach

The engineering approach bypasses the source being regulated by using general engineering information to catalog the possible technologies that could be used to meet the objective and to estimate the costs of purchasing and using those technologies. The final step in the engineering approach is to assume that the sources would use technologies that minimize cost. This produces a cost estimate for a "typical," well-informed firm.

The engineering approach has its own problems. These estimates may not approximate the actual cost of any particular firm. Unique circumstances may cause the costs of that firm to be higher, or lower, than estimated; the firm, in short, may not be typical.

The combined approach

To circumvent these problems, analysts frequently use a combination of survey and engineering approaches. The survey approach collects information on possible technologies, as well as special circumstances facing the firm. Engineering approaches are used to derive the actual costs of those technologies, given the special circumstances. This combined approach attempts to balance information best supplied by the source with that best derived independently.

In the cases described so far, the costs are relatively easy to quantify and the problem is simply finding a way to acquire the best information. This is not always the case, however. Some costs are not easy to quantify, although economists have developed some ingenious ways to secure monetary estimates even for those costs.

Take, for example, a policy designed to conserve energy by forcing more people to carpool. If the effect of this is simply to increase the average time of travel, how is this cost to be measured?

For some time, transportation analysts have recognized that people value their time, and a large amount of literature has now evolved to provide estimates of how valuable time savings or time increases would be. The basis for this valuation is opportunity cost – how the time might be used if it weren't being consumed in travel. Although the results of these studies depend on the amount of time involved, individual decisions seem to imply that travelers value their travel time at a rate not more than half their wage rates.

The treatment of risk

For many environmental problems, it is not possible to state with certainty what consequences a particular policy will have, because scientific estimates themselves often are imprecise. Determining the efficient exposure to potentially toxic substances requires obtaining results at high doses and extrapolating to low doses, as well as extrapolating from animal studies to humans. It also requires relying upon epidemiological studies that infer a pollution-induced adverse human health impact from correlations between indicators of health in human populations and recorded pollution levels.

For example, consider the potential damages from climate change. While scientists agree on potential impacts of climate change, such as sea level rise, increased storm intensity and species losses, the timing and extent of those losses are not certain.

The treatment of risk in the policy process involves two major dimensions: (1) identifying and quantifying the risks, and (2) deciding how much risk is acceptable. The first is primarily scientific and descriptive, while the second is more evaluative or normative.

Benefit-cost analysis grapples with the evaluation of risk in several ways. Suppose we have a range of policy options A, *B*, *C*, *D* and a range of possible outcomes *E*, *F*, *G* for each of these policies depending on how the economy evolves over the future. These outcomes, for example, might depend on whether the demand growth for the resource is low, medium, or high. Thus, if we choose policy *A*, we might end up with outcomes *AE*, *AF*, or *AG*. Each of the other policies has three possible outcomes as well, yielding a total of 12 possible outcomes.

We could conduct a separate benefit-cost analysis for each of the 12 possible outcomes. Unfortunately, the policy that maximizes net benefits for *E* may be different from that which maximizes net benefits for *F* or G. Thus, if we only knew which outcome would prevail, we could select the policy that maximized net benefits; the problem is that we do not. Furthermore, choosing the policy that is best if outcome *E* prevails may be disastrous if *G* results instead.

When a dominant policy emerges, this problem is avoided. A *dominant policy* is one that confers higher net benefits for every outcome. In this case, the existence of risk concerning the future is not relevant for the policy choice. This fortuitous circumstance is exceptional rather than common, but it can occur.

Other options exist even when dominant solutions do not emerge. Suppose, for example, that we were able to assess the likelihood that each of the three possible outcomes would occur. Thus, we might expect outcome *E* to occur with probability 0.5, *F* with probability 0.3, and *G* with probability 0.2. Armed with this information, we can estimate the expected present value of net benefits. The *expected present value of net benefits* for a particular policy is defined as the sum over outcomes of the present value of net benefits for that policy where each outcome is weighted by its probability of occurrence. Symbolically this is expressed as

$$EPVNB_i = \sum_{i=0}^{I} P_i PVNB_{ij}, \quad j = 1, \ldots, J,$$

where

$EPVNBj$ = expected present value of net benefits for policy j,

Pi = probability of the *i*th outcome occurring,

PVNBij = present value of net benefits for policy j if outcome i prevails,
J = number of policies being considered,
I = number of outcomes being considered.

The final step is to select the policy with the highest expected present value of net benefits.

This approach has the substantial virtue that it weighs higher probability outcomes more heavily. It also, however, makes a specific assumption about society's preference for risk. This approach is appropriate if society is risk-neutral. *Risk-neutrality* can be defined most easily by the use of an example. Suppose you were to choose between being given a definite \$50 or entering a lottery in which you had a 50 percent chance of winning \$100 and a 50 percent chance of winning nothing. (Notice that the expected value of this lottery is \$50 = 0.5(\$100) + 0.5(\$0).) You would be said to be risk-neutral if you would be indifferent between these two choices. If you view the lottery as more attractive, you would be exhibiting *risk-loving* behavior, while a preference for the definite \$50 would suggest *risk-averse* behavior. Using the expected present value of net benefits approach implies that society is risk-neutral.

Is that a valid assumption? The evidence is mixed. The existence of gambling suggests that at least some members of society are risk-loving, while the existence of insurance suggests that, at least for some risks, others are risk-averse. Since the same people may gamble and own insurance policies, it is likely that the type of risk may be important.

Even if individuals were demonstrably risk-averse, this would not be a sufficient condition for the government to forsake risk-neutrality in evaluating public investments. One famous article (Arrow and Lind, 1970) argues that risk-neutrality is appropriate since "when the risks of a public investment are publicly borne, the total cost of risk-bearing is insignificant and, therefore, the government should ignore uncertainty in evaluating public investments." The logic behind this result suggests that as the number of risk bearers (and the degree of diversification of risks) increases, the amount of risk borne by any individual diminishes to zero.

When the decision is irreversible, as demonstrated by Arrow and Fisher (1974), considerably more caution is appropriate. Irreversible decisions may subsequently be regretted, but the option to change course will be lost forever. Extra caution also affords an opportunity to learn more about alternatives to this decision and its consequences before acting. Isn't it comforting to know that occasionally procrastination can be optimal?

There is a movement in national policy in both the courts and the legislature to search for imaginative ways to define acceptable risk. In general, the policy approaches reflect a case-by-case method. We shall see that current policy reflects a high degree of risk aversion toward a number of environmental problems.

Distribution of benefits and costs

Many agencies are now required to consider the distributional impacts of costs and benefits as part of any economic analysis. For example, the U.S. EPA provides guidelines on distributional issues in its "Guidelines for Preparing Economic Analysis." According to the EPA, distributional analysis "assesses changes in social welfare by examining the effects of a regulation across different sub-populations and entities." Distributional analysis can take two forms: *economic impact analysis* and *equity analysis*. Economic impact analysis focuses on a broad characterization of who gains and who loses from a given policy. Equity analysis examines impacts on disadvantaged groups or sub-populations. The latter delves into the normative issue of equity or fairness in the distribution of costs and benefits. Loomis (2011) outlines several approaches for incorporating distribution and equity into benefit-cost analysis. Distributional weights can be helpful for equity consideration (Adler, 2016). Some issues of the distribution of benefits and costs related to energy efficiency rules for appliances were highlighted in Example 4.2.

Unintended consequences

Policies may cause indirect effects that have unintended consequences, thus reducing the effectiveness of the policy. Consider a ban on plastic bags. Later in the book, Debate 13.2 examines the unintended effects the bag ban had on the sale of other plastic bags. While well-intended, the policy failed.

Choosing the discount rate

Recall that discounting allows us to compare all costs and benefits in current dollars, regardless of when the benefits accrue or costs are charged. Suppose a project will impose an immediate cost of $4,000,000 (today's dollars), but the $5,500,000 benefits will not be earned until five years out. Is this project a good idea? On the surface it might seem like it is, but recall that $5,500,000 in five years is not the same as $5,500,000 today. At a discount rate of 5 percent, the present value of benefits minus the present value of costs is positive. However, at a 10 percent discount rate, this same calculation yields a negative value, since the present value of costs exceeds the benefits. Can you reproduce the calculations that yield these conclusions?

As Example 4.3 indicates, this has been, and continues to be, an important issue. When the public sector uses a discount rate lower than that in the private sector, the public sector will find more projects with longer payoff periods worthy of authorization. And, as we have already seen, the discount rate is a major determinant of the allocation of resources among generations as well.

EXAMPLE 4.3

The importance of the discount rate

Let's begin with an historical example. For years the United States and Canada had been discussing the possibility of constructing a tidal power project in the Passamaquoddy Bay between Maine and New Brunswick. This project would have heavy initial capital costs, but low operating costs that presumably would hold for a long time into the future. As part of their analysis of the situation, a complete inventory of costs and benefits was completed in 1959.

Using the same benefit and cost figures, Canada concluded that the project should not be built, while the United States concluded that it should. Because these conclusions were based on the same benefit-cost data, the differences can be attributed solely to the use of different discount rates. The United States used 2.5 percent while Canada used 4.125 percent. The higher discount rate makes the initial cost weigh much more heavily in the calculation, leading to the Canadian conclusion that the project would yield a negative net benefit. Since the lower discount rate weighs the lower future operating costs relatively more heavily, Americans saw the net benefit as positive.

In a more recent illustration of why the magnitude of the discount rate matters, on October 30, 2006, economist Nicholas Stern from the London School of Economics issued a report using a discount rate of 0.1 percent that concluded that the benefits of strong, early action on climate change would considerably outweigh the costs. Other economists, such as Nobel Laureate William Nordhaus of Yale University, who preferred a discount rate around 6 percent, found that optimal economic policies to slow climate change involve only modest rates of emissions reductions in the near term, followed by sharp reductions in the medium and long term.

In this debate, the desirability of strong current action is dependent (at least in part) on the size of the discount rate used in the analysis. Higher discount rates reduce the present value of future benefits from current investments in abatement, implying a smaller marginal benefit. Since the costs associated with those investments are not affected nearly as much by the choice of discount rate (remember that costs occurring in the near future are discounted less), a lower present value of marginal benefit translates into a lower optimal investment in abatement.

Far from being an esoteric subject, the choice of the discount rate is fundamentally important in defining the role of the public sector, the types of projects undertaken, and the allocation of resources across generations.

Sources: Stokey, E., & Zeckhauser, R. (1978). *A Primer for Policy Analysis*. New York: W. W. Norton, 164–165; Mikesell, R. (1977). *The Rate of Discount for Evaluating Public Projects*. Washington, D.C.: The American Enterprise Institute for Public Policy Research, 3–5; the Stern Report: http://webarchive.nationalarchives.gov.uk/20100407011151/www.hm-treasury.gov.uk/sternreview_index.htm; Nordhaus, W. (2007). A review of the Stern Review on the economics of climate change. *Journal of Economic Literature*, *XLV* (September), 686–702.

The discount rate can be defined conceptually as the social opportunity cost of capital. This cost of capital can be divided further into two components: (1) the riskless cost of capital, and (2) the risk premium. Traditionally, economists have used long-term interest rates on government bonds as one measure of the cost of capital, adjusted by a risk premium that would depend on the riskiness of the project considered. Unfortunately, the choice of how large an adjustment to make has been left to the discretion of the analysts. This ability to affect the desirability of a particular project or policy by the choice of discount rate led to a situation in which government agencies were using a variety of discount rates to justify programs or projects they supported. One set of hearings conducted by Congress during the 1960s discovered that, at one time, agencies were using discount rates ranging from 0 to 20 percent.

During the early 1970s, the Office of Management and Budget published a circular that required, with some exceptions, all government agencies to use a discount rate of 10 percent in their benefit-cost analysis. A revision issued in 1992 reduced the required discount rate to 7 percent. This circular also includes guidelines for benefit-cost analysis and specifies that certain rates will change annually.[6] This standardization reduces biases by eliminating the agency's ability to choose a discount rate that justifies a predetermined conclusion. It also allows a project to be considered independently of fluctuations in the true social cost of capital due to cycles in the behavior of the economy. On the other hand, when the social opportunity cost of capital differs from this administratively determined level, the benefit-cost analysis will not, in general, define the efficient allocation.

Example 4.3 highlights a different aspect of the choice of the discount rate for decisions involving long time horizons. It considers the question of whether or not discount rates should decline over time. Debate 4.3 explores this question.

DEBATE 4.3

Discounting over long time horizons: should discount rates decline?

As you now recognize, the choice of the discount rate can significantly alter the outcome of a benefit-cost analysis. This effect is exacerbated over long time horizons and can become especially influential in decisions about spending now to mitigate damages from climate change, which may be uncertain in both magnitude and timing. What rate is appropriate? Recent literature and some evidence argue for declining rates of discount over long time horizons. Should a declining rate schedule be utilized? A blue-ribbon panel of experts recently gathered to debate this and related questions (Arrow et al., 2012).

An unresolved debate in the economics literature revolves around the question of whether discount rates should be positive ("descriptive"), reflecting actual market rates, or normative ("prescriptive"), reflecting ethical considerations. Those who argue for the descriptive approach prefer to use market rates of return since expenditures to mitigate climate change are investment expenditures. Those who argue for the alternative prescriptive approach argue for including judgments about intergenerational equity. These rates are usually lower than those found in actual markets (Griffiths et al., 2012).

In the United States, the Office of Management and Budget (OMB) currently recommends a constant rate of discount for project analysis. The recommendation is to use 3 percent and 7 percent real discount rates in sensitivity analysis (OMB, 2003) with options for lower rates if future generations are impacted. The United Kingdom and France utilize discount rate schedules that decline over time. Is one of these methods better than the other for discounting over long time horizons? If a declining rate is appropriate, how fast should that rate decline?

The blue-ribbon panel agreed that theory provides strong arguments for a "declining certainty-equivalent discount rate" (Arrow et al., 2012, p. 21). Although the empirical literature also supports a rate that is declining over time (especially in the presence of uncertainty about future costs and/or benefits), the results from the empirical literature vary widely depending on the model assumptions and underlying data. If a declining rate schedule were to be adopted in the United States, this group of experts recommends that the EPA's Science Advisory Board be asked to develop criteria that could be used as the common foundation for determining what the schedule should look like.

Sources: Arrow, K., Maureen, J., Cropper, L., Gollier, C., Groom, B., Heal, G. M., et al. (December 2012). How should benefits and costs be discounted in an intergenerational context: The views of an expert panel. *RFFDP 12–53;* Griffiths, C., Kopits, E., Marten, A., Moore, C., Newbold, S., & Wolverton, A. (2012). The social cost of carbon: Valuing carbon reductions in policy analysis. In R. A. de Mooij, M. Keen, & I. W. H. Parry (Eds.). *Fiscal Policy to Mitigate Climate Change: A Guide for Policy Makers.* Washington, D.C.: IMF, 69–87; OMB (Office of Management and Budget). Circular A-4: Regulatory Analysis. Washington, DC Executive Office of the President. www.whitehouse.gov/omb/circulars_a004_a-4

Divergence of social and private discount rates

Earlier we concluded that producers, in their attempt to maximize producer surplus, also maximize the present value of net benefits under the "right" conditions, such as the absence of externalities, the presence of properly defined property rights, and the presence of competitive markets within which the property rights can be exchanged.

Now let's consider one more condition. If resources are to be allocated efficiently, firms must use the same rate to discount future net benefits as is appropriate for society at large. If firms were to use a higher rate, they would extract and sell resources faster than would be efficient. Conversely, if firms were to use a lower-than-appropriate discount rate, they would be excessively conservative.

Why might private and social rates differ? One reason is that the cost of capital is higher in risky industries than in no-risk industries and as such the *risk premium* we discussed previously is higher.

Another difference between private and social discount rates may stem from a difference in social and private risk premiums. If the risk of certain private decisions is different from the risks faced by society as a whole, then the social and private risk premiums may differ. One obvious example is the risk *caused* by the government.

Another divergence in discount rates may stem from different underlying rates of time preference. Such a divergence in time preferences can cause not only a divergence between private and social discount rates (as when firms have a higher rate of time preference than the public sector), but even between otherwise similar analyses conducted in two different countries.

Time preferences would be expected to be higher, for example, in a cash-poor, developing country than in an industrialized country. Since the two benefit-cost analyses in these two countries would be based upon two different discount rates, they might come to quite different conclusions. What is right for the developing country may not be right for the industrialized country and vice versa.

Although private and social discount rates do not always diverge, they may. When those circumstances arise, market decisions are not efficient.

A critical appraisal

We have seen that it is sometimes, but not always, difficult to estimate benefits and costs. When this estimation is difficult or unreliable, it limits the value of a benefit-cost analysis. This problem would be particularly disturbing if biases tended to increase or decrease net benefits systematically. Do such biases exist?

In the early 1970s, Robert Haveman (1972) conducted a major study that continues to shed some light on this question. Focusing on Army Corps of Engineers water projects, such as flood control, navigation, and hydroelectric power generation, Haveman compared the *ex ante* (before the fact) estimate of benefits and costs with their *ex post* (after the fact) counterparts. Thus, he was able to address the issues of accuracy and bias. He concluded that:

> In the empirical case studies presented, ex post estimates often showed little relationship to their ex ante counterparts. On the basis of the few cases and the a priori analysis presented here, one could conclude that there is a serious bias incorporated into agency ex ante evaluation procedures, resulting in persistent overstatement of expected benefits. Similarly in the analysis of project construction costs, enormous variance was found among projects in the relationship between estimated and realized costs. Although no persistent bias in estimation was apparent, nearly 50 percent of the projects displayed realized costs that deviated by more than plus or minus 20 percent from ex ante projected costs.[7]

In the cases examined by Haveman, at least, the notion that benefit-cost analysis is purely a scientific exercise was clearly not consistent with the evidence; the biases of the analysts were merely translated into numbers.

Does their analysis mean that benefit-cost analysis is fatally flawed? Absolutely not! Valuation methods have improved considerably since the Haveman study, but problems remain. This study does, however, highlight the enduring importance of calculating an accurate value and of including all of the potential benefits and costs (e.g., nonmarket values). As elementary as it might seem including both the benefits and the costs is necessary. As Example 4.4 illustrates, that is not always the case in practice.

EXAMPLE 4.4

Is the two for one rule a good way to manage regulatory overreach?

Environmental regulations can be costly, but they also produce economic benefits. Efficiency suggests that regulations whose benefits exceed their costs should be pursued and that is the path followed by previous Executive Orders (EOs) from Presidents Reagan (EO 12291), Clinton (EO 12866), and Obama (EO 13563).

In 2017, the Trump administration abandoned business as usual and issued EO 13771, mandating that for every new regulation issued, two must be thrown out.[8] What does economic analysis and, in particular, benefit-cost analysis have to say about this one-in, two-out prescription?

Executive Order 13771 reads, in part: "(c) . . . any new incremental costs associated with new regulations shall, to the extent permitted by law, be offset by the elimination of existing costs associated with at least two prior regulations."

In his attempt to reduce regulatory overreach President Trump's approach seems to suggest that only the costs are important when evaluating current and new regulations. Benefits don't matter. Since most of the current regulations were put into place based on benefits and costs, removing them based solely on costs would be a "blunt instrument" – one that is poorly targeted on making efficient choices.

Economist Robert Shiller further argues that regulation is in the public interest in many areas and "the world is far too complex to make it possible to count up regulations meaningfully and impose a two-for-one rule."

Alan Krupnick, economist at Resources for the Future, points out that even if a "cost only" approach was justified, it would not be easy to implement. For example "what is a cost? Is it a projected cost in the rule or actual costs as implemented? Is it present discounted costs or something else to account for cost streams over time? Is it direct costs or do indirect costs (say, to consumers) count? Is it private costs or costs to society?"

Regardless of the answer to those questions, however, benefits do matter. As Krupnick notes, "How do we determine which regulations are ineffective and unnecessary without considering their benefits? The answer is simple – we cannot."

Imagine if we only saved endangered species that cost the least to save, or cleaned up only the least expensive oil spills. Making decisions based solely on costs is misguided economics.

Sources: www.rff.org/research/publications/trump-s-regulatory-reform-process-analytical-hurdles-and-missing-benefits; www.nytimes.com/2017/02/17/upshot/why-trumps-2-for-1-rule-on-regulations-is-no-quick-fix.html;www.env-econ.net/2017/02/two-for-one-too-blunt-an-instrument-for-good-governance.html

Haveman's analysis also serves to remind us that benefit-cost analysis is not a stand-alone technique. It should be used in conjunction with other available information. Economic analysis including benefit-cost analysis can provide useful information, but it should not be the only determinant for all decisions.

Benefit-cost analysis also limited in that it does not really address the question of who reaps the benefits and who pays the cost. It is quite possible for a particular course of action to yield high net benefits, but to have the benefits borne by one societal group and the costs borne by another. This scenario serves to illustrate a basic principle – ensuring that a particular policy is efficient provides an important, but not always the sole, basis for public policy. Other aspects, such as who reaps the benefit or bears the burden, are also important considerations. Distributional benefit-cost analysis can help illuminate potential inequities.

In summary, on the positive side, benefit-cost analysis is frequently a very useful part of the policy process. Even when the underlying data are not strictly reliable, the outcomes may not be sensitive to that unreliability. In other circumstances, the data may be reliable enough to give indications of the consequences of broad policy directions, even when they are not reliable enough to fine-tune those policies. Benefit-cost analysis, when done correctly, can provide a useful complement to the other influences on the political process by clarifying what choices yield the highest net benefits to society.

On the negative side, benefit-cost analysis has been attacked as seeming to promise more than can actually be delivered, particularly in the absence of solid benefit information. This concern has triggered two responses. First, regulatory processes have been developed that can be implemented with very little information and yet have desirable economic properties. The recent reforms in air pollution control, which we cover in Chapters 3 and 10, provide some powerful examples.

The second involves techniques that supply useful information to the policy process without relying on controversial techniques to monetize environmental services that are difficult to value. The rest of this chapter deals with the two most prominent of these – cost-effectiveness analysis and impact analysis.

Even when benefits are difficult or impossible to quantify, economic analysis has much to offer. Policy makers should know, for example, how much various policy actions will cost and what their impacts on society will be, even if the efficient policy choice cannot be identified with any certainty.

Other decision-making metrics

Cost-effectiveness analysis

What can be done to guide policy when the requisite valuation for benefit-cost analysis is either unavailable or not sufficiently reliable? Without a good measure of benefits, making an efficient choice is no longer possible.

In such cases, however, it is often possible to set a policy target on some basis other than a strict comparison of benefits and costs. One example is pollution control. What level of pollution should be established as the maximum acceptable level? In many countries, studies of the effects of a particular pollutant on human health have been used as the basis for establishing that pollutant's maximum acceptable concentration. Researchers attempt to find a threshold level below which no damage seems to occur. That threshold is then further lowered to provide a margin of safety and that becomes the pollution target.

Approaches could also be based upon expert opinion. Ecologists, for example, could be enlisted to define the critical numbers of certain species or the specific critical wetlands resources that should be preserved.

Once the policy target is specified, however, economic analysis can have a great deal to say about the cost consequences of choosing a means of achieving that objective. The cost consequences are important not only because eliminating wasteful expenditures is an appropriate goal in its own right, but also to assure that they do not trigger a political backlash.

Typically, several means of achieving the specified objective are available; some will be relatively inexpensive, while others turn out to be very expensive. The problems are frequently complicated enough that identifying the cheapest means of achieving an objective cannot be accomplished without a rather detailed analysis of the choices.

Cost-effectiveness analysis frequently involves an *optimization procedure*. An optimization procedure, in this context, is merely a systematic method for finding the lowest-cost means of accomplishing the objective. This procedure does not, in general, produce an efficient allocation because the predetermined objective may not be efficient. All efficient policies are cost-effective, but not all cost-effective policies are efficient.

Earlier in this chapter we introduced the concept of the efficiency equimarginal principle. According to that principle, net benefits are maximized when the marginal benefit is equal to the marginal cost.

A similar, and equally important, equimarginal principle exists for cost-effectiveness:

> Second Equimarginal Principle (the Cost-Effectiveness Equimarginal Principle): The least-cost means of achieving an environmental target will have been achieved when the marginal costs of all possible means of achievement are equal.

Suppose we want to achieve a specific emissions reduction across a region, and several possible techniques exist for reducing emissions. How much of the control responsibility should each technique bear? The cost-effectiveness equimarginal principle suggests that the techniques should be used such that the desired reduction is achieved and the cost of achieving the last unit of emissions reduction (in other words, the marginal control cost) should be the same for all sources.

To demonstrate why this principle is valid, suppose that we have an allocation of control responsibility where marginal control costs are much higher for one set of techniques than for another. This cannot be the least-cost allocation since we could lower cost while retaining the same amount of emissions reduction. To be specific, costs could be lowered by allocating more control to the lower marginal cost sources and less to the high marginal cost sources. Since it is possible to find a way to lower cost while holding emissions constant, then clearly the initial allocation could not have minimized cost. Once marginal costs are equalized, it becomes impossible to find any lower-cost way of achieving the same degree of emissions reduction; therefore, that allocation must be the allocation that minimizes costs.

In our pollution control example, cost-effectiveness can be used to find the least-cost means of meeting a particular standard and its associated cost. Using this cost as a benchmark case, we can estimate how much costs could be expected to increase from this minimum level if policies that are not cost effective are implemented. Cost-effectiveness analysis can also be used to determine how much compliance costs can be expected to change if the EPA chooses a more stringent or less stringent standard.

Impact analysis

What can be done when the information needed to perform a benefit-cost analysis or a cost-effectiveness analysis is not available? The analytical technique designed to deal with this problem is called *impact analysis*. An impact analysis, regardless of whether it focuses on economic impact or environmental impact or both, attempts to quantify the consequences of various actions.

In contrast to benefit-cost analysis, a pure impact analysis makes no attempt to convert all these consequences into a one-dimensional measure, such as dollars, to ensure comparability. In contrast to cost-effectiveness analysis, impact analysis does not necessarily attempt to optimize. Impact analysis places a large amount of relatively undigested information at the disposal of the policy maker. It is up to the policy maker to assess the importance of the various predicted consequences and act accordingly.

On January 1, 1970, President Nixon signed the National Environmental Policy Act of 1969. This act, among other things, directed all agencies of the federal government to:

> include in every recommendation or report on proposals for legislation and other major Federal actions significantly affecting the quality of the human environment, a detailed statement by the responsible official on –
>
> i the environmental impact of the proposed action;
> ii any adverse environmental effects which cannot be avoided should the proposal be implemented;
> iii alternatives to the proposed action;
> iv the relationships between local short-term uses of the environment and the maintenance and enhancement of long-term productivity; and
> v any irreversible and irretrievable commitments of resources which would be involved in the proposed action should it be implemented.[9]

This was the beginning of the environmental impact statement, which is now a familiar, if controversial, part of environmental policy making.

Current environmental impact statements are more sophisticated than their early predecessors and may contain a benefit-cost analysis or a cost-effectiveness analysis in addition to other more traditional impact measurements. Historically, however, the tendency has been to issue huge environmental impact statements that are virtually impossible to comprehend in their entirety.

In response, the Council on Environmental Quality, which, by law, administers the environmental impact statement process, has set content standards that are now resulting in shorter, more concise statements. To the extent that they merely quantify consequences, statements can avoid the problem of "hidden value judgments" that sometimes plague benefit-cost analysis, but they do so only by bombarding the policy makers with masses of noncomparable information.

Summary

Finding a balance in the relationship between humanity and the environment requires many choices. Some basis for making rational choices is absolutely necessary. If not made by design, decisions will be made by default.

Normative economics uses benefit-cost analysis for judging the desirability of the level and composition of provided services. Cost-effectiveness analysis and impact analysis offer alternatives to benefit-cost analysis. All of these techniques offer valuable information for decision making and all have shortcomings.

A static efficient allocation is one that maximizes the net benefit over all possible uses of those resources. The dynamic efficiency criterion, which is appropriate when time is an important consideration, is satisfied when the outcome maximizes the present value of net benefits from all possible uses of the resources. Later chapters examine the degree to which our social institutions yield allocations that conform to these criteria.

Because benefit-cost analysis is both very powerful and very controversial, in 1996 a group of economists of quite different political persuasions got together to attempt to reach some consensus on its proper role in environmental decision making. Their conclusion is worth reproducing in its entirety:

> Benefit-cost analysis can play an important role in legislative and regulatory policy debates on protecting and improving health, safety, and the natural environment. Although formal benefit-cost analysis should not be viewed as either necessary or sufficient for designing sensible policy, it can provide an exceptionally useful framework for consistently organizing disparate information, and in this way, it can greatly improve the process and, hence, the outcome of policy analysis. If properly done, benefit-cost analysis can be of great help to agencies participating in the development of environmental, health and safety regulations, and it can likewise be useful in evaluating agency decision-making and in shaping statutes.[10]

Even when benefits are difficult to calculate, however, economic analysis in the form of cost-effectiveness can be valuable. This technique can establish the least expensive ways to accomplish predetermined policy goals and to assess the extra costs involved when policies other than the least-cost policy are chosen. What it cannot do is answer the question of whether those predetermined policy goals are efficient.

At the other end of the spectrum is impact analysis, which merely identifies and quantifies the impacts of particular policies without any pretense of optimality or even comparability of the information generated. Impact analysis does not guarantee an efficient outcome.

All three of the techniques discussed in this chapter are useful, but none of them can stake a claim as being universally the "best" approach. The nature of the information that is available and its reliability make a difference.

Discussion questions

1 Is risk-neutrality an appropriate assumption for benefit-cost analysis? Why or why not? Does it seem more appropriate for some environmental problems than others? If so, which ones
2 Was the executive order issued by President George W. Bush mandating a heavier use of benefit-cost analysis in regulatory rule making a step toward establishing a more rational regulatory structure, or was it a subversion of the environmental policy process? Why?

Self-test exercises

1 Suppose a proposed public policy could result in three possible outcomes: (1) present value of net benefits of $4,000,000, (2) present value of net benefits of $1,000,000, or (3) present value of net benefits of – $10,000,000 (i.e., a loss). Suppose society is risk neutral and the probability of occurrence of each of these three outcomes are, respectively, 0.85, 0.10, and 0.05, should this policy be pursued or trashed? Why?
2 a Suppose you want to remove ten fish of an exotic species that have illegally been introduced to a lake. You have three possible removal methods. Assume that q_1, q_2, and q_3 are, respectively, the amount of fish removed by each method that you choose to use so that the goal will be accomplished by any combination of methods such that $q_1 + q_2 + q_3 = 10$. If the marginal costs of each removal method are, respectively, \$$10q_1$, \$$5q_2$, and \$$2.5q_3$, how much of each method should you use to achieve the removal cost-effectively?
b Why isn't an exclusive use of method 3 cost-effective?
c Suppose that the three marginal costs were constant (not increasing as in the previous case) such that MC_1 = \$10, MC_2 = \$5, and MC_3 = \$2.5. What is the cost-effective outcome in that case?
3 Consider the role of discount rates in problems involving long time horizons such as climate change. Suppose that a particular emissions abatement strategy would result in a $500 billion reduction in damages 50 years into the future. How would the maximum amount spent now to eliminate those damages change if the discount rate is 2 percent, rather than 10 percent?

Notes

1 Actually if *B* = C, it wouldn't make any difference if the action occurs or not; the benefits and costs are a wash.
2 The monetary worth of the net benefit is the sum of two right triangles, and it equals (1/2)($5) (5) + (1/2)($2.50)(5) or $18.75. Can you see why?
3 Interagency Working Group on the Social Cost of Carbon, August 2016. Available at: www.epa.gov/sites/production/files/2016-12/documents/sc_co2_tsd_august_2016.pdf (Accessed November 18, 2017).
4 Hahn, Robert W., & Robert A. Ritz. (2015). Does the social cost of carbon matter? Evidence from US policy. *The Journal of Legal Studies*, 44(1) (January), 229–248.
5 The division between tangible and intangible benefits changes as our techniques improve. Recreation benefits were, until the advent of the travel-cost model, treated as intangible. The travel-cost model will be discussed in the next chapter.
6 Annual rates can be found at www.whitehouse.gov/omb/. 2010 rates can be found at www.whitehouse.gov/omb/circulars_a094/a94_appx-c

7 A more recent assessment of costs (Harrington et al., 1999) found evidence of both overestimation and underestimation, although overestimation was more common. The authors attributed the overestimation mainly to a failure to anticipate technical innovation.

8 Executive Order 13371, "Reducing Regulation and Controlling Regulatory Cost."

9 83 Stat. 853.

10 From Arrow, Kenneth, et al. (1996). Is there a role for benefit-cost analysis in environmental, health and safety regulation? *Science*, 272 (April 12), 221–222. Reprinted with permission from AAAS.

Further reading

Freeman, A. M. III. (2003). *The Measurement of Environmental and Resource Values*, 2nd ed. Washington, DC: Resources for the Future. A comprehensive and analytically rigorous survey of the concepts and methods for environmental valuation.

Hanley, N., & Spash, C. L. (1994). *Cost-Benefit Analysis and the Environment.* Brookfield, VT: Edward Elgar. An account of the theory and practice of this form of analysis applied to environmental problems. Contains numerous specific case studies.

Norton, B., & Minteer, B. A. (2002). From environmental ethics to environmental public philosophy: Ethicists and economists: 1973 – future. In T. Tietenberg & H. Folmer (Eds.), *The International Yearbook of Environmental and Resource Economics: 2002/2003.* Cheltenham, UK: Edward Elgar, 373–407. A review of the interaction between environmental ethics and economic valuation.

Scheraga, J. D., & Sussman, F. G. (1998). Discounting and environmental management. In T. Tietenberg & H. Folmer (Eds.), *The International Yearbook of Environmental and Resource Economics 1998–1999.* Cheltenham, UK: Edward Elgar, 1–32. A summary of the "state of the art" for the use of discounting in environmental management.

There are several federal and academic websites with guidelines for Benefit-Cost Analysis; 3 are listed here:

FEMA. *Benefit-Cost Analysis.* Available at: www.fema.gov/benefit-cost-analysis

Harvard School of Public Health. *Guidelines for Benefit-Cost Analysis.* Available at https://sites.sph.harvard.edu/bcaguidelines/

OECD. *Cost-Benefit Analysis and the Environment: Further Developments and Policy Use.* Available at: www.oecd.org/environment/cost-benefit-analysis-and-the-environment-9789264085169-en.htm

U.S. Environmental Protection Agency. (2010). *Guidelines for Preparing Economic Analyses* (Report # EPA 240-R-10-001). Available at: www.epa.gov/environmental-economics/guidelines-preparing-economic-analyses#download. The procedures prescribed by the USEPA for its analytical work.

Additional references and other historically significant references are available on this book's eResource page: www.routledge.com/9781138587595

Chapter 5

Valuing the environment
Methods and examples

> For it so falls out / That what we have we prize not to the worth / Whiles we enjoy it, but being lack'd and lost / Why, then we rack the value, then we find / The virtue that possession would not show us / Whiles it was ours.
>
> – William Shakespeare, *Much Ado About Nothing*

Introduction

Soon after the *Exxon Valdez* oil tanker ran aground on the Bligh Reef in Prince William Sound off the coast of Alaska on March 24, 1989, spilling approximately 11 million gallons of crude oil, the Exxon Corporation (now Exxon Mobil) accepted the liability for the damage caused by the leaking oil. This liability consisted of two parts: (1) the cost of cleaning up the spilled oil and restoring the site insofar as possible, and (2) compensation for the damage caused to the local ecology. Approximately $2.1 billion was spent in cleanup efforts and Exxon also spent approximately $303 million to compensate fishermen whose livelihoods were greatly damaged for the 5 years following the spill.[1] Litigation on environmental damages settled with Exxon agreeing to pay $900 million over 10 years. The punitive damages phase of this case began in May 1994. In January 2004, after many rounds of appeals, the U.S. District Court for the State of Alaska awarded punitive damages to the plaintiffs in the amount of $4.5 billion.[2] This amount was later cut almost in half to $2.5 billion and in 2008 the Supreme Court ruled that even those punitive damages were excessive based on maritime law and further argued that the punitive damages should not exceed the $507 million in compensatory damages already paid.[3]

In the spring of 2010, the Deepwater Horizon, a BP well in the Gulf of Mexico, exploded and began spewing an *Exxon Valdez-sized* oil spill every 4 to 5 days. By the time the leaking well was capped in August 2010, an estimated 134 million gallons had been spread through the Gulf of Mexico, almost 20 times greater than the *Exxon Valdez* spill, and the largest maritime spill in U.S. history. In 2016, a settlement was reached calling for total payments of $20.8 billion; $8.8 billion of this was for natural resource damages.[4] This amount is over and above the approximately $30 billion already spent on cleanup and other claims after the spill.[5] How can the economic damages from oil spills, like these that caused substantial economic and environmental harm, be calculated? Thousands of birds have been found dead in the Gulf since the BP spill, for example. What are they "worth?" Interestingly, the *Exxon Valdez* spill triggered pioneering work focused on providing monetary estimates of environmental damages, setting the stage for what is today considered standard practice for *nonmarket valuation* – the monetization of those goods and services without market prices.

In Chapter 4, we examined the basic concepts economists use to calculate these damages. Yet implementing these concepts is far from a trivial exercise. While the costs of cleanup are fairly transparent, estimating the damage (lost benefits) is far more complex. For example, how were the $900 million in damages in the Exxon case and the $20 billion in the BP case determined?

In this chapter, we explore how we can move from the general concepts to the actual estimates of compensation required by the courts. A series of special techniques has been developed to value the benefits from environmental improvement or, conversely, to value the damage done by environmental degradation. Special techniques are necessary because most of the normal valuation techniques that have been used over the years cannot be applied to environmental resources. Benefit-cost analysis requires the monetization of all relevant benefits and costs of a proposed policy or project, not merely those where the values can be derived from market transactions As such, it is also important to monetize those environmental goods and services that are not traded in any market. Even more difficult to grapple with are those nonmarket benefits associated with values unrelated to use, topics explored later on.

Why value the environment?

Many federal agencies depend on benefit-cost analyses for decision making. Ideally, the goal is to choose the most economically desirable projects, given limited budgets. Estimation of benefits and costs is used for such diverse actions as follows:

- natural resources damage assessments, such as for oil spills (National Oceanic and Atmospheric Administration);
- the designation of critical habitat under the Endangered Species Act (U.S. Fish and Wildlife Service);
- dam relicensing applications (The Federal Energy Regulatory Commission);
- estimating the costs and benefits of the Clean Air Act and the Clean Water Act.

These analyses, however, frequently fail to incorporate important nonmarket values. If the analysis does not include all the appropriate values, the results will be flawed. Is this exercise worth it? While it may prove difficult, if not impossible, to place a completely accurate value on certain environmental amenities, not making the attempt leaves us valuing them by default at $0. Will valuing them at $0 lead us to the best policy decisions? Probably not, but that does not prevent controversy from arising over attempts to replace $0 with a more appropriate value (Debate 5.1).

DEBATE 5.1

Should humans place an economic value on the environment?

Arne Naess, the late Norwegian philosopher, used the term *deep ecology* to refer to the view that the nonhuman environment has "intrinsic" value, a value that is independent of human interests. Intrinsic value is contrasted with "instrumental" value, in which the value of the environment is derived from its usefulness in satisfying human wants.

Two issues are raised by the Naess critique: (1) what is the basis for the valuing of the environment? and (2) how is the valuation accomplished? The belief that the environment may have a value that goes beyond its direct usefulness to humans is in fact quite consistent with modern economic valuation techniques. As we shall see in this chapter, economic valuation techniques now include the ability to quantify a wide range of "nonuse" values as well as the more traditional "use" values.

Controversies over how the values are derived are less easily resolved. As described in this chapter, economic valuation is based firmly upon human preferences. While some might argue that that allowing humans to determine the value of other species would have no more moral basis than allowing other species to determine the value of humans, opposition to monetizing the value of the environment creates a dilemma. When humans fail to value the environment, it frequently gets assigned a default value of zero in calculations designed to guide policy. A value of zero, however derived, will tend to justify a great deal of environmental degradation that could not be justified with proper economic valuation. As it turns out, economic valuation can be a very useful means of demonstrating when environmental degradation is senseless, even when judged from a limited anthropomorphic perspective.

Sources: Costanza, R., et al. (1998). The value of ecosystem services: Putting the issues in perspective. *Ecological Economics,* 25(1), 67–72; Daily, Gretchen, & Ellison, Katherine. (2003). *The New Economy of Nature: The Quest to Make Conservation Profitable.* Washington, D.C.: Island Press.

Valuation

While the valuation techniques we shall cover can be applied to both the damage caused by pollution and the services provided by the environment, each context offers its own unique aspects. We begin our investigation of valuation techniques by exposing some of the special challenges posed by the first of those contexts, pollution control.

In the United States, damage estimates are not only used in the design of policies, but, as indicated in the opening paragraphs of this chapter, they have also become important to the courts, who need some basis for deciding the magnitude of liability awards.[6]

The damage caused by pollution can take many different forms. The first, and probably most obvious, is the effect on human health. Polluted air and water can cause disease when ingested. Other forms of damage include loss of enjoyment from outdoor activities and damage to vegetation, animals, and materials.

Assessing the magnitude of this damage requires (1) identifying the affected categories, (2) estimating the physical relationship between the pollutant emissions (including natural sources) and the damage caused to the affected categories, (3) estimating responses by the affected parties toward mitigating some portion of the damage, and (4) placing a monetary value on the unmitigated physical damages. Each step is often difficult to accomplish.

Because the data used to track down causal relationships do not typically come from controlled experiments, identifying the affected categories is a complicated matter. Obviously, we cannot run large numbers of people through controlled experiments. If people were subjected to different levels of some pollutant, such as carbon monoxide, so that we could study the short-term and long-term effects, some might become ill and even die. Ethical concern precludes human experimentation of this type.

Statistical studies, on the other hand, deal with human populations exposed to low doses for long periods, but, as you likely know, correlation does not imply causation. To illustrate, the fact that death rates are higher in cities with higher pollution levels does not prove that the higher pollution caused the higher death rates. Perhaps those same cities averaged older populations or perhaps they had more smokers. Existing studies have been sophisticated enough to account for many of these other possible influences but, because of the relative paucity of data, they have not been able to cover them all.

The problems discussed so far arise when identifying whether a particular observed effect results from pollution. The next step is to estimate how strong the relationship is between the effect and the pollution concentrations. In other words, it is necessary not only to discover *whether* pollution causes an increased incidence of respiratory disease, but also to estimate *how much* reduction in respiratory illness could be expected from a given reduction in pollution.

The nonexperimental nature of the data makes this a difficult task. It is not uncommon for different researchers analyzing the same data to come to remarkably different conclusions. Diagnostic problems are compounded when the effects are synergistic – that is, when the effect depends, in a nonadditive way, on contributing factors such as the victims' smoking habits or the presence of other harmful substances in the air or water.

Once physical damages have been identified, the next step is to place a monetary value on them. It is not difficult to see how complex an undertaking this is. Think about the difficulties in assigning a value to extending a human life by several years or to the pain, suffering, and grief borne by both a cancer victim and the victim's family.

How can these difficulties be overcome? What valuation techniques are available not only to value pollution damage, but also to value the large number of services that the environment provides?

Types of values

Economists have decomposed the total economic value conferred by resources into three main components: (1) use value, (2) option value, and (3) nonuse or passive-use values. *Use value* reflects the direct use of the environmental resource. Examples include fish harvested from the sea, timber harvested from the forest, water extracted from a stream for irrigation, even the scenic beauty conferred by a natural vista. If you used one of your senses to experience the resource – sight, sound, touch, taste, or smell – then you have *used* the resource. Pollution can cause a loss of use value, such as when air pollution increases the vulnerability to illness, an oil spill adversely affects a fishery, or smog enshrouds a scenic vista.

Option value reflects the value people place on a future ability to use the environment. It reflects the willingness to pay to preserve the option to use the environment in the future even if one is not currently using it. Whereas use value reflects the value derived from current use, option value reflects the desire to preserve the potential for possible future use. Are you planning to go to Yellowstone National Park next summer? Perhaps not, but would you like to preserve the option to go someday?

Passive-use or *nonconsumptive use values* arise when the resource is not actually consumed in the process of experiencing it. These types of values reflect the common observation that people are more than willing to pay for improving or preserving resources that they will never use. One type of nonuse value is a *bequest value*. Bequest value is the willingness to pay to ensure a resource is available for your children and grandchildren. A second type of nonuse value, a pure nonuse value, is called *existence value*. Existence value is measured by the willingness to pay to ensure that a resource continues to exist in the absence of any interest in future use. The term existence value was coined by economist John Krutilla in his now-famous quote, "There are many persons who obtain satisfaction from mere knowledge that part of wilderness North America remains even though they would be appalled by the prospect of being exposed to it."[7] These values are "independent of any present or future use these people might make of those resources."[8]

When the Bureau of Reclamation began looking at sites for dams near the Grand Canyon, groups such as the Sierra Club rose up in protest of the potential loss of this unique resource. When Glen Canyon was flooded by Lake Powell, even those who never intended to visit recognized this potential loss. Because this value does not derive either from direct use or potential use, it represents a very different category of value.

These categories of value can be combined to produce the total willingness to pay (TWP):

$$\text{TWP} = \text{Use Value} + \text{Option Value} + \text{Nonuse Value}$$

Since nonuse or passive-use values are derived from motivations other than personal use, they are obviously less tangible than use values. Total willingness to pay estimated without nonuse values, however, will be less than the minimum amount that would be required to compensate individuals if they are deprived of this environmental asset. Furthermore, estimated nonuse values can be quite large. Therefore, it is not surprising that they are controversial. Indeed when the U.S. Department of Interior drew up its regulations on the appropriate procedures for performing natural resource damage assessment, it prohibited the inclusion of nonuse values unless use values for the incident under consideration were zero. A subsequent 1989 decision by the District of Columbia Court of Appeals (880 F. 2d 432) overruled this decision and allowed nonuse values to be included as long as they could be measured reliably.

Classifying valuation methods

Typically, the researcher's goal is to estimate the total willingness to pay for the good or service in question. This is the area under the demand curve up to the quantity consumed (recall discussion from Chapter 2). For a market good, this calculation is relatively straightforward. However, nonmarket goods and services, the focus of this chapter, require the estimation of willingness to pay either through examining behavior, drawing inferences from the demand for related goods, or through responses to surveys. And, as highlighted previously, capturing all components of value is challenging.

This section will provide a brief overview of some of the methods available to estimate these values and to convey some sense of the range of possibilities and how they are related. Subsequent sections will provide more specific information about how they are actually used.

Valuation methods can be separated into two broad categories: stated preference and revealed preference methods. Revealed preference methods are based on actual observable choices that allow resource values to be directly inferred from those choices. For example, in calculating how much local fishermen lost from the oil spill, the revealed preference method might calculate how much the catch declined and the resulting diminished value of the catch. In this case, prices are directly observable, and their use allows the direct calculation of the loss in value. Or, more indirectly, in calculating the value of an occupational environmental risk (such as some exposure to a substance that could pose some health risk), we might examine the differences in wages across industries in which workers take on different levels of risk.

Compare this with the direct stated preference method that can be used when the value is not directly observable, such as the value of preserving a species. Analysts derive this value by using a survey

Table 5.1 Economic Methods for Measuring Environmental and Resource Values

Methods	*Revealed Preference*	*Stated Preference*
Direct	Market Price Simulated Markets	Contingent Valuation
Indirect	Travel Cost Hedonic Property Values Hedonic Wage Avoidance Expenditures	Choice Experiments Conjoint Analysis Attribute-Based Models Contingent Ranking

Source: Modified by the authors from Mitchell and Carson (1989).

that attempts to elicit the respondents' willingness to pay (their "stated preference") for preserving that species.

Each of these broad categories of methods includes both indirect and direct techniques. The possibilities are presented in Table 5.1. We start with an examination of stated preference survey methods.

Stated preference methods

Stated preference methods use survey techniques to elicit willingness to pay for a marginal improvement or for avoiding a marginal loss. These methods are typically of two types, contingent valuation surveys and choice experiments. *Contingent valuation*, the most direct approach, provides a means of deriving values that cannot be obtained in more traditional ways. The simplest version of this approach merely asks respondents what they would be willing to pay for a change in environmental quality (such as an improvement in wetlands or reduced exposure to pollution) or on preserving the resource in its current state. Typically this question is framed as, "What is the maximum you are willing to pay for the change?" Alternative versions ask a "yes" or "no" question, such as whether or not the respondent would pay $X to prevent the change or preserve the species. The answers reveal either an upper bound (in the case of a "no" answer) or a lower bound (in the case of a "yes" answer).

Choice experiments, on the other hand, present respondents with a set of options. Each set consists of various levels of attributes or characteristics of the good. One of the characteristics will be the "price" of that bundle of attributes. Each choice set typically includes the status quo bundle which includes a price of $0 since it represents no change. Respondents choose their preferred option.

Contingent valuation method

The contingent valuation survey approach creates a hypothetical market and asks respondents to consider a willingness-to-pay question *contingent* on the existence of this market. Contingent valuation questions come with their own set of challenges. The major concern with the use of the contingent valuation method has been the potential for survey respondents to give biased answers. Six types of potential bias have been the focus of a large amount of research: (1) strategic bias, (2) information bias, (3) starting-point bias, (4) hypothetical bias, (5) payment vehicle bias (protest bids), and (6) the observed discrepancy between willingness to pay (WTP) and willingness to accept (WTA). The literature is rich with examples of studies aimed at reducing these biases and there are now some well accepted methods for avoiding them (See for example, Johnston et al., 2017; Haab et al., 2020 for reviews of the literature and state of the art techniques). Well-designed surveys can minimize bias, but it is useful to understand what those biases are and to know what to look for.

Strategic bias arises when the respondent intentionally provides a biased answer in order to influence a particular outcome. If a decision to preserve a stretch of river for fishing, for example, depends on whether or not the survey produces a sufficiently large value for fishing, the respondents who enjoy fishing may be tempted to provide an answer that ensures a high value, rather than the lower value that reflects their true valuation. Another variation on strategic bias is social desirability bias, which occurs when respondents try to present themselves in a favorable light; one common example is when voters claim to have voted when they did not.

Information bias may arise whenever respondents are forced to value attributes with which they have little or no experience. For example, the valuation by a recreationist of a loss in water quality in one body of water may be based on the ease of substituting recreation on another body of water. If the respondent has no experience using the second body of water, the valuation could be based on an entirely false perception.

Visual aids have been shown to reduce uncertainty and unfamiliarity with the good or service being valued, but the nature of the visual aid may affect the response. Labao et al. (2008) found that colored photographs, as opposed to black-and-white photographs, influenced respondent willingness to pay for the Philippine Eagle. The colored photographs resulted in a higher willingness to pay than black-and-white photos. Why? The authors suggest that the higher willingness to pay could be explained by photographs in color simply providing more information or by "enhancing respondents' ability to assimilate information." In any case, the nature of the visual aide seems important for revealing willingness to pay.

Starting-point bias may arise in those survey instruments in which a respondent is asked to check off their WTP from a predefined range of possibilities. How that range is defined by the designer of the survey may affect the resulting answers. A range of \$0–\$100 may produce a valuation by respondents different from, for example, a range of \$10–\$100, even if no responses are in the \$0–\$10 range. Ladenburg and Olsen (2008), in a study of willingness to pay to protect nature areas in Denmark from new highway development, found that the starting-point bias in their choice experiment was gender specific, with female respondents exhibiting the greatest sensitivity to the starting point.

Hypothetical bias (the difference between hypothetical and actual WTP) can enter the picture because the respondent is being confronted by a contrived, rather than an actual, set of choices. Since he or she will not actually have to pay the estimated value, the respondent may treat the survey casually, providing ill-considered answers. Some recent analyses of the literature suggest that hypothetical bias has been a persistent problem (List and Gallet, 2001; Murphy et al., 2005; Penn and Hu, 2018), but can be reduced by ensuring that the payment vehicle is incentive compatible and using language to ensure consequentially (making sure the respondent believes they will actually have to pay the amount in question). Using a follow-up certainty scale has been shown to be helpful in reducing hypothetical bias. With a certainty scale, respondents can be asked how certain they are they would pay the amount stated.

Ehmke et al. (2008) tested whether hypothetical bias depends on location and/or culture. In a study based on student experiments in China, France, Indiana, Kansas, and Niger, they found significant differences in bias across locations. Given that policy makers frequently rely on existing benefits estimates from other locations when making decisions, this finding should not be taken lightly. The strengths and weaknesses of using estimates derived in one setting to infer benefits in another, a technique known as *benefit transfer,* are discussed later.

Increasingly, environmental economists are using these types of experiments to try to determine the severity of some of these biases as well as to learn how to reduce bias. Some of these experiments are conducted in a laboratory setting, such as a computer lab or a classroom designed for this purpose. In one such experiment on voluntary provision of public goods (donations), Landry et al. (2006) found that for door-to-door interviews, an increase in physical attractiveness of the interviewer led to sizable increases in giving. Interestingly, physical attractiveness also led to increases in response rates, particularly by male households. Sometimes called *interviewer bias,* biases like these can be kept small through well-designed and pretested surveys.

Another challenge, *payment vehicle bias,* can arise when respondents react negatively to the choice of the payment vehicle. The payment vehicle represents how the stated WTP would be collected. Common choices include donations, taxes or increases to utility bills. If a respondent is averse to taxes or has a negative perception of the agency collecting the (hypothetical) payment, they may state $0 for their willingness to pay. If their true willingness to pay is actually greater than zero, but they are "protesting" the question or payment vehicle, this zero must be excluded from the analysis. Determining which zero bids are valid and which are protests is important The payment vehicle must be realistic, believable, and neutral in order to reduce payment vehicle bias.

The final source of bias addresses observed gaps between two supposedly closely related concepts – willingness to pay (WTP) and willingness to accept (WTA) compensation. Respondents to contingent valuation surveys tend to report much higher values when asked for their willingness to accept compensation for a specified loss of some good or service than if asked for their willingness to pay for a specified increase of that same good or service. Economic theory suggests the two should be equal. Debate 5.2 explores some of the reasons offered for the difference.

DEBATE 5.2

Willingness to pay versus willingness to accept: why so different?

Many contingent valuation studies have found that respondents tend to report much higher values for questions that ask what compensation the respondent would be willing to accept (WTA) to give something up than for questions that ask for the willingness to pay (WTP) for an incremental improvement in the same good or service. Economic theory suggests that differences between WTP and WTA should be small, but experimental findings both in environmental economics and in other microeconomic studies have found large differences. Why?

Some economists have attributed the discrepancy to a psychological endowment effect; the psychological value of something you own is greater than something you do not. In other words, you would require more compensation to be as well off without it than you would be willing to pay to get that same good, and as such, you would be less willing to give it up (WTA > WTP) (Kahneman et al., 1990). This is a form of what behavioral economists call loss aversion – the psychological premise that losses are more highly valued than gains.

Others have suggested that the difference may be explainable in terms of the market context. In the absence of good substitutes, large differences between WTA and WTP would be the expected outcome. In the presence of close substitutes, WTP and WTA should not be that different, but the divergence between the two measures should increase as the degree of substitution decreases (Hanemann, 1991; Shogren et al., 1994).

The characteristics of the good may matter as well. In their review of the evidence provided by experimental studies, Horowitz and McConnell (2002) find that for "ordinary goods" the ratio of WTA/WTP is smaller than the ratio of WTA/WTP for public and nonmarket goods. Their results support the notion that the nature of the property rights involved is not neutral.

The moral context of the valuation may matter as well. Croson et al. (working paper 2005) show that the amount of WTA compensation estimated in a damage case increases with the culpability of the party causing the damage as long as that party is also paying the damages. If, however, a third party is paying, WTA is insensitive to culpability. This difference suggests that the valuation implicitly includes an amount levied in punishment for the party who caused the damage (the valuation becomes the lost value plus a sanction).

It may also be the case that, in dynamic settings, respondents are uncertain about the value of the good. Zhao and Kling (2004) argue that in intertemporal settings, the equivalence of compensating variation/equivalent variation and WTP/WTA breaks down, in part because WTP and WTA have a behavioral component and the timing of a decision will be impacted by the consumer's rate of time preference and willingness to take risks. A buyer or seller, by committing to a purchase or sale, must forgo opportunities for additional information. These "commitment costs" reduce WTP and increase WTA. The larger the commitment costs, the larger is the divergence between the two measures.

Ultimately, the choice of which concept to use in environmental valuation comes down to how the associated property right is allocated. If someone owns the right to the resource, asking how much compensation they would require to give it up is the appropriate question. If the respondent does not own the right, using WTP to estimate the value of acquiring it is the right approach. However, as Horowitz and McConnell point out, since the holders and nonholders of "rights" value them differently, the initial allocation of property rights can have a strong influence on valuation decisions for environmental amenities. And, as Zhao and Kling note, the timing of the decision can also be an important factor.

Sources: Croson, R., Rachlinski, J. J., & Johnston, J. (Draft 2005). Culpability as an explanation of the WTA-WTP discrepancy in contingent valuation; Hanemann, W. M. (1991). Willingness to pay and willingness to accept: How much can they differ? *American Economic Review, 81,* 635–647; Horowitz, J. K., & McConnell, K. E. (2002). A review of WTA/WTP studies. *Journal of Environmental Economics and Management, 44,* 426–447; Kahneman, D., Knetsch, J., & Thaler, R. (1990). Experimental tests of the endowment effect and the Coase theorem. *Journal of Political Economy, 98,* 1325–1348; Shogren, J. F., Shin, Senung Y., Hayes, D. J., & Kliebenstein, J. B. (1994). Resolving differences in willingness to pay and willingness to accept. *American Economic Review, 84*(1), 255–270; Zhao, Jinhua, & Kling, Catherine. (2004). Willingness to pay, compensating variation, and the cost of commitment. *Economic Inquiry, 42*(3), 503–517.

Measuring willingness to pay or willingness to accept in the presence of price changes makes two new concepts relevant – compensating variation and equivalent variation. *Compensating variation* is the amount of money it would take to *compensate* for a price increase in order to make a consumer just as well off as they were before the price increase. How much the consumer was "hurt" by the price increase can be measured by the compensating variation. *Equivalent variation,* on the other hand, is the amount of money it would take to make a consumer indifferent (same income) between the money and the price increase. In other words, how much money would they pay to avoid the price increase?

If the compensating variation is greater than zero, that amount represents willingness to pay. If it is negative, it represents willingness to accept. In other words, for increases in environmental quality, compensating variation should be positive (WTP). For decreases in environmental quality, it should be negative (WTA). Equivalent variation is just the opposite – the amount of money the household would need to be given to be just as well off as before the environmental change. Equivalent variation will be positive for increases in environmental quality (WTA) and negative for decreases (WTP). In theory, in the absence of any income effects, these measures (along with consumer surplus) should be equivalent.

Much experimental work has been done on contingent valuation to determine how serious a problem biases may present. One early survey of the literature (Carson et al., 1994) uncovered 1,672 contingent valuation studies., A much more recent one gives annotations for more than 7,500 studies in 130 countries (Carson, 2011)! Are the results from these surveys reliable enough for the policy process?

Faced with the need to compute damages from oil spills, the National Oceanic and Atmospheric Administration (NOAA) convened a panel of independent economic experts (including two Nobel prize laureates) to evaluate the use of contingent valuation methods for determining lost passive-use or nonuse values. Their report, issued on January 15, 1993 (58 FR 4602), was cautiously supportive.

The committee made clear that it had several concerns with the technique. Among those concerns, the panel listed (1) the tendency for contingent valuation willingness-to-pay estimates to seem unreasonably large; (2) the difficulty in assuring the respondents have understood and absorbed the issues in the survey; and (3) the difficulty in assuring that respondents are responding to the specific issues in the survey rather than reflecting general warm feelings about public-spiritedness, known as the "warm glow" effect.[9]

But the panel also made clear its conclusion that suitably designed surveys could eliminate or reduce these biases to acceptable levels and it provided, in an appendix, specific guidelines for determining whether a particular study was suitably designed. The panel suggested that when practitioners follow these guidelines, they:

> can produce estimates reliable enough to be the starting point of a judicial process of damage assessment, including lost passive-use values. . . . [A well-constructed contingent valuation study] contains information that judges and juries will wish to use, in combination with other estimates, including the testimony of expert witnesses.

Specifically, they suggested the use of referendum-type (yes/no) willingness-to-pay questions, personal interviews when possible, clear scenario descriptions, and follow-up questions.

These guidelines have been influential in shaping subsequent studies. For example, Example 5.1 shares the results of a large contingent valuation survey, designed to estimate the value of preventing future spills. While influential, these guidelines have become dated, and, in 2017, new "contemporary guidelines" were published (Johnston et al., 2017). These guidelines provide best practice recommendations for both contingent valuation and choice experiments using what has been learned in the approximately 8,000 stated preference studies published since the NOAA guidelines were first published. The authors offer 23 recommendations including designing a survey that clearly describes the status quo or baseline scenario, selecting a random sample of the affected population and choosing an appropriate survey mode. They also recommend pretesting of the survey instrument and cite best practices for eliminating or at least reducing the potential biases listed previously. They emphasize the importance of documentation of study design, implementation, analyses and results. Finally, they give extensive guidance on when to choose contingent valuation over a choice experiment and vice versa.

EXAMPLE 5.1

Leave no behavioral trace: using the contingent valuation method to measure passive-use values

Until the *Exxon Valdez* tanker spilled 11 million gallons of crude oil into Prince William Sound in Alaska, the calculation of nonuse (or passive-use) values was not a widely researched topic. However, following the 1989 court ruling in *Ohio v. U.S. Department of the Interior* that said lost passive-use values could now be compensated within natural resources damages assessments and the passage of the Oil Pollution Act of 1990, the estimation of nonuse and passive-use values became not only a topic of great debate, but also a rapidly growing research area within the economics community.

One study (Carson et al., 2003) discusses the design, implementation, and results of a large survey designed to estimate the passive-use values related to large oil spills. In particular, the survey asked respondents their willingness to pay to prevent a similar disaster in the future by funding an escort ship program that would help prevent and/or contain a future spill. The survey was conducted for the State of Alaska in preparation for litigation in the case against the *Exxon Valdez*.

The survey followed the recommendations made by the NOAA panel for conducting contingent valuation surveys and for ensuring reliable estimates. It relied upon face-to-face interviews and the sample was drawn from the national population. The study used a binary discrete-choice (yes/no) question where the respondent was asked whether he or she would be willing to pay a specific amount, with the amount varying across four versions of the survey. A one-time increase in taxes was the chosen method of payment. They also avoided potential embedding bias (where respondents may have difficulty valuing multiple goods) by using a survey that valued a single good. The survey contained pictures, maps, and background information to make sure the respondent was familiar with the good he/she was being asked to value.

Using the survey data, the researchers were able to statistically estimate a valuation function by relating the respondent's willingness to pay to respondent characteristics. After multiplying the estimate of the median willingness to pay by the population sampled, they reported aggregate lost passive-use values at $2.8 billion (in 1990 dollars). They point out that this number is a lower bound, not only because willingness to accept compensation would be a more appropriate measure of actual lost passive-use from the spill (see Debate 5.2), but also because their median willingness to pay was less than the mean.

The *Exxon Valdez* spill sparked a debate about the measurement of nonuse and passive-use values. Laws put into place after the spill now ensure that passive-use values will be included in natural resource damage assessments. Should other parts of the world follow suit?

Source: Carson, Richard T., Mitchell, Robert C., Hanemann, Michael, Kopp, Raymond J., Presser, Stanley, & Ruud, Paul A. (2003). Contingent valuation and lost passive use: Damages from the *Exxon Valdez oil spill. Environmental and Resource Economics, 25,* 257–286.

Choice experiments

Indirect hypothetical stated preference methods include several attribute-based methods. Attribute-based methods, such as choice experiments, are useful when project options have multiple levels of different attributes. Like contingent valuation, choice experiments are also survey based, but instead of asking respondents to state a willingness to pay, they are asked to choose among alternate bundles of goods. Each bundle has a set of attributes and the levels of each attribute vary across bundles. Since one of the attributes in each bundle is a price measure, willingness to pay can be identified.

Consider an example (Landry and Mires, 2017) that surveyed North Carolina residents on their preferences and willingness to pay for marine cultural heritage sites (e.g., shipwrecks). The choice experiment included five attributes including the preservation zone, the availability of public programs and whether or not there was a walking, virtual, or diving trail. Table 5.2 reproduces the attributes and

Table 5.2 Choice Experiment: Attributes and Levels

Attributes	*Levels*
Preservation Zone	• Status quo; 30 shipwrecks protected
	• 38 more shipwrecks (68 total; 127% increase); 2192 m^2 of bottomland
	• 56 more shipwrecks (124 total; 313% increase); 13,498 m^2 of bottomland
Public Programs	• No change
	• Increase museum exhibits and provide educational workshops
	• Increase museum exhibits and provide educational workshops, plus public television series about shipwrecks and creation of boating tours to shipwrecks
Walking Trail	• Yes/No
Virtual Trail	• Yes/No
Diving Trail	• Yes/No

levels. With three attributes with three levels and two with two levels, there are 216 possible different profiles. Best practices suggests the use of a fractional factorial design and the authors chose eight versions with three choice sets per version of the survey, resulting in 24 choice sets.

Respondents were given a choice set of three different alternative management plans and the status quo (no purchase). Table 5.3 demonstrates a sample survey question. The researchers found a

Table 5.3 Sample Choice Experiment Question

I: Here is the first voting opportunity

(Please chose one of the four options that follow by putting an "X" in one of the empty boxes.)

26.	*Program 1*	*Program 2*	*Program 3*	*Status Quo*
Preservation Zone	Yellow Zone	Yellow Zone	Red Zone	Red Zone
Public Programs	Large Investment	No Investment	Large Investment	No Investment
Walking Trails	Yes	No	No	No
Virtual Trails	No	Yes	Yes	No
SCUBA Diving Trails	Yes	No	No	No
One-time Tax	$12	$55	$145	$0
*put an "X" in **one** of the boxes to the right*	☐	☐	☐	☐

27. How confident are you about this choice from these options? (Please select one)

• Very Certain • Somewhat Certain • Somewhat Uncertain • Very Uncertain • Don't Know

II: Now consider another voting opportunity with different choices

(Please choose one of the four options that follow by putting an "X" in one of the empty boxes)

28.	*Program 4*	*Program 5*	*Program 6*	*Status Quo*
Preservation Zone	Orange Zone	Orange Zone	Yellow Zone	Red Zone
Public Programs	Large Investment	No Investment	No Investment	No Investment
Walking Trails	No	Yes	No	No
Virtual Trails	No	Yes	No	No
SCUBA Diving Trails	Yes	No	Yes	No
One-time Tax	$145	$12	$55	$0
*put on "X" in **one** of the boxes to the right*	☐	☐	☐	☐

29. How confident are you about this choice from these options? (Please select one)

• Very Certain • Somewhat Certain • Somewhat Uncertain • Very Uncertain • Don't Know

III: Finally, consider this third opportunity with different choices

(Please chose one of the four options that follow by putting an "X" in one of the empty boxes.)

30.	*Program 7*	*Program 8*	*Program 9*	*Status Quo*
Preservation Zone	Red Zone	Red Zone	Yellow Zone	Red Zone
Public Programs	No Investment	Moderate Investment	Moderate Investment	No Investment
Walking Trails	Yes	No	Yes	No
Virtual Trails	Yes	No	Yes	No
SCUBA Diving Trails	No	Yes	No	No
One-time Tax	$12	$145	$55	$0
put on "X" in ***one*** *of the boxes to the right*	☐	☐	☐	☐

31. How confident are you about this choice from these options? (Please select one)

• Very Certain • Somewhat Certain • Somewhat Uncertain • Very Uncertain • Don't Know

willingness to pay of $98 per household for a moderate level of public programs on Maritime Archeology and Shipwrecks; $90/household for the Walking Trails for *the Graveyard of the Atlantic*; and $84/household for Virtual Trails for *the Graveyard of the Atlantic* (Landry and Mires, 2017).

Choice experiments have evolved from both contingent valuation and marketing studies. This approach allows the respondent to make a familiar choice (choose a bundle) and allows the researcher to derive marginal willingness to pay for an attribute from that choice.

In another example, Haefele et al. (2016) present the results of a choice experiment in which they estimated the total economic value of U.S. national parks (Example 5.2). Including both visitation values and passive-use values for U.S. residents, the total value of U.S. national parks and programs more than pays for itself at $92 billion dollars. This estimate is considered a minimum bound since international visitation values were not included.

Contingent ranking, another survey method, also falls within this final category. Respondents are given a set of hypothetical situations that differ in terms of the environmental amenity available (instead of a bundle of attributes) and are asked to rank-order them. These rankings can then be compared to see the implicit tradeoffs between more of the environmental amenity and less of the other characteristics. When one or more of these characteristics is expressed in terms of a monetary value, it is possible to use this information and the rankings to impute a value to the environmental amenity.

Sometimes more than one of these techniques may be used simultaneously. In some cases, using multiple techniques is necessary to capture the total economic value; in other cases, it may be used to provide independent estimates of the value being sought as a check on the reliability of the estimate.

EXAMPLE 5.2

The value of U.S. national parks

In 2016, the National Park Service in the United States turned 100 years old. As federal budget deficits loom, there has been some talk of selling off some of these sites. What is the value of the National Park lands, waters, and historic sites? According to the first ever comprehensive estimate, it is, at a minimum, valued at $92 billion.

Haefele et al. (2016) present the results of a survey of American households focused on estimating the total economic value (TEV) of National Parks and Programs. Previous studies have focused on the value of specific National Park or monument sites, but none had attempted to estimate the value of all of these national treasures. The goal was to calculate total economic value; visitation values and passive-use (or nonuse) values.

Using the population of all U.S. households from which to draw a sample, researchers used a mixed mode approach that utilized both mail and internet surveys with phone call reminders. Two rounds of surveys were implemented between 2013 and 2015.

In the survey, participants were asked whether protecting National Parks was important to them. Nearly 95 percent of the sample said they were, even if they did not visit them. Moreover, 93.5 percent thought it was important to protect trails, parks, and open spaces for current and future generations whether they use them or not. The language in these questions suggests bequest and passive-use values. Only 6.2 percent thought the United States should sell off some national parks. The survey also included questions on respondents' political point of view. The sample of respondents leaned to the conservative side of the aisle.

The stated preference survey design was a choice experiment in which respondents chose among bundles that included the size of cuts to programs as well as the percentages of lands sold. Choice experiments typically allow respondents to choose a status quo bundle for which the price is $0. In order to minimize hypothetical bias (respondents stating a higher willingness to pay than they would actually pay), the choice question was followed by reminders to consider their budgets. This "cheap talk" technique has been shown to significantly reduce hypothetical bias.

Respondents were asked their willingness to pay a specific amount of money to pay for the National Park Service Programs. The payment vehicle utilized was an increase in federal income tax for each of the next 10 years. As we have discussed in this chapter, protest responses must be omitted from the data since those answers do not represent willingness to pay, instead representing a scenario (usually payment vehicle) protest. Since the payment vehicle chosen was federal income tax, there was some initial concern that protest zeros would be problematic, however, only 7.5 percent of the responses were considered to be protests.

Table 5.4 Per-Household Total Economic Value (TEV) for the National Park System and NPS Programs

National Parks	*Estimated Value*
Nature-focused National Parks (79,096,632 acres)	$1,113.24
History-focused National Park (226 sites)	$874.72
Water-focused National Parks (4,818,275 acres)	$ 977.93
Per household value for all National Park acres/sites	**$2,967.00**
NPS Programs	
Historic sites and buildings protected each year (2,000)	$316.31
Acres transferred to communities each year (2,700)	$98.41
National landmarks protected each year (114)	$347.98
Schoolchildren served by NPS educational programs (4.1 million)	$682.62
Per household value for all NPS programs	**$1,445.00**

Source: Table 4 in Haefele et al. (2016)

Using econometric analysis, the marginal willingness to pay (or implicit price) for each type of National Park or National Park Service Program were estimated. These values are reproduced in Table 5.4.

These household values were then multiplied by the total number of households in the population to determine the total economic value. In order to present a minimum bound (or very conservative estimate), they assumed that households that did not return a survey were willing to pay $0.

The final tally of $92 billion includes both use values for visitors and passive-use or existence values, $62 billion of which (or two-thirds) is for the National Park Service lands and waters and historic sites, with $30 billion for programs. Of the $62 billion, the authors suggest that approximately half of that value is passive-use value. Of course, these values do not even include the willingness to pay of the millions of international tourists that visit U.S. national parks each year or those who hold passive-use values for these locations. Thus, the $92 billion TEV also represents "the minimum amount that U.S. households are willing to pay to avoid the loss of the NPS and its programs" (Haefele et al., 2016, p. 25).

According to one of the authors of the study, Linda Bilmes at Harvard University, the study shows that "Americans value the National Park Service at least 30 times more than the government spends on them." It is a happy 100th birthday indeed.

Sources: Haefele, Michelle, Loomis, John, & Bilmes, Linda. (2016). Total economic valuation of the National Park Service Lands and Programs: Results of a survey of the American public. Faculty Research Working Paper Series. RWP16–024 (June); Haefele, Michelle, Loomis, John, & and Bilmes, Linda. (2016). Total economic valuation of US National Park Service estimated to be $92 billion: Implications for policy. *The George Wright Forum,* 33(3): 335–345; National Park Foundation Press Release. (June 30, 2016). National Park Foundation announces study determining value of America's National Parks to be $92 billion.

Revealed preference methods

Revealed preference methods are "observable" because they involve actual behavior and expenditures and "indirect" because they infer a value rather than estimate it directly. Suppose, for example, a particular sport fishery is being threatened by pollution, and one of the damages caused by that pollution is a reduction in sportfishing. How is this loss to be valued when access to the fishery is free?

Travel-cost method

One way to derive this loss is through *travel-cost* methods. Travel-cost methods may infer the value of a recreational resource (such as a sport fishery, a park, or a wildlife preserve where visitors hunt with a camera) by using information on how much visitors spend in getting to the site to construct a demand curve representing willingness to pay for a "visitor day."

Freeman et al. (2014) identify two variants of this approach. In the first, analysts examine the number of trips visitors make to a site. In the second, the analysts examine whether people decide to visit a site and, if so, which site. This second variant includes using a special class of models, known as random utility models, to value quality changes.

The first variant allows the construction of a travel cost demand function. The value of the flow of services from that site is the area under the estimated demand curve for those services or for access to the site, aggregated over all who visit the site. Using this variant, individual consumer surplus can be estimated. The area below the demand curve but above the travel cost (price) is the consumer surplus.

The second variant enables an analysis of how specific site characteristics influence choice and, therefore, indirectly how valuable those characteristics are. Knowledge of how the value of each site varies with respect to its characteristics allows the analyst to value how degradation of those characteristics (e.g., from pollution) would lower the value of the site.

Travel-cost models have been used to value National Parks, mountain climbing, recreational fishing, and beaches. Travel-cost models have also been used to value losses from events such as beach closures during oil spills, fish consumption advisories, and the cost of development that has eliminated a recreation area. The methodology for both variants is detailed in Parsons (2003).

In the random utility model, a person choosing a particular site takes into consideration site characteristics and its price (trip cost). Characteristics affecting the site choice include ease of access and environmental quality. Each site results in a unique level of utility and a person is assumed to choose the site giving the highest level of utility to that person. Welfare losses from an event such as an oil spill can then be measured by the resulting change in utility should the person have to choose an alternate, less desirable site.

Example 5.3 looks at the use of travel cost methods to estimate the economic impacts of beach closures due to oil spills in Minorca, Spain.

One interesting paradox that arises with the travel cost model is that those who live closest to the site, and may actually visit frequently, will have low travel costs. These users will appear to have a lower value for that site even if their (unmeasured) willingness to pay for the experience is very high. Another challenge in this model is how to incorporate the opportunity cost of time. Usually, this is represented by wages, but that approach is not universally accepted.

EXAMPLE 5.3

Using the travel cost method to estimate recreational value: beaches in Minorca, Spain

Minorca, an island in the Mediterranean Sea, is a very popular tourist destination. Minorca's population doubles in the summer months from about 80,000 year-round residents to between 150,000 and 175,000 in the summer. The island's beaches are a major attraction.

Just how valuable are those beaches? To provide an estimate, researchers considered a hypothetical scenario in which an oil spill resulted in closure of certain beaches on the island. The analysis involved using a random utility model based upon survey data to estimate the economic impacts of these closures.

In 2008, 573 face-to-face individual surveys were conducted at 51 different beaches on the island using a discrete choice travel-cost survey. Respondents were asked some typical travel-cost survey questions such as where the trip originated, how they got to the site, how many people they were traveling with and their ages, and some questions to collect socio-economic demographics on the respondents. After being asked about their attitudes toward different beach attributes, they completed a questionnaire on the characteristics of the beach they were visiting. The characteristics included a measure of how urban the area was, the type of sand, how clean the beach was, how crowded it was, whether or not there was a toilet, presence of drink vendors, water temperature, calmness of the water, environmental quality, presence of a life guard, the direction the beach faced, and whether or not nudism was present on the beach. Travel costs included the cost of fuel and tolls plus travel time. Travel time varied by mode of transportation – using average walking and average driving speeds.

The random utility model allowed researchers to estimate the impacts on utility of the various beach characteristics identified by the surveys. Those characteristics positively affecting utility included north facing, presence of a life guard, presence of toilets and drink vendors, thin sand, presence of nudism, warm water temperatures, and good environmental quality. Characteristics negatively affecting utility included non-northern beaches, urban beaches, crowding, algae, and calm water.

Because some beach attributes were more highly valued than others, the range of estimates was dramatically affected by the details in the scenario. For example, for a closure affecting beaches on the west coast, the willingness to pay to avoid this loss was .24 euros (2008) per day per person with peak visitation of 25,000 visitors. Aggregating the per-visitor value across visitors produced a daily welfare loss from these closures of 6,000 euros. On the other extreme, a spill forcing closure of the more valuable northern beaches would cause the welfare loss to rise to 1.73 euros per day per person for a total of 43,250 euros during peak visitation.

It is easy to take highly enjoyable recreational sites for granted since they are freely provided by nature. As a result they may not be given their due when resources are allocated for their protection and enhancement. The travel-cost method can help to inform policy not only by demonstrating how truly valuable they are, but also by allowing useful distinctions to be made among various recreation resources.

Source: Pere, Riera, McConnell, Kenneth E., Giergiczny, Marek, & Mahieu, Pierre-Alexandre. (2011). Applying the travel-cost method to Minorca beaches: Some policy results. In Jeff Bennett (Ed.), *International Handbook on Non-Market Environmental Valuation.* Cheltenham, U.K.: Edward Elgar, 60–73.

Hedonic property value and hedonic wage methods

Two other revealed preference methods are the *hedonic property value* and *hedonic wage* methods. They share the characteristic that they use a statistical technique, known as multiple regression analysis, to "tease out" the environmental component of value in a related market. For example, it is possible to discover that, all other things being equal, property values are lower in polluted neighborhoods than in clean neighborhoods. (Property values fall in polluted neighborhoods because they are less desirable places to live.)

Hedonic property value models use market data (house prices) and then break down the house sales price into its attributes, including the house characteristics (e.g., number of bedrooms, lot size, and features), the neighborhood characteristics (e.g., crime rates, school quality, and so on), and environmental characteristics (e.g., air quality, percentage of open space nearby, distance to a local landfill, etc.).

Hedonic models allow for the measurement of the marginal willingness to pay for discrete changes in an attribute. Numerous studies have utilized this approach to examine the effect on property value of things such as distance to a hazardous waste site (Michaels and Smith, 1990), large farm operations (Palmquist et al., 1997), open space and land use patterns (Bockstael, 1996; Geoghegan et al., 1997; Acharya and Bennett, 2001), dams and rivers (Bohlen and Lewis, 2009; Lewis and Landry, 2017), brownfields (Mihaescu and vom Hofe, 2012), and shale oil production facilities (Gopalakrishnan and Klaiber, 2013). This approach has become commonplace with the use of geographic information systems (discussed later).[10]

Hedonic wage approaches are similar except that they attempt to isolate the environmental risk component of wages, which serves to isolate the amount of compensation workers require in order to work in risky occupations. It is well known that workers in high-risk occupations demand higher wages in order to be induced to undertake the risks. When the risk is environmental (such as exposure to a toxic substance), the results of the multiple regression analysis can be used to construct a willingness to pay to avoid this kind of environmental risk. Additionally, the compensating wage differential can be used to calculate the value of a statistical life (Taylor, 2003). Techniques for valuing reductions in life-threatening risks will be discussed later in this chapter.

Benefit transfer and meta-analysis

The NOAA panel report has created an interesting dilemma. Although it legitimized the use of contingent valuation for estimating passive-use (nonconsumptive use) and nonuse values, the panel has also set some rather rigid guidelines that reliable studies should follow. The cost of completing an "acceptable" contingent valuation study could well be so high that they will only be useful for large incidents, those for which the damages are high enough to justify their use. Yet, due to the paucity of other techniques, the failure to use contingent valuation may, by default, result in passive-use values of zero. That is not a very appealing alternative.[11]

One key to resolving the dilemma created by the possible expense of implementing the NOAA panel's recommendations may be provided by a technique called benefit transfer. Since original studies are time consuming and expensive, benefit transfer allows the estimates for the site of interest to be based upon estimates from other sites or from an earlier time period to provide the foundation for a current estimate.

Benefit transfer methods can take one of three forms: value transfers, benefit function transfers, or meta-analysis. Sometimes the actual benefit values derived from point estimates can simply be directly transferred from one context to another, usually adjusted for differences between the study site and the policy site. Function transfer involves using a previously estimated benefit function that relates site characteristics to site values. In this case, the differentiating characteristics of the site of interest are entered into the previously derived benefit function in order to derive newer, more site-specific values (Johnston et al., 2006).

Most recently, meta-analysis has been utilized. *Meta-analysis,* sometimes called the "analysis of analyses," takes empirical estimates from a sample of studies, statistically relates them to the characteristics of the studies, and calculates the degree to which the reported differences can be attributed to differences in location, subject matter, or methodology. For example, meta-analysis has been used with cross sections of contingent valuation studies as a basis for isolating and quantifying the determinants of nonuse value. Once these determinants have been isolated and related to specific policy contexts, it may be possible to transfer estimates from one context to another by finding the value consistent with the new context without incurring the time and expense of conducting new surveys each time.

Benefit transfer methods have been widely used in situations for which financial, time, or data constraints preclude original analysis. Policy makers frequently look to previously published studies for data that could inform a prospective decision. Benefit transfer has the advantage of being quick and inexpensive, but the accuracy of the estimates deteriorates as the new context tends to deviate (either temporally or spatially) the further it is from the context used to derive the estimates. Benefit transfer has not escaped controversy. Johnston and Rosenberger (2010) and Johnston et al. (2015) provide a comprehensive discussion of benefit transfer and outline some of the potential problems with the use of benefit transfer, including a lack of studies that are both of sufficiently high quality and policy relevant. Additionally, many of the published studies do not provide enough information on the attributes to allow an assessment of how they might have affected the derived value.

In response to some of these concerns, a valuation inventory database has emerged. The Environmental Valuation Reference Inventory (EVRI) is an online searchable database of over 4000 empirical studies on the economic value of environmental benefits and human health effects. It was specifically developed as a tool for use in benefit transfer.[12]

Benefit transfers are also subject to large errors. A few studies have tested the validity of environmental value transfer across sites. In those that have, the transfer errors have been sizable and wide ranging, sometimes over 100 percent for stated preference survey transfers (Brouwer, 2000; Rosenberg and Stanley, 2006). Using meta-data from 31 empirical studies, Kaul et al. (2013) find a median transfer error of 39 percent. Lewis and Landry (2017) compare original hedonic property value model results to a test of transferring those results via benefit function transfer and find errors ranging from 29 percent to 1000 percent! These results suggest caution with the use of benefit transfer.

Using geographic information systems to enhance valuation

Geographic information systems (GIS) are computerized mapping models and analysis tools. A GIS map is made up of layers such that many variables can be visualized simultaneously using overlays. GIS offers a powerful collection of tools for depicting and examining spatial relationships. Most simply, GIS can be used to produce compelling measurements and graphics that communicate the spatial structure of data and analytic results with a force and clarity otherwise impossible. But the technology's real value lies in the potential it brings to ask novel questions and enrich our understanding of social and economic processes by explicitly considering their spatial structure. Models that address environmental externalities have, almost by definition, a strong spatial component.[13]

Fundamentally spatial in nature, use of GIS in hedonic property models is a natural fit. Housing prices vary systematically and predictably from neighborhood to neighborhood. Spatial characteristics, from air quality to the availability of open space, can influence property values of entire neighborhoods; if one house enjoys abundant open space or especially good air quality, it is highly likely that its neighbors do as well.

In a 2008 paper, Lewis, Bohlen, and Wilson used GIS and statistical analysis to evaluate the impacts of dams and dam removal on local property values. In a unique "experiment," they collected data on property sales for 10 years spanning the time before and after the Edwards Dam on the Kennebec River in Maine was removed. The Edwards Dam was the first federally licensed hydropower dam in the United States to be removed primarily for the purpose of river restoration. They also collected data on property sales approximately 20 miles upstream where two dams were still in place. GIS technology enhanced this study by facilitating the calculation of the distance from each home to both the river and the nearby dams. Lewis et al. (2008) found that homeowners pay a price penalty for living close to a dam. In other words, willingness to pay for identical housing is higher the further away from the dam the house is located. They also found that the penalty near the Edwards Dam site dropped to nearly zero after the dam was removed. Interestingly, the penalty upstream also dropped significantly. While a penalty for homes close to the dams upstream remains, it fell after the downstream dam was removed. Can you think of reasons why?[14]

Example 5.4 shows how the use of GIS can enable hedonic property value models to investigate how the view from a particular piece of property might affect its value.

EXAMPLE 5.4

Using GIS to inform hedonic property values: visualizing the data

GIS offers economists and others powerful tools for analyzing spatial data and spatial relationships. For nonmarket valuation, GIS has proven to be especially helpful in enhancing hedonic property value models by incorporating both the proximity of environmental characteristics and their size or amount. GIS studies have also allowed for the incorporation of variables that reflect nearby types and diversity of land use.

Geo-coding housing transactions assign a latitude and longitude coordinate to each sale. GIS allows other spatial data, such as land use, watercourses, and census data, to be "layered" on top of the map. By drawing a circle of the desired circumference around each house, GIS can help us to calculate the amount of each amenity that is in that circle as well as the density and types of people who live there. Numerous census data are available on variables such as income, age, education, crime rates, and commuting time. GIS also makes it relatively easy to calculate straight-line distances to desired (or undesired) locations, such as parks, lakes, schools, or landfills.

In a 2002 paper entitled "Out of Sight, Out of Mind? Using GIS to Incorporate Visibility in Hedonic Property Value Models," Paterson and Boyle use GIS to measure the extent to which visibility measures affect house prices in Connecticut. In their study, visibility is measured as the percentage of land visible within one kilometer of the property, both in total and broken out for various land use categories. Finally, they added variables that measured the percentage of area in agriculture or in forest, or covered by water within one kilometer of each house.

They find that visibility is indeed an important environmental variable in explaining property values, but the nature of the viewshed matters. While simply having a view is not a significant determinant of property values, viewing certain types of land uses is. Proximity to development reduces property values only if the development is visible, for example, suggesting that out of sight really does mean out of mind! They conclude that any analysis that omits variables that reflect nearby environmental conditions can lead to misleading or incorrect conclusions about the impacts of land use on property values. GIS is a powerful tool for helping a researcher include these important variables.

Source: Paterson, Robert, & Boyle, Kevin. (2002). Out of sight, out of mind? Using GIS to incorporate visibility in hedonic property value models. *Land Economics,* 78(3), 417–425.

Averting expenditures

A final example of an indirect observable method involves examining "averting" or "avoidance" expenditures. Averting expenditures are those designed to reduce the damage caused by pollution by taking some kind of averting or defensive action. Examples include installing indoor air purifiers in response to an influx of polluted air or relying on bottled water as a response to the pollution of local drinking water supplies. Since people would not normally spend more to prevent a problem than would be caused by the problem itself, averting expenditures can provide a lower-bound estimate of the damage caused by pollution. They also cause a disproportionate hardship on poor households that cannot afford such coping expenditures. Dickie (2016) argues that ignoring averting expenditures or behavior may underestimate damages. He offers a simple example using contaminated drinking water. Suppose contaminated drinking water increases waterborne illness by 4 percent. If half the population avoids the contamination by some form of averting action such as using an alternate source of water, frequency of illness will drop to 2 percent. Only half the population is now exposed, thus reducing damages. However, the avoidance expenses must be included in the damage estimate. If they are not, the damages will be underestimated (Dickie, 2016). Example 5.5 illustrates the impact of coping or averting expenditures on residents of Kathmandu, Nepal.

EXAMPLE 5.5

Valuing the reliability of water supplies: coping expenditures in Kathmandu Valley, Nepal

Nepal, like many other poor developing countries, experiences chronic shortages of safe drinking water. The Kathmandu Valley is no exception. The National Water Supply Corporation serves 70 percent of the population, but the public water supply is neither reliable nor safe. Shortages are frequent and the water quality is frequently contaminated with fecal coliform and nitrogen-ammonia (Pattanayak et al., 2005).

How much should be invested in improving water quality depends on how valuable clean water is to this population. Quantifying those benefits requires establishing how much residents would be willing to pay for cleaner water. One pathway for quantifying willingness to pay in this context can be found in analyzing how much households spend to cope with the unreliable water supply. It turns out they purchase water from water vendors, collect water from public taps, invest in wells or storage tanks, purchase filtration systems, and/or boil water. All of these coping mechanisms have both a financial cost and a cost associated with the time devoted to coping. Using coping costs as a proxy for willingness to pay can serve as the basis for constructing a lower-bound estimate of the demand curve for water provision in settings where other more direct valuation strategies are simply not practical to implement.

In a survey of 1,500 households in five municipalities, researchers found that for households in the Kathmandu Valley, coping or averting behaviors cost the average household about 1 percent of monthly income, most of this attributed to the time spent collecting water. The authors note that these coping costs are almost twice as much as the current monthly bills paid to the water utility.

Some demographic factors were found to have influenced household coping expenditures.

- Wealthier households were found to have higher coping expenditures. As the authors note, this confirms the intuition that relatively rich households have more resources and therefore invest more in water treatment, storage, and purchases.

- More educated respondents also had higher coping costs, perhaps because these households better understood the risks of contaminated water.

If, as suggested by these two findings, the poor face higher financial and educational barriers in their quest for cleaner water, water policy in this region faces an environmental justice issue as well as an efficiency issue.

Even though averting expenditures represent only a lower bound of willingness to pay for water supply, they can provide valuable information for the estimation of benefits of water provision. In addition, these data imply that the common assertion that in poor countries the costs of supplying clean water are so high that they necessarily exceed the benefits received by water users may be a misconception – the value of water in this valley was found to be at least twice the current per unit charge even when the lower bound estimating technique was used.

Source: Pattanayak, Subhrendu K., Yang, Jui-Chen, Whittington, Dale, & Bal Kumar, K. C. (2005). Coping with unreliable public water supplies: Averting expenditures by households in Kathmandu, Nepal. *Water Resources Research,* 41(2), doi:10.1029/2003WR002443.

Challenges

Aggregation

As you have probably figured out by now, nonmarket valuation faces several challenges. One challenge involves the aggregation of estimated values into a total value that can be used in benefit-cost analysis. How large is the relevant population? Do benefits change with distance to the resource in question? Debate 5.3 explores some of these challenging issues.

DEBATE 5.3

Distance decay in willingness to pay: when and how much does location matter?

One challenge in performing benefit-cost analysis is accurately choosing the "extent of the market." The extent of the market refers to ***who benefits*** from the resource in question. Loomis (1996) argues that not accounting for the full extent of the market (i.e., including everyone who gains some benefit) can lead to **under**estimates of willingness to pay and aggregate value.

On the other hand, a more inclusive design might include respondents with vastly lower willingness to pay simply because of their location. For some resources, distant respondents have a lower willingness to pay for its improvement. It seems reasonable to expect, for example, that the benefits from a reduction in river pollution to an individual household would probably depend on its proximity to the river. Those closest to the river place the highest value on the improvement. In other words, since it seems reasonable to expect that some types of values do experience a "distance decay," in aggregating benefits this deterioration should certainly be considered.

Bateman et al. (2006) argue that not accounting for distance decay can lead to **over**estimates of willingness to pay. Those who are further away still benefit and should be counted, but at some kind of decreasing rate. Recently, the number of stated preference studies (contingent valuation and choice experiments) that focus on distance decay has increased so we have learned more about it.

What do these studies say about the circumstances that give rise to distance decay?

Interestingly, the empirical evidence suggests that both the type of value being measured (use or nonuse value) as well as the type of willingness to pay question (compensating versus equivalent variation) matter. Hanley et al. (2003) and Bateman et al. (2006) both find that distance decay does arise for use value, but very little or not at all for nonuse values. If, however, some of the current nonusers become users under the proposed scenario, their valuation would experience some distance decay. This result follows the intuition that if the willingness to pay question is framed as a marginal improvement in quality (compensating variation), then some of the nonusers might become users and that possibility would be reflected in their valuations. If the question is framed as equivalent variation (willingness to pay to avoid loss), nonuser valuations experience no distance decay, since they will remain nonusers.

These studies suggest that spatial patterns in nonmarket values have important implications not only for how benefit-cost analysis should be conducted and interpreted but also for how that analysis affects the policy evaluations. Different design choices as to the extent of the market and whether to aggregate across particular political or economic jurisdiction can lead to very different results. As Schaafsma et al. (2012) suggest, these spatial patterns should be taken into account both when drawing samples for willingness to pay surveys, and when aggregating the results.

Sources: Bateman, Ian, Day, Brett H., Georgiou, Stavros, & Lake, Ian. (September 2006). The aggregation of environmental benefit values: Welfare measures, distance decay and total WTP. Discussion paper; Hanley, Nick, Schlapfer, Felix, & Spurgeon, James. (2003). Aggregating the benefits of environmental improvements: Distance-decay functions for use and nonuse values. *Journal of Environmental Management, 68,* 297–304; Loomis, John B. (1996). How large is the extent of the market for public goods: Evidence from a nationwide contingent valuation survey. *Applied Economics,* 28, 779–782; Schaafsma, Marije, Brouwer, Roy, & Rose, John. (2012). Directional heterogeneity in WTP models for environmental valuation. *Ecological Economics,* 79(1), 21–31.

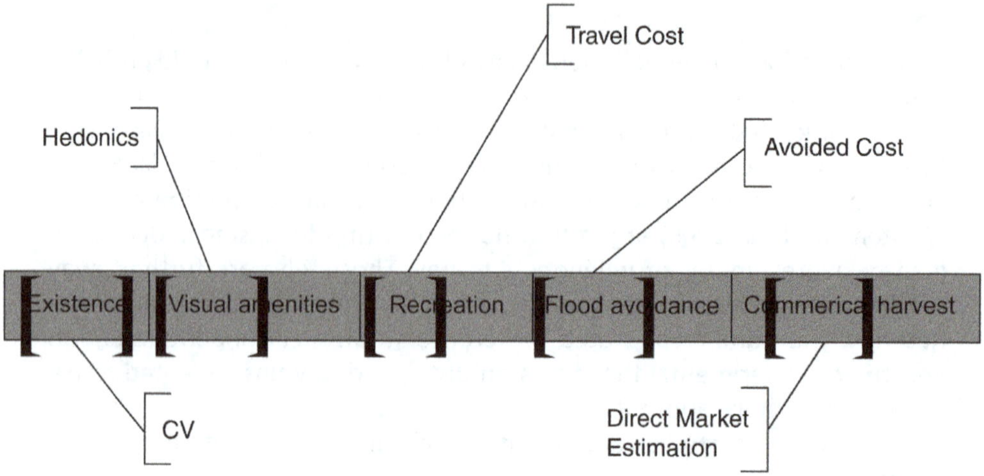

Figure 5.1 Different Methods, Different Experts, Different Data
Source: Courtesy of James Boyd, Resources for the Future

Partial values

Another large challenge for nonmarket valuation is that most studies only capture a portion of the total value of an environmental good or service. For example, ecosystems are bundles of values, but the methods outlined in this chapter are only capable of capturing a portion of the value. Consider an interesting recent example. Chami et al., (2019) estimate the value of a great whale at more than $2 million, and easily over $1 trillion for the current population great whales. What are these numbers based on? It turns out that by diving deep, whales disturb minerals that enhance the growth of phytoplankton. Phytoplankton absorb enormous amounts of carbon dioxide. So while this number seems large and certainly can be used to support whale protection policies, it only represents a partial value of a whale; the value of carbon capture. Other methods covered in this chapter would be used to estimate other values such as whale watching.

Figure 5.1 illustrates the different methods environmental economists use to capture different types of value. Each of these methods relies on different data and, many times, different experts. Rarely is the available time or money sufficient to apply all methods to a particular question.

Debate 5.4 illustrates the challenges and importance of attempts to capture the total economic value by examining a specific case study – polar bears in Canada.

DEBATE 5.4

What is the value of a polar bear?

Because polar bears are such a charismatic species, they have obviously attracted lots of popular support, but exactly how valuable are they? In 2011, the Canadian government issued a report in which it attempted to estimate the different socio-economic values of polar bears in Canada.

They commissioned the study in part to determine the economic impact of adding the polar bear to a list of at-risk species. This study represents

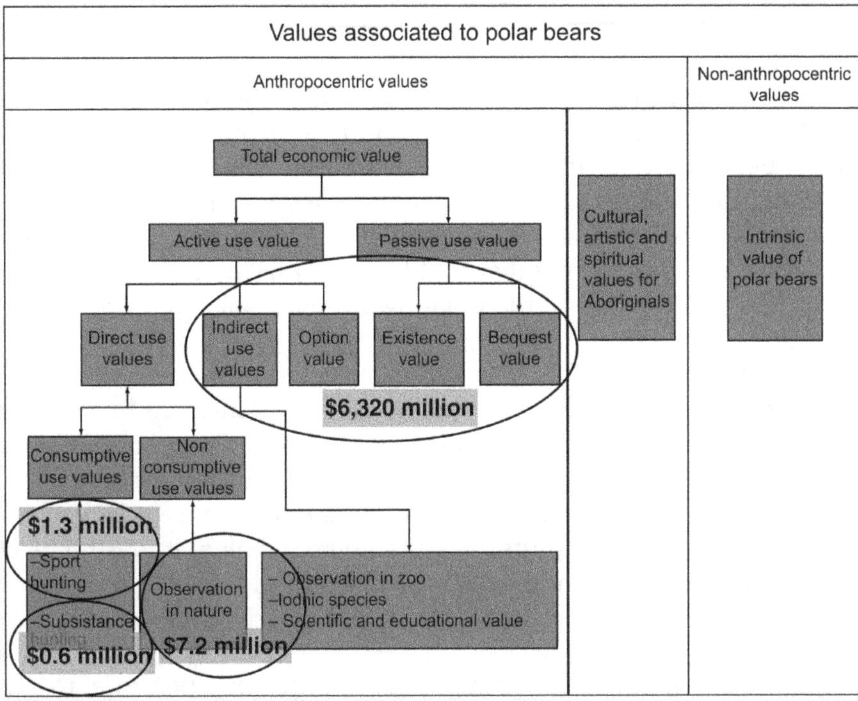

Figure 5.2 Monetary Values Associated with Polar Bears in Canada, by Value Category (Aggregate Amounts for Canada)

Source: ÉcoRessources Consultants, for Environment Canada, 2011, p. 32

one of the few studies to try to estimate the value of polar bears and the only one that tries to do it in a comprehensive fashion.

The authors tried to capture active use values (subsistence and sport hunting, polar bear viewing, and value in scientific research), as well as passive-use values (existence and bequest values). Multiple nonmarket valuation methods were used in this study including travel cost (viewing), market prices (hunting), meta-analysis, and benefit transfer (passive-use values). Time and budgetary constraints precluded the use of stated preference methods such as contingent valuation or choice experiments. The summary of their findings is reproduced in Figure 5.2. Note that the direct use values actually comprise a relatively small portion of the total value.

An effort to document the value of a species like this produces a value that is no doubt much closer to the truth than the default value of zero, but how close are these numbers to the true value? There are several caveats to consider:

- Consider the calculation for the value of polar bear meat. For this the cost, the next best substitute, which in this case was beef (for humans) and dog food was used. One could certainly argue for alternatives.

- Sport values were estimated using the benefit transfer method. Recall the challenges for using benefit transfer, in particular for a unique species like the polar bear. The study closest to this one was conducted in 1989 and focused on big game and grizzly bear hunting. For the polar bear study, the 1989 values were translated into 2009 dollars. The authors suggest their number might be an underestimate since hunting for a polar bear is such a unique experience. On the other hand, they also acknowledge that the number could just as easily be an overestimate if the charismatic image of the polar bear reduces willingness to pay for hunting.
- Finally, passive-use values were also calculated using benefit transfer. Since no study has been done on the preservation value of the polar bear in Canada, the researchers used a meta-analysis of species at risk (Richardson and Loomis, 2009). While that study calculated a total economic value, for the polar bear study the benefit transfer was specifically designed to capture only preservation value. It was relatively straightforward to remove direct uses (visitors) from the transferred value, but not the indirect use benefits such as scientific value.

Using any of these values as inputs into others creates a potential to double count, a common mistake that will be discussed further in Chapter 6. In fact, scientific values were calculated separately for the polar bear study as well as being included in the preservation value estimated via benefit transfer. As such, these numbers could overestimate the value.

What would you be willing to pay to protect the polar bear? As we have seen in this chapter, these types of questions are challenging to answer.

Sources: ÉcoRessources Consultants. (2011). Evidence of the socio-economic importance of Polar bears for Canada. Report for Environment Canada. Full report is accessible at http://publications.gc.ca/site/archivee-archived.html?url=http://publications.gc.ca/collections/collection_2012/ec/CW66-291-2011-eng.pdf; Richardson, Leslie, & Loomis, John. (2009). Total economic valuation of endangered species: A summary and comparison of the United States and the rest of the world estimates. In K. N. Ninan (Ed.), *Conserving and Valuing Ecosystem Services and Biodiversity: Economic, Institutional and Social Challenges*. London: Earthscan, 25–46.

Valuing human life

One fascinating public policy area where these various approaches have been applied is in the valuation of human life. Many government programs, from those controlling hazardous pollutants in the workplace or in drinking water, to those improving nuclear power plant safety, are designed to save human life as well as to reduce illness. How resources should be allocated among these programs depends crucially on the value of human life. In order to answer this question, an estimate of the value of that life to society is necessary and federal regulations require such estimates for benefit-cost analysis. How is life to be valued?

The simple answer, of course, is that life is priceless, but that turns out to be not very helpful. Because the resources used to prevent loss of life are scarce, choices must be made. The economic approach to valuing lifesaving reductions in environmental risk is to calculate the change in the probability of death resulting from the reduction in environmental risk and to place a value on the change. Thus, it is not life itself that is being valued, but rather a reduction in the probability that some segment of the population could be expected to die earlier than others. This *value of statistical life* (VSL) represents an individual's willingness to pay for small changes in mortality risks. It does not represent a willingness to pay to prevent certain death. It is measured as the "marginal rate of substitution between mortality risk and money (i.e., other goods and services)" (Cameron, 2010, p. 161) and as such is also called *mortality risk valuation*. Debate 5.5 examines the controversy associated with valuing changes in these mortality risks.

DEBATE 5.5

Is valuing human life immoral?

In 2004, economist Frank Ackerman and lawyer Lisa Heinzerling teamed up to write a book that questions the morality of using benefit-cost analysis to evaluate regulations designed to protect human life. In *Priceless: On Knowing the Price of Everything and the Value of Nothing* (2004), they argue that benefit-cost analysis is immoral because it represents a retreat from the traditional standard that all citizens have an absolute right to be free from harm caused by pollution. When it justifies a regulation that will allow some pollution-induced deaths, benefit-cost analysis violates this absolute right.

Economist Maureen Cropper responds that it would be immoral not to consider the benefits of lifesaving measures. Resources are scarce and they must be allocated so as to produce the greatest good. If all pollution were reduced to zero, even if that were possible, the cost would be extremely high and the resources to cover that cost would have to be diverted from other beneficial uses. Professor Cropper also suggests that it would be immoral to impose costs on people about which they have no say – for example, the costs of additional pollution controls – without at least trying to consider what choices people would make themselves. Like it or not, hard choices must be made.

Cropper also points out that people are always making decisions that recognize a trade-off between the cost of more protection and the health consequences of not taking the protection. Thinking in terms of trade-offs should be a familiar concept. She points out that people drive faster to save time, thereby increasing their risk of dying. They also decide how much money to spend on medicines to lower their risk of disease or they may take jobs that pose morbidity or even mortality risks.

In her response to Ackerman and Heinzerling, Cropper acknowledges that benefit-cost analysis has its flaws and that it should never be the only decision-making guide. Nonetheless, she argues that it does add useful information to the process and throwing that information away could prove to be detrimental to the very people that Ackerman and Heinzerling seek to protect.

Sources: Ackerman, Frank, & Heinzerling, Lisa. (2004). *Priceless: On Knowing the Price of Everything and the Value of Nothing*. New York: The New Press; Ackerman, Frank. (2004). Morality, cost-benefit and the price of life. *Environmental Forum, 21*(5), 46–47; Cropper, Maureen. (2004). Immoral not to weigh benefits against costs. *Environmental Forum, 21*(5), 47–48.

It is possible to translate the value derived from this procedure into an "implied value of statistical life." This is accomplished by dividing the amount each individual is willing to pay for a specific reduction in the probability of death by the probability reduction. Suppose, for example, that a particular environmental policy could be expected to reduce the average concentration of a toxic substance to which 1 million people are exposed. Suppose further that this reduction in exposure could be expected to reduce the risk of death from 1 out of 100,000 to 1 out of 150,000. This implies that the number of expected deaths would fall from 10 to 6.67 in the exposed population as a result of this policy. If each of the 1 million persons exposed is willing to pay $5 for this risk reduction (for a total of $5 million), then the implied value of a statistical life is approximately $1.5 million ($5 million divided by 3.33 lives saved). Alternatively, the VSL can be calculated using the change in WTP divided by the change in risk. For this example, that would be $5 divided by the change in risk of death (1/100,000–1/150,000), or $1.5 million. Thus, the VSL is capturing the rate of trade-off between money and a very small risk of death.

What actual values have been derived from these methods? One early survey (Viscusi, 1996) of a large number of studies examining reductions in a number of life-threatening risks found that most implied values for statistical life (in 1986 dollars) were between $3 million and $7 million. This same survey went on to suggest that the most appropriate estimates were probably closer to the $5 million estimate. In other words, all government programs resulting in risk reductions costing less than $5 million per life saved would be justified in benefit-cost terms. Those costing more might or might not be justified, depending on the appropriate value of a life saved in the particular risk context being examined.

In a meta-analysis, Mrozek and Taylor (2002) found much lower values for VSL. Using over 40 labor market studies, their research suggests that a range of $1.5 million to $2.5 million for VSL is more appropriate. What about age? Does the VSL change with age? Apparently so. Viscusi (2008) finds an inverted U-shape relationship between VSL and age. Specifically, using the hedonic wage model, they estimate a VSL of $3.7 million for persons ages 18–24, $9.7 million for persons ages 35–44, and $3.4 million for persons ages 55–62. According to their study, VSL rises with age, peaks, and then declines.

What about the value of statistical life across populations or countries with different incomes? Most agencies in the United States use VSLs between $5 million and $8 million.[15] These estimates are based largely on hedonic wage studies that have been conducted in the United States or in other high-income countries.[16] How might those results be translated into settings featuring populations with lower incomes?

Adjustments for income are typically derived using an estimate of the income elasticity of demand. Recall that income elasticity is the percent change in consumption given a 1 percent change in income. Hammitt and Robinson (2011) note that applying income elasticities derived for countries like the United States, might result in nonsensical VSL estimates if blindly applied to lower-income countries. While U.S. agencies typically assume a 0.4 to 0.6 percent change in VSL for a 1 percent change in real income over time, elasticities closer to 1.0 or higher are more realistic for transfers of these values between high- and low-income countries. Using the higher income elasticity number is merited since willingness to pay for mortality risk reduction as a percentage of income drops at very low incomes; what limited income is available in poorer households is reserved for basic needs.

Damage assessments: loss of ecosystem services

Another area where the quantification of nonmarket values can, and has, played a significant role is in assessing the magnitude of damage to ecosystems caused by human activities.

Oil spills are a case in point. Prior to the catastrophic 2010 Deepwater Horizon spill in the Gulf of Mexico, the Oil Pollution Act of 1990 had established a formal legal framework for determining when an oil spill results in a quantifiable adverse change in a natural resource. Through a process known as the Natural Resources Damage Assessment (NRDA), trustees of the affected ecosystem must attempt to quantify the extent of damages caused by a spill in order to seek compensation from the responsible parties. In 2016, after a 6-year study of the impacts, economists estimated the damages to the natural resources from the spill at $17.2 billion (see Chapter 13 Example 13.4 for more detail).

As a recent report from the National Research Council notes (NRC, 2013), highlighting the relationship between ecosystem services and the economy can heighten public knowledge of and support for protecting those services. That report advocated incorporating a broader ecosystem services approach to assessing damage from the spill rather than focusing only on provisioning services. By encompassing the wider array of services this broader approach could end up identifying restoration projects that would benefit not only the trustees and direct-use parties, but the larger public as well.

That process of widening the scope of assessment is complex and will ultimately take time. As of 2017, according to its records BP had paid out over $30 billion in cleanup and claims but virtually all of that is based upon direct human losses rather than the broader focus suggested by the NRC. One exception, however, involved an oyster reef project in Alabama's Mobile Bay. The restoration project was originally focused on a location that would be convenient for fishermen who lost harvests during the spill, thereby responding directly to their losses. However, the ecosystem services provided by oysters are much greater than their direct value to harvesters. The filtering action of oysters plays an important role not only in removing suspended sediments from the water column but also in cleansing the water of various pollutants. When the broader scope suggested by the NRC was applied, a location that was better suited to supply all these ecosystem services was chosen. In 2016 BP settled for an additional $20.8 billion, $8.8 billion of which will go toward environmental restoration efforts including the restoration of coastal marshes in Louisiana.

Policies to protect ecosystem services is the focus of the next chapter.

Summary: nonmarket valuation today

In this chapter, we have examined the most prominent, but certainly not the only, techniques available to supply policy makers with the information needed to implement efficient policy. Finding the total economic value of the service flows requires estimating three components of value: (1) use value, (2) option value, and (3) nonuse or passive-use values.

Our review of these various techniques included direct observation, contingent valuation, contingent choice experiments, travel cost, hedonic property and wage studies, and averting or defensive expenditures. When time or funding precludes original research, benefit transfer or meta-analysis provide alternate methods for the estimation of values. In January 2011, a panel of experts gathered at the annual meeting of the American Economics Association to reflect on nonmarket valuation 20 years after the *Exxon Valdez* spill and, unknown to any of them when the panelists were asked to participate, eight months after the *Deepwater Horizon* spill. The panelists had all worked on estimation of damages from the *Exxon Valdez* spill. The consensus among panelists was that while many of the issues with bias have been addressed in the literature, many unanswered questions remain and some areas still need work. While they all agreed that it is "hard to underestimate the powerful need for values" (i.e., some number is definitely better than no number), and we now have in place methods that can be easily utilized by all researchers, they also emphasized several problem areas. First, the value of time in travel cost models has not been resolved. What is the opportunity cost of time if you are unemployed, for example?

Second, in discussing other revealed preference methods, they asked the question, "How do the recent numerous foreclosures in the real estate market affect hedonic property value model assumptions?"[17] Third, choice experiments do not resolve all of the potential problems with contingent valuation. While choice experiments do seem to better represent actual market choices, some of the issues that arise in contingent valuation, such as the choice of the payment vehicle, also arise with choice experiments. In addition, some new challenges, such as how the sequencing of choices in choice experiments might affect outcomes, arise. The panel highlighted how this area of research has been enhanced by the field of behavioral economics, an emerging research area that combines economics and psychology to examine human behavior. And finally, they suggested that the NOAA panel recommendations be updated to reflect the new body of research. In 2017, a new set of guidelines was published to do just that. The 23 recommendations in those guidelines address these questions regarding stated preference surveys and attempt to synthesize the now large body of research that informs nonmarket valuation (Johnston et al., 2017).

Some of these same experts, along with several others, implemented a nationwide survey following the BP spill to assess what U.S. households would pay to avoid damages from another spill. Using state of the art techniques for stated preference surveys, they found that U.S. households would be willing to pay $17.2 billion to avoid the damages from another spill (Bishop et al., 2017). One author claimed, "this is proof that our natural resources have an immense monetary value to citizens of the United States who visit the Gulf and to those who simply care that this valuable resource is not damaged."

Discussion question

1 Certain environmental laws prohibit the EPA from considering the costs of meeting various standards when the levels of the standards are set. Is this a good example of appropriately prioritizing human health or simply an unjustifiable waste of resources? Why?

Self-test exercises

1 In Mark A. Cohen, "The Costs and Benefits of Oil Spill Prevention and Enforcement," *Journal of Environmental Economics and Management* Vol. 13 (June 1986), an attempt was made to quantify the marginal benefits and marginal costs of U.S. Coast Guard enforcement activity in the area of oil spill prevention. His analysis suggests (p. 185) that the marginal per-gallon benefit from the current

level of enforcement activity is $7.50, while the marginal per-gallon cost is $5.50. Assuming these numbers are correct, would you recommend that the Coast Guard increase, decrease, or hold at the current level their enforcement activity? Why?

2 Professor Kip Viscusi estimated that the cost per life saved by current government risk-reducing programs ranges from $100,000 for unvented space heaters to $72 billion for a proposed standard to reduce occupational exposure to formaldehyde.

   a Assuming these values to be correct, how might efficiency be enhanced in these two programs?
   b Should the government strive to equalize the marginal costs per life saved across all lifesaving programs?

3 a Suppose that hedonic wage studies indicate a willingness to pay $50 per person for a reduction in the risk of a premature death from an environmental hazard of 1/100,000. If the exposed population is 4 million people, what is the implied value of a statistical life?
   b Suppose that an impending environmental regulation to control that hazard is expected to reduce the risk of premature death from 6/100,000 to 2/100,000 per year in that exposed population of 4 million people. Your boss asks you to tell her what is the maximum this regulation could cost and still have the benefits be at least as large as the costs. What is your answer?

Notes

1 U.S. District Court for the State of Alaska, Case Number A89–0095CV, January 28, 2004.
2 Ibid.
3 *Exxon Shipping Company v. Baker.*
4 Bishop et al. (2017).
5 In 2017, the United States Department of the Interior released the Deepwater Horizon Response and Restoration Administrative Record, which included an estimate of the total value of damages (see Example 13.4).
6 The rules for determining these damages are defined in Department of Interior regulations. See 40 Code of Federal Regulations 300: 72–74.
7 Krutilla, John V. (1967). Conservation reconsidered. *American Economic Review*, 57(4), 777–786.
8 Ibid., p. 779.
9 A more detailed description of the methodological issues and concerns with contingent valuation with respect to the actual *Exxon Valdez* contingent valuation survey can be found in Mitchell (2002).
10 There are many examples in this category. These are just a few.
11 Whittington (2002) examines the reasons why so many contingent valuation studies in developing countries are unhelpful. Poorly designed or rapidly implemented surveys could result in costly policy mistakes on topics that are very important in the developing world. The current push for cheaper, quicker studies is risky and researchers need to be very cautious.
12 www.evri.ca
13 For examples see Bateman et al. (2002), who describe the contributions of GIS in incorporating spatial dimensions into economic analysis, including benefit-cost analysis; and Clapp et al. (1997), who discuss the potential contributions GIS can make for urban and real estate economics.
14 Interestingly, after this study was complete, one of the two upstream dams, the Fort Halifax Dam, was removed in July 2008 after years of litigation about its removal.
15 See, for example, www.epa.gov/environmental-economics/mortality-risk-valuation.
16 Many labor market estimates of VSL average near $7 million (Viscusi, 2008).
17 This question was taken up by another panel of experts at the 2012 Association of Environmental and Resource Economics annual conference and later published by Boyle et al. (2012).

Further reading

Bateman, I. J., Lovett, A. A., & Brainard, J. S. (2005). *Applied Environmental Economics: A GIS Approach to Cost-Benefit Analysis.* Cambridge: Cambridge University Press. Uses GIS to examine land use change and valuation.

Bennett, J. (Ed.). (2011). *The International Handbook on Non-Market Environmental Valuation.* Cheltenham, UK: Edward Elgar. An excellent compilation on nonmarket valuation.

Boardman, A. E., Greenberg, D. H., Vining, A. R., & Weimer, D. L. (2005). *Cost-Benefit Analysis: Concepts and Practice*, 3rd ed. Upper Saddle River, NJ: Prentice-Hall. An excellent basic text on the use of cost-benefit analysis.

Champ, P. A., Boyle, K. J., & Brown, T. C. (2016). *A Primer on Nonmarket Valuation*, 2nd ed. New York: Springer. A thorough overview of nonmarket valuation methods.

Costanza, R., et al. (1998). The value of the world's ecosystem services and natural capital. (Reprinted from *Nature*, 387, 253, 1997). *Ecological Economics*, 25(1), 3–15. An ambitious, but ultimately flawed, attempt to place an economic value on ecosystem services. This issue of *Ecological Economics* also contains a number of articles that demonstrate some of the flaws.

Johnston, R. J., Boye, K. J., Adamowicz, W., Bennett, J., Brouwer, R., Cameron, T. A., Hanemann, W. M., Hanley, N. J., Ryan, M., Scarpa, R., Tourangeau, R., & Vossler, C. A. (2017). Contemporary guidance for stated preference studies. *JAERE*, 4(2). http://dx.doi.org/10.1086/691697. This issue includes an update to the NOAA guidelines for the use of contingent valuation. It also has recommendations for the use of choice experiments.

Johnston, R. J., Rolfe, J., Rosenberger, R., & Brouwer, R. (Eds.). (2015). *Benefit Transfer of Environmental and Resource Values: A Guide for Researchers and Practitioners.* Dordrecht, the Netherlands: Springer. This article is a practical guide for the design and use of benefit transfer.

Mitchell, R. C., & Carson, R. T. (1989). *Using Surveys to Value Public Goods: The Contingent Valuation Method.* Washington, DC: Resources for the Future. A comprehensive examination of contingent valuation research with brief summaries of representative studies and recommendations for survey design.

Whitehead, J., Haab, T., & Huang, J.-C. (Eds.). (2011). *Preference Data for Environmental Valuation: Combining Revealed and Stated Approaches.* London: Routledge. A compilation of articles that use more than one valuation method or novel applications of data combinations written by nonmarket valuation economists.

Additional references and other historically significant references are available on this book's eResource page: www.routledge.com/9781138587595

Section II

Environmental policy

Chapter 6

Ecosystem goods and services

Nature's threatened bounty

Introduction

In the last chapter, we learned about the methods available for valuing environmental goods and services and damages to those goods and services. We looked at examples for use values such as recreation, but also for passive/nonuse values. Many of the ecological functions and services are not only supplied by natural processes, but nature charges nothing for their use. Examples of these ecological goods and services include pollination by bees, the aquifer recharge services by wetlands, breathable air, biodiversity, nitrogen fixation in the soil, climate regulation through carbon sequestration, as well as aesthetic and recreation services. If these services directly benefit at least one person, they are called *ecosystem services*.

In 1997 a team of researchers attempted to place a monetary global value on ecosystem services (Constanza et al., 1997). Basing their estimates on previously published studies and "a few original calculations", they found the (1997) economic value of 17 ecosystem services for 16 biomes to be in the range of US$16–54 trillion per year, with an average of US$33 trillion per year (approximately $49 trillion in 2014 dollars), a number significantly higher than global GDP. This article attracted considerable attention.

However, because the methods they used were controversial, the specific estimated values were controversial as well. In 2014, Costanza and colleagues updated their 1997 estimates. Using the same controversial methods, they suggest that the value of total global ecosystem services in 2011 was $125 trillion assuming changes to land areas and $145 trillion assuming no changes to the biomes. They also found that since the earlier study in 1997, losses to ecosystem services due to land use changes were $4.3–$20.2 trillion/year. What is not controversial, however, is the fact that ecosystems play a very valuable role in the lives of humans.

What role can economic analysis play in assuring that the value provided by these ecosystem services is not only recognized, but also protected from degradation? In this chapter we take up that question, focusing on two specific roles: (1) refining and improving the methods for quantifying the values received from natural services to increase their reliability and to demonstrate their importance, taking care to identify the specific contributions to human welfare; and (2) facilitating the design of private, public, and public-private partnership arrangements as well as incentive mechanisms that can help protect these important components of nature from degradation.

The state of ecosystem services

In 2001, U.N. Secretary-General Kofi Annan initiated the Millennium Ecosystem Assessment (MA) with the goal to assess "the consequences of ecosystem change for human well-being and to establish the scientific basis for actions needed to enhance the conservation and sustainable use of ecosystems and their contributions to human well-being."

To examine the connections and the linkages between ecosystems and human well-being, the MA divides ecosystem services into several categories.

- *Provisioning services* provide direct benefits such as water, timber, food, and fiber.
- *Regulating services* include flood control, water quality, disease prevention, and climate.
- *Supporting services* consist of such foundational processes as photosynthesis, nutrient cycling, and soil formation.
- *Cultural services* provide recreational, aesthetic, and spiritual benefits.

In 2005, the Assessment published four main findings.

- Ecosystems have changed rapidly in the last 50 years – at a rate higher than any other time period. Due to the growing demands on the earth's resources and services, some of these high rates of change are irreversible.
- Many of the changes to ecosystems, while improving the well-being of some humans, have been at the expense of ecosystem health. Fifteen of the 24 ecosystems evaluated are in decline.
- If degradation continues, it will be difficult to achieve many of the U.N. Millennium Development Goals since resources that are vital for certain especially vulnerable groups are being affected.[1] Further degradation not only intensifies current poverty, but it limits options for future generations, thereby creating intergenerational inequity.
- Finally, the Assessment suggests that reversing the degradation of ecosystems would require significant changes in institutions and policies and it specifically notes that economic instruments can play an important role in this transformation.

Another report, the Economics of Ecosystems and Biodiversity (TEEB), examines the costs of policy inaction on the decline of biodiversity worldwide. It finds that by 2050 under several "business as usual" scenarios, an additional 11 percent of remaining biodiversity could be lost, 40 percent of low-impact agriculture could be converted to intensive agriculture and 60 percent of coral reefs could be gone (perhaps as early as 2030).

Recognizing the importance of ecosystem services the Intergovernmental Platform on Biodiversity and Ecosystem Services (IPBES) was established in April 2012 as an independent intergovernmental body open to all member countries of the United Nations. IPBES provides a forum for synthesizing, reviewing, assessing, and critically evaluating relevant information and knowledge generated worldwide on biodiversity and ecosystem services.

Economic analysis of ecosystem services

Ecosystem services are flows that are generated from stocks of natural assets and that benefit humans. Tropical forests, for example, are assets that can provide carbon sequestration, habitat, watershed protection, and recreation, but also can provide flows of timber. The harvest of flows can either be sustainable or unsustainable.

Economic analysis is helpful both in identifying sources of economic degradation and in evaluating possible approaches to maintain and restore these services. Both of these tasks are enhanced by careful valuation of the flows in question.

One avenue for using these valuations is benefit-cost analysis and the scope for these analyses is wider than you might expect. They are not limited to traditional evaluation of water or land use projects. Bandara and Tisdell (2004), for example, use the results of a contingent valuation study on saving the Asian elephant to show that the WTP for the conservation of Asian elephants in Sri Lanka more than compensates for the damage caused by elephants.

Demonstrating the value of ecosystem services

The starting point for economic analysis in reversing ecosystem degradation lies in revealing the economic value forgone by the loss of these services. Quantifying those values, even imperfectly, can make it clear just how much their loss or degradation means.

Many of the services explored in this chapter are nonmarket goods or services, which means that we must use a methodology that does not depend on the availability of market prices to derive their value. As discussed in Chapter 5, two main strategies are available for eliciting these values: revealed preference methods – attributing value by observing or measuring what people spend on goods and services that contain attributes we wish to value – and stated preference methods – using surveys to ascertain willingness to pay. Other methods commonly used for valuing ecosystem services include using adjusted market prices, avoidance costs (or averting expenditures), production function methods, or damage costs avoided.[2] Here we will focus specifically on valuing services that ecosystems provide to humans either directly or indirectly.

Consider some specific contexts to illustrate both how these techniques can be applied to the valuation of ecosystem services and why the results matter.

The value of reefs

Coral reefs are an integral part of an extensive and vital landscape of coastal ecosystems. Increasingly they are in jeopardy. One of the specific areas benefited by the new field of ecosystems services research is not only the derivation of better estimates of the value of those ecosystem benefits, but also the identification of the specific sources of that value.

While some of the threat to coral reefs is due to pollution or overfishing, recently coral reef losses have accelerated significantly due to climate change. Specifically, rising water temperatures have induced coral bleaching, and excessive CO_2 dissolution in seawater is causing ocean acidification, which in turn hampers reef regeneration.

What is at stake? Just how valuable are the services provided by coral reefs? And how much do the four different categories of services contribute to the overall value?

One well-known study (TEEB, 2009) provides some relevant estimates to answer these questions by pulling together the existing literature on values of reefs in a global context. Table 6.1, drawn from that study, not only demonstrates that reefs provide valuable ecosystem services, but it also divides up the sources of value into the four categories described at the beginning of this chapter.

Note that this study finds that cultural services (particularly tourism and recreation) make the largest contribution to value. The clear implication is that studies that capture only the provisional services from coral reefs seriously underestimate this value.

One use of this type of estimate would be in calculating the reef degradation damages from climate change, a calculation that would be useful in designing climate change policy. Equivalently, the estimates could be used to derive the benefits from reducing that damage via greenhouse gas mitigation policy.

Because the TEEB study aggregates the results from a number of individual studies, it would be helpful to have some sense of what an underlying individual study might look like. What does it include? What methods are used to derive the estimates? What uses are anticipated for these estimates? Example 6.1 provides some insights from one study that help to answer these questions.

Table 6.1 Benefits from Ecosystem Services in Coral Reef Ecosystems

Coral Reefs	*Value of Ecosystem Services (in US$/ha/year – 2007 values)*		
Ecosystem Service	*Average*	*Maximum*	*Number of Studies*
Provisioning services			
Food	470	3,818	22
Raw materials	400	1,990	5
Ornamental resources	264	347	3
Regulating services			
Climate regulation	648	648	3
Moderation of extreme events	25,200	34,408	9
Waste treatment/water purification	42	81	2
Biological control	4	7	2
Cultural Services			
Aesthetic information/Amenity	7425	27,484	4
Opportunities for recreation and tourism	79,099	1,063,946	29
Information for cognitive development	2154	6461	4
Total	**115,704**	**1,139,190**	**83**
Supporting Services			
Maintenance of genetic diversity	13,541	57,133	7

Notes: These estimates are based on ongoing analyses for TEEB (TEEB Ecological and Economic Foundations, Chapter 7). As the TEEB data base and value-analysis are still under development, this table is for illustrative purposes only.
ha = hectare, a metric unit of area defined as 10,000 square meters.
Source: TEEB. (2009). Climate Issues Updated (September) Table 1, p. 7.

For the entire United States, the value of coral reefs has been estimated at $3.4 billion per year including fisheries tourism and coastal protection (NOAA, 2019). Included in this number is $94 million per year in flood damages that coral reefs help protect. In Chapter 11 we will revisit this with a discussion of increased flood risks from climate change.

EXAMPLE 6.1

The value of coral reefs in the U.S. Virgin Islands

The United States Virgin Islands (USVI) are located approximately 100 miles east of Puerto Rico by air. The four main islands are St. Croix, St. John, Water Island, and St. Thomas.

Recognizing the value of the local coral reefs and needing a baseline to provide a quantitative measure with which to compare possible alternative development/conservation plans, a study was commissioned to derive a total economic value (TEV) for these reefs. A TEV framework attempts to measure value from both use and nonuse values. This information was also felt to be useful in providing an economic basis for advocating for the preservation of these coral reefs, for establishing the basis for any damage compensation, and for determining potential user fees for residents and tourists.

This study focused on valuing the six main uses of coral reefs and adjacent habitats in selected sites on the USVI: (1) fishery value, (2) tourism value, (3) recreational and cultural value, (4) real estate value, (5) the value of shoreline protection, and (6) education/ research values.

The study involved a wide range of valuation methodologies including (1) a revealed preference study of the commercial value of the fishery, (2) a local resident survey aimed at estimating the local cultural and recreation attachment to the marine environment, (3) a tourist survey using both travel cost and choice experiment methods to get a comprehensive insight into the importance of the marine environment for visitors to the USVI, (4) an analysis of the coastal protection function of reefs, (5) a hedonic pricing analysis to discern the positive impact of healthy reefs on house prices, (6) a GIS analysis aimed at preparing value maps of the coral reefs of the USVI, and (7) an aggregation of the separate components to produce the estimation of the TEV of these coral reefs.

This study found the TEV to be $187 million per year, with the values of the component parts found to be as follows:

- Reef related tourism – $96 million
- Recreation – $48 million
- Amenity – $35 million
- Coastal protection – $6 million
- Support to commercial fisheries – $3 million

Note that tourism and recreation once again comprise the largest sources of value for this individual case as it did for the global total considered previously. Hurricanes Irma and Maria in 2017 caused widespread devastation in the Caribbean. Damages include significant losses to all of these services. In addition to displacing jobs, property and tourism, they caused devastating reef destruction and including destroying strands of Pillar Coral, a threatened species.

Source: van Beukering, P., Brander, L., van Zanten, B., Verbrugge, E., & Lems, K. (2011). The economic value of the coral reef ecosystems of the United States Virgin Islands: Final report. *IVM Institute for Environmental Studies Report Number: R-11/06*. The Netherlands: Amsterdam (August 31).

Valuing supporting services: pollination

Ecosystem valuation can also help to raise awareness of extremely valuable, but probably underappreciated, ecosystem services, especially when the continuation of those services is threatened. Pollination services supplied by bees is one such valuable ecosystem service. Many valuable agricultural crops rely on bees for pollination. Between $235 and $285 billion (U.S.) worth of annual global food production relies on the direct contribution of honey bee pollinators (Lautenbach et al., 2012).

Some 1,000,000 honeybee hives, or more than 40 percent of all the beehives in the United States, are required just for cross-pollination of the $2 billion almond crop in California. When the almond trees flower, managed honeybee hives are moved by flatbed trucks to the San Joaquin Valley to provide sufficient bees to pollinate the crop (Ratnieks and Carreck, 2010).

The benefits from pollination, however, include not only the direct economic impacts of increasing the productivity of agricultural crops but also such nonmarket impacts as aiding in genetic diversity, improving ecosystem resilience, and providing nutrient cycling. Unfortunately these important ecosystem services may be in jeopardy.

In 2006, the popular press began reporting on what has been called colony collapse disorder, an unexplained disappearance of honeybee colonies. Beekeeper surveys suggest that 33 percent of honeybee colonies in the United States died in the winter of 2010. In 2019 that number rose to 40 percent. While the exact causes are, as of yet, unknown, multiple causes are likely to blame.

Ratnieks and Carreck speculate about economic impact of potential future losses and ask an important question:

> Is the future of U.S. commercial beekeeping going to be based on pollinating a few high-value crops? If so, what will be the wider economic cost arising from crops that have modest yield increases from honey bee pollination? These crops cannot pay large pollination fees but have hitherto benefited from an abundance of honey bees providing free pollination.

The damage caused by loss of pollination services to other parts of the world could be even higher than those in the United States. One study argues that possible future global shortages of pollination services are not only likely to be profound, but have quite different economic impacts around the globe (Example 6.2).

EXAMPLE 6.2

Valuing pollination services: two illustrations

Pollinator services valued in the tens of billions of dollars worldwide are disappearing. Declining populations of pollinator insects, including wild bees, risk losses to agricultural production worldwide with disproportionate impacts on developing countries.

Wild bees from a nearby tropical forest provide pollination services to aid Costa Rican coffee production. While this coffee *(C. arabica)* can self-pollinate, pollination from wild bees has been shown to increase coffee productivity from 15 to 50 percent.

One study (Ricketts et al., 2002) examined this relationship and placed an economic value on this particular ecological service. They found that the pollination services from bees living in two specific preserved forest fragments (46 and 111 hectares, respectively) were worth approximately $60,000 per year for one large, nearby Costa Rican coffee farm. As the authors conclude:

> The value of forest in providing crop pollination service alone is . . . of at least the same order [of magnitude] as major competing land uses, and infinitely greater than that recognized by most governments (i.e., zero).

Although these estimates only partially capture the value of this forest because they consider only a single farm and a single type of ecological service, they are apparently sufficient, by themselves, to demonstrate the economic value of preserving this particular forest.

Recognizing that this kind of partial analysis, which focuses on an individual case, should be complemented by studies with a more macro focus has encouraged different methodologies with a more global focus. One of these studies, which used a multiregion, computable general equilibrium (CGE) model of agricultural production and trade, examined the global economic impacts of pollinator declines (Bauer and Wing, 2010).

CGE models produce numerical assessments of economy-wide consequences of various events or programs. They include not only the direct effects on the crop sector, but also the indirect, noncrop effects. Using this type of model allows the authors to estimate the impacts of a decline in pollination services in different geographic regions. The also are able to estimate how these impacts are affected by the presence of different local substitutes for pollination services.

The authors find that the annual global losses to the crop sector attributable to a decline in direct pollination services are estimated to be $10.5 billion, but economywide losses (noncrop sectors) are estimated to be much larger, namely $334 billion. Clearly estimates based only a direct services would seriously underestimate the value of pollination services.

They also find that some regions of the world, especially western Africa, are likely to suffer disproportionately. Their enhanced vulnerability is due not only to the larger share that pollinator-dependent crops make up in western Africa's agricultural output, but also to the relatively higher importance of the agriculture sector in the African economy.

Richer countries are not immune. In early 2017, the rusty patched bumble bee *(Bombus affinis),* a key pollinator of blueberries, tomatoes, and wildflowers, became the first bumble bee and the first wild bee of any kind to be listed on the Endangered Species list in the United States. Wild bumble bees are important pollinators of one-third of U.S. crops. Pollination services in the United States have been estimated at $3 billion per year (Gorman, 2017).

Sources: Ricketts, T. H. et al. (August 24, 2002). Economic value of tropical forest to coffee production. *PNAS (Proceedings of the National Academy of Science),* 101(34), 12579–12582; Bauer, D. M., & Wing, I. S. (October 2010). Economic consequences of pollinator declines: A synthesis. *Agricultural and Resource Economics Review,* 39(3), 368–383. Gorman, S. (January 11, 2017). U.S. lists a bumble bee species as endangered for the first time. *Scientific American.*

Valuing supporting services: forests and coastal ecosystems

Valuation methods have been used extensively to value forest ecosystem services, coastal and marine ecosystem services, and biodiversity. In his summary of the literature on coastal and marine ecosystem services (CMEs) valuation, Barbier (2012) notes that losses to fishery nurseries, mangroves that provide storm protection, coral reefs that are a rich source of biodiversity, filtering services of wetlands, and sea grasses have now been measured worldwide. Quantifying the benefits of these services can provide an empirical foundation for decision making and for setting priorities.

The TEEB (2009) presents several other examples that demonstrate the numerous and diverse possible sources of benefits. One such example derives the ecosystem benefits from protecting a forest with high biodiversity in Madagascar. Benefits flowing from that resource include medicines (estimated net present value of $1.57 million), erosion control (estimated NPV of $380,000), carbon storage (estimated NPV of $105 million), recreation, and forest products (estimated value of $9.4 million).

This study also notes the complicated scale dimension of ecosystem services by demonstrating how benefits flow from developing countries to a distant city, in this case London. These transboundary benefits include medicines, fish, coffee, flood control, and existence value. Valuing services that simultaneously affect several different scales (local, regional, global) can be challenging, but not including all scales can produce a serious underestimate.

Challenges and innovation in ecosystem valuation

In order for valuations to be useful, their derivations must be based upon consistent methodologies. Consistency is important not only to assure that various valuation projects can be directly compared but also so that benefit transfers are facilitated. (Recall from Chapter 5 that benefit transfer involves using values from one study site to provide the basis for valuing services at another policy site.)

Achieving this kind of consistency requires precise definitions of the services as well as agreement on how these services contribute to value. It also requires that the valuation procedures avoid double counting.

For nonmarket goods and services these issues are especially challenging. While market goods have well-defined units based on actual purchases, nonmarket goods and services may offer a large variety of attributes, each of which could have value. If different analysts choose different attributes to value, the result will not only be inconsistent valuations, but inconsistent valuations make policy-relevant benefit transfer impossible (Johnston et al., 2005).

The Millennium Ecosystem Assessment (2005) provides a classification of ecosystem services that has been widely cited, but unfortunately these classifications are vulnerable to double counting. "Water purification" and the "provision of freshwater" are listed as separate services, for example (Balmford et al., 2011; Boyd and Banzhaf, 2007). Double counting can also occur if an ecosystem service provides both an intermediate good and a final good. When both are separately valued and simply added together, a common mistake, the resulting values are inflated. On the other hand intermediate services cannot simply be ignored since they are one source of the final value (Johnston and Russell, 2011).

Given these challenges, how do nonmarket valuation methods fare in practice? Because ecosystem service valuation is relatively new, the quest for clean, reliable estimates is still evolving. For example, Boyd and Krupnick (2009) note in their survey of the stated preference literature that a lack of consistency in definitions is still relatively common. Johnston and Russell (2011) also lament the lack of clarity in definitions of final ecosystem goods and services.

Researchers using stated preference methods are beginning to grapple with this aspect of inconsistency – how to distinguish between intermediate and final goods. The specific challenge for economists using stated preference techniques is to design surveys that identify commodities that are both true to the ecological science and meaningful and understandable to respondents (Boyd and Krupnick, 2009; Johnston et al., 2012). This is no easy undertaking.

For revealed preference methods, it is sometimes difficult to know the specific underlying source of value. For example, if a hedonic property value study finds that being near beaches raises land value, which attributes of the beaches are the source of that value. Is it the beach width? The sand quality? Both?

One emerging solution to this dilemma involves combining stated and revealed preference data. (Note that the study in Example 6.1 uses both.) By combining the two methods, the source of the revealed preference value can be explored in greater depth using the more specific stated preferences of the respondent. The downside is that implementing two studies is obviously more expensive than one.

Moore et al. (2011) provide a useful example of how an attribute-based study can bring greater clarity to the question of *what* is being valued. In their study aimed at estimating marginal values of forest protection programs, they utilized a stated preference survey that asked respondents to consider two different types of conservation sites – one with distinct use values like recreation and easy access, versus another with high ecological values like a richer biodiversity or providing habitat for endangered species. Identifying and valuing these specific attributes, as opposed to deriving only an overall value for the site, allows for the estimation of the marginal value of each type of service. Note that estimating separate marginal values for specific ecosystem services also facilitates more precise benefit transfers.

One response to the high cost of conducting new site-specific studies for each ecosystem service is to use meta-analysis, the technique (discussed in Chapter 5) that can draw insights from a large number of previously completed studies. This approach has the advantage that not only will the service value be based on a large number of studies but it can also identify the study characteristics that seem to play a role in the resulting value. Despite the challenges, the role for nonmarket valuation is already clear and numerous studies have highlighted the benefits of protection of one or more ecosystem service in ways that have made for better policy.

Institutional arrangements and mechanisms for protecting nature's services

Valuation is only one of the contributions economic analysis can make to the maintenance and protection of important ecosystem services. Another is using economics to help design institutions and policies that can bring economic incentives to bear.

Payments for environmental services

One avenue where economic analysis has been helpful in this regard lies in identifying ways to create institutional arrangements in which the providers of ecosystem services can be compensated for nonmarket services. This would not only create better incentives for maintaining and enhancing those services, but also provide a revenue source that could be used to further that purpose. While we have previously provided some examples of these arrangements, a few additional examples may prove helpful in conveying some sense of the scope of the options.

Costa Rica's Pago por Servicios Ambientales (PSA) program

One of the earliest examples of this approach can be found in Costa Rica. Built upon an existing forestry law, the PSA program includes four specific environmental services provided by forest ecosystems: (1) greenhouse gas emission mitigation; (2) water services for human consumption, irrigation, and energy production; (3) biodiversity conservation; and (4) scenic beauty for recreation and ecotourism. For our purposes in this chapter the water services component is the most interesting and we shall focus on it.

The program started with voluntary agreements involving payments to private landowners from water users in return for conserving certain forested areas that served as recharge or purification areas in the watershed. Bottlers, municipal water supply systems, irrigation water users, and hotels have all chosen to participate in these agreements. Whereas early agreements saw water users paying for a quarter of conservation costs (since water services were only one of four services that the law enumerated as provided by forests), in more recent agreements water users are not only paying the entire cost of conservation, but the administrative costs as well. These agreements typically cover a five-year period.

As the program has matured, a water tariff has been added to finance the payments, effectively transforming one aspect of the program from a voluntary one into a mandatory one. Interestingly the voluntary agreements are still occurring not only because the payments made under these agreements are deducted from the amounts owed under the tariff, but the voluntary agreements give somewhat more control to the signatory over exactly how the payment will be used.

Pagiola (2008) reports that the PSA program has been very popular with landowners (with requests to participate far outstripping available financing) and that recipients had a higher percentage of their forest under conservation than nonrecipients. He also points out, however, that the program does have some specific inefficiencies. In particular, because the PSA program offers a relatively low, undifferentiated, and mostly untargeted payment, it tends to attract participants whose opportunity cost of participation is low or negative. As a result some socially desirable land use practices are not adopted because the payment being offered is insufficient.

This program also provides a good opportunity to discuss an issue of some importance to these types of programs – economic sustainability. Programs will only be successful over the long term if they create the means to sustain themselves financially after the initial enthusiasm. This can occur either because (1) the incentives created by the program are large enough to cause private benefits to be higher than costs for both payees and recipients or (2) sufficient required financing is provided by law.

Indeed, some payments for service arrangements (including some in the PAS program) are funded by limited-term grants from international organizations. These are no doubt helpful in setting up the program and providing some initial successes, but many times what happens after these grants run out is not clear. In the case of the PSA water services program the existence of the tariff coupled with the apparent private landowner interest in participating suggest that outlook for the economic sustainability of this program seems relatively good.

Other watershed payment programs

Investing in watershed services is a broad category that covers payments for watershed services, water quality trading markets, instream buybacks, and water funds. Bennett et al. (2013) report on the state of watershed payments and find 205 active programs in 29 countries as of 2011. Sixty-seven of these are in the United States and 61 are in China. In 2011, $8.17 billion was transacted, though not all payments were in cash. In-kind payments, training programs, or agriculture inputs are also included.

Of the programs tracked, 66 of them include the stacking or "bundling" of other benefits. Most of these include co-benefits of biodiversity. Others include the bundling of carbon offsets or aesthetics. Concern for endangered species has also been a primary impetus for many of these programs.

Having users pay for services that they previously received for free can serve to produce an efficient outcome by providing both an incentive and revenue to protect those services. Suppose, however, the provider threatens to cut off supplies of those services unless the desired payments are forthcoming. Is this extortion or simply good business? (See Debate 6.1.)

DEBATE 6.1

Paying for ecosystem services or extortion?: the case of Yasuni National Park

Designated a UNESCO Biosphere Reserve in 1989, Yasuni National Park is one of the most biologically diverse places on earth. It is also the location for an estimated 846 million barrels of crude oil, 20 percent of Ecuador's reserves. As a developing country Ecuador was faced with a classic dilemma – should it preserve the parkland or extract the oil?

To avoid the environmental destruction caused by oil exploration in one of the areas with the greatest biological and cultural diversity of the Amazon, the government proposed permanently forgoing oil production in the Ishpingo-Tambococha-Tiputini (ITT) oil fields, located in Yasuni, if the world community would contribute 50 percent of the forgone income (estimated to be US$3.6 billion over a 13-year period).

Supporters argued that the payments would pay for global climate change benefits resulting from the CO_2 emissions avoided. They calculated 407 million metric tons of CO_2 emissions would be saved due to non-extraction and burning of oil and another 800 million metric tons of CO_2 from avoided deforestation.

Detractors suggested that this was extortion – "pay us or we will destroy the planet."

Regardless of whether it was a good idea or not, it failed. In August 2013, Ecuador's president announced that, since the initiative had attracted only a fraction of the cash it had aimed to raise, he ended it.

Sources: Ecuador Yasuni ITT Trust Fund. Retrieved from http://mptf.undp.org/yasuni; Ecuador approves Yasuni park oil drilling in Amazon rainforest. Retrieved from www.bbc.co.uk/news/world-latin-america-23722204

EXAMPLE 6.3

Trading water for beehives and barbed wire in Bolivia

Amboro National Park in Bolivia supports a very biologically diverse ecosystem. The park and surrounding areas are under intense pressure from illegal land incursions. Migrants from the surrounding highlands, with encouragement from local political leaders, extract timber from the park and clear areas for agriculture. Lack of well- defined property rights for local communities leaves few alternative options. Due to increased timber harvesting and increased agriculture, the Los Neros River dries up earlier than it did in the past, causing suffering among the local communities that depend on the river for irrigation.

Asquith (2006) describes a unique solution to this property rights problem involving payments for environmental services. Natura Bolivia, an environmental group, helped negotiate an agreement through which downstream water users would pay for the protection of native vegetation in the watershed. Instead of financial compensation though, payment would be in the form of one beehive and training in honey production per 10 hectares of cloud forest protected. In 2003, 60 beehives were provided to farmers in exchange for 600 hectares of cloud forest conserved. In 2004, the municipal government provided another 11 hives to farmers. By 2006, 2100 hectares had been protected.

The Los Negros scheme is slowly building a market for environmental services and helping to define property rights in the region. In 2006, when contracts were renewed, some farmers requested barbed wire, instead of beehives, in order to help them strengthen their land claims. Combining a market mechanism (payment for environmental services) with developing a local enforcement mechanism and strengthening local property rights has proven to be a successful scheme so far.

Source: Asquith, N. (December 2006). Bees and barbed wire for water on the Bolivian frontier. *PERC, 24(4)*. Available at www.perc.org/articles/bees-and-barbed-wire-water

Water is not the only service to be involved in a payments scheme and sometimes the payments can be in kind rather than in cash (see Example 6.3).

Tradable entitlement systems

Another program approach recognizes that not only more land but also land better suited for supplying environmental services could be supplied if those services were treated separately in land titles. Some land may be especially good at providing environmental services while having a low opportunity cost, but other land may have a very high opportunity cost. If all land is required to meet the same environmental service provision requirements, the cost of the program will soar. Suppose, however, that the landowner has to supply those services, but not necessarily on the specific piece of land facing the requirement. This is the premise of a number of programs including wetlands banking and carbon sequestration credits.

Wetlands banking

Several U.S. administrations, both Republican and Democratic, have pledged that wetlands should experience "no net loss."[3] Despite these bipartisan pledges to protect wetlands, as the pressure on coastal and shorefront properties has increased, the economic benefits from developing wetlands (and political pressures to remove obstacles to development) have significantly increased as well.

One policy instrument for attempting to preserve wetlands in the face of this pressure is known as Wetlands Mitigation Banking and involves providing incentives for creating off-site "equivalent" wetlands services when adverse impacts on the original site are unavoidable and when on-site compensation is either not practical or use of a mitigation bank is environmentally preferable to on-site compensation. According to the U.S. EPA, "The objective of a mitigation bank is to provide for the replacement of the chemical, physical, and biological functions of wetlands and other aquatic resources which are lost as a result of authorized impacts."[4]

Mitigation banks involve wetlands, streams, or other aquatic resource areas that have been restored, established, enhanced, or (in certain circumstances) specifically preserved for the purpose of providing compensation for unavoidable impacts to aquatic resources. Mitigation banks involve a form of "third-party" compensatory mitigation in which the responsibility for compensatory mitigation implementation and success is assumed by someone other than the party who, by causing an adverse impact to a wetland, is required by law to provide mitigation.

A mitigation bank may be created when a government agency, corporation, nonprofit organization, or other entity undertakes mitigation activities under a formal agreement with a regulatory agency. The value of those activities is defined in "compensatory mitigation credits." In principle, the number of credits available for sale is based upon the use of ecological assessment techniques to certify that the credited areas provide the specified ecological functions.

How has the program performed? As one recent review (Salzman and Ruhl, 2006) concludes:

> Despite policies mandating that habitat trading ensure equivalent value and function, the experience is that most programs are not administered this way. In practice, most habitat trades to date in wetlands programs have been approved on the basis of acres, in many instances ensuring equivalence in neither value nor function.

This experience is instructive. Merely assuring that the compensation involves a similar number of acres falls short of true equivalence unless the replacement ecological functions supplied by those acres are also the same.

Carbon Sequestration Credits

To the extent that landowners do not receive all the benefits of landownership, they may discount or ignore the benefits that accrue to others. Carbon sequestration credits are an attempt to rectify one such imbalance. Is this an efficient remedy?

As will be discussed in Chapter 8, carbon dioxide is a greenhouse gas, which means that excessive concentrations of carbon dioxide in the atmosphere can contribute to climate change. Through photosynthesis, trees absorb (sequester) carbon dioxide, thereby removing it from the atmosphere and lowering its threat to the climate.

Carbon sequestration credits attempt to internalize the carbon-absorption benefit externality by giving forest (or marsh) owners credit for the additional carbon they remove from the atmosphere. They can earn this credit by investing in additional carbon sequestration (by planting new trees, or protecting a salt marsh, for example). This credit (or offset) can be sold to those who can use these reductions in fulfillment of their legal obligations to meet specified carbon-emissions targets. Some evidence suggests that reducing carbon in this way would be cheaper than many other measures. The Reducing Emissions from Deforestation and Forest Degradation (REDD) program, run by the United Nations, is an example of this approach (see Example 6.4).

We will return to this concept in Chapters 8 and 10.

EXAMPLE 6.4

Reducing Emissions from Deforestation and Forest Degradation (REDD): A Twofer?

According to the United Nations, deforestation and forest degradation, through agricultural expansion, conversion to pastureland, infrastructure development, destructive logging, fires, and so on, account for nearly 20 percent of global greenhouse gas emissions, more than the entire global transportation sector and second only to the energy sector. In response, the United Nations has set up a program to reduce these emissions by reducing the forest degradation in developing countries. REDD is an effort to create a financial value for the carbon stored in forests, offering incentives for developing countries to reduce emissions from forested lands and to invest in low-carbon paths to sustainable development. According to this scheme, nations would receive payments for emissions-reduction credits determined on the basis of actual reductions in forest emissions measured against agreed-upon baselines. These credits can be sold in the international compliance carbon markets (where they could be used in combination with domestic reductions to meet assigned national targets) or voluntary carbon markets (where they could be used to pursue other organizational goals, such as demonstrating carbon neutrality). Data from the Forest Trends Ecosystem Marketplace indicate that as of 2016 forest carbon projects are protecting 28 million hectares of forest.

The promise of this program is that it offers opportunities to make progress on two goals at once: (1) reducing forest degradation, and (2) reducing emissions that contribute to climate change. The challenges, which are far from trivial, are to establish baselines that are both fair and effective and to assure that monitoring and verification procedures are sufficiently rigorous as to provide reliable, accurate measures of actual emissions reductions. Otherwise the emissions authorized by the credits might exceed the actual emissions reductions that the credits are based upon.

Sources: Government of Norway. (2009). Reducing emissions from deforestation and forest degradation (REDD): An options assessment report. An electronic co py of this report is available at the United Nations REDD website: www.un-redd.org/; Forest Trends Ecosystem Marketplace. (2016). View from the understory: State of forest carbon finance 2016. Available at www.forest-trends.org/documents/files/doc_5388.pdf (accessed February 10, 2017).

Ecotourism

Ecotourism provides another prominent example of an activity that attempts to create a revenue stream based upon environmental services that can serve to fund protection of those services.

According to several organizations such as the International Ecotourism Society and International Union for Conservation of Nature, ecotourism can be defined as follows:

> Environmentally responsible travel to natural areas, in order to enjoy and appreciate nature (and accompanying cultural features, both past and present) that promotes conservation, has a low visitor impact and provides for beneficially active socioeconomic involvement of local peoples.

Not all ecotourism projects turn out to be consistent with this definition. Increasing the number of visitors to sensitive natural areas in the absence of appropriate oversight and control can threaten the integrity of both ecosystems and local cultures (see Debate 6.3). Additionally, the possible instabilities in this revenue source posed by climate fluctuations, volatile exchange rates, and political and social upheaval could make an excessive reliance upon tourism a risky business.

Another major threat to wildlife comes from poaching. Poaching is the illegal taking of game or domestic livestock. Normally we consider adequate enforcement to be the solution to poaching, but in some settings assuring adequate enforcement is easier said than done. Can trophy hunting help?

DEBATE 6.3

Does ecotourism provide a pathway to sustainability?

One of the ways ecotourism can promote conservation is by providing the necessary funds to implement an effective conservation program. Take the example of Bolivia's Eduardo Avaroa Reserve. This diverse landscape includes hot springs and geysers surrounded by volcanoes and majestic mountains. Its freshwater and saltwater lakes provide habitat for year-round flocks of pink flamingos and other birds, while nearby 23 types of mammals and almost 200 species of plants flourish in the desert-like environment. With over 40,000 visitors per year, the park is Bolivia's most visited.

When a conservation planning initiative determined that tourism was a major threat to the reserve, The Nature Conservancy worked with the Bolivian National Park System to develop a visitor-fee system. The program, which reportedly generated over half a million dollars in new funds, allows the reserve to fund efforts to mitigate these tourism-related threats. The visitor-fee approach is now being extended across the Bolivian Park System. It is estimated that the national protected areas system could generate more than $3 million per year in new income for conservation.

Quite a different take on ecotourism is provided by a British academic Rosaleen Duffy. Speaking about Belize – a popular ecotourist destination in Central America – Duffy relates stories of how scuba diving and snorkeling visitors have spoiled fragile corals and otherwise-harassed marine wildlife.

"In their pursuit of reefs, rainforests, and ruins," writes Duffy, "they did not reflect on the environmental impact of the construction of hotels, the use of airlines, the manufacture of diving equipment, the consumption of imported goods or even something as visible as taking a motorboat out to the reef, which polluted the water." As a *Time* article on her book notes, "To Duffy, it seems, the only good tourist is the one who stays home."

Sources: Duffy, D. (2002). *A Trip too Far – Ecotourism, Politics and Exploitation.* Washington, D.C.: Island Press; Bird, M. A. (2002). Ecotourism or egotourism. *TIME* online. Retrieved May 24, 2007, from http://content.time.com/time/magazine/article/0,9171,338585,00.html; The Nature Conservancy, Ecotourism and Conservation Finance. Retrieved May 24, 2007, from www.nature.org/aboutus/travel/ecotourism/about/art14824.html

Consider, for example, how the economics of poaching might be used to enhance enforcement in the case of African wildlife. From an economic point of view, poaching can be discouraged if it is possible to raise the relative cost of illegal activity. In principle that can be accomplished by increasing the sanctions levied against poachers, but it is effective only if monitoring can not only detect the illegal activity but also apply the sanctions to those who engage in it. In many places that is a tall order, given the large size of the habitat to be monitored and the limited budgets for funding enforcement. Example 6.5 shows, however, how economic incentives can be enlisted to promote more monitoring by local inhabitants as well as to provide more revenue for enforcement activity.

EXAMPLE 6.5

Payments for ecosystem services – wildlife protection in Zimbabwe

In the late 1980s, an innovative program was initiated in Zimbabwe that stands out as a success among other African wildlife protection schemes. It transformed the role of wildlife from a state-owned treasure to be preserved into an active resource controlled and used by both commercial farmers and smallholders in communal lands. The transformation has been good for the economy and the wildlife.

The initiative is called the Communal Areas Management Program for Indigenous Resources (CAMPFIRE). It was originally sponsored by several different agencies in cooperation with the Zimbabwean government, including the University of Zimbabwe's Center for Applied Study, the Zimbabwe Trust, and the Worldwide Fund for Nature (WWF). The U.S. federal government currently provides resources to CAMPFIRE, principally through USAID. Under the CAMPFIRE system, villagers collectively utilize local wildlife resources on a sustainable basis. Trophy hunting by foreigners is perhaps the most important source of revenue, because hunters require few facilities and are willing to pay substantial fees to kill a limited number of large animals. The government sets the prices of hunting permits as well as quotas for the number of animals that can be taken per year in each locality. Individual communities sell the permits and contract with safari operators who conduct photographic and hunting expeditions on community lands.

The associated economic gains accrue to the villages, which then decide how the revenues should be used. The money may either be paid to households in the form of cash dividends, which may amount to 20 percent or more of an average family's income, or they may be used for capital investments in the community, such as schools or clinics. In at least one area, revenues compensate citizens who have suffered property loss due to wild animals. Households may also receive nonmonetary benefits, such as meat from problem animals or culled herds. By consistently meeting their needs from their own resources on a sustainable basis, local communities have become self-reliant. This voluntary program has been steadily expanding since its inception, and now includes 28 wildlife districts of which 15 are hunting districts.

The program has been working. In 2010, 40 elephants were poached. In 2015, this number had dropped to five. Additionally, it has been estimated that households participating in CAMPFIRE increased their incomes by 15–25 percent. Between 1989 and 2006, CAMPFIRE dividends disbursed to communities was $20.8 million.

In 2014, the United States suspended ivory imports from Tanzania and Zimbabwe in an effort to reduce poaching of elephants. American clients generally constitute 76 percent of hunters in CAMPFIRE areas for all animals hunted each year. The ban resulted in the cancellation of 108 out of 189 (57 percent) elephant hunts booked by U.S. citizens in CAMPFIRE areas. The resulting drop in CAMPFIRE income has been significant. Revenues dropped from $2.3 million in 2013, to $2.1 million in 2014 to $1.6 million in 2015.

The decreased revenues reduce funds for protection of wildlife and also remove the incentives for community members to protect the elephants. While well intended, the American ban could backfire if poaching resumes.

Sources: Frost, P. G., & Bond, I. (2008). The CAMPFIRE programme in Zimbabwe: Payments for wildlife services. *Ecological Economics,* 65(4), 776–787; http://campfirezimbabwe.org/index.php/news-spotlight; Jonga, C. and Pangeti, G. (2015). https://firstforwildlife.wordpress.com/2015/08/18/the-campfire-program-in-zimbabwe/; Barbier, E. (1992). Community based development in Africa. In T. Swanson & E. Barbier (Eds.), *Economics for the Wilds: Wildlife, Diversity, and Development*. Washington, D.C.: Island Press, 107–118; Bojo, J. (February 1996). The economics of wildlife: Case studies from Ghana, Kenya, Namibia and Zimbabwe. *AFTES Working Paper No. 19.* The World Bank; and the website www.Colby.edu/personal/thtieten/end-zim.html

Other types of incentives have also proved successful. In Kenya, for example, a compensation scheme has helped Maasai tribesmen to transition from hunting lions to protecting them. Maasai from the Mbirikani ranch are now compensated for livestock killed by predators. They receive $80 for each donkey and $200 for each cow killed. The Mbirikani Predator Fund has compensated herders for the loss of 750 head of livestock each year since the program began in 2003. As an additional collective incentive, if any herder kills a lion, no one gets paid.[5]

Rearranging the economic incentives so that local groups have an economic interest in preservation can provide a powerful means of protecting some biological populations. Open access undermines those incentives.

Poverty and debt

Poverty and debt are major sources of pressure on ecosystem services. In eastern and southern Africa, for example, positive feedback loops have created a downward cycle in which poverty and deforestation reinforce each other. Most natural forests have long since been cut down for timber and fuelwood and for producing crops from the cleared land. As forests disappear, the rural poor are forced to divert more time toward locating new sources of fuel. Once fuelwood is no longer available, dried animal waste is burned, thereby eliminating it as a source of fertilizer to nourish depleted soils. Fewer trees lead to more soil erosion and soil depletion leads to diminished nutrition. Diminished nutrition reinforces the threats to human health posed by an inability to find or afford enough fuel, wood, or animal waste for cooking and boiling unclean water. Degraded health saps energy, increases susceptibility to disease, and reduces productivity. Survival strategies may necessarily sacrifice long-term goals simply to ward off starvation or death; the forest is typically an early casualty.

At the national level, poverty takes the form of staggering levels of debt. Repaying this debt and the interest payments flowing from it reduces the capacity of a nation to accumulate foreign exchange earnings. In periods of high real interest rates, servicing these debts commands most if not all foreign exchange earnings. Using these foreign exchange earnings to service the debt eliminates the possibility of using them to finance imports for sustainable activities to alleviate poverty.

According to the "debt-resource hypothesis," large debts owed by many developing countries encourage these countries to overexploit their resource endowments to raise the necessary foreign exchange. Timber exports represent a case in point. One strategy that has been employed to help and has had some success is debt-for-nature swaps.

Debt-for-nature swaps

One strategy involves reducing the pressure on the forests caused by the international debt owed by many developing countries. One of the more innovative policies that explores common ground in international arrangements has become known as the debt-for-nature swap. A debt-for-nature swap involves the purchase (at a discounted value in the secondary debt market) of a developing country's debt, frequently by an environmental nongovernmental organization (NGO). The new holder of the debt, the NGO, offers to cancel the debt in return for an environmentally related action on the part of the debtor nation.

The first debt-for-nature swap took place in Bolivia in 1987. Since then debt-for-nature swaps have been arranged or explored in many developing countries, including Ecuador, the Philippines, Zambia, Jamaica, Madagascar, Guatemala, Venezuela, Argentina, Honduras, and Brazil.

A brief examination of the Madagascar case can illustrate how these swaps work. Recognized as a prime source of biodiversity, the overwhelming majority of Madagascar's land mammals, reptiles, and plants are found nowhere else on earth. Madagascar is also one of the poorest countries in the world, burdened with high levels of external debt. Because of its limited domestic financial resources, Madagascar could not counter the serious environmental degradation it was experiencing.

Between 1989 and 1996, Conservation International, the Missouri Botanical Garden, and the World Wildlife Fund negotiated nine commercial debt-for-nature swaps in Madagascar. These arrangements generated $11.7 million in conservation funds. Agreements signed by Madagascar's government and the participating conservation organizations identified the programs to be funded. One such program trained over 320 nature protection agents, who focused on involving local communities in forest management.

Other arrangements involving different governments and different environmental organizations have since followed this lead. The main advantage of these arrangements to the debtor nation is that a significant foreign exchange obligation can be paid off with domestic currency. Debt-for-nature swaps offer the realistic possibility to turn what has been a major force for unsustainable economic activity (the debt crisis) into a force for resource conservation.

Extractive reserves

One strategy specifically designed to protect the indigenous people of the forest as well as to prevent deforestation involves the establishment of extractive reserves. These areas would be reserved for the indigenous people to engage in the traditional hunting-gathering activities.

Extractive reserves have already been established in the Acre region of Brazil. Acre's main activity comes from the thousands of men who tap the rubber trees scattered throughout the forest, a practice dating back 100 years. Under the leadership of Chico Mendes, a leader of the tappers who was subsequently assassinated, four extractive reserves were established in June 1988 by the Brazilian government to protect the rubber tappers from encroaching development.

The World Heritage Convention

The World Heritage Convention came into being in 1972 with the primary mission of identifying and preserving the cultural and natural heritage of outstanding sites throughout the world, and ensuring their protection through international cooperation. Currently, some 178 countries have ratified the convention.

Ratifying nations have the opportunity to have their natural properties of outstanding universal value added to the World Heritage List. The motivation for taking this step is to gain international recognition for this site, using the prestige that comes from this designation to raise awareness for heritage preservation and the likelihood that the site can be preserved.

A ratifying nation may receive both financial assistance and expert advice from the World Heritage Committee as support for promotional activities for the preservation of its properties as well as for developing educational materials.

Responsibility for providing adequate protection and management of these sites falls on the host nations, but a key benefit from ratification, particularly for developing countries, is access to the World Heritage Fund. This fund is financed by mandatory contributions from ratifying nations, calculated at 1 percent of the country's contribution to UNESCO, the administering agency. Annually, about $3 million (U.S.) are made available, mainly to low-income countries to finance technical assistance and training projects, as well as for assistance preparing their nomination proposals or to develop conservation projects. Emergency assistance may also be made available for urgent action to repair damage caused by human-made or natural disasters.

Royalty payments

A potential source of revenue for biodiversity preservation involves taking advantage of the extremely high degree of interest by the pharmaceutical industry in searching for new drugs derived from these biologically diverse pools of flora and fauna. Establishing the principle that nations containing these biologically rich resources within their borders would be entitled to a stipulated royalty on any and all products developed from genes obtained from these preserves provides both an incentive to preserve the resources and some revenue to accomplish the preservation.

Nations harboring rich biological preserves have begun to realize their value and to extract some of that value from the pharmaceutical industry. The revenue is in part used for inventorying and learning more about the resource as well as preserving it. For example, in 1996, Medichem Research, an Illinois-based pharmaceutical company, entered into a joint venture with the Sarawak government. The organization created by this joint venture has the right to file exclusive patents on two compounds that offer some promise as cancer treatments.

The agreement specified a 50–50 split from royalties once the drug is marketed. The Sarawak government was given the exclusive right to supply the latex raw material from which the compounds are derived. Furthermore, Sarawak scientists are involved in screening and isolating the compounds and Sarawak physicians are involved in the clinical trials.

This agreement not only provides a strong rationale for protecting the biological source, but also enables the host country to build its capacity for capturing the value of its biodiversity in the future (Laird and Ten Kate, 2002). These arrangements are particularly significant because they facilitate transboundary sharing of the costs of preservation. It is unrealistic to expect countries harboring these preserves to shoulder the entire cost of preservation when the richer countries of the world are the major beneficiaries. It may also be unrealistic to assume that pharmaceutical demand is sufficient to fund efficient preservation (see Example 6.6).

Debt-for-nature swaps, extractive reserves, and royalty payments, all involve recognition of the fact that resolving the global externalities component of deforestation requires a rather different approach from resolving the other aspects of the deforestation problem. In general, this approach involves financial transfers from the industrialized nations to the tropical nations, transfers that are constructed so as to incorporate global interests into decisions about the future of tropical forests.

Recognizing the limited availability of international aid for the preservation of biodiversity habitat, nations have begun to tap other revenue sources. Tourist revenues have become an increasingly popular source, particularly where the tourism is specifically linked to the resources that are targeted for preservation. Rather than mixing these revenues with other public funds, nations are earmarking them for preservation (see Example 6.7).

EXAMPLE 6.6

Does pharmaceutical demand offer sufficient protection to biodiversity?

The theory is clear – incentives to protect plants are stronger when the plants are valuable to humans. Is the practice equally clear?

The case of Taxol is instructive. Derived from the slow-growing Pacific yew, Taxol is a substance that has proved effective in treating advanced forms of breast and ovarian cancers. As of 1998, it was the best-selling anticancer drug ever.

Since the major site for this tree was in the old-growth forests of the Pacific Northwest, the hope of environmental groups was that the rise in the importance of Taxol might provide both sustainable employment and some protection for old-growth forests.

In fact, that is not how it worked out. The Taxol for the chemical trials was derived from the bark of the tree. Stripping the tree of its bark killed it. And supplying enough bark for the chemical trials put a tremendous strain on the resource.

Ultimately, the private company that marketed Taxol, Bristol-Squibb, developed a semi-synthetic substitute that could be made from imported renewable tree parts.

The Pacific yew, the original source of one of the most important medical discoveries in the twentieth century, was left completely unprotected. And the industry that had grown up to supply the bark collapsed. In the end, its value proved transitory and its ability to support a sustainable livelihood in the Pacific Northwest was illusory. Not all seemingly good ideas produce the expected outcomes. The details matter.

Source: Goodman, J., & Walsh, V. (2001). The Story of Taxol: Nature and Politics in the Pursuit of an Anti-Cancer Drug. *New York: Cambridge University Press.*

EXAMPLE 6.7

Trust funds for habitat preservation

How can local governments finance biodiversity preservation when faced with limited availability of both international and domestic funds? One option being aggressively pursued involves trust funds. Trust funds are moneys that are legally restricted to be used for a specific purpose (as opposed to being placed in the general government treasury). They are administered by trustees to assure compliance with the terms of the trust. Most, but not all, trust funds are protected endowments, meaning that the trustees can spend the interest and dividends from the funds, but not the principal. This assures the continuity of funds for an indefinite period.

Where does the money come from? Many nations that harbor biodiversity preserves cannot afford to spend the resources necessary to protect them. One possibility is to tap into foreign demands for preservation. In Belize, the revenue comes from a "conservation fee" charged to all arriving foreign visitors. The initial fee, $3.75, was passed by Belize's parliament in January 1996, raising $500,000 in revenues each year for the trust fund. These fees, along with grants and donations, provide the Protected Areas Conservation Trust (PACT) with a sustainable source of funding for protected areas.

Currently in Belize 482 projects in some 103 protected areas form a vast national protected areas system, with categories that encompass forest reserves, nature reserves, national parks, marine reserves, private reserves, wildlife sanctuaries, natural monuments, bird sanctuaries, spawning aggregation reserves, and archaeological reserves. Similar trust funds have been set up in Mexico, Honduras, and Guatemala.

Biodiversity preservation that depends on funds from the general treasury becomes subject to the vagaries of budgetary pressures. When the competition for funds intensifies, the funds may disappear or be severely diminished. The virtue of a trust fund is that it provides long-term, sustained funding targeted specifically on the protection of biodiversity.

Source: www.pactbelize.org (accessed October 31, 2019)

The special problem of protecting endangered species

Suppose a specific species is found to be endangered and listed as such under the U.S. Endangered Species Act (ESA). How can economics help to create incentive-based programs to enhance the likelihood of survival for this species?

Conservation biologists have found that one key to reducing the threat to endangered species is to prevent their habitat from become fragmented into smaller parcels. In response, economists have developed programs that attempt to reduce habitat fragmentation.

Conservation banking

One such program, conservation banking, enlists a tailored transferable credits program into endangered and threatened species conservation. A conservation bank is a parcel of land containing natural-resource values that are conserved and managed, in perpetuity, through a conservation easement held by an entity responsible for enforcing the terms of the easement. Banks of especially suitable land are established for specified listed species (under the Endangered Species Act) and used to offset impacts to the species occurring on nonbank lands by providing a larger, less fragmented habitat for them.

Access to the habitat services provided by these banks is provided by the creation of saleable quantified "credits," where each credit provides a specified amount of habitat provision designed to satisfy the requirements of the ESA. Project proponents are, therefore, able to complete their ESA obligations through a one-time purchase of credits from the conservation bank (see Example 6.8).

EXAMPLE 6.8

Conservation banking: the gopher tortoise conservation bank

In rapidly growing Mobile County, Alabama, the gopher tortoise faced survival problems due to the disappearance of its habitat. Since the tortoise is federally listed as a threatened species under the Endangered Species Act (ESA), small landowners were forced to observe some rather severe restrictions on their use of the land. Because these restrictions were quite burdensome for the landowners and the resulting fragmented, patchy habitat proved ineffective in protecting the tortoise, these restrictions created quite a conflict in the community.

A conservation bank established by the Mobile Area Water and Sewer System (MAWSS) in 2001 reduced the conflict, allowing development to continue in other areas while restoring and permanently protecting a much more suitable large tract of the long- leaf pine habitat that the tortoise prefers.

MAWSS owns a 7000-acre forest that buffers and protects the county's water supply. Under the terms of its conservation bank, MAWSS has agreed to set aside 222 acres, forgo any development on that land, and manage it in perpetuity for the benefit of gopher tortoises. Landowners who want to build on tortoise habitat elsewhere in Mobile County can purchase "credits" from the bank, and thereby be relieved of their ESA responsibilities to set aside a small patch of their land. The tortoises benefit because the large tract of contiguous, suitable habitat is vastly superior to a network of small, unconnected patches of land, while the landowners can now develop their land by helping to fund (through the purchase of credits) this tortoise habitat.

Source: Environmental Defense's Center for Conservation Incentives. (February 24, 2003). Gopher tortoise conservation bank: Mobile area landowners and wildlife get help. Retrieved from www.edf.org/?from=splash_continue&_ga=1.202011924.401743717.1469651799

The agglomeration bonus

Another strategy to reduce fragmentation, known as the *agglomeration bonus,* has been proposed by Smith and Shogren (2002). The agglomeration bonus is a voluntary incentive mechanism that is designed to protect endangered species and biodiversity by reuniting fragmented habitat across private land in a manner that minimizes landowner resistance.

Many states currently have programs that encourage landowners to conserve land, but how can these owners be further encouraged to give priority to land that connects with other land? Under this bonus payment scheme the landowner receives an additional payment (the bonus) for each retired acre that shares a common border with another retired acre. If both landowners retire land at their common border, both can profit from their neighbor's retired acres. With this bonus each landowner has an explicit incentive to give priority to retiring acres that are adjacent to his or her neighbor's retired acres. Notice that the agglomeration bonus pays for connected land not any specific piece of land – landowners are free to select any land that shares a common border with other retired land.

This mechanism provides an incentive for landowners to give preference to land that would form a contiguous reserve across their common border. The government agency's role would be to target the critical habitat and to integrate the agglomeration bonus into the compensation package, but the landowners would have the ultimate power to decide whether or not to participate.

An analysis of the properties of this mechanism using experimental economics (Parkhurst et al., 2002) found that in the lab the absence of a bonus always created fragmented habitat, whereas with the bonus players cooperated to establish the optimal habitat reserve.

Safe harbor agreements

Safe harbor agreements are a means of conserving endangered and threatened species on privately owned land.[5] These agreements approach the problem of landowner incentives from a different perspective, mainly seeking to overcome some rather severe unintended consequences that can flow from the Endangered Species Act (ESA).

Under the ESA many landowners are actually inhibited from implementing practices likely to benefit endangered species because of the repercussions that might arise from these apparently benign activities. Under the approach taken by the ESA, the presence of an endangered species on a property may result in new legally imposed restrictions on any activities deemed harmful to that species. Thus, if landowners were simply to restore wildlife habitats on their property, and those habitats attracted endangered animals, they might find themselves faced with many new restrictions on their use of the land. As a result, some landowners are not only unwilling to take such risks, but they may actually actively manage property to prevent endangered species from occupying their land.

Safe harbor agreements overcome these perverse incentive problems. Any landowner who agrees to carry out activities expected to benefit an endangered species is guaranteed that no added ESA restrictions will be imposed as a result. A landowner's ESA responsibilities are effectively frozen at their current levels for a particular species if he or she agrees to restore, enhance, or create habitat for that species. Safe harbor agreements do not, however, confer a right to harm any endangered species already present when the agreement is entered into (established by the landowner's "baseline" responsibilities). Those responsibilities are unaffected by a safe harbor agreement.

Preventing invasive species

Invasive species are nonnative plants and animals that have been introduced (intentionally or accidentally). They tend to spread quickly, causing damage to ecosystem and human health. The literature on the economics of invasive species is relatively new, but there is agreement that prevention is much less expensive than mitigation. As such prevention is a preferable policy option to control once a species has taken over a new location (see for example, Finnoff et al., 2007; Kaiser and Burnett, 2010). This is frequently called the *precautionary principle* in economics.

On the other hand, many species have already been introduced or there is a concern they have reached a particular location. Example 6.9 looks at the role of community science in the detection and monitoring of invasive species.

EXAMPLE 6.9

The changing economics of monitoring and its role in invasive species management

An old adage states that you can't manage what you don't measure. Measurement, however, has typically not been cheap, posing a dilemma for managers who want to make solid decisions with limited budgets.

One area where this has been true is in fisheries. In many cases managers don't even know all the species that inhabit the marine and freshwater environments in their areas.

New technology may change that. Scientists have developed simple techniques involving Environmental DNA or eDNA that allow scientists to extract filtered water from a water course for testing. These tests, which can be done for anywhere from $50 to $150 a test, are powerful enough to detect any species that have been present in that water in the last day or two. The presence of a single cell is sufficient. These costs are sufficiently low and the results sufficiently reliable that the U.S. Forest Service has launched a project to collect DNA from all rivers and streams across the western United States to create an Aquatic Environmental DNA Atlas.

Another common use of this approach is to detect the presence of invasive species. Researchers at Cornell University faced the daunting task of monitoring New York state's 7,600 lakes and 70,000 miles of rivers and streams for these species. The challenge was finding a way to acquire the samples at reasonable cost.

To meet this challenge, they started a community science project with cooperating science teachers across the state. Detection kits were sent to participating classes. The students in those classes gathered the water samples as part of their class and sent the collected samples to the university. When the results were returned, the students entered them in a database.

With the low labor costs associated with this form of gathering the samples and the new technology that makes the DNA tests not only possible, but simple enough that community scientist results can be reliable, monitoring can now take place on a scale that was formerly inconceivable. And the community scientists can participate in "hands-on" science.

Source: Robbins, Jim. (2017). A splash of river water now reveals the DNA of all its creatures. *Yale Environment 360* (March 9). http://e360.yale.edu/features/edna-rivers-fish-bull-trout-forest-service (accessed March 9, 2017)

Moving forward

Ecosystem goods and services may be the ultimate resources that humans rely on. This chapter has highlighted some of the ways that economic analysis can place values on these goods and services to assist policy makers in decision making. We have also looked at multiple examples of economic incentives and mechanisms to encourage the provision of ecosystem goods and services and to reduce their degradation.

As we have seen with these examples the theory is relatively straight forward, but in practice, developing innovative mechanisms like payments for ecosystem services or carbon sequestration credits is challenging, especially in developing countries.

Summary

Ecosystems provide a host of services to humans, but the continued existence of those services is threatened. In this chapter we explore how two different kinds of economic analysis can contribute to protecting, maintaining, and enhancing these ecosystems.

The first step involves providing quantitative estimates of the value of these ecosystem services both to demonstrate their importance in general and to provide metrics that can be included in cost-benefit analyses that are being used for making choices that affect ecosystems. For commercial species such as fish, forests, and commercial resources such as water the valuation task is made somewhat easier by the ready availability of prices.

For other ecosystem services the task is more difficult, but over time some of those barriers are beginning to fall as techniques such as avoided cost, stated preference surveys and travel cost studies are used to value ecosystem services. These methodologies are increasingly being applied to such different problems as valuing pollination services, assessing the economic impact of ecosystem-degrading events such as oil spills, and quantifying the role and economic benefits of natural water purification systems derived from wetlands or stream buffer zones. Newer methods such as computable general equilibrium (CGE) models allow analysts to capture not only the direct values to humans, but the indirect values as well. These studies not only corroborate and quantify the general sense that ecosystems services are valuable and deserve protection but they also identify the many pathways that provide these provisioning, regulating, supporting, and cultural services.

This chapter also examines the other main protection avenue – designing institutions and mechanisms that can eliminate or at least reduce perverse incentives that intensify degradation. Specifically we have examined innovative schemes that provide payments from service users to service providers for historically nonmarketed services to assure that the providers have an incentive to refrain from converting the land to some other incompatible use. Another category of approaches focuses on creating new transferable entitlements to service flows. Not only do they give rise to new markets (such as wetlands banking, conservation entitlements for fish, or carbon sequestration credits) that can provide more economic sustainability to these flows by returning revenue to those who protect those services, but they also provide a new venue for potentially reducing resource conflicts.

And finally we note how economic incentives can be used to protect the most vulnerable species – those that have already been classified as endangered. Environmental organizations have turned to economic approaches such as conservation banking to provide incentives for the market to preserve more of the most suitable endangered species habitat and safe harbor programs to counteract some of the more perverse habitat-destroying incentives for landowners that were inadvertently created by the Endangered Species Act.

As we point out in this chapter this relatively new subfield is experiencing some growing pains, but early successes and new innovations indicate that its future is promising.

Discussion questions

1 Consider the issues raised by the debate over Ecuador's proposal to preserve the Yasuni National Park from oil extraction. What is your view? Is this simply another payment for ecosystem services or was this extortion? Is this case different from some of the other payment for services cases described previously? If so, how is it different?
2 Consider the issues raised by the debate over using ecotourism to promote sustainability. What is your view? Is ecotourism always a pathway to sustainability? Never a pathway to sustainability? Sometimes a pathway to sustainability? Does your view suggest an appropriate role for government in managing ecotourism or should the entire process be left to the private sector? Why?
3 In 2016, *Outside Magazine* ran an obituary for the Great Barrier Reef in Australia (www.outside-online.com/2112086/obituary-great-barrier-reef-25-million-bc-2016). It was meant to be in part a spoof, yet recent evidence suggests that, while the whole reef is not dead, large portions of it are, and recovery might not be possible. What is the value of the Great Barrier Reef? Which ecosystem services values might be lost?
4 One approach to protecting ecosystem services involves dedicating specific habitat to wildlife (such as parks or reserves), a strategy that prohibits residential development in those areas. Other strategies (wetlands and conservation banking) accommodate residential development at a specific site, while attempting to offset the adverse effects on that site with requirements for preservation activities at other sites as a condition of allowing development at the original site. In your mind, does one of these strategies always dominate the other? Is so, why? If not, does the context matter? How would an economist think about these questions?

Self-test exercises

1 Several of the policy options discussed in this chapter rely on transferable entitlements of one kind or another. The prominence of these approaches raises the question of what transferability adds to mix. For each of the following options describe why making the entitlement transferable increases its efficiency.

   a Carbon reduction credits
   b Conservation banking.

2 Suppose that a fishery has two sectors: (1) a commercial fishery that harvests fish to sell them to a processor, and (2) a recreational fishery where boat captains take individuals out to catch some fish for the sport of it. Each sector has a catch share. Suppose further that the demand for sport fishing goes up considerably relative to the commercial fishery. This development would create a conflict because the recreational fishery would no doubt argue that its catch share is now unfairly low. Compare how this conflict might be dealt with depending on whether the catch shares are transferable between sectors or not. Think about how the incentives of each sector to resolve this conflict are affected by the possibility of inter-sector transferability of the catch shares.

Notes

1 The Millennium Development Goals (MDGs) include reducing the world's biodiversity losses and loss of environmental resources, as well as reducing the number of people without access to such services as safe drinking water (https://www.un.org/millenniumgoals/).
2 For a description of these approaches and the role they play in ecosystem service evaluation see Bateman et al. (2011).

3 This section benefited from Salzman and Ruhl (2006).

4 Conservation International, June 21, 2007, www.conservation.org/NewsRoom/pressreleases/Pages/062107-Saving-Africa%E2%80%99s-Free-Roaming-Lions.aspx

5 This section benefited from the information in Environmental Defense's Center for Conservation Incentives. For more information on safe harbor agreements, see the website at www.environmentaldefense.org/article.cfm?ContentID=399

Further reading

Agricultural *and Resource Economics Review* (continues the *Northeastern Journal of Agricultural and Resource Economics*), 42(1), April 2013: This special issue is devoted entirely to the economics of ecosystem services valuation, measurement, and analysis.

Millennium Ecosystem Assessment. (2005). *Ecosystems and Human Well-Being: A Synthesis.* Washington, DC: Island Press. A summary of the findings of the U.N. Ecosystem Assessment.

National Research Council of the National Academies of Science (NRC). (2013). *An Ecosystem Services Approach to Assessing the Impacts of the Deepwater Horizon Oil Spill in the Gulf of Mexico.* Washington, DC: National Academies Press. Discusses the benefits and challenges associated with using an ecosystem services approach to damage assessment, and offers suggestions for areas of future research.

Pattanayak, S. K., Wunder, S., & Ferraro, P. J. (2010). Show me the money: Do payments supply environmental service in developing countries? *Review of Environmental Economics and Policy,* 4(2), 254–274. Survey of the literature on payments for ecosystem services with a particular emphasis on their use in developing countries.

Ruckelshaus, M., McKenzie, E., Taillis, H., Guerry, A., Daily, G., Kareiva, P., Polasky, S., Ricketts, T., Bhagabati, N., Wood, S., & Bernhardt, J. (2013). Notes from the field: Lessons learned from using ecosystem service approaches to inform real-world decisions. *Ecological Economics.* http://dxdoi.org/10.1016Zj.ecolecon2013.07.009. Offers six lessons from recent assessments of biodiversity and ecosystem services.

TEEB. (September 2009). The economics of ecosystems and biodiversity: Climate issues update. A report that examines the impacts of climate change on ecosystems and biodiversity with a special emphasis on coral reefs and forests.

Additional references and other historically significant references are available on this book's eResource page: www.routledge.com/9781138587595

Chapter 7

Fisheries policy

Introduction

In 2009, the World Bank and the Food and Agriculture Organization of the United Nations (FAO) released a report called *The Sunken Billions: The Economic Justification for Fisheries Reform*. According to this report, economic losses in marine fisheries due to overfishing, poor management, and economic inefficiency are approximately $50 billion per year (US$). Over the last 30 years, those losses sum to over $2 trillion! The report goes on to argue that well-managed marine fisheries could provide sustainable economic benefits for millions of fisheries, coastal villages, and cities. In this chapter we explore the role of economics in designing well-managed fisheries.

Humans share the planet with many other living species. How those biological populations are treated depends in part on whether they are commercially valuable and whether the institutional framework set up to manage the harvesting of a given resource provides sufficient conservation incentives to those who are best positioned to protect the resource.

In the last two chapters, we learned about environmental goods and services that are not traded in a typical market place. In this chapter, we consider those ecosystem services that are commercially valuable such as commercial fisheries. A commercially valuable species is like a double- edged sword. On one side, the value of the species to humans provides a strong and immediate reason for human concern about its future. On the other hand, its value may promote excessive harvest. Commercially exploited biological resources can become depleted to the point of extinction if the population is drawn down beyond a critical threshold.

Extinction, although important, is not the only critical renewable resource-management issue. Since any sustainable level of harvest will avoid extinction, how do we choose among them? What sustainable level of harvest is appropriate? In this chapter, we consider how the process of fisheries management could be reformed to improve both efficiency and sustainability.

Biological populations belong to a class of renewable resources we will call *interactive resources*, wherein the size of the resource stock (population) is determined jointly by biological considerations and by actions taken by society. The postharvest size of the population, in turn, determines the availability of resources for the future. Thus, humanity's actions affect the flow of these resources over time. Because this flow is not purely a natural phenomenon, the rate of harvest has intertemporal effects. Tomorrow's harvesting choices are affected by today's harvesting behavior.

Using the fishery as a case study, we begin by examining what is meant by an efficient and sustainable level of harvest. We then investigate whether efficiency is a sufficiently strong criterion to avoid extinction. Will efficient harvests always result in sustainable outcomes? Having shown how our two social choice criteria apply to fisheries, we turn to an examination of how well our institutions fulfill those criteria. Are normal incentives compatible with efficient sustainable harvest levels?

Unfortunately, we shall discover that in many cases normal incentives are compatible with neither efficiency nor sustainability. Many commercial fisheries can be classified as open access, common-pool resources (Chapter 2), and, as such, suffer from overharvesting. The FAO estimates that as of 2015 approximately 90 percent of the world's fish stocks were either fully exploited or overexploited (FAO, 2018). Only 7 percent of fisheries are classified commercially as underfished. When the asset value of the resource cannot be protected by existing institutions, a *tragedy of the commons*[1] can result. As we shall see, with so many fisheries experiencing overfishing, finding solutions that meet both efficiency and sustainability criteria is challenging.

Efficient allocations – bioeconomics theory

The biological dimension

Like many other studies, our characterization of the fishery rests on a biological model originally proposed by Schaefer (1957). The Schaefer model posits a particular average relationship between the growth of the fish population and the size of the fish population. This is an average relationship in the sense that it abstracts from such influences as water temperature and the age structure of the population. The model therefore does not attempt to characterize the fishery on a day-to-day basis, but rather in terms of some long-term average in which these various random influences tend to counterbalance each other (see Figure 7.1).

The size of the population is represented on the horizontal axis and the growth of the population on the vertical axis. The graph suggests that there is a range of population sizes ($\underline{S}$– S^*) where population growth increases as the population increases and a range (S^* – $\bar{S}$) where initial increases in population lead to eventual declines in growth. We can shed further light on this relationship by examining more closely the two points ($\bar{S}$ and $\underline{S}$) where the function intersects the horizontal axis and therefore growth

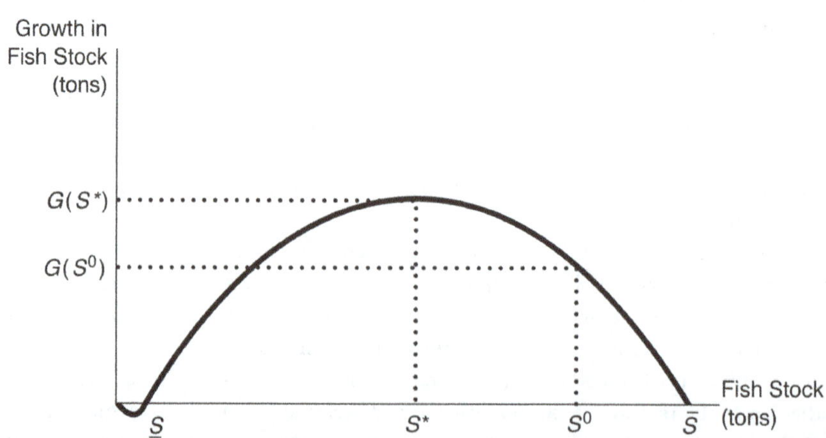

Figure 7.1 Relationship between the Fish Population (Stock) and Growth

in the stock is zero. $\bar{S}$ is known as the natural equilibrium, since this is the population size that would persist in the absence of outside influences. Reductions in the stock due to mortality or out-migration would be exactly offset by increases in the stock due to births, growth of the fish in the remaining stock, and in-migration.

This natural equilibrium would persist because it is stable. A *stable equilibrium* is one in which movements away from this population level set forces in motion to restore it. If, for example, the stock temporarily exceeded $\bar{S}$, it would be exceeding the capacity of its habitat (called *carrying capacity*). As a result, mortality rates or out-migration would increase until the stock was once again within the confines of the carrying capacity of its habitat at $\bar{S}$.

This tendency for the population size to return to $\bar{S}$ works in the other direction as well. Suppose the population is temporarily reduced below $\bar{S}$. Because the stock is now smaller, growth would be positive and the size of the stock would increase. Over time, the fishery would move along the curve to the right until $\bar{S}$ is reached again.

What about the other points on the curve? $\underline{S}$ known as the *minimum viable population*, represents the level of population below which growth in population is negative (deaths and out-migration exceed births and in-migration). In contrast to $\bar{S}$, this equilibrium is unstable. Population sizes to the right of $\underline{S}$ lead to positive growth and a movement along the curve toward S and away from $\underline{S}$. When the population moves to the left of $\underline{S}$, the population declines until it eventually becomes extinct. In this region, no forces act to return the population to a viable level.

A catch level is said to represent a *sustainable yield* whenever it equals the growth rate of the population, since it can be maintained over time. As long as the population size remains constant, the growth rate (and hence the catch) will remain constant as well.

S^* is known in biology as the *maximum sustainable yield population*, defined as the population size that yields the maximum growth; hence, the maximum sustainable yield (catch) is equal to this maximum growth and it represents the largest catch that can be perpetually sustained. Since the catch is equal to the growth, the sustainable yield for any population size (between $\underline{S}$ and $\bar{S}$) can be determined by drawing a vertical line from the stock size of interest on the horizontal axis to the point at which it intersects the function, and drawing a horizontal line over to the vertical axis. The sustainable yield is the growth in the biomass defined by the intersection of this line with the vertical axis. Thus, in terms of Figure 7.1, $G(S^0)$ is the sustainable yield for population size S^0. Since the catch is equal to the growth, population size (and next year's growth) remains the same.

It should now be clear why $G(S^*)$ is the maximum sustainable yield. Larger catches would be possible in the short run, but these could not be sustained; they would lead to reduced population sizes and eventually, if the population were drawn down to a level smaller than $\underline{S}$, to the extinction of the species.

Static efficient sustainable yield

Is the maximum sustainable yield synonymous with efficiency? The answer is no. Recall that efficiency is associated with maximizing the *net* benefit from the use of the resource. If we are to define the efficient allocation, we must include the costs of harvesting as well as the benefits.

Let's begin by defining the efficient sustainable yield without worrying about discounting. The static efficient sustainable yield is the catch level that, if maintained perpetually, would produce the largest annual net benefit. We shall refer to this as the *static efficient sustainable yield* to distinguish it from the *dynamic efficient sustainable yield*, which incorporates discounting. The initial use of this static concept enables us to fix the necessary relationships firmly in mind before dealing with the more complex role discounting plays. Subsequently, we raise the question of whether or not efficiency always dictates the choice of a sustainable yield as opposed to a catch that changes over time.

We condition our analysis on three assumptions that simplify the analysis without sacrificing too much realism: (1) the price of fish is constant and does not depend on the amount sold, (2) the marginal cost of a unit of fishing effort is constant, and (3) the amount of fish caught per unit of effort expended is proportional to the size of fish population (the smaller the population, the fewer fish caught per unit of effort).

Given these assumptions, we can construct the economic model. Under assumption (3), we can overlay harvest-effort functions onto the population function in Figure 7.1. Since the amount of fish caught per unit effort is held constant, the relationship between catch and stock for given levels of effort can be portrayed by the linear functions in Figure 7.2. Notice that increasing effort rotates the harvest function up and to the left (E2 > E1). The sustained yield associated with each level of effort is the point of intersection of these two curves. If we plot the series of points associated with the possible levels of effort and the sustained yield associated with each effort level, we will have our sustainable yield function defined in terms of effort rather than population as portrayed in Figure 7.3. (Effort could be measured in vessel years, hours of fishing, or some other conventional metric.)

To avoid confusion, notice that increasing fishing effort in Figure 7.2 would result in smaller population sizes and would be recorded as a movement from right to left. Because the variable on the horizontal axis in Figure 7.3 is effort, and not population, an increase in fishing effort is recorded as a movement from left to right.

So far so good. To turn this into a complete economic model, we need to determine benefits and costs or, equivalently in this case, total revenue and total costs. From assumption (1) we know that the shape of the biological function dictates the shape of the revenue function. Simply multiplying each sustained yield (harvest) in Figure 7.3 by the constant price, we can turn the physical units (harvest) into monetary units (total revenue). Under assumption (2) we can characterize the final component of our model; the linear function that depicts the total cost is simply calculated as the level of effort times the constant marginal cost of each unit of effort. The resulting figure (Figure 7.4) portrays the benefits (revenues) and costs as a function of fishing effort.

In any sustainable yield, annual catches, population, effort levels, and net benefits, by definition, remain constant over time. The static efficient sustainable yield allocation maximizes the constant annual net benefit.

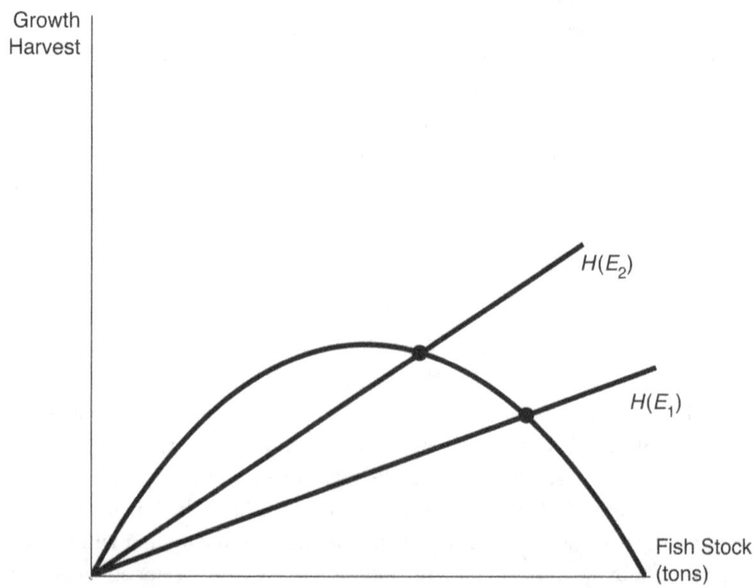

Figure 7.2 Relating Equilibrium Effort, Harvest, and Stock Size

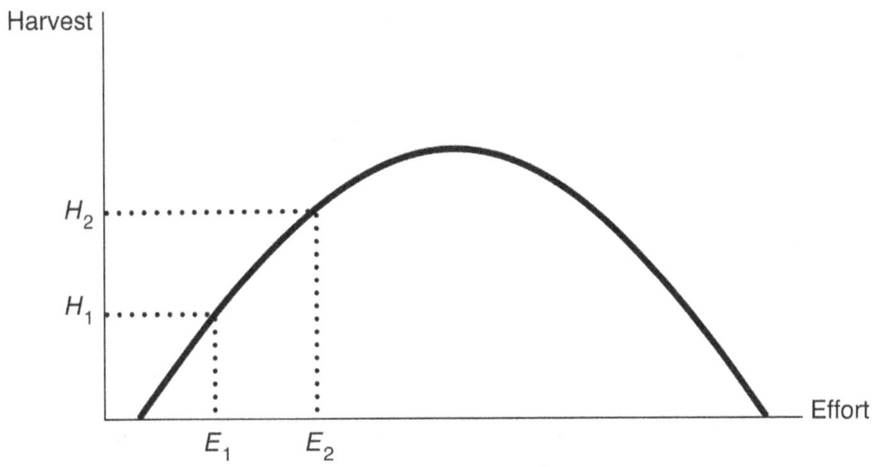

Figure 7.3 Sustainable Harvest (Yield)

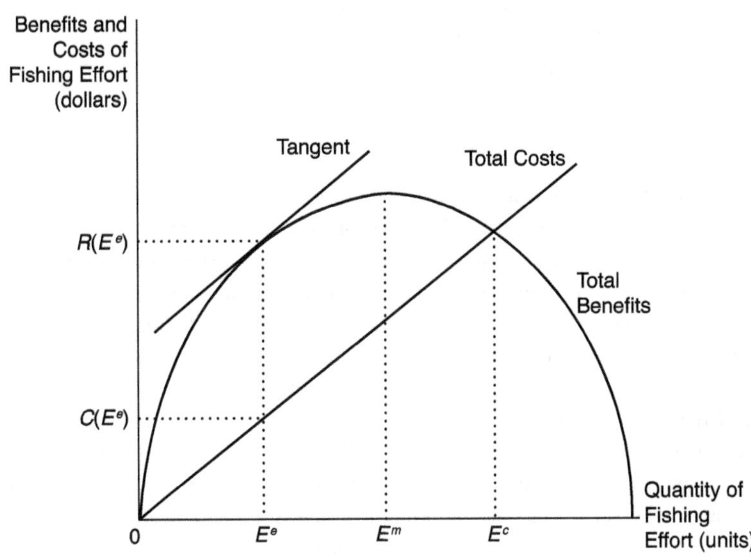

Figure 7.4 Efficient Sustainable Yield for a Fishery

As sustained levels of effort are increased, eventually a point is reached (E^m) at which further effort reduces the sustainable catch (and revenue) for all years. That point, of course, corresponds to the maximum sustainable yield on Figure 7.1 (S^*), meaning that both points reflect the same population and growth levels. Every effort level portrayed in Figures 7.3 and 7.4 corresponds to a specific population level in Figure 7.1.

The net benefit is presented in the diagram as the difference (vertical distance) between benefits (price times the quantity caught) and costs (the constant marginal cost of effort times the units of effort expended). The efficient level of effort is E^e, or the point in Figure 7.4 at which the vertical distance between benefits and costs is maximized.

E^e is the efficient level of effort because it is where marginal benefit (which graphically is the slope of the total benefit curve) is equal to marginal cost (the *constant* slope of the total cost curve). Levels of effort higher than E^e are inefficient because the additional cost associated with them exceeds the additional value of the fish obtained. Can you see why lower levels of effort are also inefficient?

Now we are armed with sufficient information to determine whether or not the maximum sustainable yield is efficient. The answer is clearly no. The maximum sustainable yield would be efficient only if the marginal cost of additional effort were zero. Can you see why? (*Hint:* What is the marginal benefit at the maximum sustainable yield?) Since at E^m the marginal benefit is lower than marginal cost, the efficient level of effort is *less* than that necessary to harvest the maximum sustainable yield. Thus, the static efficient level of effort leads to a *larger* fish population, but a lower annual catch than the maximum sustainable yield level of effort.

To fix these concepts firmly in mind, consider what would happen to the static efficient sustainable yield if a technological change were to occur (e.g., better sonar detection) that lowered the marginal cost of fishing. The lower marginal cost would result in a rotation of the total cost curve to the right. With this new cost structure, the old level of effort would no longer be efficient. The marginal cost of fishing (slope of the total cost curve) would now be lower than the marginal benefit (slope of the total benefit curve). Since the marginal cost is constant, the equality of marginal cost and marginal benefit can result only from a decline in marginal benefits. This implies an increase in effort. The new static efficient sustainable yield equilibrium implies more annual effort, a lower population level, a larger annual catch, and a higher net benefit for the fishery.

Dynamic efficient sustainable yield

The static efficient sustainable yield turns out to be the special case of the dynamic efficient sustainable yield where the discount rate is zero. It is not difficult to understand why: the static efficient sustained yield is the allocation that maximizes the (identical) net benefit in every period. Any effort levels higher than this would yield temporarily larger catches (and net benefit), but this would be more than offset by a reduced net benefit in the future as the stock reached its new lower level. Thus, the undiscounted net benefits would be reduced.

The effect of a positive discount rate for the management of a fishery is similar to its influence on the allocation of depletable resources – the higher the discount rate, the higher the cost (in terms of forgone current income) to the resource owner of maintaining any given resource stock. When positive discount rates are introduced, the efficient level of effort increases beyond that suggested by the static efficient sustained yield with a corresponding decrease in the equilibrium population level.

The increase in the yearly effort beyond the efficient sustained yield level would *initially* result in an increased net benefit from the increased catch. (Remember that the amount of fish caught per unit effort expended is proportional to the size of the population.) However, since this catch exceeds the sustained yield for that population size, the population of fish would be reduced and future population and catch levels would be lower. Eventually, as that level of effort is maintained, a new, lower equilibrium level would be attained when the size of the catch once again equals the growth of the population. Colin Clark (1976) has shown mathematically that, in terms of Figure 7.4, as the discount rate is increased, the dynamic efficient level of effort is increased until, with an infinite discount rate, it would become equal to E^c, the point at which net benefits go to zero.

It is easy to see why the use of an infinite discount rate to define the dynamic efficient sustainable yield results in allocation E^c. We have seen that temporally interdependent allocations over time give rise to a marginal user cost measuring the opportunity cost of increasing current effort. This opportunity cost reflects the forgone future net benefits when more resources are extracted in the present. For efficient interdependent allocations, the marginal willingness to pay is equal to the marginal user cost plus the marginal cost of extraction.

With an infinite discount rate, this marginal user cost is zero, because no value is received from future allocations. (Do you see why?) This implies that (1) the marginal cost of extraction equals the marginal willingness to pay, which equals the constant price, and (2) total benefits equal total costs.[2] Earlier we demonstrated that the static efficient sustained yield implies a larger fish population than the maximum sustainable yield. Once discounting is introduced, it is inevitable that the dynamic efficient sustainable yield would imply a smaller fish population than the static efficient sustainable yield and it is possible, though not inevitable, that the sustained catch would be smaller. Can you see why? In Figure 7.4 the sustained catch clearly is lower for an infinite discount rate.

The likelihood of the population being reduced below the level supplying the maximum sustainable yield depends on the discount rate. In general, the lower the extraction costs and the higher the discount rate, the more likely it is that the dynamic efficient level of effort will exceed the level of effort associated with the maximum sustainable yield. This is not difficult to see if we remember the limiting case discussed earlier. When the marginal extraction cost is zero, the static efficient sustainable yield and the maximum sustainable yield are equal.

Thus, with zero marginal extraction costs and a positive discount rate, the dynamic efficient level of effort necessarily exceeds not only the static efficient level of effort, but also the level of effort associated with the maximum sustainable yield. Higher extraction costs reduce the static efficient sustainable yield but not the maximum sustainable yield. (Remember that it is a biological, not an economic, concept.) By reducing efficient effort levels, higher extraction costs reduce the likelihood that discounting would cause the population to be drawn below the maximum sustainable yield level.

Could a dynamically efficient management scheme lead to extinction of the fishery? As Figure 7.4 shows, it would not be possible under the circumstances described here because E^c is the highest dynamically efficient level possible in this model, and that level falls short of the level needed to drive the population to extinction. However, in more complex models, extinction certainly can be an outcome.

For extinction to occur under a dynamic efficient management scheme, the benefit from extracting the very last unit would have to exceed the cost of extracting that unit (including the costs on future generations). As long as the fish population growth rate exceeds the discount rate, this will not be the case. If, however, the growth rate is lower than the discount rate, extinction can occur even in an efficient management scheme if the costs of extracting the last unit are sufficiently low.

Why does the biomass rate of growth have anything to do with whether or not an efficient catch profile leads to extinction? Rates of growth determine the productivity of conservation efforts.[3] With high rates of growth, future generations can be easily satisfied. On the other hand, when the rate of growth is very low, it takes a large sacrifice by current generations to produce more fish for future generations. In the limiting case, where the rate of growth is zero, we have a resource with fixed supply and therefore this fishery would become an exhaustible resource. Total depletion would occur whenever the price commanded by the resource is high enough to cover the marginal cost of extracting the last unit.

We have shown that the dynamic efficiency criterion is not automatically consistent with sustaining constant yields perpetually for an interactive renewable resource, since it is mathematically possible for an efficient allocation of a fishery to lead to extinction of the resource. How likely are these criteria to conflict in practice?

It is not as likely as this basic model might imply. Actual fisheries differ from the standard model in two key ways. First, harvesting marginal costs are typically not constant (as they are in the model discussed previously), but rather increase as the remaining stock size diminishes. Second, while the model we discussed holds prices constant, the size of the harvest can affect prices; larger harvests can depress them. Both of these modifications of the basic model suggest additional incentives for conserving the stock.

How empirically important are these incentives? Grafton et al. (2007) examine their importance for four specific fisheries and find not only that extinction is not the efficient outcome in any of the four fisheries but also in general, in this reformulated model, the stock level that maximizes the present value of net benefits is actually *larger* than the stock level that supports the maximum sustainable yield. Their results seem to hold both for relatively high discount rates and relatively long-lived fish. (The orange roughy fishery, discussed in more detail later on, was one of the four they studied.)

Appropriability and market solutions

We have defined an efficient allocation of the fishery over time. The next step is to characterize the normal market allocation and to contrast these two allocations. Where they differ we can entertain the possibility of various public policy corrective means.

Let's first consider the allocation resulting from a fishery managed by a competitive sole owner. A sole owner would have a well-defined property right to the fish. We can establish the behavior of a sole owner by elaborating on Figure 7.4 as is done in Figure 7.5. Note that the two panels share a common horizontal axis, a characteristic that allows us to examine the effect of various fishing effort levels on both graphs.

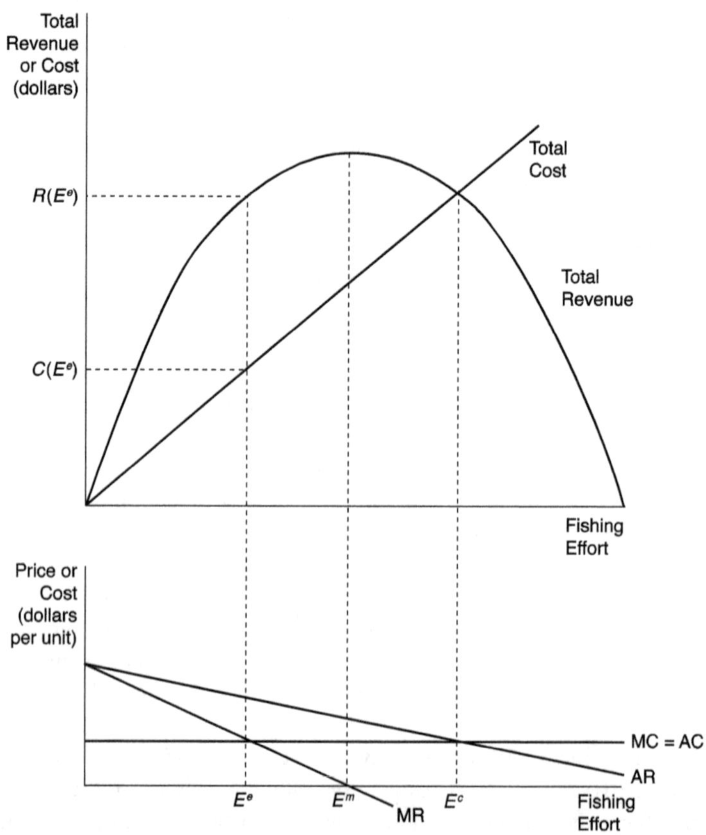

Figure 7.5 Market Allocation in a Fishery

A sole owner would want to maximize his or her profits.[4] Ignoring discounting for the moment, the owner can increase profits by increasing fishing effort until marginal revenue equals marginal cost. This occurs at effort level E^e, the static efficient sustainable yield, and yields positive profits equal to the difference between $R(E^e)$ and $C(E^e)$.

In ocean fisheries, however, sole owners are unlikely. Ocean fisheries are typically open- access resources – no one exercises complete control over them. Since the property rights to the fishery are not conveyed to any single owner, no fisherman can exclude others from exploiting the fishery.

What problems arise when access to the fishery is completely unrestricted? Open-access resources create two kinds of external costs: a contemporaneous external cost and an intergenerational external cost. The contemporaneous external cost, which is borne by the current generation, involves the over commitment of resources to fishing – too many boats, too many fishermen, too much effort. As a result, current fishermen earn a substantially lower rate of return on their efforts. The intergenerational external cost, borne by future generations, occurs because overfishing reduces the stock, which, in turn, lowers future profits from fishing.[5]

We can use Figure 7.5 to see how these external costs arise.[6] Once too many fishermen have unlimited access to the same common-pool fishery, the property rights to the fish are no longer efficiently defined. At the efficient level, each boat would receive a profit equal to its share of the scarcity rent. This rent, however, serves as a stimulus for new fishermen to enter, pushing up costs and eliminating the rent. Open access results in overexploitation.

The sole owner chooses not to expend more effort than E^e because to do so would reduce the profits of the fishery, resulting in a personal loss to her. When access to the fishery is unrestricted, a decision to expend effort beyond E^e reduces profits to the fishery as a whole but not to that individual fisherman. Most of the decline in profits falls on the other fishermen.

In an open-access resource, the individual fisherman has an incentive to expend further effort until profits are zero. In Figure 7.5, that point is at effort level E^c, at which average revenue and average cost are equal. It is now easy to see the contemporaneous external cost – too much effort is being expended to catch too few fish, and the cost is substantially higher than it would be in an efficient allocation.

If this point seems abstract, it shouldn't. Many fisheries are plagued by precisely these problems. In a productive fishery in the Bering Sea and Aleutian Islands, for example, one early study (Huppert, 1990) found significant overcapitalization. While the efficient number of motherships (used to take on and process the catch at sea, so the catch boats do not have to return to port as often) was estimated to be nine, the actual level was 140. As a result, a significant amount of net benefits was lost ($124 million a year). Had the fishery been harvested more slowly, the same catch could have been achieved with fewer boats used closer to their capacity.

In Chapter 2, we stated that the resource owner who can exclude others balances the use value against the asset value. When access to the resource is unrestricted, exclusivity is lost. As a result, it is rational for a fisherman to ignore the asset value, since he or she can never appropriate it, and simply maximize the use value. In the process, all the scarcity rent is dissipated. The allocation that results from allowing unrestricted access to the fishery is identical to that resulting from a dynamic efficient sustainable yield when an infinite discount rate is used.

Open-access resources do not automatically lead to a stock lower than (S^*), the one that maximizes the sustained yield. It is possible to draw a cost function with a slope sufficiently steep that it intersects the benefit curve at a point to the left of E^m. Nonetheless, mature, open-access fisheries can be exploited well beyond the point of maximum sustainable yield.

As noted previously, open-access fishing may or may not pose the threat of species extinction. It depends on the nature of the species and the benefits and costs of an effort level above E^m that would have the effect of driving the stock level below the minimum viable population. One species that may face that risk is the northern bluefin tuna. Considered critically endangered, it is still being harvested at unsustainable levels due to the high market price fishermen receive as a result of its popularity in sushi restaurants. The threat of extinction cannot be determined purely from theory; it must be determined by empirical studies on a case-by-case basis.

Are open-access resources and common-pool resources synonymous concepts? They are not. Not all common-pool resources allow unlimited access. Informal arrangements among those harvesting the common-pool resource, which may be fostered by harvester cooperation, can serve to limit access (Example 7.1 presents one such arrangement).

EXAMPLE 7.1

Harbor gangs of Maine and other informal arrangements

Unlimited access to common-pool resources reduces net benefits so drastically that this loss encourages those harvesting the resource to band together to restrict access, if possible. The Maine lobster fishery is one setting where those informal arrangements have served to limit access with some considerable success.

Key among these arrangements is a system of territories that establishes boundaries between fishing areas. Particularly near the offshore islands, these territories tend to be exclusively harvested by close-knit, disciplined groups of harvesters. These "gangs" restrict access to their territory by various means. (Some methods, although effective, are covert and illegal, such as the practice of cutting the lines to lobster traps owned by new entrants, thereby rendering the traps irretrievable.)

Acheson (2003) found that in every season of the year the pounds of lobster caught per trap and the size of those lobsters were greater in defended areas. Not only did the larger number of pounds result in more revenue, but also the bigger lobsters brought in a higher price per pound. Informal arrangements were successful in this case, in part, because the Maine lobster stock is also protected by regulations limiting the size of lobsters that can be taken (imposing both minimum and maximum sizes) and prohibiting the harvest of egg-bearing females.

It turns out that many other examples of community *co-management* also offer encouraging evidence for the potential of sustainability. One example, the Chilean abalone (a type of snail called *loco*) is Chile's most valuable fishery. Local fishers began cooperating in 1988 to manage a small stretch (two miles) of coastline. Today, the co-management scheme involves 700 co-managed areas, 20,000 artisanal fishers, and 2,500 miles of coastline.

While it would be a mistake to assume that all common-pool resources are characterized by open access, it would also be a mistake to assume that all informal co-management arrangements automatically provide sufficient social means for producing efficient harvests such that stronger public policy would be unnecessary. One study (Gutiérrez et al., 2011) examined 130 fisheries in 44 developed and developing countries. It found that co-management can work, but only in the presence of strong leadership, social cohesion, and complementary incentives such as individual or community quotas. They find that effective community-based co-management can both sustain the resource and protect the livelihoods of nearby fishermen and fishing communities. The existence of nearby protected areas was also found to be an important determinant of success.

Sources: Acheson, J. M. (2003). Capturing the Commons: Devising Institutions to Manage the Maine Lobster Fishery. Hanover, NH: University Press of New England; Gutiérrez, N. L., Hilborn, R., & Omar Defeo, O. (2011). Leadership, social capital and incentives promote successful fisheries. Nature, 470 (17 February), 386–389. Retrieved from www.nature.com/nature/journal/v470/n7334/full/nature09689.html

Open-access resources generally violate the efficiency criterion and may violate the sustainability criteria. If these criteria are to be fulfilled, some restructuring of the decision-making environment may be necessary. The next section examines the possible role for government in accomplishing that outcome.

Public policy toward fisheries

What can be done? A variety of public policy responses is possible. Perhaps it is appropriate to start with circumstances where allowing the market to work can improve the situation.

Raising the real cost of fishing

Perhaps one of the best ways to illustrate the virtues of using economic analysis to help design policies is to show the harsh effects of policy approaches that ignore it. Because the earliest approaches to fishery management had a single-minded focus on attaining the maximum sustainable yield, with little or no thought given to maximizing the net benefit, they provide a useful contrast.

One striking concrete example is the set of policies originally designed to deal with overexploitation of the Pacific salmon fishery in the United States. The five species of Pacific salmon are particularly vulnerable to overexploitation and even extinction because of their migration patterns. Pacific salmon are spawned in the gravel beds of rivers. As juvenile fish, they migrate to the ocean, only to return as adults to spawn in the rivers of their birth. After spawning, they die. When the adults swim upstream, with an instinctual need to return to their native streams, they can easily be captured by traps, nets, or other catching devices.

Recognizing the urgency of the problem, the government took action. To reduce the catch, they raised the cost of fishing. Initially this was accomplished by preventing the use of any barricades on the rivers and by prohibiting the use of traps (the most efficient catching devices) in the most productive areas. These measures proved insufficient, since mobile techniques (trolling, nets, and so on) proved quite capable by themselves of overexploiting the resource. Officials then began to close designated fishing areas and suspend fishing in other areas for stipulated periods of time. In Figure 7.4, these measures would be reflected as a rotation of the total cost curve to the left until it intersected the total benefits (revenue) curve at a level of effort equal to E^e. The aggregate of all these regulations had the desired effect of curtailing the yield of salmon.

Were these policies efficient? They were not even though they resulted in the efficient catch! This statement may seem inconsistent, but it is not. Efficiency implies not only that the catch must be at the efficient level, but also it must be extracted at the lowest possible cost. It was this latter condition that was violated by these policies (see Figure 7.6).

Figure 7.6 reflects the total cost in an unregulated fishery (TC_1) and the total cost after these policies were imposed (TC_2). The net benefit received from an efficient policy is shown graphically as the vertical distance between total cost and total benefit. Notice that after the policy, the net benefit was reduced to zero. Why?

The net benefit was squandered on the use of excessively expensive means to catch the desired yield of fish. Rather than use traps to reduce the cost of catching the desired number of fish, traps were prohibited. Larger expenditures on capital and labor were required to catch the same number of fish. This additional capital and labor represent one source of the waste.

The limitations on fishing times had a similar effect on cost. Rather than allowing fishermen to spread their effort out over time so the boats and equipment could be more productively utilized, fishermen were forced to buy larger boats to allow them to take as much as possible during the shorter seasons. (As one extreme example, Tillion (1985) reported that the 1982 herring season in Prince William Sound lasted only four hours and the catch still exceeded the area quota.) Significant overcapitalization produced gross inefficiency.

Regulation imposed other costs as well. It was soon discovered that while the preceding regulations were adequate to protect the depletion of the fish population, they failed to curb the incentive for individual fishermen to increase their share of the take. Even though the profits would be small because of high costs, new technological change would allow adopters to increase their shares of the market and put others out of business.

To protect themselves, the fishermen were eventually driven to introducing bans on new technology. These restrictions took various forms, but two are particularly noteworthy. The first was the

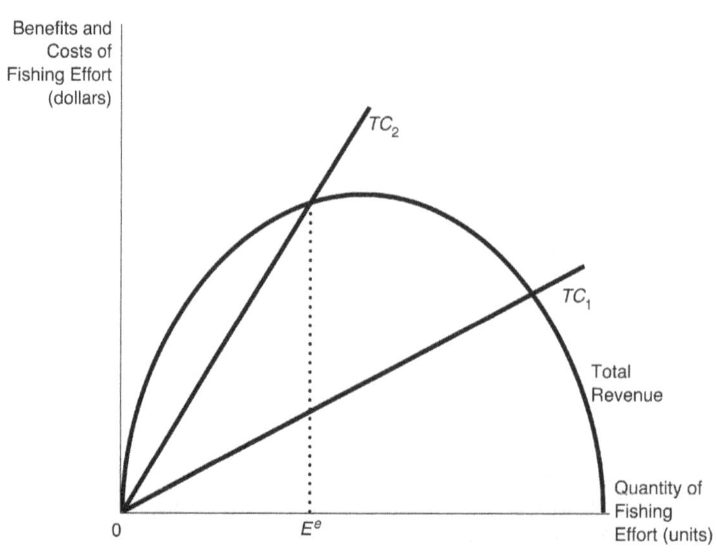

Figure 7.6 Effect of Regulation

banning of the use of thin-stranded, monofilament net. The coarse-stranded net it would have replaced was visible to the salmon in the daytime and therefore could be avoided by them. As a result, it was useful only at night. By contrast, the thinner monofilament nets could be successfully used during the daylight hours as well as at night. Monofilament nets were banned in Canada and the United States soon after they appeared.

The most flagrantly inefficient regulation was one in Alaska that barred gill netters in Bristol Bay from using engines to propel their boats. This regulation lasted until the 1950s and heightened the public's awareness of the anachronistic nature of this regulatory approach. The world's most technologically advanced nation was reaping its harvest from the Bering Sea in sailboats, while the rest of the world – particularly Japan and the Soviet Union – was modernizing their fishing fleets at a torrid pace!

Guided by a narrow focus on biologically determined sustainable yield that ignored costs, these policies led to a substantial loss in the net benefit received from the fishery. Costs are an important dimension of the problem, and when they are ignored, the incomes of fishermen suffer. When incomes suffer, further conservation measures become more difficult to implement, and incentives to violate the regulations are intensified.

Technical change presents further challenges to attempts to use cost-increasing regulations to reduce fishing effort. Technical innovations can lower the cost of fishing, thereby offsetting the increases imposed by the regulations. In the New England fishery, for example, Jin et al. (2002) report that the introduction of new technologies such as fish finders and electronic navigation aids in the 1970s and 1980s led to higher catches and declines in the abundance of the stocks despite the extensive controls in place at the time.

Taxes

Is it possible to provide incentives for cost reduction while assuring that the yield is reduced to the efficient level? Can a more efficient policy be devised? Economists who have studied the question believe that more efficient policies are possible.

Consider a tax on effort. In Figure 7.6, taxes on effort would also be represented as a rotation of the total cost line and the after-tax cost to the fishermen would be represented by line TC_2. Since the after-tax curve coincides with TC_2, the cost curve for all those inefficient regulations, doesn't this imply that the tax system is just as inefficient? No! The key to understanding the difference is the distinction between *transfer costs* and *real resource costs.*

Under a regulation system of the type described earlier in this chapter, all of the costs included in TC_2 are real resource costs, which involve utilization of resources. Transfer costs, by contrast, involve transfers of resources from one part of society to another, rather than their dissipation. Transfers do represent costs to that part of society bearing them, but are exactly offset by the gain received by the recipients. Unlike real resource costs, resources are not used up with transfers. Thus, the calculation of the size of the net benefit should subtract real- resource costs, but not transfer costs, from benefits. For society as a whole, transfer costs are retained as part of the net benefit; who receives it is affected, but not the size of the net benefit.

A tax on catch would yield a similar result, but in this case the total revenue curve would shrink (price minus tax) rather than total cost increasing. Both types of taxes would help move the equilibrium toward E*. Can you draw this using Figure 7.6?

In Figure 7.6, the net benefit under a tax system is identical to that under an efficient allocation. The net benefit represents a transfer cost to the fisherman that is exactly offset by the revenues received by the tax collector. This discussion should not obscure the fact that, as far as the individual fisherman is concerned, tax payments are very real costs. Rent normally received by a sole owner is now received by the government. Since the tax revenues involved can be substantial, fishermen wishing to have the fishery efficiently managed may object to this particular way of doing it. They would prefer a policy that restricts catches while allowing them to keep the rents. Is that possible?

Catch share programs

Catch share programs offer this option. Catch share programs allocate a portion of the total allowable catch to individuals, communities, or cooperatives. Programs in this category include individual fishing quotas (IFQs), individual transferable quotas (ITQs), individual vessel quotas (IVQs), territorial use rights fisheries (TURFs), fishing cooperatives, and community fishing quotas.[7] An ITQ program is a specific IFQ program where harvesting privileges can be transferred subsequent to initial allocations, IVQs are sometimes transferable, while TURFs grant rights to a geographic area. All of these create a type of harvest entitlement either in the fishery as a whole or in a specific geographic area.[8]

Catch share programs exist in 22 countries and on all continents (Table 7.1).

Table 7.1 Countries with Individual Transferable Quota Systems

Country	*Number of Species Covered*
Argentina	1
Australia	26
Canada	52
Chile	9
Denmark	1
Estonia	2
Falkland Islands	4
Greenland	1
Iceland	25
Italy	1
Mauritius	1*
Morocco	1*
Mozambique	4
Namibia	10
The Netherlands	7
New Zealand	97
Portugal	1*
South Africa	1*
United States	6

*Complete species list unavailable. Norway, Peru, and Russia also use ITQ systems as part of their fisheries management.
Sources: Adapted from Chu, C. (2009). Thirty years later: The global growth of ITQs and their influence on stock status in marine fisheries. *Fish and Fisheries, 10,* 217–230; Arnason, R. (Summer 2012). Property rights in fisheries: How much can individual transferable quotas accomplish? *Review of Environmental Economics and Policy,* 6(2), 217–236; Jardine, S. L. & Sanchirico, J. N. (2012). Catch share programs in developing countries: A survey of the literature. *Marine Policy, 36,* 1242–1254

ITQs

Let's first consider individual transferable quotas. Several of their identifiable characteristics serve to enhance efficiency:

1 The quotas entitle the holder to catch a specified share of the total authorized catch of a specified type of fish.
2 The catch authorized by the quotas held by all fishermen should be equal to the efficient catch for the fishery.
3 The quotas should be freely transferable among fishermen and markets should send appropriate price signals about the value of the fishery.

Each of these three characteristics plays an important role in obtaining an efficient allocation. Suppose, for example, the quota was defined in terms of boats rather than in terms of catch – not an uncommon type of quota. With a limit on the number of boats an inefficient incentive still remains for each boat owner to build larger boats, to place extra equipment on them, and to spend more time fishing. These actions would expand the capacity of each boat and cause the actual catch to exceed the target (efficient) catch. In a nutshell, the boat quota limits the number of boats fishing but does not limit the amount of fish caught by each boat. If we are to reach and sustain an efficient allocation, the catch must ultimately be limited.

While the purpose of the second characteristic (setting the right catch quota) is obvious, the role of transferability deserves more consideration. With transferability, the entitlement to fish flows naturally to those gaining the most benefit from it because their costs are lower. Because it is valuable, the transferable quota commands a positive price. Those who have quotas but also have high costs find they make more money selling the quotas than using them. Meanwhile, those who have lower costs find they can purchase more quotas and still make money.

Transferable quotas also encourage technological progress. Adopters of new cost-reducing technologies can make more money on their existing quotas and make it profitable to purchase new quotas from others who have not adopted the technology. Therefore, in marked contrast to the earlier regulatory methods used to raise costs, both the tax system and the transferable quota system encourage the development of new technologies without threatening the sustainability of the fishery.

How about the distribution of the rent? In a quota system, the distribution of the rent depends crucially on how the quotas are initially allocated. There are many possibilities with different outcomes. The first possibility is for the government to auction off these quotas. With an auction, government would appropriate all the rent and the outcome would be very similar to the outcome of the tax system. If the fishermen do not like the tax system, they would not like the auction system either.

In an alternative approach, the government could give the quotas to the fishermen, for example, in proportion to their historical catch. The fishermen could then trade among themselves until a market equilibrium is reached. All the rent would be retained by the current generation of fishermen. Fishermen who might want to enter the market would have to purchase the quotas from existing fishermen. Competition among the potential purchasers would drive up the price of the transferable quotas until it reflected the market value of future rents, appropriately discounted.[9]

Thus, this type of quota system allows the rent to remain with the fishermen, but only the current generation of fishermen. Future generations see little difference between this quota system and a tax system; in either case, they have to pay to enter the industry, whether it is through the tax system or by purchasing the quotas.

Worldwide, ITQs are currently used by 22 countries to manage hundreds of different species (Table 7.1). The annual global catch taken under ITQs may be as large as a quarter of the global harvest (Arnason, 2012). The fact that ITQ systems are spreading to new fisheries so rapidly suggests that their potential is being increasingly recognized. This expansion does not mean the absence of any concerns. In 1997, the United States issued a moratorium on the implementation of new ITQ programs, which expired in 2002. Issues about the duration of catch shares, whether shareholders need to be active in the fishery and the distributional implications all remain contentious. As of 2015, there were 16 catch-share programs in the United States and five fisheries that were considering catch-shares.

One of the most established ITQ programs is in New Zealand. In 1986, a limited ITQ system was established in New Zealand to protect its deep-water trawl fishery (Newell et al., 2005). Although this was far from being the only, or even the earliest, application of ITQs, it is the world's largest and provides an unusually rich opportunity to study how this approach works in practice. Some 130 species are fished commercially in New Zealand.[10] The Fisheries Amendment Act of 1986 that set up the program covered 17 inshore species and nine offshore species.

Because this program was newly developed, allocating the quotas proved relatively easy. The New Zealand Economic Exclusion Zone (EEZ) was divided geographically into quota-management regions. The total allowable catches (TACs) for the seven basic species were divided into individual transferable quotas by quota-management regions. By 2000, 275 quota markets were in existence.

Quotas were initially allocated to existing firms based on their average historical catch. However, because fishing is characterized by economies of scale, simply reducing everyone's catch proportionately wouldn't make much sense. That would simply place higher costs on everyone and waste a great deal of fishing capacity as all boats sat around idle for a significant proportion of time. A better solution would clearly be to have fewer boats harvesting the stock. That way each boat could be used closer to its full capacity without depleting the population. Which fishermen should be asked to give up their livelihood and leave the industry?

The economic-incentive approach addressed this problem by having the government buy back catch quotas from those willing to sell them. Initially, this was financed out of general revenues; subsequently, it was financed by a fee on catch quotas. Essentially, each fisherman stated the lowest price that he or she would accept for leaving the industry; the regulators selected those who could be induced to leave at the lowest price, paid the stipulated amount from the fee revenues, and retired their licenses to fish for this species. It wasn't long before a sufficient number of licenses had been retired and the population was protected. Because the program was voluntary, those who left the industry did so only when they felt they had been adequately compensated. Meanwhile, those who paid the fee realized that this small investment would benefit them greatly in the future as the population recovered. A difficult and potentially dangerous pressure on a valuable natural resource had been alleviated by the creative use of an approach that changed the economic incentives.

Toward the end of 1987, however, a new problem emerged. The stock of one species (orange roughy) turned out to have been seriously overestimated by biologists. Since the total allocation of quotas was derived from this estimate, the practical implication was that an unsustainably high level of quotas had been issued; the stock was in jeopardy. The New Zealand government began buying some quotas back from fishermen, but this turned out to be quite expensive with NZ$45 million spent on 15,000 tons of quotas from inshore fisheries.

Faced with the unacceptably large budget implications of buying back a significant number of quotas, the government ultimately shifted to a percentage-share allocation of quotas. Under this system, instead of owning quotas defined in terms of a specific quantity of fish, fishermen own percentage shares of a total allowable catch. The total allowable catch was determined annually by the government. In this way the government could annually adjust the total allowable catch, based on the latest stock assessment estimates, without having to buy back (or sell) large amounts of quota. This approach affords greater protection to the stock but increases the financial risk to the fishermen. By 2004, New Zealand's ITQ program had expanded to cover 70 species. Newell et al. (2005) found that the export value of these species ranged from NZ $700/metric ton for jack mackerel to NZ $40,000/metric ton for rock lobster. They also found that by 2000 some 70 percent of quote holders engaged in transactions in the ITQ market.

Despite this activity, some implementation problems have emerged. Fishing effort is frequently not very well targeted. Species other than those sought (known as "bycatch") may well end up as part of the catch. If those species are also regulated by quotas and the fishermen do not have sufficient ITQs to cover the bycatch, they are faced with the possibility of being fined when they land the unauthorized fish. Dumping the bycatch overboard avoids the fines, but the jettisoned fish frequently do not survive. Dumping the bycatch represents a double waste – not only is the stock reduced, but also the harvested fish are wasted.

Managers have also had to deal with "high-grading," which can occur when quotas specify the catch in terms of weight of a certain species, but the value of the catch is affected greatly by the size of the individual fish. To maximize the value of the quota, fishermen have an incentive to throw back the less valuable (typically smaller) fish, keeping only the most valuable individuals. As with bycatch, when release mortality is high, high-grading results in both smaller stocks and wasted harvests.

Although ITQ systems are far from perfect, frequently they offer the opportunity to improve on traditional fisheries management (see Example 7.2). In its 2012 annual report, to Congress, NOAA reported that 32 stocks have been rebuilt. Some 41 stocks (19 percent) are still overfished, but that is down from 45 just a year earlier.

Costello et al. (2008) examined the global effectiveness of these polices in over 11,000 fisheries from 1950 to 2003. Fisheries with catch share rules, including ITQs, experienced much less frequent collapse than fisheries without them. In fact, they found that by 2003 the fraction of fisheries with ITQs that had collapsed was only half that of non-ITQ fisheries. They suggest that this might be an underestimate since many fisheries with ITQs have not had them for very long. This large study suggests that well-designed property rights regimes (catch shares or ITQs more specifically) may help prevent fisheries collapse and/or help stocks of some species recover. Chu (2009) examined 20 stocks after ITQ programs were implemented and found that 12 of those had improvements in stock size. Eight, however, continued to decline. Apparently, ITQs can sometimes help, but they are no panacea. In the next chapter we will consider whether ITQs can help to conserve different marine species such as whales.

EXAMPLE 7.2

The relative effectiveness of transferable quotas and traditional size and effort restrictions in the Atlantic sea scallop fishery

Theory suggests that individual transferable quotas will produce more cost-effective outcomes in fisheries than traditional restrictions, such as minimum legal size and maximum effort controls. Is this theoretical expectation compatible with the actual experience in implemented systems?

In a fascinating study, economist Robert Repetto (2001) examined this question by comparing Canadian and American approaches to controlling the sea scallop fishery off the Atlantic coast. While Canada adopted a transferable quota system, the United States adopted a mix of size, effort, and area controls. The comparison provides a rare opportunity to exploit a natural experiment since scallops are not migratory and the two countries use similar fishing technologies. Hence, it is reasonable to presume that the differences in experience are largely due to the difference in management approaches.

What were the biological consequences of these management strategies for the two fisheries?

- The Canadian fishery was not only able to maintain the stock at a higher level of abundance, but it was also able to deter the harvesting of undersized scallops.
- In the United States, stock abundance levels declined and undersized scallops were harvested at high levels.

What were the economic consequences of these differences?

- Revenue per sea-day increased significantly in the Canadian fishery, due largely to the sevenfold increase in catch per sea-day made possible by the larger stock abundance.
- In the United States, fishery revenue per sea-day fell, due not only to the fall in the catch per day that resulted from the decline in stock abundance, but also to the harvesting of undersized scallops.
- Although the number of Canadian quota holders was reduced from nine to seven over a 14-year period, 65 percent of the quota remained in its original hands. The evidence suggests that smaller players were apparently not at a competitive disadvantage.

What were the equity implications?

- Both U.S. and Canadian fisheries have traditionally operated on the "lay" system, which divides the revenue among crew, captain, and owner according to preset percentages, after subtracting certain operating expenditures. This means that all parties remaining in the fishery after regulation shared in the increasing rents.

In these fisheries at least, it seems that the expectations flowing from the theory were borne out by the experience.

Source: Repetto, R. (2001). A natural experiment in fisheries management. *Marine Policy, 25*, 252–264.

Catch share programs

Catch shares include Individual Quotas, Individual Transferable Quotas, Individual Vessel Quotas, Cooperatives, and Territorial Use Rights for Fishing (TURFs) with catch limits. As of 2013, there were nearly 200 rights-based management programs worldwide in 40 countries covering more than 500 species. As more fisheries convert to rights-based management, the number of programs has increased.

CATCH SHARE PROGRAMS IN THE UNITED STATES

In the United States, the Magnuson Stevens Act authorizes several types of catch share approaches under its "limited access privilege" program. In the United States there are 16 active catch share programs (Table 7.2). Most of these are individual fishing quotas (IFQs), but more recently cooperatives and community development quotas (CDCs) have emerged.

EUROPEAN COMMON FISHERIES POLICY

The Common Fisheries Policy is the fisheries policy of the European Union (EU). It sets total allowable catch (TAC) for member states. Each country receives a national quota based on a percentage of the TAC. For each stock, different allocation percentages per country are applied. EU member countries can trade these quotas with other EU countries. Each member state is then responsible for enforcing its quota.[11] The 2015 TACs covered 36 species.[12]

TERRITORIAL USE RIGHTS FISHERIES (TURFS)

An alternative to ITQs is to allocate rights to a specific area for a specific species or group of species, rather than to a portion of the total allowable catch. Such geographic-based rights systems are called territorial use rights fisheries or TURFs. Like ITQs, TURFs typically grant access rights, not ownership rights, to harvesters.

TURFs could allow access to a layer of the water column (such as the bottom of the ocean or the surface, for example) in a specific zone. They could also allow access to a specific oyster bed or a raft

Table 7.2 Catch-Shares in the United States by Fisheries Management Region

New England • Atlantic Sea Scallops IFQ (2010) • New England Multispecies Sectors (2010)	**Mid-Atlantic** • Surf Clam & Ocean Quahog ITQ (1990) • Golden Tilefish IFQ (2009)
South Atlantic • Wreckfish ITQ (1991)	**Pacific** • Pacific Sablefish Permit Stacking IFQ (2001) • Pacific Coast Groundfish Trawl Rationalization IFQ (2011)
North Pacific • Halibut & Sablefish IFQ (1995) • Western Alaska CDQ (1992) • Bering Sea AFA Pollock Cooperative (1999) • Groundfish (non-Pollock) Cooperatives (2008) • Bering Sea King & Tanner Crab IFQ (2005) • Central Gulf of Alaska Rockfish Cooperative (2011)	**Gulf of Mexico** • Red Snapper IFQ (2007) • Grouper & Tilefish IFQ (2010) Atlantic Highly Migratory Species • Individual Bluefin Tuna Quota (2015)
Caribbean • No catch share programs	**Western Pacific** • No catch share programs

Source: Adapted from NOAA Fisheries (2019). www.fisheries.noaa.gov/national/laws-and-policies/catch-shares.

for mollusks. They could be granted to individuals, communities, corporations, or even to nations. An economic exclusion zone (EEZ) is a TURF granted to an individual nation.

Early examples of operating TURFs can be found in Japan. These now well-established TURFs allocate zones to local fisher organizations called Fishery Cooperative Associations (FCAs). Approximately 1,300 FCAs now operate in Japan (Wilen et al., 2012). They can also be found in Chile. With its 3,000-mile shoreline, Chile has created management and exploitation areas (MEAs) along its near-shore. These TURFs help manage the economically important Chilean abalone and sea urchin (Wilen et al., 2012). Other examples of TURFs can be found in Bangladesh, Fiji, Grenada, India, Papau New Guinea, Philippines, Solomon Islands, Turkey, and Vietnam (Jardine and Sanchirico, 2012).

TURFs can allow for more economically efficient use of the fishery resource by creating a form of property right, albeit a different property right from that conveyed by an ITQ. Despite their differences, both types of property rights create incentives to protect the future value of the resource, which in turn can incentivize self-enforcement mechanisms. They also can improve the welfare of small fishing communities.

While TURFs do help reduce the open-access problem, the value of a TURF is complicated by the fact that fish are mobile and therefore do not stay in one location. Since a TURF is site specific, its value is impacted by capture outside of the TURF. Obviously, for stocks that do not migrate far, the value of a TURF is enhanced.

Some researchers have suggested that some combination of TURF and ITQ policies may be most efficient. Debate 7.1 considers this question.

DEBATE 7.1

ITQs or TURFs? species, space, or both?

ITQs and TURFs can improve economic efficiency and help protect fisheries from overexploitation. Is one management method better than another? Can they be usefully combined?

Species-based ITQs have proven very popular and they can, in theory, create efficient harvesting and conservation incentives. However, in practice enforcement can be challenging and they suffer from several externalities. Some of the most prominent externalities, including gear impacts on ecosystems, spatial externalities, and cross-species interactions, might actually be increased by ITQs. Let's see how.

Typically the total allowable catch (TAC) is divided amongst several, perhaps numerous, owners. Although they do not compete over the size of their catch (since that is fixed by their catch share), they do still compete over the timing of that catch. Timing might matter a great deal when the most productive harvesting periods (in terms of reducing the private effort required per unit catch) turn out to be precisely the periods that impose the largest external costs (say by increasing the likelihood of bycatch or negatively impacting the juvenile stock). As such, they help solve one problem (assuring a sustainable total catch), while creating another (encouraging a harvest timing that increases external costs).

The Coase theorem (Chapter 2) suggests that these ownership rights should, in principle, create incentives to solve the remaining externalities, as well, but in practice, the transaction costs of such negotiations are apparently prohibitively high.

What about TURFs? TURFs help solve the problem of managing harvests over time and space and can help protect sensitive areas given that an individual or group has sole rights to that area. Local cooperatives have the advantage of being able in principle to manage interspecies interactions and habitat destruction, but in practice TURFs tend to suffer from conflict and coordination problems. Another common criticism of TURFs is that the scale must match the range of the species and many TURFs do not (or cannot) achieve this size.

Rather than framing the issue as whether ITQs or TURFs are the best choice, it may be that each has its own niche. Certainly, in developing countries with weak institutional structures, TURFs offer many advantages over species- based ITQs. TURFs also may be most appropriate for small, local populations. On the other hand, ITQs have been used successfully for many marine fisheries. Clearly, one size does not fit all for fisheries policy.

Source: Wilen, J. E., Cancino, J., & Uchida, H. (Summer 2012), The economics of territorial use rights fisheries, or TURFs. *Review of Environmental Economics and Policy*, *6*(2), 237–257.

Conflict resolution in open-access resources via transferable entitlements

As we have seen, when marine resources and services suffer from free access problems, ITQs are one option for reducing the overfishing problem. We have also seen in Chapter 6, that tradable entitlement systems have been used to protect ecosystem services. Might they be used to protect marine resources for conservation rather than extraction?

Arnason (2012) argues that a properly designed ITQ system could also provide another, quite different, benefit, namely facilitating the resolution of marine resource conflicts between recreational and commercial fisheries as well as conflicts between fishing and other marine resource uses. Making the entitlements transferable creates both an economic means and an economic incentive for the entitlements to move to their highest valued use as circumstances change, but careful design and adequate enforcement would be key to achieving success in conflict resolution.

Have ITQs helped to resolve conflicts? Not yet, but some ITQ holders are beginning to coordinate with other users of marine resources. In New Zealand, the scallop fishery has formed an association that coordinates activities not only with other open-water fisheries, but also with aquaculture (Arnason, 2012).

One difficult international area of conflict involves the management of whale populations. Could tradable entitlements possibly help to resolve this conflict? (See Debate 7.2.)

DEBATE 7.2

Tradable quotas for whales?

The International Whaling Commission banned whaling in 1986. Yet approximately 2,000 are still harvested each year – approximately 1,000 by Japan for "scientific purposes," 600 by Iceland and Norway, who do not recognize the ban, and 350 for subsistence (Costello et al., 2012). In 2010, some nations proposed allowing limited whaling with the hope that taking this step would reduce the number of whales actually harvested. This proposal never materialized due to disagreements between whaling and nonwhaling nations.

Costello et al. (2012) argue that this conflict could be reduced using tradable quotas for whale harvesting thus "creating a market that would be economically, ecologically and socially valuable for whalers and whales alike" (p. 139). Under their scheme both whalers and conservationists could bid for quotas and whalers could earn profits from whaling or from selling their quotas to conservationists. They propose allocating "whale shares" in sustainable numbers to all the member nations of the International Whaling Commission (IWC). (Note that this means that nonwhaling nations would also get a share. These shares could only be acquired by the whaling nations by buying them from the nonwhaling nations.) Shares would be traded in a global market and could be exercised or retired in perpetuity. The size of the harvest would depend on who bought the shares and could fall between zero (conservationists purchase all) and the sustainable total quota. Since trades are voluntary, in principle this market mechanism has the potential to make all parties better off (including the whales)!

Opponents note that multiple challenges exist including determining the sustainable quota, obtaining agreement on how the shares to this quota would be initially allocated among the parties, and creating a trading system with adequate transparency and enforcement. Additionally those who oppose putting a price tag on whales as a matter of principle certainly are opposed to this idea. However, as Costello et al. point out, this lack of a real price tag could well be what has hindered anti-whaling operations.

What about costs and benefits? Conservation organizations such as Greenpeace spend millions of dollars on anti-whaling campaigns. The authors estimate that Greenpeace USA, Greenpeace International, Sea Shepherd Conservation Society, and the World Wildlife Fund spend approximately $25 million annually on anti-whaling activities. The estimated profit from one minke whale is approximately $13,000, while the profit is $85,000 for a fin whale (2012 market prices and costs). Costello et al. estimate that the 350 whales saved by the Sea Shepherd in 2008 could simply have been purchased for less than $4 million.

Instead of spending money on anti-whaling, these groups would have the option to simply purchase the whales, thereby preventing anyone from harvesting them. The authors think it could be a win-win situation! Do you think they are right?

Source: Costello, C., Gaines, S., & Gerber, L. R. (January 12, 2012). Conservation science: A market approach to saving the whales. Nature, 481, 139–140.

Aquaculture

Having demonstrated that inefficient management of the fishery results from treating it as an open-access resource, one obvious solution is to allow some fisheries to be privately held. This approach can work when the fish are not very mobile, when they can be confined by artificial barriers, or when they instinctively return to their place of birth to spawn.

The advantages of such a move go well beyond the ability to preclude overfishing. The owner is encouraged to invest in the resource and undertake measures that will increase the productivity (yield) of the fishery. (For example, adding certain nutrients to the water or controlling the temperature can markedly increase the yields of some species.) The controlled raising and harvesting of fish is called *aquaculture*. Probably the highest yields ever attained through aquaculture have resulted from using rafts to raise mussels. Some 300,000 kilograms per hectare of mussels, for example, have been raised in this manner in the Galician bays of Spain. This productivity level approximates those achieved in poultry farming, widely regarded as one of the most successful attempts to increase the productivity of farm-produced animal protein.

Japan became an early leader in aquaculture, undertaking some of the most advanced aquaculture ventures in the world. The government has been supportive of these efforts, mainly by creating private property rights for waters formerly held in common. The governments of the prefectures (which are comparable to states in the United States) initiate the process by designating the areas to be used for aquaculture. The local fishermen's cooperative associations then partition these areas and allocate the subareas to individual fishermen for exclusive use. This exclusive control allows the individual owner to invest in the resource and to manage it effectively and efficiently.

Another market approach to aquaculture involves *fish ranching* rather than *fish farming*. Whereas fish farming involves cultivating fish over their lifetime in a controlled environment, fish ranching involves holding them in captivity only for the first few years of their lives.

Fish ranching relies on the strong homing instincts in certain fish, such as Pacific salmon or ocean trout, which permits their ultimate return and capture. The young salmon or ocean trout are hatched and confined in a convenient catch area for approximately 2 years. When released, they migrate to the ocean. Upon reaching maturity, they instinctually return to the place of their births, where they are harvested.

Fish farming has certainly affected the total supply of harvested fish. Aquaculture represents 48 percent of global catch and 53 percent if you include non-food uses (FAO, 2018). Aquaculture is currently the fastest-growing animal food production sector. In China, aquaculture now represents more than two-thirds of fisheries production. China has become the largest producer (and exporter) of seafood, producing 62 percent of the global supply of farmed fish. Shrimp, eel, tilapia, sea bass, and carp are all intensively farmed. Aquaculture is certainly not the answer for all fish. Today, it works well for certain species, but other species will probably never be harvested domestically. Furthermore, fish farming can create intensive environmental problems. Salmon farming and shrimp farming, especially, create negative externalities, as do fish farmed in contaminated water (see Debate 7.3). Nonetheless, it is comforting to know that aquaculture can provide a safety valve in some regions and for some fish and in the process take some of the pressure off the overstressed natural fisheries. The challenge will be to keep aquaculture sustainable.

DEBATE 7.3

Aquaculture: does privatization cause more problems than it solves?

Privatization of commercial fisheries, namely through fish farming, has been touted as a solution to the overfishing problem. For certain species, it has been a great success. Some types of shellfish, for example, are easily managed and farmed through commercial aquaculture. For other species, however, the likelihood of success is not so clear-cut.

Atlantic salmon is a struggling species in the northeastern United States and for several rivers, is listed as "endangered." Salmon farming takes the pressure off of the wild stocks. Atlantic salmon are intensively farmed off the coast of Maine, in northeastern Canada, in Norway, and in Chile. Farmed Atlantic salmon make up almost all of the farmed salmon market and more than half of the total global salmon market. While farmed salmon offer a good alternative to wild salmon and aquaculture has helped meet the demand for salmon from consumers, it is not problem-free.

Farmed fish escapees from the pens threaten native species, pollution that leaks from the pens creates a large externality, and pens that are visible from the coastline degrade the view of coastal residents. The crowded pens also facilitate the prevalence and diffusion of several diseases and illnesses, such as sea lice and salmon anemia. Antibiotics used to keep the fish healthy are considered dangerous for humans. Diseases in the pens can also be transferred to wild stocks. In 2007, the Atlantic Salmon Federation and 33 other conservation groups called on salmon farms to move their pens farther away from sensitive wild stocks.

And the concerns do not end there. Currently, many small species of fish, like anchovies or herring, are being harvested to feed carnivorous farmed fish. Scientists argue that this is not an efficient way to produce protein, because it takes 3–5 pounds of smaller fish to produce 1 pound of farmed salmon.

Pollution externalities associated with the increased production include contaminated water supplies for the fish ponds and heavily polluted wastewater. Some farmers raising their fish in contaminated water have managed by adding illegal veterinary drugs and pesticides to the fish feed, creating food safety concerns. Some tested fish flesh has been found to contain heavy metals, including mercury, and flame retardants.

While solving some problems, intensive aquaculture has created others. Potential solutions include open-ocean aquaculture (moving pens out to sea), closing pens, monitoring water quality, and improving enforcement. Clearly, sole ownership to the fishery isn't a silver bullet when externalities are prevalent.

Is shrimp farming any better? Over half of the shrimp consumed worldwide are farmed, mostly in Asia and Central America, while the markets are mostly in the United States and China. Developing countries that farm shrimp have cut down valuable mangroves in order to create fish farms. These mangroves provided storm protection and important coastal habitat (recall Example 2.2). Things are changing, however. Some shrimp farms are experimenting with inland ponds that treat their own waste. They are also exploring using vegetable protein as a food source. The challenge will be scale. Can new technology be expanded to meet the demand?

Sources: Atlantic Salmon Federation, www.asf.ca/main.html; Barboza, D. (December 15, 2007). China's seafood industry: Dirty water, dangerous fish. *New York Times*; Urry, Amelia. (2014). Grist. http://grist.org/food/is-there-a-sustainable-future-for-americas- most-popular-seafood/

Subsidies and buybacks

Excess fleet capacity or overcapitalization is prevalent in many commercial fisheries. Overcapacity encourages overfishing. Many subsidies exacerbate this effect by encouraging overcapacity and overcapitalization. Fuel subsidies, tax exemptions, fish price supports, and grants for new vessels are common forms of subsidies in fisheries. By enhancing profits, these subsides create perverse incentives to continue fishing even while stocks are declining.

A rather different type of subsidy is intended to discourage overfishing. If vessel owners do not have alternative uses for their vessels, they may resist catch restrictions or other measures meant to help depleted stocks. Management options have included buyback or, equivalently, decommissioning subsidies to reduce fishing capacity. In 2004, the U.S. government spent $100 million to buy out 28 of the 260 Alaskan snow crab fishery vessels. Payments used to buy out excess fishing capacity are useful subsidies in that they reduce overcapacity, but if additional capacity seeps in over time, they are not as effective as other management measures. If fishermen come to anticipate a buyback, they may acquire more vessels than they otherwise would have, which would lead to even greater levels of overcapacity.

Exclusive economic zones – the 200-mile limit

The final policy dimension concerns the international aspects of the fishery problem. Obviously, the various policy approaches to effective management of fisheries require some governing body to have jurisdiction over a fishery so that it can enforce its regulations.

Currently, this is not the case for many of the ocean fisheries. Much of the open water of the oceans is a common-pool resource to governments as well as to individual fishermen. No single body can exercise control over it. As long as that continues to be the case, the corrective action will be difficult to implement. In recognition of this fact, there is now an evolving law of the sea defined by international treaties. One of the concrete results of this law, for example, has been some limited restrictions on whaling. Whether this process ultimately yields a consistent and comprehensive system of management remains to be seen, but it is certainly an uphill battle.

The United Nations Convention on the Law of the Sea grants countries bordering the sea ownership rights that extend some 200 miles out to sea. Within these Exclusive Economic Zones (EEZs), the countries have exclusive jurisdiction and can implement effective management policies. These zones are essentially very large TURFs. These "exclusive zone" declarations have been upheld and are now firmly entrenched in international law. Thus, very rich fisheries in coastal waters can be protected, while those in the open waters await the outcome of an international negotiations process. The European Union has the largest EEZ in the world.

Unfortunately, EEZs do not sufficiently protect highly migratory fish stocks such as tunas and sharks and as such, 58 percent of the ocean (the high seas) is overexploited and overfished for many species (White and Costello, 2014).

Marine protected areas and marine reserves

Regulating only the amount of catch leaves the type of gear that is used and locations where the harvests take place uncontrolled. Failure to control those elements can lead to environmental degradation of the habitat on which the fishery depends even if catch is successfully regulated. Some gear may be particularly damaging, not only to the targeted species (e.g., by capturing juveniles that cannot be sold, but that don't survive capture), but also to nontargeted species (bycatch). Similarly, harvesting in some geographic areas (such as those used for spawning) might have a disproportionately large detrimental effect on the sustainability of the fishery.

Conservation biologists have suggested complementing current policies with the establishment of a system of marine protected areas (MPAs). The U.S. federal government defines MPAs as "any area of the marine environment that has been reserved by federal, state, tribal, territorial, or local laws or regulations to provide lasting protection for part or all of the natural and cultural resources therein."[13] Restrictions range from minimal to full protection. A marine reserve, a marine protected area with full protection, is an area that prohibits harvesting and enjoys a very high level of protection from other threats, such as pollution.

Biologists believe that marine protected areas can perform several maintenance and restorative functions. First, they protect *individual species* by preventing harvest within the reserve boundaries. Second, they reduce *habitat damage* caused by fishing gear or practices that alter biological structures. Third, in contrast to quotas on single species, reserves can promote *ecosystem balance* by protecting against the removal of ecologically pivotal species (whether targeted species or bycatch) that could throw an ecosystem out of balance by altering its diversity and productivity (Palumbi, 2002).

Reducing harvesting in these areas protects the stock, the habitat, and the ecosystem on which it depends. This protection results in a larger population and, ultimately, if the species swim beyond the boundaries of the reserve, larger catches in the remaining harvest areas.

Simply put, reserves promote sustainability by allowing the population to recover. Their relationship to the welfare of current users, however, is less clear. Proponents of MPAs suggest that they can promote sustainability in a win-win fashion (meaning current users benefit as well). This is an important point because users who did not benefit might mount political opposition to marine reserve proposals, thereby making their establishment very difficult.

Would the establishment of a marine protected area maximize the present value of net benefits for fishermen? If MPAs work as planned, they reduce harvest in the short run (by declaring areas previously available for harvest off-limits), but they increase it in the long run (as the population recovers and spills over the boundaries of the protected areas). However, the delay would impose costs. (Remember how discounting affects present value?) To take one concrete example of the costs of delay to harvesters, they may have to pay off a mortgage on their boat. Even if the bank grants them a delay in making payments, total payments will rise due to interest. So, by itself, a future rise in harvests does not guarantee that establishing the reserve maximizes present value unless the rise in catch is large enough and soon enough to compensate for the costs imposed by the delay.[14]

Since the present value of this policy depends on the specifics of the individual cases, a case study can be revealing. In an interesting case study of the California sea urchin industry, Smith and Wilen (2003) state the following:

> Our overall assessment of reserves as a fisheries policy tool is more ambivalent than the received wisdom in the biological literature. . . . We find . . . that reserves can produce harvest gains in an age-structured model, but only when the biomass is severely overexploited. We also find . . . that even when steady state harvests are increased with a spatial closure, the discounted returns are often negative, reflecting slow biological recovery relative to the discount rate.
>
> (p. 204)

This certainly does not mean that MPAs or marine reserves are a bad idea! In some areas, they may be a necessary step for achieving sustainability; in others, they may represent the most efficient means of achieving sustainability. It does mean, however, that we should be wary of the notion that they always create win-win situations; sacrifices by local harvesters might be required. MPA policies must recognize the possibility of this burden and deal with it directly, not just assume it doesn't exist.

Some international action on marine reserves is taking place as well. The 1992 international treaty called the Convention on Biological Diversity lists as one of its goals the conservation of at least 10 percent of the world's ecological regions, including, but not limited to, marine ecoregions. Progress has been significant for terrestrial ecoregions, but less so for coastal and marine ecoregions.

One creative proposal to incentivize the creation of new MPAs as well as incentivize sustainable fishing practices is to link eco-labeling to adjacent MPAs. Lester et al. (2013) propose building on recent surges in demand for green products and sustainable fisheries ecolabeling such as the Marine Stewardship Council's (MSC) label and the Monterey Aquarium Seafood Watch Program. They explore providing credit for adjacent MPAs in seafood certification and labeling. The impacts of MPAs on fish stocks is clear and could be used to provide "sustainability credits." They argue that making this link more explicit in labeling could help protect fish stocks.

Enforcement – illegal, unreported, and unregulated fish stocks

Illegal, unreported, and unregulated (IUU) fishing is a growing global problem. Approximately 90 percent of the seafood consumed in the United States is imported, either caught by foreign fishing vessels or sent abroad for processing and then reimported. Half of this is wild-caught seafood. It has been estimated that 20–32 percent of wild-caught seafood imports into the United States are from IUU sources (Pramod et al., 2014). The global market is complex and large and when seafood changes hands multiple times, it seems likely that even perceived legal imports contain IUU catch. Some regulations are difficult to enforce, such as the High Seas Driftnet Moratorium Protection Act which specifies that commerce in products caught with driftnets is illegal. Monitoring, control, and surveillance are prohibitively expensive in many cases.[15]

Another illegal activity is "high-grading," which can occur when fisherman have already met their quota, but then catch larger more valuable fish and discard the low-valued fish overboard. Often quotas specify the catch in terms of weight of a certain species, but the value of the catch is affected greatly by the size of the individual fish. One possible strategy is simply banning discarding, but due to the difficulties of monitoring and enforcement, that is not as straightforward a solution as it may seem. Kristofersson and Rickertsen (2009) examine whether a ban on discarding has been effective in the Icelandic cod fishery. They use a model of a fishery with an ITQ program and apply it to the Icelandic cod fishery. They estimate that longline vessels would discard up to 25 percent of the catch of small cod and gillnet vessels up to 67 percent. Their analysis found that quota price did not seem to be an influencing factor, but the existence of a system of quotas and the size of the hold in which the harvested fish are kept do matter. They suggest that to get the "most bang for the buck," enforcement efforts should be directed at gillnet vessels and on fisheries with small hold capacities.

Some fisheries managers have successfully solved both problems by allowing fishermen to cover temporary overages with allowances subsequently purchased or leased from others. As long as the market value of the "extra" fish exceeds the cost of leasing quotas, the fishermen will have an incentive to land and market the fish and the stock will not be placed in jeopardy.

Clearly, high-grading and other discards are still a significant problem. Zeller et al. (2017) estimate discards at 10–20 percent of global catch. Some of this is high-grading, other discards are from catch that is diseased, or isn't the target species.

Poaching (illegal harvesting) can introduce the possibility of unsustainability even when a legal structure to protect the population has been enacted. For example, in 1986 the International Whaling Commission set a ban on commercial whaling, but under a loophole in this law, Japan had continued to kill hundreds of whales each year. In November 2007, a fleet embarked on a five-month hunt in the Antarctic despite numerous international protests. While originally intending to target humpback whales, in response to the protests Japan eventually stopped harvesting that species. Since humpback whales are considered "vulnerable," commercial hunts have been banned since 1966, but Japan had claimed that harvests for research were not covered by this ban.

Bluefin tuna is another very valuable commercial species that is threatened and has been brought under international control. The population of bluefin tuna has plummeted 1970, with most of that loss occurring in the last decade (ICCAT.org). A recent report issued by the International Scientific Committee for Tuna and Tuna-like Species in the North Pacific Ocean (ISC 2016), the Pacific bluefin has declined 97! Much of the decline is due to overfishing and illegal harvesting (harvesting more than the quota allotment). Japan is the largest consumer of bluefin tuna, which is prized for sushi. Fleets from Spain, Italy, and France are the primary suppliers.

In the United States, the National Marine Fisheries Service manages the Atlantic Highly Migratory Species regulations which include a catch-share program for the U.S. portion of the International Commission for the Conservation of Atlantic Tunas (ICCAT) quota of endangered bluefin tuna. The 2014 amendment 7 to the 2006 rule "allocates U.S. bluefin tuna quota among domestic fishing categories; implements measures applicable to the pelagic longline fishery, including Individual Bluefin Quotas (IBQs), two new Gear Restricted Areas, closure of the pelagic longline fishery when annual bluefin tuna quota is reached," among other rules on bycatch and monitoring.[16] It also requires vessels to account for incidental bluefin tuna landings and dead discards using individual bluefin quota allocation.

A rather different approach to protect the species was tried in the international forum. In 2009, a petition to ban trade in the Atlantic bluefin tuna went before the U.N. Convention on International Trade in Endangered Species (CITES). This was the first time that a major commercial fishery has been addressed by CITES. While conservationists and biologists supported the CITES listing, many industry groups were opposed. The National Fisheries Institute president, John Connelly, wrote in opposition:

> Commercially-exploited aquatic species are fundamentally different from the other species that CITES regulates. . . . Unlike these other species, fish and seafood stocks are not generally threatened with biological extinction. While they can and do become overfished, the resulting loss of return on investment for fishermen prevents them from driving commercial fish stocks toward biological extinction.
>
> (Gronewold, 2009)

In early 2010, CITES voted against the ban. In January 2011, a record price was set for a northern bluefin. A giant, 754-pound bluefin brought 32.5 million yen, or nearly $400,000. Do you think this price is a sufficient incentive to protect the bluefin tuna from extinction? Why or why not? See Debate 7.4.

DEBATE 7.4

Bluefin tuna: difficulties in enforcing high-value species

The International Commission for the Conservation of Atlantic Tunas (ICCAT) is responsible for the conservation of highly migratory species, including several species of tuna. ICCAT reports fish biomass as well as catch statistics and is responsible for setting total allowable catch by species each year.

Since ICCAT has never successfully enforced their quotas, it is not clear that they have a credible enforcement capability. Monitoring statistics consistently show catch well above the TAC.

Additionally, international pressure from the fishing industry frequently results in a TAC higher than scientists recommend. In 2009, for example, having reviewed the current biomass statistics, which showed the current stock to be at less than 15 percent of its original stock, ICCAT scientists recommended a total suspension of fishing. Ignoring their scientists' recommendation, ICCAT proceeded to set a quota of 13,500 tons. They did, however, also agree to establish new management measures for future years that will allow the stock to rebuild with an estimated 60 percent degree of confidence. While that sounds good, it turns out that if enforcement is less than perfect, and the resulting catch is above 13,500, the probability that the stock will recover cannot reach the 60 percent level by 2022 (Table 7.3).

Table 7.3 Probabilities of Stock Rebuilding at $SSBF_0.1$ by Years and TAC Levels

	Percentage				
TAC	*2010*	*2013*	*2016*	*2019*	*2022*
0	0	2	25	69	99
2,000	0	1	21	62	99
4,000	0	1	18	55	99
6,000	0	0	14	47	97
8,000	0	0	11	40	92
10,000	0	0	9	33	84
12,000	0	0	6	26	73
13,500	0	0	5	21	63
14,000	0	0	4	20	59
16,000	0	0	3	14	46
18,000	0	0	2	10	34
20,000	0	0	1	6	24

Note: Gray color highlights the catch at which the 60 percent probability would not be achieved.
Source: Report of the 2010 Atlantic bluefin tuna stock assessment session (Table 1); ICCAT, www.iccat.int/en

Sources: International Commission for the Conservation of Atlantic Tunas 2009 annual ICCAT meeting press release (November 16, 2009); ICCAT, www.iccat.org; Gronewold, G. (October 14, 2009). Is the bluefin tuna an endangered species? *Scientific American.* Retrieved from www.scientificamerican.com/article.cfm?id=bluefin-tuna-stocks- threatened-cites-japan-monaco; Draft amendment 7 to the Consolidated Atlantic Highly Migratory Species Fishery Management Plan, *National Marine Fisheries Service*, August 2013. Retrieved from www.scribd.com/doc/161801821/NOAA-Draft-Bluefin-Tuna-Amendment.

Summary

Unrestricted access to commercially valuable species will generally result in overexploitation. This overexploitation, in turn, results in overcapitalization, depressed incomes for harvesters, and depleted stocks. Even extinction of the species is possible, particularly for populations characterized by easy, low-cost extraction. Where extraction costs are higher, extinction is unlikely, even with unrestricted access.

Both the private and public sectors have moved to ameliorate the problems associated with past mismanagement of commercial fisheries. By reasserting private property rights, many countries have stimulated the development of aquaculture. Governments in Canada and the United States have moved to limit overexploitation of the Pacific salmon. International agreements have been instituted to place limits on whaling. It is doubtful that these programs fully satisfy the efficiency criterion, although it does seem clear that more sustainable catches will result.

Using data from 4713 fisheries worldwide, representing 78 percent of global reported fish catch, Costello et al. (2016) estimate global maximum sustained yield to be 98 million metric tons (not including illegal fishing). They forecast that business-as-usual fisheries management will result in the continued collapse of many of the worlds fisheries. They suggest that commonsense reforms could increase both fish abundance (and hence food security) along with profits.

Creative strategies for sharing the gains from moving to an efficient level of harvest could prove to be a significant weapon in the arsenal of techniques designed to protect a broad class of biological resources from overexploitation. An increasing reliance on individual transferable quotas (ITQs) and TURFs offers the possibility of preserving stocks without jeopardizing the incomes of those men and women currently harvesting those stocks. Strengthening property rights is a key component in generating both efficient and sustainable harvests. Approximately 20 percent of developing countries have implemented space-based (mostly in Asia and Pacific regions) or quota-based (mostly found in African nations) allocation systems.

It would be folly to ignore barriers to further action, such as the reluctance of individual harvesters to submit to many forms of regulation, the lack of a firm policy governing open- ocean waters, and the difficulties of enforcing various approaches. Whether these barriers will fall before the pressing need for effective management remains to be seen. Climate change is already affecting the marine environment, so looming challenges remain.

In this chapter we have focused on fisheries as an example of a renewable biological resource, but the models and the insights that flow from them can be used to think about managing other wildlife populations as well. This topic will be taken up in the next chapter.

Discussion questions

1 Is the establishment of the 200-mile limit a sufficient form of government intervention to ensure that the tragedy of the commons does not occur for fisheries within the 200-mile limit? Why or why not?
2 With discounting it is possible for the efficient fish population to fall below the level required to produce the maximum sustained yield. Does this violate the sustainability criterion? Why or why not?

Self-test exercises

1 Assume that the relationship between the growth of a fish population and the population size can be expressed as $g = 4P-0.1\,P^2$, where g is the growth in tons and P is the size of the population (in thousands of tons). Given a price of $100 a ton, the marginal benefit of smaller population sizes (and hence larger catches) can be computed as $20P-400$.

   a Compute the population size that is compatible with the maximum sustainable yield. What would be the size of the annual catch if the population were to be sustained at this level?
   b If the marginal cost of additional catches (expressed in terms of the population size) is $MC = 2(160-P)$, what is the population size that is compatible with the efficient sustainable yield?

2 Assume that a local fisheries council imposes an enforceable quota of 100 tons of fish on a particular fishing ground for one year. Assume further that 100 tons per year is the efficient sustained yield. When 100 tons have been caught, the fishery would be closed for the remainder of the year.

   a Is this an efficient solution to the common property problem? Why or why not?
   b Would your answer be different if the 100-ton quota were divided into 100 transferable quotas, each entitling the holder to catch 1 ton of fish, and distributed among the fishermen in proportion to their historical catch? Why or why not?

3 In the economic model of the fishery developed in this chapter, compare the effect on fishing effort of an increase in cost of a fishing license with an increase in a per-unit tax on fishing effort that raises the same amount of revenue. Assume the fishery is private property. Repeat the analysis assuming that the fishery is a free-access common property resource.
4 When trying to reduce the degree of inefficiency from an open-access fishery, would a regulation that increases the marginal cost of fishing effort by banning certain types of gear or a tax on effort be equally efficient? Why or why not?
5 a In the typical economic model of an efficient fishery, would a fall in the price of fish generally result in a larger or a smaller sustainable harvest? Why?
   b Suppose the fishery allowed free access. Would a fall in the price of fish generally result in a larger or a smaller harvest? Why?

6 Suppose that a particular fishery experiences a technological change such that the fixed cost of fishing increases, but the marginal cost of fishing decreases. The change is such that the before and after total cost curves cross at an effort level higher than that associated with the before efficient sustained yield, but lower than the free-access level of effort.

   a What would the effect of this technological change be on the static efficient level of effort and the size of the static efficient level of harvest? Would they increase or decrease or are the effects ambiguous?
   b What would the effect of this technological change be on the level of effort and the size of the harvest in a free-access fishery? Would they increase or decrease or are the effects ambiguous?

Notes

1 Hardin, Garrett. (1968). The tragedy of the commons. *Science*, 162, 1243–1247.

2 This is not difficult to demonstrate mathematically. In our model, the yield (h) can be expressed as $h = qES$, where q is the proportion of the population harvested with one unit of effort, S is the size of the population, and E is the level of effort. One of the conditions a dynamic efficient allocation has to satisfy with an infinite discount rate is $P = a/qS$, where P is the constant price, a is the constant marginal cost per unit of effort, and qS is the number of fish harvested per unit of effort. By multiplying both sides of this equation by h and collecting terms, we obtain $Ph = aE$. The left-hand side is total benefits, while the right is total cost, implying net benefits are zero.

3 Note the parallel with the role of the growth rate in efficient timber harvesting in Chapter 11.

4 Note that we are ruling out monopoly behavior via our assumption that the price is not affected by effort level.

5 This will result in fewer fish for future generations as well as smaller profits if the resulting effort level exceeds that associated with the maximum sustainable yield. If the open-access effort level is lower than the maximum sustainable yield effort level (when extraction costs are very high), then reductions in stock would increase the growth in the stock, thus supplying more fish (albeit lower net benefits) to future generations.

6 This type of analysis was first used in Gordon (1954).

7 NOAA Catch Share Policy. Available at: www.nmfs.noaa.gov/sfa/management/catch_shares/about/documents/noaa_cs_policy.pdf (Accessed June 2017).

8 NOAA keeps a thorough catch share bibliography on its website. www.nmfs.noaa.gov/sfa/management/catch_shares/resources/references.html

9 This occurs because the maximum bid from any potential entrant would be the value to be derived from owning that permit. This value is equal to the present value of future rents (the difference between price and marginal cost for each unit of fish sold). Competition will force the purchaser to bid near that maximum value, lest he or she lose the quota.

10 Ministry of Fisheries, New Zealand. Available at: www.fish.govt.nz/en-nz/default.htm

11 European Commission. (2017). Available at: https://ec.europa.eu/fisheries/cfp_en

12 https://ec.europa.eu/fisheries/sites/fisheries/files/docs/body/poster_tac2015_en.pdf

13 For information and maps of marine protected areas of the United States, see http://marineprotectedareas.noaa.gov/. For a worldwide atlas, see www.mpatlas.org/

14 The distribution of benefits and costs among current fishermen also matters. Using a case study on the Northeast Atlantic Cod fishery, Sumaila and Armstrong (2006) find that the distributional effects of MPAs depend significantly on the management regime that was in place at the time of the development of the MPA and the level of cooperation in the fishery.

15 The FAO keeps statistics on IUU fishing that can be accessed at www.fao.org/iuu-fishing/en/

16 www.federalregister.gov/documents/2014/12/02/2014-28064/atlantic-highly-migratory-species-2006-consolidated-atlantic-highly-migratory-species-hms-fishery

Further reading

Acheson, J. M. (2003). *Capturing the Commons: Devising Institutions to Manage the Maine Lobster Industry*. Hanover, NH: University Press of New England. An impressive synthesis of theory and empirical work, combined with an insider's knowledge of the institutions and the people who run them, makes this a compelling examination of the history of one of America's most important fisheries.

Adler, J. H., & Stewart, N. (2013). Learning how to fish: Catch shares and the future of fisheries conservation. *UCLA Journal of Environmental Law & Policy*, 31(1), 150–197. A useful summary of the history, law, and economics of catch shares.

Clark, C. W. (1990). *Mathematical Bioeconomics: The Optimal Management of Renewable Resources*, 2nd ed. New York: Wiley-Interscience. Careful development of the mathematical models that underlie current understanding of the exploitation of renewable resources under a variety of property rights regimes.

Food and Agriculture Organization of the United Nations. (2018). *State of the World Fisheries and Aquaculture*. Data and figures on catch and farmed fisheries around the world as well as statistics on labor and consumption in fisheries. Accessed at www.fao.org/state-of-fisheries-aquaculture.

NOAA Catch Share Policy: Executive Summary. (2013). Available at: www.nmfs.noaa.gov/sfa/domes_fish/catchshare/docs/noaa_cs_policy.pdf. A useful review of U.S. Fisheries Policy.

Review *of Environmental Economics and Policy*, 6(2), Summer (2012). This special issue contains several summary articles from the Symposium: Rights-Based Fisheries Management.

Schlager, E., & Ostrom, E. (1992). Property right regimes and natural resources: A conceptual analysis. *Land Economics*, 68, 249–262. A conceptual framework for analyzing a number of property rights regimes; the authors use this framework to interpret findings from a number of empirical studies.

Additional references and other historically significant references are available on this book's eResource page: www.routledge.com/9781138587595

Chapter 8

Climate change I

The nature of the challenge

Introduction

As pollutants flow beyond national boundaries, the political difficulties of implementing comprehensive, cost-effective control measures are compounded. Pollutants crossing national boundaries impose spatial external costs; neither emitters nor the political jurisdictions within which they emit have the proper incentives for controlling the emissions.

Compounding the problem of improper incentives is the scientific uncertainty that limits our understanding of these complex problems. Our knowledge about various relationships that form the basis for our understanding of the magnitude of the problems and the effectiveness of various strategies to control them is impressive, but far from complete. Unfortunately, the problems are so important and the potential consequences of inaction so drastic that procrastination is not usually an optimal strategy. To avoid having to act in the future under emergency conditions when the remaining choices have dwindled, strategies to preserve options with desirable properties must be formulated now on the basis of the available information, as limited as it may be.

Unfortunately, as we shall see, meeting the challenges of global problems requires international cooperation, but achieving the type and depth of international cooperation that would be required is exceedingly difficult. In addition international cooperation is also likely to be hampered by the potential for future international conflicts to be heightened by impending climate-intensified scarcities (water, for example) and the expected border-crossing surge of refugees fleeing extreme weather-related disasters.

In this chapter we survey the evidence on the unique challenges and opportunities posed by climate change. We consider not only the additional important aspect of the international context associated with climate change, but also the physical features of this pollutant that differ from the other air pollutants. As we shall see, both of these aspects of this challenge affect policy design.

The science of climate change

One class of global pollutants, greenhouse gases (GHGs), absorb the long-wavelength (infrared) radiation from the earth's surface and atmosphere, trapping heat that would otherwise radiate into space.

The mix and distribution of these gases within the atmosphere is in no small part responsible for both the hospitable climate on the earth and the inhospitable climate on other planets, but changing the mix of these gases is modifying our climate.

Several greenhouse gases exist, but the major ones are carbon dioxide, methane, and nitrous oxide. In 2018 the World Meteorological Organization reported that the concentrations of all three in the atmosphere were at all-time highs.

Carbon dioxide (CO_2): Although the combustion of fossil fuels (coal, natural gas, and oil), is the major source of CO_2emissions, burning wood and certain chemical reactions used in manufacturing products such as cement are also sources.

Methane (CH_4): Leakage from the production and transport of coal, natural gas, and oil are the major sources of methane emissions, but they also result from livestock and other agricultural practices and from the decay of organic waste in municipal solid waste landfills.

Nitrous oxide (N_2O): Nitrous oxide is emitted in the nitrogen cycle in natural ecosystems and has a variety of anthropogenic sources, including the use of synthetic fertilizers in agriculture, motor vehicle exhaust, and some manufacturing processes.

Global climate is also influenced by natural factors that determine how much of the sun's energy enters and leaves the Earth's atmosphere and by natural climate cycles that affect temperatures and weather patterns in the short term, especially regionally. However, the unambiguous long-term warming trend in global average temperature over the last century cannot be explained by natural factors alone.

As the U. S. Global Change Research Program's Fourth National Climate Assessment put it:

> This assessment concludes, based on extensive evidence, that it is extremely likely that human activities, especially emissions of greenhouse gases, are the dominant cause of the observed warming since the mid-20th century. For the warming over the last century, there is no convincing alternative explanation supported by the extent of the observational evidence.[1]

The warming impacts of these three GHGs on global temperatures differ widely.[2] These differences are derived from two important characteristics of a greenhouse gas: (1) how well the gas absorbs energy (preventing it from immediately escaping into space), and (2) how long the gas stays in the atmosphere. These impact differentials among the gases are usually measured by a metric called the Global Warming Potential (GWP). It is a relative measure of the total energy that a gas absorbs over a particular period of time (usually 100 years), compared to carbon dioxide.

The GWP potential for CO_2 is 1.0 by definition. CO_2 remains in the atmosphere for a very long time – once they enter the atmosphere CO_2emissions can persist for up to thousands of years.

Methane (CH_4) has a GWP more than 20 times higher than CO_2 for a 100-year time scale. Once emitted its lasts for only about a decade in the atmosphere, but on average, on a pound-for-pound basis, CH_4 absorbs more energy than CO_2, making its GWP higher.

Global Nitrous Oxide (N_2O) has a GWP 300 times that of CO_2 for a 100-year timescale. N_2O emitted today remains in the atmosphere for more than 100 years, on average.

The GWP metric has several uses. For one a GWP weighted average of the impact of the GHGs can be used to create a single metric, called CO_2e (carbon dioxide equivalent). This mixture metric captures the total warming impact of any mixture of these emissions. A single metric like this is useful, for example, in comparing the impacts of emissions from different countries, since those emissions contain different mixes of gases. The CO_2e metric can be (and has been) also used to set the necessary emission limits that must be achieved if international targets for limiting temperature-increases are to be met.

The nature of the threats

The U. S. Global Change Research Program[3] was started in 1989 during the administration of George H. W. Bush and mandated by Congress in 1990, to "assist the Nation and the world to understand, assess, predict, and respond to human-induced and natural processes of global change." This process coordinates the work of some 13 Federal agencies that deal with climate change issues. In 2018 this group issued a major report[4] called "Fourth National Climate Assessment, Vol. I: The Climate Science Special Report."

Some of its main findings include:

- Global annually averaged surface air temperature has increased by about 1.8°F (1.0°C) over the last 115 years (1901–2016). This period is now the warmest in the history of modern civilization.
- Thousands of studies conducted by researchers around the world have documented changes in surface, atmospheric, and oceanic temperatures; melting glaciers; diminishing snow cover; shrinking sea ice; rising sea levels; ocean acidification; and increasing atmospheric water vapor.
- Global average sea levels are expected to continue to rise – by at least several inches in the next 15 years and by one to four feet by 2100. Sea level rise will be higher than the global average on the east and gulf coasts of the United States.
- Heatwaves have become more frequent in the United States since the 1960s, while extreme cold temperatures and cold waves are less frequent.
- The incidence of large forest fires in the western United States and Alaska has increased since the early 1980s and is projected to further increase in those regions as the climate changes, with profound changes to regional ecosystems.
- Without major reductions in emissions, the increase in annual average global temperature relative to pre-industrial times could reach 9°F (5°C) or more by the end of this century. With significant reductions in emissions, the increase in annual average global temperature could be limited to 3.6°F (2°C) or less.
- Continued growth in CO_2 emissions over this century and beyond would lead to an atmospheric concentration not experienced in tens to hundreds of millions of years. There is broad consensus that the further and the faster the Earth system is pushed towards warming, the greater the risk of unanticipated changes and impacts, some of which are potentially large and irreversible.

The military and climate scientists characterize the role of climate change on the damages caused by such natural disasters as floods, intense storms, forest fires, and drought as a threat multiplier. The intended implication is that they don't typically cause the disasters, but they intensify the damages that result from them. While most scientists accept this view of the state of the science, not all observers do. And some are even willing to put their money where their mouth is (Example 8.1).

EXAMPLE 8.1

Betting on climate science

In 2011 Economist Chris Hope was at a conference at Cambridge, UK. As he describes the situation in an article in *The Guardian*:

> most of the participants were skeptical about the influence of humans on the climate. I took the microphone and asked if any of them would care to make a £1,000 bet with me about whether 2015

would be hotter than 2008. Two brave souls, Ian Plimer and Sir Alan Rudge, agreed.

Cole then found a climate scientist, James Annan, who was willing make a side bet that would give Cole 5 to 1 odds against 2015 being cooler than 2008. (Specifically, if 2015 were warmer Cole would pay Annan £666 and if 2015 were colder Annan would pay Cole £3,333.) Although the numbers look a bit odd, in fact this side bet provided a perfect hedge for Cole. He would win £1,333 if 2015 were cooler than 2008, and £1,334 if it were warmer. This side bet had shifted the downside risk (the risk of losing) to Annan, who was willing to accept it due to his confidence that this risk was very small.

We now know that 2015 was hotter than 2008 and Plimer and Rudge each lost £1,000, which was split between Cole (£1,334) and Annan (£666) based upon their side bet.

Did the specific starting and ending dates matter in this bet? While global temperatures have in general been rising, it turns out this was a particularly bad set of dates for betting against climate change. To start with, 2008 was a relatively cool year. According to the NASA Goddard Institute for Space Studies, a strong cyclical effect known as La Niña caused much of the Pacific Ocean to be cooler than the long-term average for that year.

In contrast, the ending year, 2015, was the hottest year on record up to that time. Notice that every bet against a warmer temperature involving an ending date of 2015 would have lost.

Would a different set of 7-year intervals involving earlier starting and ending dates have produced a different result? Gather the data, do the calculations and find out for yourself. Start with 1998 and examine every 7-year period, ending with the 2008 period used in this bet. In general, what do these data show about the wisdom of betting against climate change?

Sources: Hope, Chris. (July 28, 2016). Making a safe bet on climate change. In his Keeping an Eye on Climate Change blog. Available at: www.chrishopepolicy.com/2016/07/making-a-safe-bet-on-dangerous-climate-change/; NASA Goddard Institute for Space Studies (GISS). (February 23, 2009). 2008 was earth's coolest year since 2000. Available at: www.nasa.gov/topics/earth/features/2008_temps.html

Characterizing the broad strategies for managing the risk

Clearly this report suggests that the U. S. (and the broader global community) face substantial risks from a changing climate. What can be done to manage these risks??

Four broad strategies have been identified: (1) sequestration, (2) adaptation (3) mitigation, and (4) restoration.

- Carbon *sequestration* is the process of capturing and storing atmospheric carbon dioxide. It reduces the amount of carbon dioxide in the atmosphere by trapping carbon dioxide that would otherwise end up in the atmosphere. Natural processes of sequestration include carbon dioxide uptake by the oceans and plants. Policy can become involved in such diverse ways as encouraging planting new forests or scrubbing gases from power plants. Captured carbon dioxide can be stored under geological formations or injected into drilling sites to draw up the last bits of oil. Researchers and startups are also exploring ways to use carbon dioxide to produce alternative fuels, building materials, and other products and to develop new materials that capture and store carbon dioxide from the air.
- *Adaptation* strategies involve efforts to modify natural or human systems in order to reduce or eliminate harm from climate change impacts. Examples include modifying development planning to increase the resilience of damage-prone areas, such as relocating transportation systems and waste treatment facilities away from areas vulnerable to sea-level rise, and preparing public health facilities to handle the larger burdens resulting from the changing disease impacts of a warmer climate.
- *Mitigation* attempts to moderate the temperature rise by using strategies designed to reduce emissions of GHGs.
- *Restoration* involves cleaning up and restoring areas damaged by climate-involved events such as severe storms, floods, forest fires, etc.).

In this chapter we shall focus on the challenges posed not only by the scientific findings, but also posed for developing politically viable international risk management strategies to manage those challenges. In the next chapter we focus on energy's significant and special role in managing the risk of climate change. Carbon dioxide emissions can be reduced either by using less energy or by using alternative energy sources (such as wind, photovoltaics, or hydro) that produce less or no carbon dioxide. Any serious reduction in carbon dioxide emissions would involve significant changes in our energy-consumption patterns and those changes could come with an economic cost. Thus, the debate over how vigorously this strategy of energy transition should be followed is a controversial public-policy issue. Economics has much to add to that discussion, as you will see.

In our third chapter in this section on climate change we consider both the potential role of carbon pricing strategies and how well the current experiences conform with that potential role. As we shall see carbon pricing has some interesting, unique characteristics.

In the fourth chapter we examine adaptation strategies and how they fit into the overall policy mix. What kinds of strategies are available? Are they substitutes or complements to emission-reduction strategies? How does the mix of mitigation and adaptation strategies affect the cost of action and the cost of inaction?

Economic insights on targets and timing

What light can economics shed on the fundamental questions of how much control of emissions should be undertaken and what is the optimal timing of those investments? In principle this is an easy question to answer. Efficiency is achieved when the marginal cost of controlling an additional unit of emissions becomes equal to the marginal reduction in damages that results from controlling (rather than emitting) that unit of emissions.

Unfortunately while we can calculate the optimal point for a specific set of assumptions, each different set of assumptions results in a different optimal level of emissions reduction. Why are different sets of assumptions involved? Two main reasons involve the choice of the discount rate and the uncertainty associated with the damage estimates.

Remember that in benefit-cost analysis when benefits and costs are distributed over time, it is appropriate to convert them to present values so they can be easily compared across time periods. When the benefits and costs are spread over long time horizons, the magnitude of the discount rate matters a lot. In general the use of a higher discount rate will call for a lower degree of optimal control and a more relaxed period of implementation, while a lower discount rate will call for more control achieved more rapidly.

Why not simply pick the "right" discount rate and use it to define the optimum? Unfortunately which discount rate is "right" depends on the framework you are using to define it. Since multiple frameworks can be justified (especially for a long-lived problem like climate change), multiple acceptable discount rates are possible.

Generally the two main perspectives on discounting in the climate change context lies between *normative* discounting and *opportunity cost* discounting. While the former is derived from ethical principles about the treatment of future generations, the latter focuses on the observed opportunity cost of capital. Not surprisingly the former leads to a lower recommended discount rate (in the 1–2 percent range, for example) than the latter (in the 3–7 percent range, for example). Both have strong arguments and powerful spokespersons articulating the two different points of view. Reasonable economists can disagree on which discount rate is best.[5]

A second problem arises from the uncertainty of the estimates underlying the calculations. Consider just one example. As the planet warms, a layer of frozen tundra (permafrost) begins to thaw. This layer is composed of dead plants and animals that have been frozen deep in permafrost for thousands of years. As long as this organic matter remains frozen, it will remain in the permafrost. However, if it thaws, it will decay, releasing carbon dioxide or methane into the atmosphere. As we noted earlier methane is a very powerful greenhouse gas so the thawing of the permafrost could speed up the warming process, perhaps considerably. While we know that this will happen (indeed in some places it is happening now), we know less about exactly how fast the process will take place.

Fortunately even when exact estimates of the optimal degree and speed of reduction cannot be agreed upon, economics still has a lot to offer policy makers. Suppose for example we ask the simpler question "should we be undertaking more emissions reduction now?"

The answer to that is pretty clear. Recall that when the marginal cost of reducing a unit of emissions is less than the marginal social damage that would have been caused by that unit of emissions, we should increase control. (Can you see why?)

What do we know about the relative magnitudes of those numbers now?

First for the marginal social damage we have a concept called the social cost of carbon. This term designates the economic cost caused by an additional ton of CO_2 emissions or CO_2e emissions (if multiple gases are considered.). More precisely, it is the change in the discounted value of economic welfare from an additional unit of CO_2e emissions.

How can we find the current marginal cost of control? From Chapter 4 we know that emitters facing a price on carbon minimize their costs by setting their marginal cost of control to the carbon price. This means we can infer the marginal cost of control from current carbon prices in those areas that have put a price on carbon.

Fortunately World Bank Reports[6] keep track of these prices. In their 2017 report they found that three quarters of the emissions covered by a carbon price are priced at less than US\$10/tonCO_2e.

If we compare these to the social cost of carbon estimates, these prices are typically lower (sometimes much lower) than the most commonly preferred social cost of carbon results. (For example, 2018 Nobel Laureate William Nordhaus used a figure of roughly \$30/ton CO_2e for 2015 emissions.)[7] Other estimates are typically somewhat higher.

The implication, of course, from comparing these two numbers is that action now is more efficient than waiting. Every ton controlled will reduce the present value of the resulting damages by more than the cost of preventing the emission of that ton. It is therefore not surprising that most studies find that action to mitigate emissions enhances, rather than reduces, future economic well-being.

Furthermore the costs of taking action have dropped considerably over time. Not only have the costs of procuring renewable energy sources like solar and wind fallen, but the costs of electricity storage to counteract the intermittency of these sources have become much cheaper as well. Some studies have now even found that a *global* transition to 100 percent renewable energy across all sectors – power, heat, transport and even desalination before 2050 is not only feasible, but it is cheaper than the current system.[8] That, of course, is only an estimate, but it is interesting that it is even possible to forecast the feasibility of such a large change from existing data.

What can economics say about how the costs are affected by delay? The rise in atmospheric emissions means that the costs of mitigation rise as well. A recent study by the MIT Joint Program on the Science and Policy of Global Change found that delaying the abatement policy would substantially increase the mitigation cost. To be specific they found that delaying the start of policy to 2030, as opposed to starting it in 2010, raises the mitigation costs in 2050 and 2100 by 52.0 percent and 26.4 percent, respectively.[9]

So how does uncertainty about both the costs and the benefits of climate change affect the choice between action and waiting. As William Nordhaus has put it:[10]

> The ranges of uncertainty for future emissions, concentrations, temperature, and damages are extremely large. However, this does not reduce the urgency of taking strong climate change policies *today*. When taking uncertainties into account, the desirable strength of policy (as measured by the social cost of carbon or the optimal carbon tax) would increase, not decrease.

The case for governments to act now comes through strongly even without complete knowledge.

Economic analysis also points out, that the risks of being wrong are clearly asymmetric. If it turns out in retrospect that the chosen policy controlled more emissions than ultimately necessary, current generations could bear a mildly larger-than-necessary control cost. On the other hand, if current generations act too timidly (less control than needed) and the problem turns out to be as serious as the predictions indicate, catastrophic and largely irreversible damage to the planet could be inflicted on future generations. Further we don't have to proceed in an unchanged manner. As we learn more over time, the targets can be adjusted. If they turn out, in the future to be too strict, they can be relaxed. If they turn out to be too weak, they can be tightened. Starting to act, however, is imperative.

Yohe et al. (2004) investigated both consequences of being wrong using a standard, well-respected global climate model. Their model investigates what happens when decision makers would choose global mitigation policies that would be in effect for 30 years, but after 30 years the policy makers would be able to modify the policies to take into account the better understanding of climate change consequences that would have been afforded by the intervening years. The specific source of uncertainty in their model results from our imperfect knowledge about the relationship between the atmospheric greenhouse gas concentrations and the resulting change in climate impacts. The specific question they examine is "What is the best strategy now?"

They found at that time that a hedging strategy that involved modest reductions dominated a "wait-and-see" strategy. Not only did current action initiate the capital turnover process and provide incentives for technical change, but also it allowed the avoidance of very costly and potentially irreversible mistakes later. That finding has turned out to be prescient. A number of economists, William Nordhaus included, now believe we have delayed so long that that it is now unlikely that nations can achieve the 2°C increase target that is referenced in international agreements, even if ambitious policies are introduced in the near term.

Having discussed the compelling nature of the evidence that action now is efficient, the question of "how much action?" remains. Theoretically the answer is easy. Just choose the efficient level of control. We know that has been achieved when the marginal cost of control becomes equal to the margin social damage. Unfortunately, as noted previously, the models are not sufficiently precise as to produce a universally accepted optimal level of control. In part this is due to the fact that while we know there are temperature thresholds (called tipping points), where the process could be abruptly accelerated, we don't know exactly where those thresholds lie.

As one way to handle that uncertainty the international community settled on an agreed-upon target of controlling emissions so as to prevent the increase of temperature from going beyond 2°C. Why that target? According to one observer, the international community concluded that if the temperature rise could be limited to an increase of 2°C, the benefits would likely be sufficient to offset the cost of the mitigation policy; if the temperature rose over 2°C, it would probably result in quicker, more unpredictable, and more dangerous climate response that could prove to be irreversible.

Once the temperature increase target was accepted, it was necessary to translate that temperature target into an emissions target, since emissions are the basis for defining specific mitigation actions. This was done in two steps: (1) figuring out the GHG concentration level in the atmosphere that would be consistent with staying within the temperature increase target and (2) deriving the amount of increased cumulative CO_2e emissions (called the carbon budget) that would be consistent with not exceeding that concentration. Keeping all nations collectively within that carbon budget would provide a ballpark estimate of what needed to be done.

Once the carbon budget was established negotiations among the countries could take place to craft an international agreement that lays out feasible pathways for mitigating emissions to a level consistent with that target, as well as a process for monitoring compliance with those pathways. These agreements need to be designed so that countries would not only be willing to join the agreement, but would continue to live up to their assigned responsibilities, once the agreement went into effect.

How can we systematically think about agreement designs that provide the appropriate incentives for countries not only to participate, but to comply? The challenge is particularly tricky because the outcomes are jointly determined. In other words the incentives for any country depend on the choices being made by the other involved countries. An area of economics known as game theory is helpful in identifying the forces affecting this class of negotiations and how those forces shape both the design of these agreements and the ultimate outcomes that could be achieved.

Game theory as a window on global climate negotiations

Game theory has been used to study the incentives in situations where participant outcomes are jointly determined. Outcomes are jointly determined when the payoff to any nation from its decision whether to participate in and comply with an international agreement or not depends not only on its decisions, but also on the decisions of other nations.

One particularly interesting strain of game theory investigates the conditions that support *self-enforcing agreements* (Barrett, 1994) – namely those where the incentives are sufficient to encourage both joining the agreement and, once a member, continuing to abide by the rules. Since no country can be forced to sign an international agreement, and signatories can always withdraw after signing, self-enforcing agreements are those where the incentives are most likely to create successful, stable coalitions.

A main difficulty in constructing self-enforcing agreements is the *free-rider* effect. Climate change involves a global pollutant and the effects of emissions reductions are a public good. In this case that means all nations receive the benefits of emissions reductions whether those nations contributed to those reductions or not. Individual nations therefore bear all of the costs of their reductions, but gain only a portion of the resulting benefits. This means the *private* marginal benefit for any nation's reduction effort is lower than the *social* marginal benefit, which is the sum of the marginal benefits received by all nations. Therefore when an individual nation reduces emissions until its *private* marginal cost of reduction is equal to its *private* marginal benefit, this private optimum results in too little reduction.

The Barrett model assumes that when a country joins the international agreement the other signatories respond by increasing their abatement levels, and hence reward the country for participating in the agreement; when a country withdraws, the remaining signatories reduce their abatement levels, and hence punish the country for withdrawing from the agreement. These punishments and rewards are credible, because the signatories always choose their abatement levels in order to maximize their collective net benefits. The questions of interest are: (1) under what conditions is a stable, successful coalition achieved? and (2) how well do these conditions fit the current climate negotiations?

The Barrett analysis finds that a stable successful agreement can only be achieved when the difference between the cooperative (where all nations actually cooperate so that *collective* net benefits are maximized) and noncooperative outcomes (where each nation simply acts independently in pursuit of its own self-interest) is small. Why? Unless the free-rider effect is small in this agreement it seriously undermines cooperation. Unfortunately, this analysis demonstrates that in precisely those cases where the gains from cooperation are greatest, the incentives for individual nations to become free-riders are also greatest, thereby inhibiting the formation of a stable successful agreement.

More recent work (Barrett, 2013) has focused on whether the existence of a catastrophe threshold (a tipping point) ups the ante sufficiently such that cooperation is more likely. This analysis finds that when the specifics of a climate catastrophe threshold are known with certainty and the benefits of avoiding catastrophe are high relative to the costs, self-enforcing treaties can coordinate countries' behavior so as to avoid the catastrophe. Where the net benefits of avoiding catastrophe are lower relative to the costs, however, agreements typically fail to avoid catastrophe; only modest cuts in emissions would be sustained. This analysis also finds that uncertainty about the magnitude of the temperature rise that would trigger the catastrophic threshold normally causes coordination to collapse as well. Since our understanding of the precise temperatures that trigger various tipping points is in fact limited, this is a concerning result.

Another game theory study (Jacquet, 2013), which relies on a lab experiment, reveals even more barriers to cooperation – the nature and timing of the payoffs to cooperation. At the start of this experiment, which is played with real money for ten rounds, each of six participants is allotted a fixed amount of money (40 euros) to invest in a climate account. Each round these players choose how much of their allotted money they want to put into the account.

At the end of ten rounds, if the climate account grows to 120 euros from the contributions made by the six players over the ten rounds, the participants in that game are deemed to have won their game (averted "dangerous climate change"). Each participant in a game that successfully averts dangerous climate change receives a bonus in addition to the money they each have left over after their contributions to the climate account. However, if after ten rounds the climate account ends up smaller than 120 euros, the participants in that game are deemed to have lost the game and they receive no bonus.

The game was played with three different sets of rules. The first treatment involved 10 groups, while the second and third involved 11. In the first scenario, where the earned bonus (45 euros) would be received the next day, 7 out of the ten groups averted dangerous climate change. In the second scenario, where the earned bonus (still 45 euros) would be received seven weeks later, only 4 of the 11 groups succeeded. In the final scenario, where the bonus was used to plant oak trees in order to sequester carbon, and thus provide the greatest benefit to future generations, none of the 11 groups reached the target. Apparently, the fact that payoffs from action on climate change occur with a lag is yet another factor that makes successful agreements harder to achieve and nations are more likely to participate if the bonuses accrue to them rather than use to enhance the global good.

In general these results are very discouraging because they suggest that under precisely the conditions currently prevailing in the climate policy arena, a close examination of the incentives facing nations seeking to form stable, effective agreements to mitigate greenhouse gases suggests that global cooperation is at best an elusive outcome.

Fortunately, the current climate arena also includes some more positive aspects of international cooperation that are not included in these models, but that suggest possibly more reliable pathways for success. One such area involves bringing the management of co-benefits, the benefits from a reduction in nontargeted pollutants that occurs as a result of the process of mitigating greenhouse gases. One important example is the reduction in adverse human health impacts from reduced particulate pollution when low- or no-carbon fuels are substituted for coal. Since all the health benefits from reducing the concentrations of these local pollutants are received by the mitigating nation, the free-rider effect does not come into play for that portion of the benefits. Co-benefits can add a powerful additional incentive for individual participants receiving those co-benefits to mitigate. Some argue that this can explain, for example, China's recent increased interest in reducing greenhouse gases.

Another strategy designed to improve the odds of a successful agreement involves "issue linkage" in which countries simultaneously negotiate a climate change agreement and a linked economic agreement. Typical candidates for linkage are agreements on trade liberalization, or cooperation on either research and development (R&D) or international debt. The intuition behind this approach is that some countries gain from resolving the first issue, while others gain from the second. Linking the two issues increases the chances that cooperation may result in mutual gain and, hence, increases the incentives of both parties to join and abide by the combined agreement.

To understand how this works, consider a research-and-development example from Cararro (2002). To counteract the incentive to free ride on the benefits from climate change, suppose only ratifiers of both agreements can share in the insights gained from research and development in the ratifying countries. The fact that this benefit can only be obtained by ratifying both the climate change agreement and the R&D agreement provides an incentive to ratify both since these benefits do not create a free-rider effect. Nations choosing not to ratify can be excluded from the research-and-development benefits; they would have to join the agreement to gain this benefit.

Another strategy for encouraging participation involves transfers from the gainers to the losers. Some countries have more to gain from an effective agreement than others. If the gainers were willing to share some of those gains with reluctant nations who have more to lose, the reluctant nations could be encouraged to join. Some interesting early work (Chandler and Tulkens, 1997) has shown that it is possible to define a specific set of transfers such that each country is better off participating than not participating. That is a powerful, comforting result, but has it proved to be a successful pathway for these agreements in practice?

In terms of operationalizing the concept of using transfers as an inducement to join the agreement, the Bali Climate Change Conference in 2007 established a funding mechanism for adaptation. It was established to finance specific adaptation projects and programs in developing countries that are parties to the Kyoto Protocol (www.adaptation-fund.org). Note that while this fund is directed toward adaptation, rather than mitigation, the fact that it is available only to parties to the agreement provides an incentive for potential holdouts to participate.

As a complementary measure, the Conference of Parties (COP) to the United Nations Framework Convention on Climate Change (UNFCCC) decided in 2010 to also establish the Green Climate Fund, which would raise significantly more funding than described in the previous paragraph. This fund is intended to provide support to developing countries as they limit or reduce their greenhouse gas emissions and as they adapt to the impacts of climate change, focusing especially on those developing countries that are particularly vulnerable to the adverse effects of climate change.[11] As of May 2019 some 102 proposals had been approved.

And, finally, choosing cost-effective policies can positively affect the level of participation. Since cost-effective policies reduce the cost, but not the benefits, of participation, those policies should make participation more likely by increasing the net benefits from joining the agreement.

How have all of these factors interacted in the process of seeking agreements? Historically, climate change agreements have been based upon a top-down approach where the goals and responsibilities were defined collectively by the agreement itself and imposed on participants. That was not producing the intended results because many of the world's countries, especially the developing countries, remained on the sidelines.

The Paris Accord, which was passed in December 2015 and went into force in October 2016, shifted to a more bottom-up approach. Each individual country was asked to define their own contribution, called a nationally determined contribution (NDC), to achieve the worldwide goal. The NDCs are not binding (enforceable) as a matter of international law.

After the Paris Accord was concluded, experts did the calculations to find out if the sum of all NDCs would be large enough to meet the temperature increase goals embodied in the agreement, assuming that all counties lived up to their commitments in their NDC. Not surprisingly, given what we have learned from game theory, the experts found that the sum of the NDCs would not be sufficient to keep global emissions within the temperature-increase targets. Additionally, soon after he won the 2016 U.S. presidential election, Donald Trump announced his intention to withdraw the United States from the Paris Accord. Apparently so far it seems that the public good effects outweigh the effects of co-benefits, linkages, and financial transfers.

The precedent: reducing ozone-depleting gases

Fortunately not all international agreements designed to manage global pollutant challenges have had such a dismal experience. Are there lessons to be learned from those earlier agreements? Perhaps. Consider the experience of the Montreal Protocol, which was designed to control ozone-depleting gases.

In the stratosphere, the portion of the atmosphere lying just above the troposphere, rather small amounts of ozone present have a crucial positive role to play in determining the quality of life on the planet. The ozone layer absorbs a portion of ultraviolet light called UVB. By absorbing the ultraviolet wavelengths, stratospheric ozone shields people, plants, and animals from harmful radiation, and by absorbing infrared radiation, it is a factor in determining the earth's climate.

Several chemical compounds involving bromine or chlorine can, when they enter the atmosphere, deplete the ozone layer. One major class of ozone-layer depleting chemicals is chlorofluorocarbons (CFCs. These chemical compounds were used as aerosol propellants and in cushioning foams, packaging, and insulating foams, industrial cleaning of metals and electronics components, food freezing, medical instrument sterilization, refrigeration for homes and food stores, and air-conditioning of automobiles and commercial buildings.

Responding to the ozone-depletion threat, an initial group of 24 nations signed the *Montreal Protocol* in September 1988. A subsequent series of new agreements generally broadened the number of covered substances and established specific schedules for phasing out their production and use. The Protocol now has 197 countries participating and resulted in the phase-out of 99 percent of nearly 100 ozone-depleting chemicals. In terms of reducing its target emissions the protocol is generally considered to have been a noteworthy success. The ozone layer is now expected to return to its pre-1980 levels no later than 2075.

How did this treaty avoid the free-rider pitfalls identified previously? One reason for the success of this approach was an early recognition of the need to solicit the active participation of developing countries. One component of the success in eliciting that participation resulted from offering later phaseout deadlines for developing countries. Another involved the creation of a *Multilateral Fund.*

In 1990 the parties agreed to establish the Multilateral Fund, which was designed to cover the incremental costs that developing countries incur as a result of taking action to eliminate the production and use of ozone-depleting chemicals. Contributions to the Multilateral Fund come from the industrialized countries. The fund has been replenished multiple times. As of April 2013, the contributions made to the Multilateral Fund by some 45 countries (including countries with economies in transition, or CEIT countries) totaled over U.S. $3.09 billion.

The fund promotes technical change and facilitates the transfer of more environmentally safe products, materials, and equipment to developing countries. Developing countries that have ratified the agreement have access to technical expertise, information on new replacement technologies, training and demonstration projects, and financial assistance for projects to eliminate the use of ozone-depleting substances.

The existence of the Multilateral Fund, however, does not deserve the bulk of the credit for the success of the Montreal Protocol. The success of ozone protection was possible in no small measure because producers were able to develop and commercialize alternatives to ozone-depleting chemicals. In many cases the companies that would be forced to stop producing ozone-depleting chemicals were the same companies that would produce the substitutes. Countries and producers ended the use of CFCs faster and cheaper than was originally anticipated due both to the availability of these substitutes and the fact that profit from their sale would offset any losses from stopping production of the ozone-depleting chemicals.

In retrospect we now know that one class of the substitutes, HFCs, had a detrimental side effect – it turned out to be a potent greenhouse gas. Although HFCs have a shorter residence time in the atmosphere than carbon dioxide, they turn out to be a much more powerful greenhouse gas on a pound for pound basis.

Responding to this challenge a deal to phase out HFCs was reached in Kigali, Rwanda, in October 2016. This agreement could on its own prevent a 0.5°C (0.9°F) rise in temperature by 2100 and, hence, be a healthy complement to the Paris Accord.

Summary

Economic analysis of the climate change problem not only defines the need for action, but also sheds light on effective forms that action might take. The empirical studies suggest that it makes sense to not only mitigate emissions, but to do it soon. Delay raises the costs of taking action.

Economics also sheds light on the barriers to effective participation in climate change agreements and some potential solutions as well. Game theory studies reveal that the free-rider effect is a significant barrier to participation as is the long horizon over which the effects of current polices are felt. Game theory studies with a broader scope, however, point out specific strategies (such as international transfers and issue linkage) that can be used to build stronger incentives for participation. Some international cost sharing is also likely to be a necessary ingredient in a successful attack on the climate problem as it was in the earlier ozone-depletion case.

The first global pollutant problem confronted by the international community arose when ozone-depleting gases were implicated in the destruction of the stratospheric ozone shield that protects the earth's surface from harmful ultraviolet radiation. Because these are accumulating pollutants, an efficient response to this problem involves reducing their emissions over time.

To restrict their accumulation in the atmosphere, the international agreements on ozone-depleting substances created a system of limits on production and consumption. Internationally, this system is considered a success in part because the Multilateral Fund and other incentives, such as delayed compliance deadlines, facilitated the participation of developing countries and in part because the losses imposed on producers of ozone-depleting chemicals when those chemicals were phased out were offset by the profits gained by many of the same producers as they produced and sold the substitutes.

Climate change is appropriately considered a more difficult problem. At the top of the list is the fact that in this case controlling greenhouse gases means controlling energy use from fossil fuels, the lynchpin of modern society. It is therefore perhaps not surprising that current international agreements on climate change that have been set up to efficiently manage the pending threats posed by climate change are falling well short of achieving outcomes that would be sufficient to meet the internationals targets.

Our knowledge is sufficient to know what we have to do to efficiently manage this challenge, but the political will is not yet sufficient to put the necessary policies in place.

Discussion question

1 What is your national, regional, or state government doing about climate change? Has it adopted a form of carbon pricing? If so, how is it working out? Is anyone working on an adaptation plan in your area?

Self-test exercise

1 "In negotiations over a public good such as a greenhouse gas emissions reduction, a cooperative agreement always produces higher aggregate benefits than a noncooperative agreement so cooperation will dominate noncooperation." Discuss.

Notes

1 Wuebbles, D.J., D.W. Fahey, K.A. Hibbard, B. DeAngelo, S. Doherty, K. Hayhoe, R. Horton, J.P. Kossin, P.C. Taylor, A.M. Waple, and C.P. Weaver. (2017). Executive summary. In: *Climate Science Special Report: Fourth National Climate Assessment*, Volume I, D.J. Wuebbles, D.W. Fahey, K.A. Hibbard, D.J. Dokken, B.C. Stewart, and T.K. Maycock (eds.). U.S. Global Change Research Program, Washington, DC, USA, pp. 12–34. doi: 10.7930/J0DJ5CTG.

2 See www.epa.gov/climateleadership/atmospheric-lifetime-and-global-warming-potential-defined.

3 See www.globalchange.gov/about for more details.

4 Wuebbles, D.J., D.W. Fahey, K.A. Hibbard, B. DeAngelo, S. Doherty, K. Hayhoe, R. Horton, J.P. Kossin, P.C. Taylor, A.M. Waple, & C.P. Weaver. (2017). Executive summary. In *Climate Science Special Report: Fourth National Climate Assessment*, Volume 1, D.J. Wuebbles, D.W. Fahey, K.A. Hibbard, D.J. Dokken, B.C. Stewart, & T.K. Maycock (eds.). Washington, DC, USA: U.S. Global Change Research Program, pp. 12–34. doi: 10.7930/J0DJ5CTG.

5 One of the most famous debates about the "correct" discount rates involved Nicholas Stern (who used a 1.40 percent rate) and William Nordhaus (who used a 4.30 percent rate). See Stern, N. (2007). *The Economics of Climate Change: The Stern Review*. Cambridge, UK: Cambridge University Press and Nordhaus, W.D. (2008). *A Question of Balance: Weighing the Options on Global Warming Policies*. New Haven, CT: Yale University Press.

6 World Bank, Ecofys and Vivid Economics. (2017). *State and Trends of Carbon Pricing 2017 (November)*. Washington, DC: World Bank. doi: 10.1596/978-1-4648-1218-7

7 See Table 3 in Nordhaus, William. (2018).

Projections and uncertainties about climate change in an era of minimal climate policies. *American Economic Journal: Economic Policy*, 10(3), 333–360. https://doi.org/10.1257/pol.20170046

8 Ram, M., D. Bogdanov, A. Aghahosseini, A. Gulagi, A.S. Oyewo, M. Child, U. Caldera, K. Sadovskaia, J. Farfan, L.S.N.S. Barbosa, M. Fasihi, S. Khalili, B. Dalheimer, G. Gruber, T. Traber, F. De Caluwe, H.-J. Fell, & C. Breyer. (2019). *Global Energy System Based on 100% Renewable Energy: Power, Heat, Transport and Desalination Sectors*. Study by Lappeenranta University of Technology and Energy Watch Group, Lappeenranta, Berlin, March.

9 Chen, Y.-H.H., M. Babiker, S. Paltsev, & H. Reilly. (2016). Costs of climate mitigation policies. MIT Joint Program on the Science and Policy of Climate Change Report 292. Available at: https://globalchange.mit.edu/publication/15766 (Accessed June 14, 2017).

10 Nordhaus, William. (2018). Projections and uncertainties about climate change in an era of minimal climate policies. *American Economic Journal: Economic Policy*, 10(3), 333–360. https://doi.org/10.1257/pol.20170046

11 How difficult these negotiations are can be illustrated by the fact that the magnitude of U.S. pledges to the Green Climate Fund was one example President Trump gave of the United State's unfair burden under the Paris Accord. Although the Green Climate Fund actually precedes the Paris Accords by about five years, it wasn't until 2013 that the GCF started its first round of fundraising.

Further reading

Barron Alexander, R., et al. (2018). Policy insights from the EMF 32 study on U.S. carbon tax scenarios. *Climate Change Economics*, 9(1), 1840003. doi: 10.1142/S2010007818400031. An exercise 32 (EMF 32) using 11 different models to assess emissions, energy, and economic outcomes from a plausible range of economy-wide carbon price policies to reduce carbon dioxide (CO_2) emissions in the United States.

Calvo, E., & Santiago, J. R. (2012). Dynamic models of international environmental agreements: A differential game approach. *International Review of Environmental and Resource Economics*, 6, 289–339. A survey of dynamic models of international environmental agreements.

Mendelsohn, R., Dinar, A., et al. (2006). The distributional impacts of climate change on rich and poor countries. *Environment and Development Economics*, 11, 159–178. This economic analysis concludes that poor countries will suffer the bulk of the damages from climate change, due primarily to their location.

Pizer, W., et al. (5 December, 2014). Using and improving the social cost of carbon. *Science*, 346(6214), 1189–1190. Examines the challenges faced in constructing the SCC, and proposes both an institutional process for regular SCC review and revision when used in government policy-making and how scientists might contribute to improved SCC estimates.

Stern, N. (2008). The economics of climate change. *American Economic Review*, 98(2), 1–37. As assessment by the former chief economist of the World Bank.

U.S. Environmental Protection Agency. (2016). *Climate Change Indicators in the United States*, 4th ed. EPA 430-R-16–004. Available at: www.epa.gov/climate-indicators. This report presents 37 indicators to help readers understand changes observed from long-term records related to the causes and effects of climate change, the significance of these changes, and their possible consequences for people, the environment, and society.

Additional references and other historically significant references are available on this book's eResource page: www.routledge.com/9781138587595

Chapter 9

Climate change II
The role of energy policy

If it ain't broke, don't fix it!

– Old Maine proverb

Introduction

Energy is one of our most critical resources; without it life would cease. We derive energy from the food we eat. Through photosynthesis, the plants we consume – both directly and indirectly when we eat meat – depend on energy from the sun. The materials we use to build our houses and produce the goods we consume are extracted from the earth's crust, and then transformed into finished products with expenditures of energy.

Currently, many industrialized countries depend on oil and natural gas for the majority of their energy needs. According to the International Energy Agency (IEA), these resources together supply 59 percent of all primary energy consumed worldwide. (Adding coal, another fossil fuel resource, increases the share to 86 percent of the total.) Fossil fuels are depletable, nonrecyclable sources of energy and when they are burned, they contribute CO_2 to the atmosphere, thereby contributing to climate change.

Since energy plays such a large role in contributing to both the productivity of the economy and to changing the climate, it is not surprising that energy policy is high on the policy agenda. Energy is a driving force in our economy and is likely to remain that way. How can we continue to use energy productively, while lowering energy's impact on the climate?

Two main paths forward suggest themselves: (1) improving energy efficiency and (2) fuel switching. Energy efficiency is sometimes defined as the amount of input energy required to provide a given service or output. Improving energy efficiency therefore involves lowering the amount of input energy to provide that service or output. For example an energy *in*efficient heating system in a home would require more fuel to keep the home at a comfortable temperature than an energy efficient heating system. Insulating a home, thereby retaining energy that would otherwise escape through leaky walls, can also improve a home's energy efficiency. Energy efficiency investments help to meet the climate challenge by lowering how much energy is needed per unit of output, thereby lowering emissions along with crafting a more efficient use of fuels.

Table 9.1 Carbon Content of Fuels: Pounds of CO_2 Emitted per Million Btu of Energy

Coal (anthracite)	228.6
Coal (bituminous)	205.7
Coal (lignite)	215.4
Coal (subbituminous)	214.3
Diesel fuel & heating oil	161.3
Gasoline	157.2
Propane	139.0
Natural gas	117.0

Source: Energy Information Administration. Retrieved from www.eia.gov/tools/faqs/faq.cfm?id=73&t=11. Last visited on January 28, 2017.

The second major pathway, fuel switching, starts from a recognition that some fuels contribute more to climate change risk than others. The most obvious way is when they are combusted to produce some specific type of useful energy (say producing electricity or powering your car). How much of a risk to climate change is posed by combustion of a particular fuel depends on the amount of carbon contained within that fuel. As can be seen from Table 9.1, among the fossil fuels, coal contains the most carbon per unit of energy produced and natural gas contains the least.

Combusting higher carbon fuels contributes more greenhouse gas emissions per unit of input energy than low-carbon fuels. It follows therefore that switching from high-carbon fuels to low-carbon fuels, all other things being equal, can lower emissions.

A less obvious way to lower emissions is curbing leakage from natural gas production and distribution. Natural gas is a naturally occurring hydrocarbon gas mixture consisting primarily of methane. Since methane is an especially powerful greenhouse gas, natural gas leakage intensifies the climate change risk. Leakage can occur from a well as gas is being recovered or from a pipeline used to distribute the gas to customers.

The role of fracking

Natural gas production remained relatively stable from the mid-1970s until the middle of the first decade of the twenty-first century, when a new technology dramatically changed the cost of accessing new sources of natural gas in shale, a type of sedimentary rock.[2] Hydraulic fracturing, or "fracking" as it is known popularly, combines horizontal drilling with an ability to fracture deep shale deposits using a mixture of high pressure water, sand, and chemicals. Not only does the fractured shale release large quantities of natural gas, but this extraction process also costs less than accessing more conventional sources.

The introduction of this new technology has increased production dramatically in the United States and fracked gas is likely to play an even larger role over the next few decades according to the Energy Information Agency, the statistical and data arm of the U.S. Department of Energy. If ever there were an example of the profound effect a technical change can have, this is it!

This new form of production has dramatically changed the energy situation in the United States, but that change comes with some controversy (see Debate 9.1).

DEBATE 9.1

Does the advent of fracking increase net benefits?

While fracking will no doubt lower U.S. dependency on energy imports (the subject of the next section) and provide an economic boost by lowering energy costs in the United States as it displaces more expensive fuels, it also comes with some costs. The main short-term concerns involve water contamination (fracking chemicals leaking into local wells), water depletion (the extraction process uses large quantities of water), air quality issues (some of the toxic fracking chemicals can escape into the surrounding air).

Methane leakage from wells and pipelines also directly adds to the climate threat and offsets some of the gains achieved by the fact that natural gas is a lower carbon fuel. Over the longer run, according to the International Energy Agency, an excessive reliance on natural gas would be incompatible with reaching proposed climate policy goals.

If fracking comes with high benefits and high costs, does it make economic sense? The simple answer is that we don't know yet. Even if a benefit-cost analysis could be revealing, many of the components of that analysis are not yet known with sufficient certainty to provide much confidence in the answers this early in the game. To take just one example of our ignorance, if the leakage rate exceeds 3.2 percent, natural gas is apparently no better for the climate than coal or oil. Unfortunately, we have a firm grasp on the leakage rate for only a few specially studied wells. Furthermore, the expected costs from the associated water and air contamination are not yet fully known either. Finally, even if we were able to derive a reasonable answer for the current period prior to much regulation, the answer is likely to be much more favorable to fracking once a regulatory framework to reduce the problems is in place.

Fortunately, studies are underway to fill in the information gaps and regulations that control the most negative net benefit aspects of the industry are likely to follow. Stay tuned.

Sources: Alvarez, R. A., Pacala, S. W., Winebrake, J. J., Chameides, W. L., & Hamburg, S. P. (2012). Greater focus needed on methane leakage from natural gas infrastructure. PNAS, 109, 176435–176440; Jackson, R. B., et al. 2013. The environmental costs and benefits of fracking. Annual Review of Environment and Resources, 39, 327–362.

On the surface the role of energy policy in managing the climate threat sounds simple enough – we just need to combine more energy efficiency with a transition to low-carbon fuels. Like many problems, however, the devil is in the details. In this chapter we shall take a close look at some of those details.

Fossil fuels: national security considerations

We begin by examining the question of the role of imports in an efficient energy policy. Vulnerable strategic imports such as oil have an added cost that is not reflected in the marketplace. National security is a classic public good. No individual corporate importer correctly represents our collective national security interests in making a decision on how much to import. Hence, leaving the determination of the appropriate balance between imports and domestic production to the market generally results in an excessive dependence on imports in terms of both climate change and national security considerations (see Figure 9.1).

In order to understand the interaction of these factors, five supply curves are relevant. Domestic supply is reflected by two options. The first, S_{d1}, is the long-run domestic supply curve without considering the climate change damages resulting from burning more oil, while the second, S_{d2}, is the domestic supply curve that includes these per-unit climate damages.

The upward slopes of these supply curves reflect increasing availability of domestic oil at higher prices, given sufficient time to develop those resources. Imported foreign oil is reflected by three supply curves: P_{w1} reflects the observed world price, P_{w2} includes a "vulnerability premium" in addition to the world price, and P_{w3} adds in the per-unit climate change damages due to consuming more imported oil. The vulnerability premium reflects the additional national security costs caused by imports. All three curves are drawn horizontally to the axis to reflect the assumption that any single importing country's action on imports is unlikely to affect the world price for oil.

As shown in Figure 9.1, in the absence of any correction for national security and climate change considerations, the market would generally demand and receive D units of oil. Of this total amount, A would be domestically produced and $D - A$ would be imported. Why?

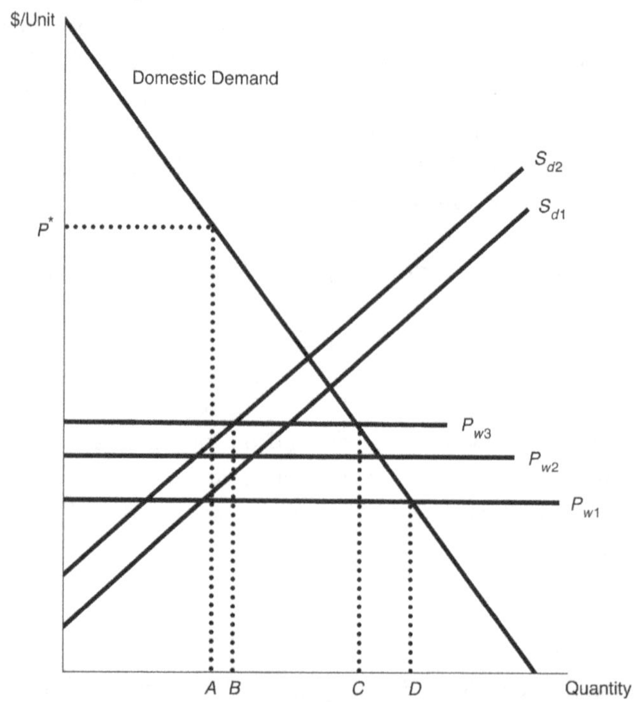

Figure 9.1 The National Security Problem

In an efficient allocation, incorporating the national security and climate change considerations, only C units would be consumed. Of these, B would be domestically produced and $C - B$ would be imported. Comparing these two outcomes, note that, because national security and climate change are externalities, the market in general tends to consume too much oil and vulnerable imports exceed their efficient level.

What would happen during an embargo? Be careful! At first glance, you would guess that we would consume where domestic supply equals domestic demand, but that is not right. Remember that S_{d1} is the domestic supply curve, *given enough time to develop the resources*. If an embargo hits, developing additional resources cannot happen immediately (multiple-year time lags are common). Therefore, in the short run, the supply curve becomes perfectly inelastic (vertical) at A. The price will rise to $P^{\star}$ to equate supply and demand. As the graph indicates, the loss in consumer surplus during an embargo can be very large indeed.

How can importing nations react to this inefficiency? As Debate 9.2 shows, several strategies are available.

The importing country might be able to become self-sufficient in energy, but should it? If Figure 9.2 adequately represents the situation, then the answer is clearly no. The net benefit from self-sufficiency (the allocation where domestic supply S_{d1} crosses the demand curve) is clearly lower than the net benefit from the efficient allocation (C).

DEBATE 9.2

How should countries deal with the vulnerability of imported oil?

Many countries import most of their oil. Since oil is a strategic material, how can the resulting vulnerability to import disruption be addressed?

One vision focuses on a strategy of increasing domestic production, not only of oil, but also of natural gas and coal. This vision includes opening up new oil fields in such places as coastal waters or public lands, as well as expanding the production of newer sources such as tar sands or oil shale. Tax incentives and subsidies could be used to promote domestic production.

Another vision emphasizes energy efficiency and transitioning to renewable resources. Pointing out that expanded domestic production of oil could exacerbate climate change as well as other environmental problems, this vision promotes such strategies as mandating standards for fuel economy in automobiles, enacting energy efficiency standards for appliances, and switching to more solar, wind and hydro sources of power.

Using economic analysis, figure out what the effects of these two different strategies would be on the implementing country with respect to (1) oil prices in the short run and the long run, (2) emissions affecting climate change, and (3) imports in the short run and the long run. What strategy or strategies would you like to see chosen by your country? Why?

Why, you might ask, would self-sufficiency be inefficient when embargoes obviously impose so much damage and self-sufficiency could grant immunity from this damage? Why would we want any imports at all when national security is at stake?

The simple answer is that the vulnerability premium is lower than the cost of becoming self-sufficient, but that response merely begs the question, "why is the vulnerability premium lower?" It is lower for three primary reasons: (1) embargoes are not certain events – they may never occur; (2) steps can be taken to reduce vulnerability of the remaining imports; and (3) expanding current domestic production via subsidies would lower the domestic amounts available to future users.

The expected damage caused by one or more embargoes depends on the likelihood of occurrence, as well as the intensity and duration. This means that the P_{w2} curve will be lower for imports having a lower likelihood of being embargoed. Imports from countries less hostile to our interests are more secure and the vulnerability premium on those imports is smaller.[4]

For any remaining vulnerable imports, certain contingency programs can be adopted to reduce the damage an embargo would cause. The most obvious measure is to develop a domestic stockpile of oil to be used during an embargo. The United States has taken this route. The stockpile, called the *strategic petroleum reserve,* was originally designed to contain 1 billion barrels of oil). A 1 billion-barrel stockpile could replace 3 million barrels a day for slightly less than 1 year or a larger number of barrels per day for a shorter period of time. This reserve could serve as a temporary alternative domestic source of supply, which, unlike other oil resources, could be rapidly deployed on short notice. It is, in short, a form of insurance. If this protection can be purchased cheaply, implying a low P_{w2}, imports become more attractive.

We have established the fact that government can reduce our vulnerability to imports, which tends to keep the risk premium as low as possible. Certainly for oil, however, even after the stockpile has been established, the risk premium is not zero; P_{w1} *and* P_{w2} will not coincide. Consequently, the government must also concern itself with achieving both the efficient level of consumption and the efficient share of that consumption borne by imports. Let's examine some of the policy choices.

As noted in Debate 9.2, energy conservation is one possible approach to the problem. One way to accomplish additional conservation is by means of a tax on fossil fuel consumption. Graphically, this approach would be reflected as a shift inward of the after-tax demand curve. Such a tax could reduce energy consumption and emissions of greenhouse gases to an efficient level. It could not, however, achieve the efficient share of imports, since the tax falls on *all* energy consumption, whereas the security problem involves only imports. While energy conservation may increase the net benefit, it cannot ever be the sole policy instrument used or an efficient allocation will not be attained.

Another strategy, the expansion of domestic supply, is already occurring due to fracking in places such as the Bakken Formation. According to the U.S. Geological Survey, one of the larger domestic discoveries in recent years of unconventional oil can be found in the Bakken and associated formations in Montana and North Dakota. Parts of these shale formations extend into the Canadian Provinces of Saskatchewan and Manitoba. The introduction of hydraulic fracturing technology to the region in 2008 caused a boom in production and a reduction in imports.

As Example 9.1 points out, however, even a local community that takes advantage of that boom can be in for a rocky ride if its economy depends exclusively or primarily on that single commodity.

Diagrammatically, the effect of the fracking induced expansion in domestic oil production would be portrayed in Figure 9.2 as a shift of the domestic supply curve to the right. Notice that one effect would be to reduce the share of imports in total consumption (an efficient result) and that is already happening. Net energy imports (imports minus exports) peaked in 2005. Since 2005, imports have declined while exports have increased (see Figure 9.2).

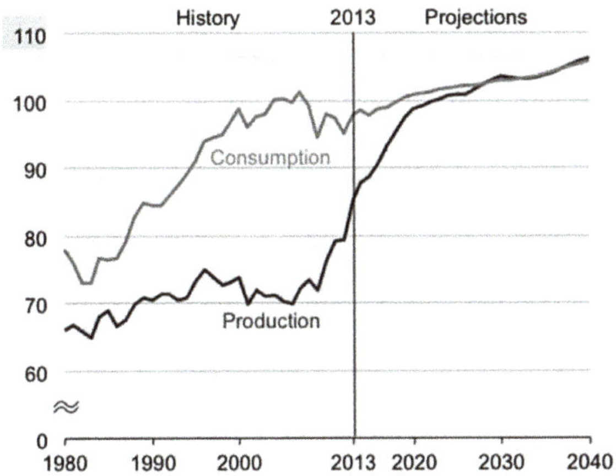

Figure 9.2 Total Energy Production and Consumption 1980–2040

Source: U.S. Energy Information Administration, Annual Energy Outlook 2015, p. 17

EXAMPLE 9.1

Fuel from shale: the Bakken experience

The boom in oil production made possible by fracking resulted in North Dakota becoming the most rapidly growing state in the nation. Population increased in response to rising wages and lots of retail activity and public infrastructure was built to accommodate the rising population.

Then in 2014 dropping oil prices (in part due to an oil glut resulting from increased production from domestic shale) reversed the process. As the prices fell, small rural towns were hit particularly hard.

Williston, North Dakota, for example, experienced job losses both in the oil industry and in the retail sectors built up to serve the influx of new workers. Not only did the population begin to decline, but the investments in public infrastructure made to accommodate the larger population become more difficult to finance. During the boom Williston had built a new $57 million high school, but declining economic activity caused by the lower prices caused a decline in the tax base needed to pay for that school.

Boom-and-bust cycles can be especially devastating to small, resource-dependent communities like Williston. With little diversification of their economic base they become especially vulnerable to swings in the prices of the resources on which they depend so heavily.

Sources: USGS releases new oil and gas assessment for Bakken and Three Forks formations. Retrieved from www2.usgs.gov/blogs/features/usgs_top_story/usgs-releases-new-oil-and-gas-assessment-for-bakken-and-three- forks-formations/; Hydraulic fracturing, www.epa.gov/hydraulicfracturing (accessed February 4, 2016); Oldham, Jennifer, & Philips, Matthew. (2016). The Bakken bust hits North Dakota hard (February 4), *www.bloomberg.com/news/articles/2016-02-04/the-bakken-bust-hits-north-dakota-hard* (accessed October 11, 2016); Millsap, Adam. (2016). What the boom and bust of Williston, North Dakota teaches us about the future of cities (June 7), *www.forbes.com/sites/adammillsap/2016/06/07/* williston-nd-and-the-rise-and-fall-of-american-cities/#66ae277a6c81 (accessed October 11, 2016).

The domestic supply expansion would, however, increase climate change emissions (an inefficient result). This strategy also tends to drain domestic reserves faster, which could make the nation more vulnerable in the long run (another inefficient result). The expansion of domestic fossil fuels reduces imports, but the lower prices and resulting increased consumption also tend to intensify the climate change problem.

A third approach would tailor the response more closely to the national security problem. One could use either a tariff on imports equal to the vertical distance between P_{w1} *and* P_{w2} or a quota on imports equal to $C - B$. With either of these approaches, the price to consumers would rise to P_1, total consumption would fall to C, and imports would be $C - B$. This achieves the appropriate balance between imports and domestic production (an efficient result), but it does not internalize the climate change cost from increasing domestic production (an inefficient result). As developed in more detail in the next chapter, imposing a separate price on carbon would be a necessary component of the package in order to internalize the climate externality.

Electricity: the evolving role for depletable resources

Most observers who think about energy futures see electricity as assuming an increasingly large role in the total energy picture. Evolving technologies for using electricity for both heating and cooling (heat pumps) and transportation (electric vehicles) figure importantly in this perspective.

What energy sources should be used to generate that electricity? While the industrialized world currently depends on conventional sources of oil, coal, and gas for most of our energy, over the long run, in terms of both climate change and national security issues, the obvious solution involves a transition to domestic renewable sources of energy that do not emit greenhouse gases. What role does that leave for depletable resources such as natural gas and uranium, which are currently used to generate a considerable amount of electricity?

Although some observers believe the transition to renewable sources of electricity will proceed so rapidly that using these fuels as a bridge will be unnecessary, many others believe that depletable fuels will continue to play a significant transition role for some time. In the United States, coal, previously a contender, has been losing out to natural gas, which is now cheaper. In 2018, the consumption of coal hit a four-decade low in the United States when a total of 19 coal-fired plants closed that year. That was one of the largest waves of such retirements in the single year.

Although other contenders do exist, the fuel other than natural gas receiving the most attention (and controversy) as a transition energy source is nuclear energy. Unfortunately nuclear has its own limitations – safety and economics.

With respect to safety, two sources of concern stand out: (1) nuclear accidents or sabotage, and (2) the storage of radioactive waste. Is the market able to make efficient decisions about the role of nuclear power in the energy mix? In both cases, the answer is no, given the current decision-making environment. Let's consider these issues one by one.

The production of electricity by nuclear reactors involves radioactive elements. If these elements escape into the atmosphere and come in contact with humans in sufficient concentrations, they can induce birth defects, cancer, or death. Although some radioactive elements may also escape during the normal operation of a plant, the greatest risk of nuclear power is posed by the threat of nuclear accidents or deliberate sabotage.

As the accident in Fukushima, Japan, in 2011 made clear, nuclear accidents could inject large doses of radioactivity into the environment. Unlike other types of electrical generation, nuclear processes continue to generate heat long after the reactor is turned off. This means that the nuclear fuel must be continuously cooled, or the heat levels will escalate beyond the design capacity of the reactor shield. If the high heat causes the reactor vessel to fracture, clouds of radioactive gases and particulates that are dangerous to human health will be released into the atmosphere.

An additional concern arises from the need to store nuclear wastes. The waste-storage issue relates to both ends of the nuclear fuel cycle – the disposal of uranium tailings from the mining process and spent fuel from the reactors – although the latter receives most of the publicity. Uranium tailings contain several elements, the most prominent being thorium-230, which decays with a half-life of 78,000 years to a radioactive, chemically inert gas, radon-222. Once formed, this gas has a very short half-life (38 days).

The spent fuel from nuclear reactors contains a variety of radioactive elements with quite different half-lives. In the first few centuries, the dominant contributors to radioactivity are fission products, principally strontium-90 and cesium-137. After approximately 1000 years, most of these elements will have decayed, leaving the transuranic elements, which have substantially longer half-lives. These remaining elements would remain a risk for up to 240,000 years. Thus, decisions made today affect not only the level of risk borne by the current generation – in the form of nuclear accidents – but also the level of risk borne by a host of succeeding generations (due to the longevity of radioactive risk from the disposal of spent fuel).

Nuclear power has also been beset by economic challenges. New nuclear power plant construction has become much more expensive than previously, in part due to the increasing regulatory requirements designed to provide a safer system.

The transition to lower carbon fuels has created some renewed interest in the nuclear option. The first new nuclear generator in the United States in 20 years entered commercial operation in Tennessee in 2016, a year in which globally nuclear power plants provided a bit over 11 percent of the world's electricity. The World Nuclear Association announced in 2016 that some 440 nuclear power reactors were operating in 31 countries and that over 60 power reactors were currently being constructed in 13 countries. China was constructing eight new reactors a year.

What future role nuclear power will play in other countries after Fukushima remains to be seen.

Electricity: transitioning to renewables

Ultimately, our energy needs will have to be fulfilled from renewable energy sources, either because the depletable energy sources have been exhausted or, as is more likely, the environmental costs of using the depletable sources have become so high that renewable sources will be cheaper.

Many of these renewable sources of energy, such as hydroelectric power, wind, photovoltaics, and ocean tidal power are used to generate electricity. These sources not only allow electricity generation to lower carbon emissions, but they are also renewable and hence sustainable.

Renewable energy comes in many different forms. Different sources will have different comparative advantages so, ultimately, a mix of sources will be necessary. The extent to which these sources will penetrate the market will depend upon their relative cost and consumer acceptance. New systems are usually initially less reliable and more expensive than old systems. Once they mature, reliability normally increases and cost declines; experience is a good teacher.

Since early producers and consumers – the pioneers – experience both lower reliability and higher costs, procrastination can be an optimal individual strategy. From an individual point of view, waiting until all the bugs have been worked out and costs come down reduces the risk of making the investment.

From a social point of view, however, if each producer and consumer procrastinates about switching, the industry will never be able to reach a sufficient scale of operation and will not be able to gain enough experience to reach the level of reliability and lower cost that will be necessary to reach the specified renewable goals. How can these initial barriers be overcome?

One strategy involves establishing specific renewable resource goals with deadlines for meeting them. For example, the original EU Renewable Resource Directive, which establishes an overall policy for the production and promotion of energy from renewable sources in the EU, requires at least 20 percent of its total energy needs be filled by renewables by 2020. In addition, under the directive all EU countries must also ensure that at least 10 percent of their transport fuels come from renewable sources by 2020.

More recently, EU countries have agreed on strengthening their initial renewable target to assure that at least 27 percent of final energy consumption is met from renewables in the EU as a whole by 2030. One of the expanding sources is offshore wind. In June 2017 Germany, Denmark, and Belgium backed a pledge to install 60 gigawatts of new offshore wind power next decade, more than five times the world's existing capacity.

Another strategy subsidizes pioneer investments via the tax code. This is commonly done, for example, with production or investment tax credits. Once the market is sufficiently large that it can begin to take advantage of economies of scale and overcome the initial sources of unreliability, the subsidies could be eliminated.

Another common policy approach for overcoming these obstacles involves combining Renewable Portfolio Standards (RPS) for electricity generation with Renewable Energy Credits (RECs). Renewable portfolio standards stipulate a minimum percentage of the total electricity generated by each generator that must come from specified renewable sources such as wind, hydro, or solar. The generating entity can either meet that standard directly by generating the requisite proportion from the specified renewable sources, or indirectly by purchasing renewable energy credits from independent generators.

An independent generator that produces electricity from a specified renewable source actually produces two saleable commodities. The first is the electricity itself, which can be sold to the grid, while the second is the renewable energy credit that turns the environmental attributes (such as the fact that it was created by a qualifying renewable source) into a legally recognized form of property that can be sold separately. Generally, renewable generators create one REC for every 1,000 kilowatt-hours (or, equivalently, 1 megawatt-hour) of electricity placed on the grid.

Providing this form of flexibility in how compliance with the RPS is achieved lowers the compliance cost, not only in the short run (by allowing the RECs to flow to the areas of highest need) but also in the long run (by making renewable source generation more profitable in areas not under an RPS mandate than it would otherwise be). By 2013 some 29 states and the District of Columbia had a renewable portfolio standard, with seven more having non-binding goals. Many of those also had REC programs.

How cost-effective have these polices been? Example 9.2 discusses a study that looks specifically at that question.

EXAMPLE 9.2

The relative cost-effectiveness of renewable energy policies in the United States

The United States depends on both renewable portfolio standards, and a suite of production and investment tax credits to promote renewable resources that reduce carbon emissions. A completely different approach, one that puts a price directly on those emissions, is used to directly reduce carbon emissions. How cost-effective are these policies targeted exclusively on promoting renewable resources?

Using a highly detailed model of regional and interregional electricity markets Palmer et al. (2011) examine this question over a time horizon covering the period from 2010 to 2035. The analysis evaluates each of these policy approaches in terms of their relative effectiveness and cost-effectiveness in reducing carbon emissions, their effectiveness in promoting renewable resource electricity generation, and their effects on electricity prices.

Between these two renewable resource policies the tax credit was found to be the least cost-effective, with the renewable portfolio somewhat better. Because it involves a subsidy and the other polices do not, the tax credit leads to relatively lower electricity prices. These lower prices promote greater electricity consumption and hence relatively larger emissions. This offsetting increase in emissions diminishes the tax credit's cost-effectiveness.

However the best policy turned out to be the third, a particular form of carbon pricing. As we shall see in more detail in the next chapter, carbon pricing creates very cost-effective incentives for emissions reduction. Additionally it is the only policy considered in this study that increases the relative cost of using *nonrenewable* higher carbon sources. Neither the tax credit nor the renewable portfolio standard discourages the use of high-carbon nonrenewable technologies at all; they apply only to renewable sources.

Source: Palmer, K., Paul, A., Woerman, M., & Steinberg. D. C. (2011). Federal policies for renewable electricity: Impacts and interactions. *Energy Policy*, 39(7), 3975–3991.

Another quite different approach to promoting the use of renewable resources in the generation of electric power is known as a *feed-in tariff*. Used more commonly in Europe than in the U. S., a feed-in tariff specifies the prices received by anyone who installs qualified renewable generation capacity that sells electricity to the grid. The level of these prices (typically determined in advance by the rules of the program) is based upon the costs of supplying the power. Specifically they are set sufficiently high so as to assure installers that they will receive a reasonable rate of return on their investment. While in Germany this incentive payment is guaranteed for 20 years for each installed facility, each year the magnitude of the payment for each cohort of newly constructed generators is reduced (typically in the neighborhood of 1–2 percent per year) in order to reflect expected technological improvements and economies of scale.

A feed-in tariff actually offers two different incentives: (1) it provides a price high enough to promote the desired investment and (2) it guarantees the stability of that price over time rather than forcing investors to face the market uncertainties associated with fluctuating fossil fuel prices or subsidies that come and go.

Of course, when higher prices are paid to renewable investors, these costs must be borne by someone. In Germany the higher costs associated with the feed-in tariffs were typically passed along to electricity ratepayers. German electricity rates have been, as a result, relatively high. In principle these higher costs should be temporary, since rising fossil fuel costs would be expected to rise above the relatively stable prices dictated by feed-in tariffs. Time will tell. Stay tuned.

Spain took a different approach that produced different results. It refused to allow its electric utilities to pass on the increased cost of electricity resulting from the feed-in tariffs to consumers. As a result, its electricity system's financial deficit became unsustainable, and in 2013 Spain halted new feed-in tariff contracts for renewable energy.

As we have seen so often in other policy circumstances, the implementation details matter.

Electricity: storage and targeted distributed energy

One downside of renewable resources such as solar or wind is that they supply power intermittently. The sun does not shine at night and the wind does not always blow. The secret of matching the availability of the electrical power to the need for it both seasonally and diurnally is being able to store electricity in surplus times and draw upon it in deficit times. A wide variety of storage means exist from batteries to pumped storage. Fortunately the cost of electricity from batteries has decreased by 76 percent from 2012 to 2018, making renewable energy combined with battery storage increasingly competitive with coal and gas generation.[1]

Pumped hydroelectric storage facilities store energy in the form of water in an upper reservoir, pumped from another reservoir at a lower elevation. During periods of high electricity demand, power is generated by releasing the stored water through turbines in the same manner as a conventional hydropower station. During periods of low demand (usually nights or weekends when electricity is also lower cost), the upper reservoir is resupplied by using lower-cost electricity from the grid to pump the water back to it. Pumped storage hydroelectric projects have been providing energy storage capacity and transmission grid ancillary benefits in the United States and Europe since the 1920s.

One desirable characteristic of distributed energy sources, such as solar, wind, or even energy efficiency, is that they can be located near users. Contrast this with large power plants, which are centrally located. By locating close to users, distributed energy sources can lower the distance (and hence the cost) of transporting electricity from source to user.

Could targeting these distributed sources at areas facing transmission constraints eliminate the expense of building new transmission lines and hence be a cost-effective component in the energy mix needed by that region? As Example 9.3 points out, in the right circumstances, it can.

EXAMPLE 9.3

Thinking about cost reduction outside of the box: the Boothbay pilot project

The Boothbay Harbor region, a popular summer tourist destination on the Maine coast at the end of a peninsula, has a problem. The existing electricity transmission line serving the area does not have the capacity to handle its large and growing summer electrical demand. The traditional response, upgrading the transmission line, would be very expensive. Could the problem be solved at lower cost in another way?

The Maine Public Utilities Commission decided to discover whether non-transmission alternatives (NTAs) – such as distributed generation, efficiency, storage, and new smart grid technologies – could solve electric grid reliability needs at lower cost and with less pollution than new transmission lines or transmission system upgrades. In 2012, the Commission established the Boothbay Smart Grid Reliability Pilot project to test the NTA hypothesis. In its first 3-year initial phase, the Boothbay Pilot sought to provide experienced-based evidence on whether a portfolio of NTAs could reduce electricity load under peak conditions on specific transmission assets in the Boothbay subregion of Central Maine by 2 megawatts (MW), thereby avoiding an estimated $18 million transmission line rebuild.

What did the pilot project show? Based upon the results for the initial phase of this project the evidence suggests that the net cost of the accepted NTAs, together with administrative and operational expenses, is projected to be less than 33 percent of the cost of building a new transmission line and would save ratepayers approximately $18.7 million (including energy savings) over the 10-year project life through 2025.

These results suggest that targeting an integrated package of distributed solutions at those geographic areas facing transmission constraints can produce grid benefits well beyond the direct services they provide to individual customers.

Source: Grid Solar LLC, Final report: Boothbay Sub-Region Smart Grid Reliability Pilot Project (January 19, 2016).

Another new niche for distributed energy sources is to supply remote areas (in developing countries, for example) that previously have never had access to the electrical grid. As Example 9.4 points out, townships in Africa are using solar microgrids and novel, technology-based financing models to supply these remote areas.

EXAMPLE 9.4

The economics of solar microgrids in Kenya

Entrepreneurs are constructing solar photovoltaic microgrids in remote rural areas of Kenya. Microgrids in Kenya are small electricity generation and distribution systems that can operate independently of larger grids. Due to their small scale they typically cannot supply electricity as cheaply as the larger grid, but for remote areas that do not have access to the larger grid, the electricity from solar microgrids is typically cheaper than the other local energy alternatives such as producing electricity via diesel generators.

Installing these microgrids requires capital investment and these villages are typically poor and do not have access to this capital. How do they get around this significant barrier? Entrepreneurs supply the capital, own the solar panels, and sell the electricity to local homes and businesses. The product is electricity, not panel installation.

In one financial model, cloud-based software keeps track of consumption and payments via smart meters. The smart meters measure and control power to each customer in town by communicating remotely with payments software. Although power is cut off when the prepaid credit is exhausted, customers can top up their credit whenever they wish, in amounts as small as a few cents.

One problem is that the greatest demand for power is at night when the sun is not shining, but that problem is overcome with battery storage units that typically hold up to 24 hours of electrical consumption. Storage adds to the cost, but the cost increase apparently is not enough to eliminate the economic advantages of the microgrid to local residents or the profitability to the entrepreneurs. Analysis at the Lawrence Berkeley National Lab suggests that wind and solar can now be economically and environmentally competitive for a large portion of Africa.

Sources: Pearce, Fred. (2015). African lights: Solar microgrids bring power to Kenyan villages (October 27) Yale Environment 360. Available at: http://e360.yale.edu/features/african_lights_microgrids_are_bringing_power_to_rural_kenya; Lawrence Berkeley National Laboratory. (2017). The economic case for wind, solar energy in Africa. *ScienceDaily* (March 27). Available at: www.sciencedaily.com/releases/2017/03/170327172829.htm.

Energy efficiency

As the world grapples with creating the right energy portfolio for the future, energy-efficiency policy is playing an increasingly complementary role. In recent years the amount of both private and public money being dedicated to promoting energy efficiency has increased a great deal, in no small part due to its ability to reduce emissions and save money at the same time.

The role for energy efficiency in the broader mix of energy polices depends, of course, on how large the opportunity is. Estimating the remaining potential is not a precise science, but the conclusion that significant opportunities remain seems inescapable

The existence of these opportunities can be thought of as a necessary, but not sufficient, condition for government intervention. Depending upon the level of energy prices and the discount rate, the economic return on these investments could be too low to justify intervention. In that case the costs of the policy intervention would exceed any gains that would result.

The strongest case for government intervention flows from the existence of externalities. Markets are not likely to internalize these external costs on their own. The natural security and climate change externalities mentioned in the previous chapter, as well as other external co-benefits such as community health effects from reducing health-impairing pollution imply that the market undervalues investments in energy efficiency; the persons making those investments can capture only a portion of the total benefits.

The analysis provided by economic research in this area, however, makes it clear that the case for policy intervention extends well beyond externalities. Internalizing externalities is a very important, but incomplete, motivator for a policy response.

Consider just a few of the other foundations for policy intervention. Inadequately informed consumers can impede rational choice, as can a limited access to capital (preventing paying the up-front costs for the more energy-efficient choice even when the resulting energy savings would justify the additional expense in present value terms). As Example 9.5 points out, however, on-bill financing coupled with monthly energy savings that exceed the cost of the efficiency investments means that the consumers save money.

EXAMPLE 9.5

On-bill financing in Hawaii: solving the up-front cost problem

On April 8, 2019 Hawaii announced its Green Energy Money $aver (GEM$) on-bill financing program, a statewide initiative to make clean energy more affordable for homes and small businesses. This program provides easy-access financing for cost-effective energy efficiency upgrades as well as for rooftop solar panels and other renewable distributed energy systems. Most importantly, on-bill financing can save participants money immediately by approving only cash-flow positive projects, those that provide average savings that exceed the cost of the monthly repayments.

Under this system the investment in clean energy is conveniently repaid through a line item on the participant's monthly electric bill, **with no upfront costs**. Since a good history of utility bill payment is sufficient, credit checks are unnecessary. Because the investment is tied to the utility meter (rather than to an individual), both the financing and the energy savings can easily be transferred from one participant to another (as homes are sold, for example). This enables longer repayment periods, which, along with cost-effective investments, allows a cash-flow positive outcome.

Source: https://www.eesi.org/articles/view/a-closer-look-at-hawaiis-innovative-financing-model-for-green-energy-investments.

Could policies to increase energy efficiency (such as subsidizing the cost of weatherizing your home) trigger offsetting responses that actually end up undermining their effectiveness? As Example 9.6 points out that is a distinct possibility.

EXAMPLE 9.6

Energy efficiency: rebound and backfire effects

Energy efficiency policies can trigger offsetting feedbacks that lower their effectiveness. The literature distinguishes two possible outcomes – the rebound effect and the backfire effect.

Consider an example. A weatherization subsidy could provide an incentive to lower both the amount and cost of energy needed to heat or cool the space in your home. If temperatures in the home were unaffected by this investment, no rebound effect would occur. Suppose a homeowner, however, responds to that lower cost by turning up (or down) the thermostat to provide a warmer (or cooler) ambiance than before? Any *increased* energy consumed in response to its lower cost is known as a rebound effect. Its counterpart, the backfire effect, occurs when the rebound effect is so large that a weatherization subsidy actually causes an increased amount of energy consumed; the increase in energy from the change in temperature is larger than the savings from lowering the amount of energy needed to maintain the same temperature.

What is the evidence on the existence and magnitude of these effects? A review of the studies seeking to answer this question finds "that the existing literature does not support claims that energy efficiency gains will be reversed by the rebound effect" (Gillingham et al., 2016, p. 85). In other words the existing literature provides little, if any, support for a backfire effect. It does, however, find evidence of rebound effects that can, depending upon the context, range as high as 60 percent.

What does this imply for the effectiveness of energy efficiency policy? The authors conclude that this evidence does imply that energy efficiency policies may be less effective in reducing energy (and reducing carbon emissions) than generally thought, since rebound effects can offset to some degree the direct energy-reducing effects of the policy.

They also, however, note that the welfare effects of the rebound effects are ambiguous. The rebound effect results in an offsetting increase in damaging climate change impacts, but it raises the consumer net benefits of having more comfortable homes. The existing literature does not provide answers as to which is larger.

Source: Gillingham, Kenneth, Rapson, David, & Wagner, Gernot. (2016). The rebound effect and energy efficiency policy. *Review of Environmental Economics and Policy*, *10*(1) (Winter), 68–88.

Promoting energy efficient vehicles – the U.S. approach

Since transportation emissions are a large and growing portion of total carbon emissions, can energy efficiency investments pay off in this arena as well? The Corporate Average Fuel Economy (CAFE) program, established in the United States in1975, was designed at that time primarily to reduce American dependence on foreign oil by producing more fuel-efficient vehicles. It was later expanded to be a way of reducing vehicular carbon emissions

The program requires each automaker to meet government-set miles-per-gallon targets (CAFE standards) for all its car and light truck fleets sold in the United States each year. The unique feature is that the standard is a fleet average, not a standard applied to each vehicle. As a result, automakers can sell some low-gas mileage vehicles as long as they sell enough high-gas mileage vehicles to raise the average to the standard. The CAFE standards took effect in 1978, mandating a fleet average of 18 miles per gallon (mpg) for automobiles. The standard increased each year until 1985, when it reached 27.5 mpg. Most observers believe that the CAFE standards did, in fact, reduce oil imports. During the 1977–1986 period, oil imports fell from 47 to 27 percent of total oil consumption. The CAFE standard remained at 27.5 mpg until 2005 when a new set of rules was announced.

CAFE standards, however, have had their share of problems. When Congress instituted the CAFE standards, light trucks were allowed to meet a less stringent fuel-economy standard because they constituted only 20 percent of the vehicle market and were used primarily as work vehicles. Light truck standards were set at 17.2 mpg for the 1979 model year and went up to 20.7 mpg in 1996 (combined two-wheel and four-wheel drive). With the burgeoning popularity of SUVs, which are counted as light trucks, trucks now comprise nearly half of the market. In addition, intense lobbying by the auto industry resulted in an inability of Congress to raise the standards from 1985 until 2004. As a result of the less stringent standards for trucks and SUVs, the absence of any offsetting increase in the fuel tax, and the increasing importance of trucks and SUVs in the fleet of on-road vehicles, the average miles per gallon for all vehicles declined, rather than improved. In 2005 the standard for light trucks saw its first increase since 1996 to 21 miles per gallon.

Rules passed during the Obama administration called for a fleetwide fuel-efficiency average of 46.7 miles per gallon by 2026.

In 2018 President Trump moved not only to roll back these higher standards, but also to strip California of its special authority to set its own fuel economy levels for autos. Under this plan cars and light-duty trucks will only have to average about 37 mpg by 2026, rather than the Obama targets. The policy debate continues.

Since new fuel economy standards only affect new vehicles, overall fuel economy for the entire transportation fleet takes a long time to improve – up to 15 years or until all the older cars are off the roads. This, combined with a vehicular "rebound effect," (better fuel economy increases miles driven), raises the question of how fuel taxation and fuel economy standards differ in their impacts. See Debate 9.3.

DEBATE 9.3

Comparing CAFE Standards with Fuel Taxes

Increasing the fuel efficiency of oil consumption could, in principle, be accomplished by increasing either fuel taxes or fuel-efficiency standards. By raising the cost of driving, the former would encourage auto purchasers to seek more fuel-efficient vehicles, while the latter would ensure that the average new vehicle sold was fuel efficient. Does it make a difference which strategy is followed?

It turns out that it does, and economics can help explain why. Think about what each strategy does to the marginal cost of driving an extra mile. Increased fuel taxes raise the marginal cost per mile driven, but fuel-economy standards lower it. In the first case, the marginal cost per mile rises because the tax raises the cost of the fuel. In the second case, the more fuel-efficient cars use less fuel per mile so the cost has gone down.

Following economic logic leads immediately to the conclusion that even if both strategies resulted in the same fuel economy, the tax would reduce oil consumption by more because it would promote fewer miles driven. On these grounds, a tax is better than a fuel-economy standard.

Austin and Dinan (2005) test these ideas with a simulation model in which they compare an increase in the CAFE standards to a gasoline tax designed to save the same amount of gasoline. Using a 12 percent discount rate, they estimate that a per gallon tax designed to save the same amount of gasoline as a stipulated fuel economy standard would cost 71 percent less than the comparable change in fuel-economy standards!

Supporters of fuel-economy standards, however, counter with two arguments: (1) in the United States, sufficiently high gasoline taxes to produce that level of reduction could never have passed Congress, so the fuel-economy standards were better, indeed much better, than no policy at all, and (2) at least one careful empirical study has found that the increase in driving resulting from the fuel economy standards in practice is likely to be very small, and may even be nonexistent. This latter finding implies that studies like the one discussed previously are likely to considerably overstate the cost-effectiveness advantage of a gasoline tax. Can you see why?

Sources: Austin, D., & Dinan, T. (2005). Clearing the air: The costs and consequences of higher CAFE standards and increased gasoline taxes. Journal of Environmental Economics and Management, 50, 562–582; West, Jeremy, Hoekstra, Mark, Meer, Jonathan, & Puller, Steven L. (May 2015). Vehicle miles (not) traveled: Why fuel economy requirements don't increase household driving. National Bureau of Economic Research Working Paper #21194.

Fuel economy standards in the European Union

The European Union (EU) has tackled the externalities from fuel consumption primarily through gas taxes and has some of the highest gas taxes in the world. Fuel economy standards are also higher than in the United States. The European Union standards are set to rise annually from the 2012 standard of 45 miles per gallon (5L/100 km). They also have a carbon dioxide target of 130 grams per kilometer. The European Union also combines standards with very high fuel taxes, which creates a larger demand for small cars (Anderson et al., 2011). EU countries also tax diesel at lower rates than gasoline and as such diesel's share of passenger cars has grown significantly. The Netherlands, Norway, Germany, and Sweden used differential tax rates to encourage consumers to purchase (and manufacturers to produce) low-emitting cars before subsequent regulations required all cars to be low emitting. Tax differentiation confers a tax advantage (and, hence, after-tax price advantage) on cleaner cars. The amount of the tax usually depends on (1) the emissions characteristics of the car (heavier taxes being levied on heavily polluting cars), (2) the size of the car (in Germany, heavier cars qualify for larger tax advantages to offset the relatively high control requirements placed upon them), and (3) the year of purchase (the tax differential is declining since all cars will eventually have to meet the standards).

Additionally Europe not only has much higher gasoline prices, but also it has developed strategies to make better use of transportation capital. Its intercity rail system is better developed than the one in the United States, and public transit ridership is typically higher within cities. Context does matter.

Summary

Dimensions of the energy problem, such as climate change and national security, suggest the need for some government role. Insecure foreign sources require policies such as tariffs and strategic reserves to reduce vulnerability and to balance the true costs of imported and domestic sources. In addition, government must ensure that the costs of energy fully reflect not only the potentially large environmental costs, including climate change, but also the national security costs associated with a dependence on foreign sources of energy.

Economic analysis reveals that no single strategy is sufficient to solve the national security and climate change problems simultaneously. Subsidizing domestic supply, for example, would reduce the share of imports in total consumption (an efficient result), but it would reduce neither consumption nor climate change emissions (inefficient results). On the other hand, energy conservation (promoted by a tax on energy consumption, for example) would reduce energy consumption and the associated emissions (efficient outcomes) but would not achieve the efficient share of imports (an inefficient result) since an energy tax falls on *all* energy consumption, whereas the national security problem involves only imports. An energy tax also would fail to produce a fully efficient resolution for climate impacts since it would focus on energy per se, not the actual emissions emitted by that energy use, a factor that varies widely among fuels. A carbon tax, not an energy tax, would be needed to make this kind of distinction among fuels.

Given the environmental difficulties with all of the depletable transition fuels (tar sands, fracked oil and gas, as well as coal and uranium), energy efficiency and the promotion of renewable sources of energy are now playing (and will presumably continue to play) a larger role.

Renewable energy sources have the advantages that they are sustainable and, as distributed technologies, they can be located closer to consumers, thereby saving transmission and distribution costs. On the other hand they are intermittent sources which means that the peak generation times will not automatically not coincide with periods of peak demand. The solution to this diurnal and seasonal mismatch is increasingly depending on developing a complementary storage capacity. Fortunately battery storage, a major component of this capacity, is experiencing falling prices as the technology advances.

The menu of energy options as the economy transitions to renewable sources offers a large number of choices. It is far from clear what the ultimate mix will turn out to be, but it is very clear that government policy is a necessary ingredient in any smooth transition to a sustainable-energy future. Since many of the most important costs of energy use are externalities, an efficient transition to these renewable sources will not occur unless the playing field is leveled by internalizing the externalities, especially those associated with carbon emissions. The potential for an efficient and sustainable allocation of energy resources by our economic and political institutions clearly exists, even if historically it has not always been achieved.

Discussion questions

1 Should benefit-cost analysis play the dominant role, a complementary role, or no role in deciding the proportion of electric energy to be supplied by nuclear power? Why or why not?

2 Economist Abba Lerner once proposed a tariff on oil imports equal to 100 percent of the import price. This tariff is designed to reduce dependence on foreign sources as well as to discourage OPEC from raising prices (since, due to the tariff, the delivered price would rise twice as much as the OPEC increase, causing a large subsequent reduction in consumption). Should this proposal become public policy? Why or why not?

3 Does the fact that the strategic petroleum reserve has never been used to offset shortfalls caused by an embargo mean that the money spent in creating the reserve has been wasted? Why or why not?

Self-test exercises

1 Some time ago, a conflict between a paper company and a coalition of environmental groups arose over the potential use of a Maine river for hydroelectric power generation. As one aspect of its case for developing the dam, the paper company argued that without hydroelectric power the energy cost of operating some specific paper machines would be so high that they would have to be shut down. Environmental groups countered that the energy cost was estimated to be too high by the paper company because it was assigning all of the high-cost (oil-fired) power to these particular machines. That was seen as inappropriate because all machines were connected to the same electrical grid and therefore drew power from all sources, not merely the high-cost sources. They suggested, therefore, that the appropriate cost to assign to the machines was the much lower average cost. Revenue from these machines was expected to be sufficient to cover this average cost. Who was right?

2 Peaking plants, those that are only called into service during times of peak demand, are typically cheaper to build (compared to base-load plants, which operate all of the time), but have relatively high operating costs. Explain why it makes sense for utilities to use this lower-capital, high-operating-cost type of plant for peaking and the high-capital, lower-operating-cost type of plant for base load.

3 Explain why the existence of a renewable energy credit market would lower the compliance costs for utilities forced to meet a renewable portfolio standard.

4 Using Figure 9.1, show how the level of oil imports and the price level would be affected if the country represented in that figure acted to internalize national security issues, but ignored climate change impacts.

5 a Some new technologies, such as LED light bulbs, have the characteristic that they cost more to purchase than more conventional incandescent alternatives, but they save energy. How could you use the present value criterion to decide how cost-effective these new technologies are? What information would you need to do the calculations? How would the calculations be structured? How would you use the results of these calculations to decide on their cost-effectiveness?

b Some typical monthly electrical bills have two components: (1) a fixed monthly change (e.g., \$10 a month) and (2) a usage component (e.g., \$0.14 per kilowatt-hour consumed). If a utility is planning to raise the amount they charge customers for electricity, would you expect that increase to discourage, encourage, or have no effect on the demand for LED light bulbs? Does it depend on which component they change? Why or why not?

6 Electric heat pumps are technologies that in the right circumstances can be cost-effective sources of heating. In a cold climate they frequently complement more typical energy sources such as oil or natural gas boilers in order to reduce total energy costs. In order to be cost-effective, however, the savings on oil and natural gas from using the heat pumps must be large enough to justify both their initial costs and the subsequent cost of the additional electricity to run them. Would you expect the number of heat pump sales to be affected by the magnitude of local interest rates? Why or why not?

Note

1 www.utilitydive.com/news/electricity-costs-from-battery-storage-down-76-since-2012-bnef/551337/

Further reading

Anthoff, D., & Hahn, R. (2010). Government failure and market failure: On the inefficiency of environmental and energy policy. *Oxford Review of Economic Policy*, 26(2), 197–224. A selective survey of the literature to highlight what is known about the efficiency of particular kinds of policies, laws, and regulations in managing energy and environmental risk.

Gillingham, K., Newell, R. G., & Palmer, K. (2009). Energy efficiency economics and policy. *Annual Review of Resource Economics*, 1, 597–620. Reviews economic concepts underlying decision-making in energy efficiency and conservation and the related empirical literature.

Gillingham, K., Rapsony, D., & Wagner, G. (2016). The rebound effect and energy efficiency policy. *Review of Environmental Economics and Policy*, 10(1), 68–88. One argument against energy efficiency, called the rebound effect, occurs when the actual energy savings are lower than initially expected due to offsetting consumption increases. This article reviews the outstanding literature on the magnitude and policy implications of the rebound effect.

Schmalensee, R. (2009). Evaluating policies to increase electricity generation from renewable energy. *Review of Environmental Economics and Policy*, 6, 45–64. Evaluates policies aimed at increasing the generation of electricity from renewable sources based upon on a review of experience in the United States and the European Union.

Additional references and other historically significant references are available on this book's eResource page: www.routledge.com/9781138587595

Chapter 10

Climate change III
Carbon pricing

Introduction

The previous chapter has focused on climate policies that target aspects of the energy sector such as balancing imports versus domestic production as well as the role of fuel substitution and energy efficiency in decarbonization. Targeting energy use makes sense because it is such an important component of the total problem.

Energy policies, however, are not likely to be a sufficient response to the threats from climate change. Carbon pricing is not only a more comprehensive approach that is focused directly on emissions, but that direct approach is more cost-effective. In this chapter we shall not only examine the logic behind its superior cost-effectiveness, including the necessary conditions for cost-effectiveness to occur, but also how the existing carbon pricing programs are working out in practice.

Carbon pricing and emissions mitigation policy

Decisions about energy choices are important components for making headway on the inefficiencies associated with climate change. They are not, however, the only game in town and they do have disadvantages.

Carbon pricing is unique in its comprehensiveness, including its ability to control emissions sources other than energy. Once a price is put on CO_2e it promotes: (1) fuel switching to lower carbon fuels, (2) energy efficiency by raising the amount of cost savings per unit of emissions reduced, (3) reductions in emissions from non-energy sources and (4) technological innovation to come up with new fuels or new energy-saving and emission-reducing techniques.

To see why a well-designed carbon tax is the most cost-effective strategy for reducing emissions recall the cost-effectiveness equimarginal principle (in Chapter 2). It stipulates that a cost-effective mitigation outcome is achieved only when the marginal cost of reducing the last ton of emissions is equalized across all reduction opportunities. Although any normal mix of energy policies would be likely to satisfy this condition only by coincidence, carbon pricing would normally satisfy it.

When any emitter faces a price on all its greenhouse gas emissions (measured as CO_2e to assure each ton has a comparable impact), it minimizes its costs by abating its emissions until the marginal cost of the next CO_2e ton reduced is equal to the price.

Every emitter would have that same incentive. If they all face the same CO_2e price, every emitter would set its marginal cost of control equal to that price, which implies that all of the marginal costs of abatement would be equal. The conditions for cost-effectiveness would have been satisfied.

Notice what practical policy insights follow from this analysis. First to be cost-effective the price on emissions should be applied to all greenhouse gases (via CO_2e), not just carbon dioxide, and to all sources of those gases, not merely some. Otherwise the marginal costs would be equalized for a subset of the gases and sources, but not them all. In the many carbon pricing programs around the world today not all greenhouse gases are priced and not all sources of even the included gases are covered; many programs focus exclusively on some sources of some gases.

Second, all emitters should face the *same* price per ton of CO_2e; otherwise the different prices would result in different marginal costs, a violation of the condition for cost-effectiveness. Notice that this implies a single world price, but in practice the large number of existing carbon pricing programs currently have quite different prices. So while carbon pricing can in principle be cost-effective under the right conditions, so far those conditions are not commonly found in practice.

This analysis also suggests why other policies such as renewable portfolio standards or gas taxes would only be cost-effective by coincidence. Not only do they not result in equal marginal control costs, but they only are only able to deal with some emissions sources.

Forms of carbon pricing

Carbon pricing has historically been applied in two different forms: (1) carbon taxes or (2) emissions trading (also known as cap-and-trade) programs. In the former the government sets the carbon price and the market determines the resulting level of emissions. In the latter the government determines the allowed amount of emissions and the market determines the price that will achieve that level. Seen in this light they are mirror images of each other. For any allowed level of emissions there is a price that will result in that level of emissions. Conversely if that price is imposed as a tax, that same level of emissions will result from that tax.

Early in climate change negotiations it became clear that using cost-effective mitigation strategies was an international priority. At that time Europe had historically tended to favor carbon taxes, while the United States had preferred cap-and-trade. In practice, as shown in Table 10.1, we now have experience with both approaches.

According to the World Bank[1] in 2019 some 57 carbon pricing initiatives involving some 46 national jurisdictions had been implemented or were scheduled for implementation. Some 28 of these involved national programs. These initiatives cover 19.6 percent of global GHG emissions. Of the scheduled or implemented programs about 52 percent of them involved carbon taxes with the rest being cap-and-trade programs.

Providing context: a brief look at two illustrative carbon pricing programs

While cap-and-trade and a carbon tax are both forms of carbon pricing, but they operate rather differently. To provide some feel for how these two types of programs work in practice consider two examples: (1) the British Columbia carbon tax, and (2) the European Union's Emissions Trading Scheme.

Table 10.1 Selected Carbon Market and Carbon Tax Programs

Carbon Markets	*Carbon Taxes*
The Kyoto Protocol's Clean Development and Joint Implementation Mechanisms (2005)	Finland (1990)
The European Union Emissions Trading Scheme (2005)	Sweden (1991)
Regional Greenhouse Gas Initiative U.S. (2009)	Norway (1991)
New Zealand (2010)	United Kingdom (2001)
California, U.S.A. (2013)	Denmark (2005)
Quebec, Canada (2013)	Alberta, Canada (2007)
Nova Scotia (2019)	Switzerland (2007)
Peoples Republic of China Pilot Programs (2013) and National Program (2020)	British Columbia, Canada (2008)
South Korea (2015)	India (2010)
	Japan (2012)

Source: World Bank Carbon Pricing Dashboard. https://carbonpricingdashboard.worldbank.org/map_data (accessed May 23, 2019)

British Columbia carbon tax program

Since 2008, British Columbia has imposed a carbon tax on each metric ton of carbon dioxide equivalent (CO_2e) emissions from the combustion of fuel. The tax rose from 10 Canadian dollars per ton of carbon dioxide in 2008 to 30 dollars in 2012. This program affects an estimated 77 percent of British Columbia's total greenhouse gas (GHG) emissions.

Under this program, CO_2e is defined as the amount of CO_2, methane, and nitrous oxide (N_2O) released into the atmosphere, with the methane and N_2O emission levels adjusted to account for their impact on global warming relative to CO_2. Certain fuels, such as fuel for commercial aviation and ships, are exempted. To facilitate implementation, the carbon tax is applied and collected at the wholesale level, using the traditional administrative channels for collecting motor fuel taxes. The cost of the tax is ultimately passed forward to consumers via higher prices.

This carbon tax program is revenue neutral (i.e., all revenue generated is returned to British Columbians through rebates or cuts in other taxes rather than retained to finance new or expanded programs). The corporate income tax was cut to 10 percent from 12 percent, to stimulate a flagging economy in 2010. Though it returned to 11 percent, it is still the lowest among Canada's provinces.

To help protect low-income households, the Low Income Climate Action Tax Credit program provides adult residents with lump sum tax credits that are reduced by 2 percent of net family income above specified income thresholds.

Analyses suggest that the British Columbia policy reduced emissions 5–15 percent by 2015 and per-capita gasoline demand dropped 15 percent between 2007 and 2014.[2] Meanwhile, provincial real GDP grew more than 17 percent from 2007 to 2015, outpacing the rest of Canada.

When a new government took over in 2012, it retained the program, but it stopped the annual rise in the tax rate. Carbon emissions in BC started rising again after the province froze the tax. In part the new government did not want to get too far ahead of other nations, lest they start losing their competitive edge.

Since then, Canadian Prime Minister Justin Trudeau has established his proposed national climate plan, which requires all provinces and territories to put in place either a carbon tax or a cap-and-trade plan by 2022.

European Union Emissions Trading Scheme (EU ETS)

Launched in 2005, the EU ETS operates in 31 countries and has been the largest emissions trading system in the world. The program establishes a cap on the total amount of certain GHGs[3] that can be emitted from installations covered by the system. Under this cap, companies receive emission allowances, which they can sell to, or buy from, one another as needed. At the end of the year each company must surrender enough allowances to cover all its emissions for that year or pay penalties on any excess. Companies can bank any spare allowances for future sale or for covering their future needs. The cap (and, hence, the number of allowances) is reduced over time so that total emissions will fall.

The EU ETS operates in all 28 EU countries plus Iceland, Liechtenstein, and Norway. It limits emissions from more than 11,000 heavy energy-using installations (power stations and industrial plants) as well as airlines operating between these countries, and it covers around 45 percent of the EU's greenhouse gas emissions.

Emissions in the EU were reduced by 22 percent between 1990 and 2015 while the economy grew by 50 percent over the same period. According to the European Environment Agency (EEA) the decrease was mostly driven by emissions reductions in power generation. Emission reductions slowed down in the later period as an excess of allowances for sale developed.

Carbon markets and taxes: how have these approaches worked in practice?

Cost savings

Two types of studies have conventionally been used to assess cost savings: *ex ante* analyses, based on computer simulations, and *ex post* analyses, which examine actual implementation experience. A substantial majority, though not all, of the large number of *ex ante* analyses have found that a change from more traditional regulatory measures based upon source-specific limits to more cost-effective market-based measures such as emissions trading or pollution taxes would potentially achieve either similar reductions at a much lower cost or much larger reductions at a similar cost. The evidence also finds, as the theory would lead us to expect, that these two instruments typically produce more emissions reduction per unit expenditure than other types of polices such as renewable resource subsidies or mandates.

Although the number of existing detailed *ex post* studies, drawn from the experiences of existing programs, is small, they typically find, however, that the cost savings from shifting to these market-based measures are positive, but less than would have been achieved if the final outcome had been fully cost-effective. In other words, while both taxes and emissions trading are fully cost-effective in principle, they fall somewhat short of that in practice.

Emissions reductions

In one study that attempts to control for other factors that could affect emissions outcomes, Lin and Li (2011) compared the change in per capita CO_2 emissions over time between countries that do and do not use carbon pricing (specifically a carbon tax). They found that in general emissions were reduced more in countries with carbon taxes, but the role of carbon taxes was found to be a statistically significant factor only for Finland. The authors attributed this lack of statistical significance for the other countries to the relatively common political practice of granting tax exemptions to certain energy intensive industries.

Among emissions trading markets, as noted previously, emissions in the EU were reduced by 22 percent between 1990 and 2015. In the northeastern United States, the Regional Greenhouse Gas Initiative (RGGI) emissions from all covered sources were reduced 37 percent during the 2008–2015 period despite a rather weak cap. While the recession played some role, the main sources of the RGGI reductions were (1) substituting to renewable resources and lower-carbon fossil fuels (specifically natural gas) aided considerably by lower natural gas prices, and (2) energy efficiency investments, that reduced the amount of energy used per unit of output.

Not all countries or regions regulate their greenhouse gases, of course, and that raises the specter of leakage. Leakage can occur when pressure on the regulated source to reduce emissions results in a diversion of emissions to unregulated, or lesser regulated, locations. Common channels for this diversion involve firms moving their polluting factories to countries with lower environmental standards or consumers increasing their reliance on imported products from countries with unregulated or less-regulated sources. When leakage occurs it means that the actual emissions reductions are smaller than those recorded at the regulated site, because some emissions have been merely transferred to another location, not reduced. Generally, to date, however, the evidence suggests that actual carbon leakage effects have been rather small despite initial concerns that they might be quite large.[4]

Economic impacts

An analytical exercise by the Stanford University Energy Modeling Forum used 11 different models to assess emissions, energy, and economic outcomes from carbon price policies to reduce carbon dioxide (CO_2) emissions in the United States. Across all models, they found that carbon prices lead to significant reductions in CO_2 emissions as well as conventional pollutants. Most of the reductions occurred in the electricity sector. They found that the expected economic costs are "modest," and in any case those costs would be more than offset by benefits from avoided climate damages and health benefits from reductions in conventional air pollution.[5]

A different study that specifically focused on employment effects,[6] found find that while imposing a pollution tax causes substantial reductions in employment in the carbon-intensive polluting industry, these effects would be expected to be largely offset by increased employment in other sectors. While the policy causes a substantial shift in employment between industries, the study found that the net effect on overall employment (and unemployment) was small.

The authors also noted that while some studies find larger employment effects, most of those focus exclusively on the polluting sector and do not take into consideration the offsetting increases in jobs in the other sectors.

And finally a study,[7] conducted by the Organization for Economic Cooperation and Development (OECD) compared financial data from around 2,000 regulated firms operating in the European Union Emissions Trading Scheme with data from similar-sized unregulated firms from the same countries and sectors. It found that ETS regulations had no negative effect on revenue, profits, fixed assets or jobs, and, in fact, firms subject to the ETS tended to perform better. Another study by the OECD discovered that these general results for carbon pricing were found for a larger set of environmental regulations.[8]

Price levels

It is important to distinguish between what *could be* accomplished by a well-designed carbon price program and what *has been* actually accomplished by implemented carbon price programs. One area where this is particularly important involves the level of the carbon prices in existing programs. The fact that a program following the optimal price trajectory could achieve optimal results is of little comfort if actual price trajectories do not live up to the optimality trajectory.

What is the evidence? Fortunately this is a topic covered by the World Bank's review of the State of Carbon Pricing 2018.[9] They found:

> most initiatives are still below the US\$40/tCO_2e to US\$80/tCO_2e range needed in 2020 to stay consistent with achieving the temperature goal of the Paris Agreement. . . . Even taking planned price increases into account in existing and upcoming initiatives, there remains a clear gap and a crucial need for significant progress to align these initiatives with the ambition of the Paris Agreement.

In this dimension, with a few notable exceptions, carbon pricing has yet to live up to its promise.

Four carbon pricing program design issues

Using the revenue

Either form of carbon pricing (auctioning allowances or a carbon tax) can raise revenue while reducing emissions. What difference do the various choices about revenue use make?

Revenues could be used to reduce the financial burden of the policy on low-income populations, to boost the economy, to increase the magnitude of the emissions reductions, to aid workers displaced by the policy, and even to increase the likelihood that a carbon-pricing policy might be enacted in the first place. While in some cases particular revenue choices can simultaneously achieve multiple objectives, others require political trade-offs.

Various strategies have been designed to achieve one or more of these objectives. They include: (1) giving the revenue back to households in the form of a lump-sum rebate on a per capita basis, (2) lowering various taxes such as the corporate tax, the income tax, the capital gains tax, the payroll tax, and so on, (3) subsidizing further emissions reductions, or (4) helping workers who are displaced by the shift to a lower-carbon energy supply.

Some of these revenue strategies can be designed to be "revenue-neutral." By definition, no revenue from a revenue neutral policy can be used to fund new or expanded programs. Revenue neutrality can be achieved either by rebating the carbon-pricing revenues to households, by lowering other tax rates such that the lost revenue to the government from the lower rates is equal to the revenue derived from carbon pricing or some combination of the two. Revenue neutrality is seen as potentially helpful in building support for the policy among those who do not want to see an increase in the size of government.

Without considering the use of the revenue, a carbon tax has been generally found to be regressive. In other words the burdens of a carbon tax disproportionately fall on low-income households. However, most other energy policies seeking to reduce carbon emissions are also regressive. How does a carbon tax compare in terms of its distributional fairness compared to policies such as fuel economy standards, renewable portfolio standards, building codes, and so on?

A recent study[10] that examines this issue found that carbon pricing has an advantage in achieving more progressive outcomes than these other policies because it generates revenue. The revenue from carbon pricing can be used to offset the regressive aspects of the tax itself. Generally other polices do not generate revenue that can be used for this purpose.

How can the carbon-pricing revenue be used to make a carbon tax less regressive? The secret is to use the revenue in a way that has a strong progressive impact (meaning benefitting the poor more than the rich). If this effect is large enough, it can more than offset the regressive nature of the carbon tax itself.

Issuing lump-sum rebates to households (for example, a fixed monthly check for each member of every eligible household up to four) is an effective strategy for reducing the burden from carbon pricing on lower-income populations. Indeed economic studies find that of the various strategies lump-sum rebates are the most effective choice in pursuing this particular objective. Further the rebates do boost the economy, but they are not the most effective revenue-using choice for boosting the economy.

Economists have found that using the revenue to lower tax rates on such taxes as the capital gains tax or the corporate income tax would produce the largest boost to the economy. However, because the beneficiaries from these tax-reduction approaches are primarily upper-income groups, they would have the least effect on reducing the burden on the low-income populations.

Some programs that are not revenue neutral use the revenue to incentivize greater emissions reductions. Common strategies include using the revenue to pick up part of the cost for those households or businesses who invest in energy efficiency or in renewable energy such as wind or solar. Some energy efficiency programs have been shown to boost the economy in high energy cost regions not only by lowering the energy costs, but also by keeping the revenue in the local area rather than exporting it to import fuels. Studies find, however, that energy efficiency incentives are not as effective in boosting the economy as lowering the capital gains or corporate tax rates. Although energy efficiency programs frequently target some of the subsidies at the poor and the resulting investments do lower participants' energy cost, they are not particularly effective at lowering the burden on low-income populations in general since only those that choose to participate actually benefit.

Fortunately, in a particularly interesting finding, economic studies have also found that it is not necessary to make an either-or decision among these revenue-using choices. Because substantial revenue is commonly involved in carbon pricing programs, multiple strategies can be used simultaneously, thereby covering several bases at once.

Offsets

While both emissions trading and a carbon tax control emissions from sources specifically subject to those programs, offsets allow emissions reductions from sources that are not subject to either the tax or the cap to be certified as offsets. Offsets, like allowances, can be used to cover emissions in a cap-and-trade program. They can also be used to reduce the tax base in carbon taxation. Offsets or offset tax credits perform several roles in pricing GHGs:

- First, increasing the number of reduction opportunities lowers the cost of compliance.
- Second, lowering the cost of compliance could increase the likelihood of enacting a carbon-pricing program by making compliance easier.
- Third, offsets extend the reach of a program by providing economic incentives for reducing sources that are not covered by the tax or cap.
- Finally, because offsets separate the source of financing from the source providing the reduction, it secures some reductions (in developing countries, for example) that for affordability reasons might not be secured otherwise.

The challenge for establishing an effective offset program is assuring that the primary requirements (namely, that the reductions be quantifiable, enforceable, and additional) are all met. One obstacle is the tradeoff between the administrative costs associated with verifying the validity of offsets and the degree of offset validity. Assuring valid offsets is not always cheap.

In response to concerns over the validity of offsets, most programs now try to limit their use. One historical approach has been to restrict the use of offsets (domestic, foreign, or both) to some stipulated percentage of the total required allowances. In the Regional Greenhouse Gas Initiative (RGGI) in the northeastern United States, for example, CO_2 offset allowances may be used to satisfy only 3.3 percent of a source's total compliance obligation during a control period, although this may be expanded to 5 percent and 10 percent if certain CO_2 allowance price thresholds are reached. In contrast, in 2011, Germany announced that it would not allow *any* offsets to be used to pursue its reduction goals.

The role of price volatility

A tax system fixes prices, and unless some administrative intervention changes those fixed prices, carbon price volatility is not an issue. This is not the case with emissions trading in either principle or practice.

Experience not only validates the concern that emissions trading can be plagued by volatile prices, but also demonstrates that price volatility is not a rare event. In the EU ETS case, two early price declines were attributable to (1) inadequate public knowledge of actual emissions relative to the cap and (2) a failure to permit allowances in the first phase to be banked for use in the second phase. A subsequent dramatic price decline in 2012 stemmed from an overallocation of allowances, recession, and long-term uncertainty about the stability of climate policy.

Experience has demonstrated that the design of an emissions trading system is vulnerable to unstable prices in two rather fundamental ways:

- First, because the cap establishes a fixed supply of allowances, demand shifts (due, for example, to other regulatory actions, recessions, or shifts in prices of lower carbon fuels) can trigger large changes in allowance prices since supply cannot respond.
- Second, the demand for allowances is derived from the need to satisfy compliance obligations. Changing circumstances (due either to external factors or simply greater than anticipated success in lowering carbon emissions) can create a surplus of allowances. This surplus may cause the price to drop precipitously since lower prices do not stimulate any increase in the quantity demanded for compliance. Both the RGGI and the EU ETS markets have experienced precisely this kind of price-dropping surplus.

Although declining prices reflect falling costs of emissions reductions, they have a downside as well. Low prices can decrease the incentive to innovate and innovation is a key to promoting the transformations required to decarbonize the economy.

In the last decade, cap-and-trade programs have created different mechanisms to address falling prices[11]. The first element involves a price floor. The Regional Greenhouse Gas Initiative (RGGI), which includes nine states in the northeast and mid-Atlantic, and the Western Climate Initiative (WCI), a trading program including California, Ontario, and Quebec, have adopted minimum prices in their allowance auctions, below which no allowances are sold. While addressing excessively low prices, a price floor, by itself, does nothing to prevent fear about prices that could temporarily rising to politically unacceptable levels, thereby undermining the political basis for implementing the program. The collar works by making additional allowances available to emitters when prices threaten to rise above expected levels when the agreement was established.

Two types of price collars are either in use or scheduled to be used in the near future.

A "hard collar" places no limits on the number of allowances that can added to the system at the ceiling price. It therefore can add enough allowances, when necessary, to keep the price from rising above a stipulated trigger price. The trigger prices are usually derived from the forecasts of price expectations presented during the process used to establish the implementation rules of the program.

A "soft collar" sets a limit on the number of allowances that can be added to the system from a fixed allowance reserve. While the use of this reserve to add allowances to the market will reduce the price rise that would otherwise occur, the limited size of the reserve may not necessarily be large enough prevent the price from slipping above the trigger price.

Additionally RGGI has added a new feature – a cost containment reserve (CCR), which, when combined with the price floor, is known as a *soft* price collar.[12] The CCR allows for the sale of a *fixed* number of allowances in addition to the cap when the clearing price in the quarterly auction reaches a pre-stipulated CCR Trigger Price. (The Trigger Price was $10 in 2017 and it rises over time.) The CCR is replenished at the start of each calendar year. In 2015, 2016, 2017, and 2018 the CCR had a withdrawal limit of ten million allowances, and the CCR Trigger Prices were $6.00, $8.00, $10.00, and $10.25 respectively. All 15 million allowances were sold from the CCR for the period from 2014 to 2015, but the CCR was not triggered in 2016, 2017, or 2018.

As of 2019, California had a similar soft price collar, but in their post-2020 program they will initiate a hard collar with an unlimited amount of emissions available to ensure that the market price does not rise above the specified trigger price. Although both types of price collars provide a check on price volatility, a hard collar provides more certainty that prices will not rise above politically unacceptable levels. A carbon tax, however, provides the greatest certainty.

Uncertainty of hitting the environmental target

Historically virtually all environment management targets have been specified in quantitative, not price, terms. For example, we have the allowable temperature increase targets in international climate change policy or the human health targets for other water or air pollutants. Cap-and-trade programs typically have less uncertainty about whether the program will hit a designated quantity target at the designated time than a carbon tax. This follows from the fact that the cap is also a quantitative measure.

As discussed in Chapter 8 the normal procedure for setting a quantitative cap is to derive a quantitative carbon budget from the increased temperature target. This quantitative aggregate emissions target can also be used to set the cap in an emissions trading program.

While this procedure for deriving the cap in a cap-and-trade program is not a completely certain one, it is certainly more direct and more certain than deriving the appropriate tax rate from the temperature target. In some ways this is the mirror image of price volatility problem. Cap-and trade program provide less certainty about price and more about emissions reductions, while carbon tax programs provide more certainty about future prices and less about emissions reductions.

Controversy: the morality of emissions trading

Emissions trading has not avoided controversy. One element of that controversy raises the rather important question of whether the greenhouse gas trading concept violates conventional norms of international ethics (see Debate 10.1).

DEBATE 10.1

Is global greenhouse gas trading immoral?

In a December 1997 editorial in the *New York Times*, Michael Sandel, a Harvard government professor, suggested that greenhouse gas trading is immoral. He argued that treating pollution as a commodity to be bought and sold not only removes the moral stigma that is appropriately associated with polluting, but also trading reductions undermines an important sense of shared responsibilities that global cooperation requires. He illustrated the point by suggesting that legitimizing further emission by offsetting it with a credit acquired from a project in a poorer nation would be very different from penalizing the firm for emitting, even if the cost of the credit were equal to the penalty. Not only would the now-authorized emission become inappropriately "socially acceptable" but also the wealthier nation would have met its moral obligation by paying a poorer nation to fulfill a responsibility that should have been fulfilled by a domestic emissions reduction.

Published responses to this editorial countered with several points. First, it was pointed out that since it is voluntary, international emissions trading typically benefits both nations; one nation is not imposing its will on another. Second, the historical use of these programs has resulted in much cleaner air at a much lower cost than would otherwise have been possible, so the ends would seem to justify the means. Third, with few exceptions, virtually all pollution-control regulations allow some emission that is not penalized; this is simply a recognition that zero pollution is rarely either efficient or politically feasible.

Source: Sandel, M. J. (December 17, 1997). It's immoral to buy the right to pollute. With replies by Steven Shavell, Robert Stavins, Sanford Gaines, and Eric Maskin. *New York Times;* excerpts reprinted in Stavins, R. N. (Ed.) (2000). *Economics of the Environment: Selected Readings,* 4th ed. New York: W.W. Norton & Company, 449–452.

Summary

Energy policies focused on fuel switching and energy efficiency are important, but incomplete solutions to the climate problem. Unlike energy efficiency, for example, carbon pricing has no rebound effect. Further carbon pricing is the only policy we know of that in principle not only can be comprehensive, but it can, under the right conditions, result in a cost-effective means of reducing emissions.

Since carbon pricing is the main means for achieving cost-effective policy on climate change, the fact that the number of existing regional and national carbon pricing programs is growing and the list of participating countries includes some important players is good news indeed.

The empirical evidence drawn from these existing programs demonstrates that they are achieving emissions reductions in a relatively cost-effective manner, but current programs are not completely cost effective. In part that is due to the fact that they are not fully comprehensive in the sense that in general they cover only some greenhouse gases and some emission sources.

The negative economic impact of these programs is pretty modest and job losses in some sectors are largely balanced by gains in others. Further if revenue is used in an appropriate way, the burdens of the policy can be distributed in a progressive, rather than a regressive manner.

Carbon pricing, however, has some problems of its own. In general current prices are too low to support a transition to the low-carbon future in time to hold temperature increases below international goals. Some other issues, such as volatile prices in cap-and trade markets and the appropriate role for offsets, are still in the process of being resolved.

Although carbon pricing is, in principle, the most cost-effective approach, in practice if it can't be enacted in a form that provides emissions reductions quickly enough or deep enough, it may not dominate other approaches. Other policies, though less cost-effective in principle, in practice may be able to achieve larger emissions reductions more rapidly. It is therefore quite possible they could ultimately be more efficient. If they reduce more climate damages more quickly and more thoroughly than carbon pricing, these large climate damage reductions could more than offset their higher costs. In any case the chances of getting a handle on the threats posed by a modified climate will be enhanced if policy-makers have a larger menu of policy options to work with than a smaller one.

In terms of risk management it seems clear that current action dominates inaction even in the presence of uncertainly about outcomes. Disagreements among reasonable people about the severity and timing of the risks posed by a modified climate should not be a recipe for policy paralysis.

During the next few decades, options must not only be preserved, they must be enhanced. Responding in a timely and effective fashion to global pollution problems will not be easy. Our political institutions are not configured in such a way as to make decision making on a global scale simple. International organizations exist at the pleasure of the nations they serve. Only time will tell if the mechanisms described in this chapter will prove equal to the task.

Discussion questions

1 Concerned individuals can now seek to reduce their carbon footprint by buying offsets. Air travelers, for example, are now asked if they wish to purchase offsets when they buy their ticket. Is this a complement or substitute for a national climate change policy? Why?

2 What is your national, regional, or state government doing about climate change? Has it adopted a form of carbon pricing? If so, how is it working out? Is anyone working on an adaptation plan in your area? Do the basics of those approaches seem consistent with some of the characteristics of an efficient strategy discussed in this chapter? Why or why not?

Self-test exercises

1 Explain why a climate policy using emissions-charge revenue to provide capital and operating subsidies for carbon capture technologies is less cost-effective than an emissions-charge policy alone.

2 The revenues from an emissions-charge approach to controlling climate change would be unusually large in comparison to other pollutants. What circumstances would lead to high revenues?

3 Label the following as true, false, or uncertain, and explain your choice. (Uncertain means that it can be either true or false depending upon the circumstances.)

   a The imposition of a tax on currently uncontrolled greenhouse gas emissions would represent a move toward efficiency.

   b Relying on a series of regional systems (like the EU ETS), rather than a true global system, for controlling greenhouse gases increases the importance of the leakage problem.

4 Suppose two countries with domestic cap-and-trade policies are considering linking their two systems. Country A has a cap of 20 tons of emissions, a domestic marginal cost of abatement of \$10 and an uncontrolled emissions level of 60 tons, while Country B has a cap of 40 tons, a domestic marginal cost of abatement of \$1q, where q = the tons of emission abatement, and an uncontrolled emissions level of 80 tons.

   a Before linkage what would be the prices in the two separate markets and how much abatement would each country choose?

   b If these two markets were linked by allowing each country to buy from and sell allowances to the other, what would be the prices in the two markets? How much would each country abate? Describe the transfer of allowances, if any, that would take place between the two countries.

Notes

1 The World Bank Carbon Pricing Dashboard can be accessed at https://carbonpricingdashboard.worldbank.org

2 www.canada.ca/en/services/environment/weather/climatechange/climate-action/pricing-carbon-pollution/estimated-impacts-federal-system.html

3 The covered gases include: (1) carbon dioxide (CO_2) emissions from power and heat generation, from energy-intensive industry sectors and from civil aviation, (2) nitrous oxide (N2O) from production of nitric, adipic and glyoxylic acids and glyoxal and (3) perfluorocarbons (PFCs) from aluminum production

4 For an example see: Verde, Stefano F. (2018). The impact of the EU emissions trading system on competitiveness and carbon leakage. Working Paper Series/Number: EUI RSCAS; 2018/53; Florence School of Regulation. Available at: http://fsr.eui.eu/publications/the-impact-of-the-eu-emissions-trading-system-on-competitiveness-and-carbon-leakage/

5 Barron Alexander, R., et. al. (2018). Policy insights from the EMF 32 study on U.S. carbon tax scenarios. *Climate Change Economics*, 9(1), 1840003

6 Hafstead, Marc A.C., & Roberton C. Williams, III. (2018). Unemployment and environmental regulation in general equilibrium. *Journal of Public Economics*, 160, 50–65.

7 www.oecd.org/newsroom/eu-emissions-trading-system-does-not-hurt-firms-profitability.htm

8 Dechezleprêtre, Antoine, Tomasz Kozluk, Tobias Kruse, Daniel Nachtigall, & Alain de Serres. (2019). Do environmental and economic performance go together? A review of micro-level empirical evidence from the past decade or so. *International Review of Environmental and Resource Economics*, 13, 1–118.

9 https://openknowledge.worldbank.org/bitstream/handle/10986/29687/9781464812927.pdf?sequence=5&isAllowed=y. See Figure 7.

10 Deryugina, Tatyana, Don Fullerton, & William A. Pizer. (2019). An introduction to energy policy trade-offs between economic efficiency and distributional equity. *Journal of the Association of Environmental and Resource Economists*, 6(S1) (March).

11 Burtraw, Dallas, & Amelia Keyes (2018). European union reforms its carbon emissions market. Resources: RFF's online magazine Issue 198 | Summer 2018 Available at: www.resourcesmag.org/archives/european-union-reforms-its-carbon-emissions-market/

12 Potomac Economics. Annual report on the market for RGGI CO_2 allowances: 2018. Prepared for: RGGI, Inc., on behalf of the RGGI Participating States (April, 2019).

Further reading

Barron Alexander, R., et al. (2018). Policy insights from the EMF 32 study on U.S. carbon tax scenarios. *Climate Change Economics*, 9(1), 1840003. doi: 10.1142/S2010007818400031. Exercise 32 (EMF 32) uses 11 different models to assess emissions, energy, and economic outcomes from a plausible range of economy-wide carbon price policies to reduce carbon dioxide (CO_2) emissions in the United States.

Burtraw, D., & Keyes, A. (2018). European union reforms its carbon emissions market. Resources: RFF's online magazine Issue 198 | Summer 2018. Available at: www.resourcesmag.org/archives/european-union-reforms-its-carbon-emissions-market/

Deryugina, T., Fullerton, D., & Pizer, W. A. (March 2019). An introduction to energy policy trade-offs between economic efficiency and distributional equity. *Journal of the Association of Environmental and Resource Economists*, 6(S1). http://dx.doi.org/10.1086/701515. This article and the articles that it introduces examine the important question of how the distributional consequences of a carbon tax compare with a host of energy policies that have also been used to reduce carbon emissions.

Fankhauser, S. (2016). Adaptation to climate change. Grantham Research Institute on Climate Change and the Environment Working Paper No. 255. Available at: www.lse.ac.uk/GranthamInstitute/publication/adaptation-to-climate-change/. Last accessed on April 1, 2017. A survey of the economics of adaptation.

Fell, H., Burtraw, D., Morgenstern, R. D., & Palmer, K. L. (2012). Soft and hard price collars in a cap-and-trade system: A comparative analysis. *Journal of Environmental Economics and Management*, 64(2), 183–198. Compares price collars (price ceilings and floors) in a cap-and-trade system involving uncertainty with respect to the level of baseline emissions and costs.

Goulder, L. H., & Schein, A. R. (2013). Carbon taxes versus cap and trade: A critical review. *Climate Change Economics*, 4(3), 1350010. https://doi.org/10.1142/S2010007813500103. Assessing the similarities and differences between carbon taxes and carbon cap-and-trade.

Metcalf, G. E. (2019). The distributional impacts of U.S. energy policy. *Energy Policy*, 129, 926–929. Surveys energy policy in the United States from a distributional perspective.

Phillips, B., & Reilly, J. (2019). Designing successful greenhouse gas emission reduction policies: A primer for policymakers: The perfect or the good? *Joint Program Report Series Report*, 335, February, 14 p. Available at: http://globalchange.mit.edu/publication/17200. This paper evaluates four types of greenhouse gas emission reduction policies, carbon taxes, cap and trade (C&T) programs, tradeable performance standards (TCES) and technology-neutral clean energy standards (CES).

Stavins, R. N. (2008). Addressing climate change with a comprehensive US cap-and-trade system. *Oxford Review of Economic Policy*, 24(2), 298–321. Describes considerations for designing a cap-and-trade policy to control greenhouse gas emissions in the United States.

Stern, N. (2008). The economics of climate change. *American Economic Review*, 98(2), 1–37. As assessment by the former chief economist of the World Bank.

Tietenberg, T. H. (Summer 2013). Reflections: Carbon pricing in practice. *Review of Environmental Economics and Policy*, 7, 313–329. A review of the existing carbon pricing programs that considers their effectiveness and the emerging design lessons.

U.S. Environmental Protection Agency. (2016). *Climate Change Indicators in the United States*, 4th ed. EPA 430-R-16-004. Available at: www.epa.gov/climate-indicators. This report presents 37 indicators to help readers understand changes observed from long-term records related to the causes and effects of climate change, the significance of these changes, and their possible consequences for people, the environment, and society.

Williams, R. C., III. (June 2016). Environmental taxation. Resources for the Future Discussion Paper 16–24. Available at: www.rff.org/files/document/file/RFF-DP-16-24.pdf. This paper evaluates the economic and environmental effects of potential environmental tax reforms, based on a review of recent economic research.

Additional references and other historically significant references are available on this book's eResource page: www.routledge.com/9781138587595

Chapter 11

Climate change IV
Adaptation

Introduction – the role of adaptation policy

Mitigation polices, the subject of the last chapter, are important tools for reducing emissions. Mitigation of emissions is absolutely necessary, but not sufficient. As we reach tipping points, certain impacts of climate change are becoming unavoidable. While the degree of damage associated with those impacts can, in part, be mitigated with carbon pricing, not all impacts are preventable. Climate adaptation, the subject of this chapter, is an inevitable component of the mix of policies needed to manage the risks from climate modification.

The IPCC defines climate adaptation as

> Adaptation to climate change refers to adjustments in human and natural systems in response to actual or expected climatic variation, with a view to moderating harm or exploiting beneficial opportunities.
>
> (IPCC, 2001)

The Intergovernmental Panel on Climate Change (IPCC) outlines two types of adaptation policies: 1) *pro-active* policies, which involve taking action in anticipation of a climate change impact; or 2) *reactive* policies, which are taken in response to a climate change impact that has already occurred

Reactive adaptation policies have been the most common practices in many places – responding to damages from hazards such as wind, floods, and fires. As the intensity and frequency of these events is expected to grow, reactive polices become very expensive. How do individuals, towns, cities and countries prioritize among the many possible proactive policies?

Adaptation planning first involves conducting a vulnerability assessment to determine who and what is at risk and to what extent? The IPCC outlines this process in the schematic in Figure 11.1.

The vulnerability of a particular location is determined by examining the level of exposure to the risks and the number and types of hazards faced (IPCC, 2014). While hazards are driven by changes in the climate, vulnerability and exposure are influenced to a large extent by the socio-economic conditions and as such, adaptation policies are very context and location specific. For example, rising sea levels is a hazard faced by many locations, but some have a higher capacity to adapt.

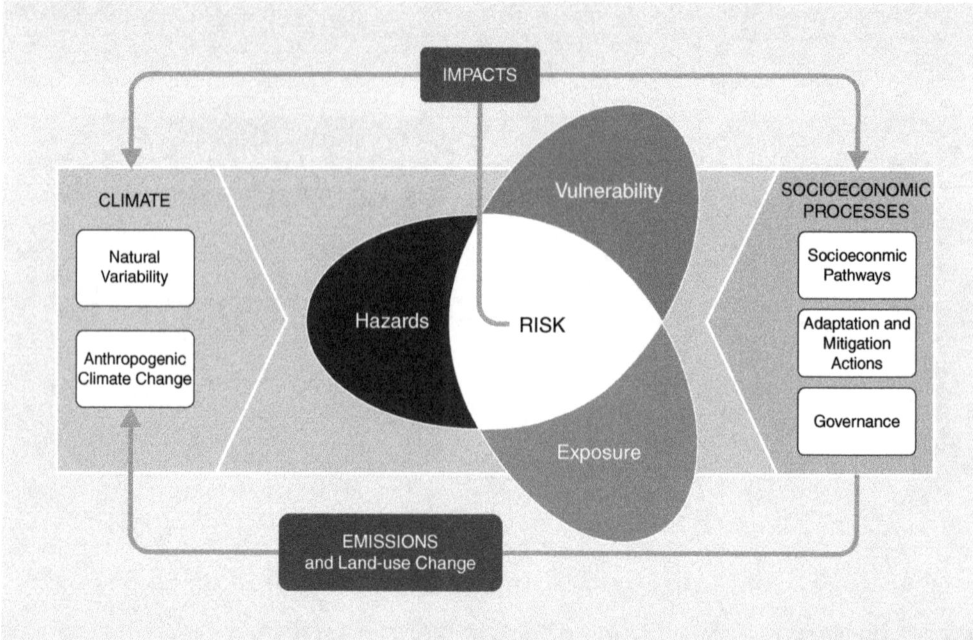

Figure 11.1 Perspectives on Vulnerability and Risk
Source: Figure SPM.1 from IPCC, 2014: Climate Change 2014: Impacts, Adaptation, and Vulnerability – Summary for Policymakers. Contribution of Working Group II to the Fifth Assessment Report of the Intergovernmental Panel on Climate Change [Field, C.B, V.R. Barros, D.J. Dokken, K.J. Mach, M.D. Mastrandrea, T.E. Bilir, M. Chatterjee, K.L. Ebi, Y.O. Estrada, R.C. Genova, B. Girma, E.S. Kissel, A.N. Levy, S. MacCracken, P.R. Mastrandrea, and L.L. White (eds.)]. Cambridge University Press, Cambridge, UK and New York, USA.

The Netherlands, with its considerable experience with managing the risks from an encroaching ocean and the resources at its disposal, is well positioned to cope effectively. On the other hand others, such as some poor island nations, have much lower capacity to adapt and thus have higher vulnerability.

Adaptation and mitigation – complements or substitutes?

Whereas mitigation strategies try to limit damage by limiting the emissions that cause the impacts, adaptation tends to limit damage by reducing the damage caused by the impacts that do occur. The two strategies are complements in the sense that the optimal policy response contains both adaptation and mitigation. Since the marginal cost function for each strategy is upward-sloping, this normally means that an optimal strategy would employ both mitigation and adaptation. Deviating from this optimum necessarily means that costs would be higher than necessary.

In another, equally meaningful sense the two strategies are also substitutes: more of one typically means less is needed of the other. To understand how they can be substitutes remember that the optimal level of either strategy would be to invest up to the point where the marginal cost of an additional unit of that strategy is equal to the marginal damages reduced by that unit. So for either strategy higher marginal damages imply a higher demand for investing more in that strategy.

If the strategies are substitutes, a reduction in the marginal cost of mitigation, for example, should lower the demand for adaptation. Why? Let's think this through. In an optimal policy a lower marginal cost of mitigation with an unchanged marginal damage would imply a higher optimal level of mitigation. This increased level of mitigation would lower the resulting marginal damage not only for additional units of mitigation, but for additional units of adaptation as well. The lower resulting marginal damages for adaptation would lower the demand for it. In this sense mitigation and adaptation are substitutes: increase the amount of one and the efficient amount of the other decreases.

If you search the internet you will discover that some pundits think about mitigation and adaptation as an either/or choice. They further suggest that policy makers should choose the one that is cheaper. Economic analysis points out that this is a false choice.

- First of all, as noted previously, upward-sloping marginal cost functions for each strategy normally mean that an optimal approach would employ both strategies. Deviating from this optimum causes the costs to be higher than necessary.
- Second, to the extent that adaptation and mitigation are substitutes, they are not perfect substitutes. Adaptation strategies are necessarily targeted at specific problems in specific geographic areas, whereas mitigation strategies have broader, global damage-reduction effects.
- Third, to some extent their timing may differ. Mitigation is necessarily done early to prevent emissions from building up in the atmosphere. Some adaptation can be done early as well, but some can also be delayed until a better understanding of the intensity and location of damages emerges.

As one World Bank study put it:

> There is a need for an integrated portfolio of actions ranging from avoiding emissions (mitigation) to coping with impacts (adaptation) and to consciously accepting residual damages . . . . However, some irreversible losses cannot be compensated for. Thus, mitigation might be in many cases the cheapest long-term solution to climate change problems and the most important to avoid thresholds that may trigger truly catastrophic consequences.[1]

While mitigation strategies can be regional, national or international, adaptation strategies are very localized. Adaptation, by necessity, is location and context specific. Unlike mitigation strategies, it is frequently less obvious which adaptation strategies might be best. The decision-making tools of economics can be very helpful in these situations. Measuring costs and benefits of adaptation strategies, considering *who* benefits and why, and acknowledging the time sensitivity makes benefit-cost analysis and cost-effectiveness analysis powerful tools for decision making (recall Chapter 4). Efficient adaptation is the minimization of the sum of damage costs from climate change plus the cost of adaptive actions.

What forms can adaptation strategies take? They can involve a mix of public and private strategies. They range from large-scale infrastructure changes – such as building sea walls to protect against sea-level rise – to behavioral shifts as when individuals waste less water, farmers plant different crops, and households relocate their dwellings to higher land for flood protection

In the rest of this chapter, we examine examples of policies and strategies used to enhance adaptation. Although the range of possibilities is large and to some extent location-specific, to illustrate the role economics can play we focus on two areas: flooding caused by increased storm frequency and intensity as well as from sea level rise; and water scarcity from increased frequency of drought.

Flood risks: storms, sea level rise, and storm surges

One threat to sustainability comes from natural disasters such as hurricanes, floods, and wildfires, which are intensified by climate change. In its 2012 report The National Research Council notes:

> In 2011 the United States was struck by multiple disasters – including 14 related to weather and climate – that caused more than $55 billion in economic damages, breaking all records since these data were first reported in 1980. Nearly 600 Americans died, and many thousands more were displaced.

The report goes on to suggest that building a culture of resilience could reduce the nation's vulnerability to disasters as well as the costs they impose.

What exactly is resilience? According to the report, "Resilience is the ability to prepare and plan for, absorb, recover from, and more successfully adapt to adverse events."

How much difference could an increase in resilience make? A study conducted by the Multihazard Mitigation Council found that for every dollar spent on pre-disaster investments in resilience to prepare for earthquakes, wind, and flooding, about $4 were saved in post-disaster damages.

Readers of this book will recognize some of the strategies that could promote resilience. One involves providing better information to homeowners, businesses, and governments to apprise them of both the risks being faced and cost-effective ways of mitigating those risks. Another would be to implement policies that provide incentives for private risk reduction investments.

Flood insurance in the United States

Floods are one of the most prevalent and most costly types of natural disasters. One instrument that can be used to promote resilience in the face of flood risk is flood insurance.

The National Flood Insurance Program (NFIP) was established in 1968 with the passage of The National Flood Insurance Act. Frequent flooding of the Mississippi River in the early 1960s led to the perception that floods were uninsurable risks and as such, there was a lack of availability of private insurance. One of the reasons for this is that private insurance companies rely on pooled risk. In any population of people, not all of them are expected to use their insurance, so those people subsidize those who need to file a claim. People are willing to pay annual premia to ensure that they do not lose larger amounts of money at one point in time. With floods, the entire community is typically affected and as such the insurance company must pay out a significant amount of money, typically more than they took in in premiums.

The NFIP is managed by the Federal Emergency Management Administration (FEMA). The goals are:

1 To provide flood insurance;
2 To improve floodplain management; and
3 To develop floodplain maps.

In principle a well-designed flood insurance program could both reduce the economic damages caused and provide funds to lower the recovery time following a flood. With climate change intensifying flood risks, enhanced insurance-financed resilience could be especially cost-effective.

As Example 11.1 points out, however, the insurance program has to be both well-designed and implemented appropriately if it is to be effective; otherwise it can end up increasing the damages. The devil really is in the details.

EXAMPLE 11.1

Enhancing resilience against natural disasters with flood insurance

Among other characteristics an efficient flood insurance design requires (1) premium levels high enough to cover the claims and (2) a structure of premiums that reflects the actual severity of the risk faced by the individual premium payers.

In the United States NFIP flood insurance isn't mandatory, but homes and businesses in designated flood-prone areas must carry flood insurance to qualify for federally backed mortgages. Maps are used not only to designate areas that are flood-prone, but also to characterize their degree of risk.

In practice does this program meet the two efficiency tests? In a nutshell . . . it does not.

Premium levels have historically been too low to cover the claims. In 2018 the NFIP debt, resulting from claims exceeding premium revenue, was $20.5 billion. Furthermore attempts by Congress to raise premiums produced a backlash, resulting in a political inability to raise premiums to the efficient level.

An added factor involves the maps that are used to characterize the risk. Since climate change is intensifying flood risk, older maps necessarily underestimate the risk. Unfortunately the process of updating the maps has not kept pace, so underestimates are common.

Some problems with the structure of premiums have emerged as well. In efficient policy designs policy-holders who undertake measures that lower the risk to their structures should face lower premiums to reflect the lower risk. These premium discounts would provide the motivation for homeowners and businesses to reduce risks. As Kousky and Shabman (2016) report, the NFIP has been offering substantial premium reductions for elevating the structures, but not for other effective flood mitigation measures. As a result those other measures are underutilized and damages are higher than necessary. As a practical matter the program mainly enables people to rebuild in the same areas without doing enough to mitigate future risks.

One would expect that these incentives would lead to higher future claims.

A study by the Natural Resources Defense Council found that some 2109 NIFP- covered properties across the United States have flooded more than ten times, and the NFIP paid to rebuild them after each flood. One covered home has flooded 40 times and received a total of $428,379 in flood insurance payments.

The mere existence of a flood insurance program is not, by itself, evidence of efficient resilience.

Sources: National Research Council. (2012). *Disaster Resilience: A National Imperative*. Washington, D.C.: The National Academies Press; Kousky, Carolyn, & Shabman, Leonard A. (July 29, 2016). The role of insurance in promoting resilience. This blog is available at: www.rff.org/blog/2016/role-insurance-promoting-resilience; Moore, Rob. (August 11, 2016). Flood, rebuild, repeat: The need for flood insurance reforms. This blog is available at: www.nrdc.org.

Increased frequency and intensity of storms and flooding has challenged the financial viability of the NFIP. Hurricane Katrina in 2005, followed closely in the same year by Rita and Wilma, created a huge debt burden for the NFIP.

2017 was the second highest flood damages claims year in NFIP's 50 year history. Hurricanes Harvey, Irma and Maria saw claim payouts and projected payouts totaling over $10 billion, well over revenues from that same year. 2018 was similar with Hurricane Matthew and the impacts of the Louisiana floods causing millions of dollars in damages. The NFIP borrows money from the U.S. Treasury to cover shortfalls, but since 2005, the program has been in financial distress (Figure 11.2).

With increased frequency and intensity of large storm events, programs such as the NFIP are starting to move from reactive polices to those that are more pro-active.

Pro-active versus reactive adaptation strategies

Rebuilding after a flood or hurricane is a reactive strategy. The way it currently works subsidized flood insurance actually provides *a perverse incentive*, meaning it incentivizes an inefficient

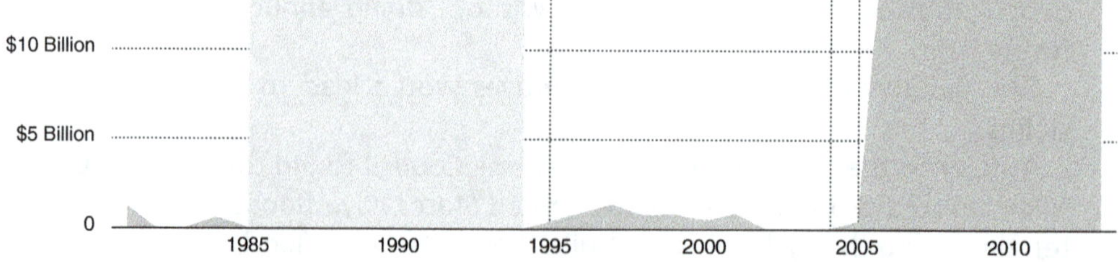

Figure 11.2 NFIP Debt

Source: Union of Concerned Scientists, Congressional Research Service Report. Estimate for Sandy debt from July 2013 GAO reports. Chart by Lam Thuy Vo.

behavior. If the government pays, people will rebuild. Current rules that require funds to be used to rebuild in the same place exacerbate what is already a *moral hazard*. Recall from introductory economics, a moral hazard is a situation in which there is a lack of incentive to protect against risk. In this case that lack of incentive follows from the fact that subsidized insurance protects policy holders from its consequences. The extra risks of living in a high-risk area are passed along to taxpayers.

These types of perverse incentives can intensify the risks in the long run. The National Flood Insurance Program has hit its borrowing ceiling several times and some debt has been forgiven, the amount of debt the program is carrying is not sustainable. Several policies and programs have been put into place to try to remedy those perverse incentives some more proactive than others.

Recent reforms have been aimed at strengthening the program. The Biggert-Waters Flood Insurance Reform Act of 2012 attempted to make the program more financially and structurally sound by raising flood insurance rates, by no longer subsidizing second homes and repeat-loss homes (those that had been flooded more than once). The Homeowner Flood Insurance Affordability Act of 2014 capped rate increases at 18 percent annually and repealed certain rate increases in order to keep flood insurance affordable. It also allowed properties that are in newly mapped flood zones to buy flood insurance at a preferred risk rate for one year.

None of these policies prevent building in the flood zones, but there are some other programs aimed at making communities less prone to high flood damages. The National Flood Insurance Program and the Federal Emergency Management Agency take some measures aimed at encouraging adaptation. Federal hazard mitigation grants provide funds for communities to invest in adaptation infrastructure. As we will see later in this chapter, these programs pass a benefit-cost test by wide margins.

Another program is the Community Rating System (CRS).[2] CRS communities receive flood insurance premium discounts for actions that reduce the damages from flood events. Communities that join the CRS program receive a score of 1 to 10. A community at high risk with no protections in place would receive a score of 10 and residents and businesses pay full premiums for flood insurance. Communities that undertake adaptation measures[3] receive points that can reduce their score. For every point a score drops, communities receive a 5 percent discount in flood insurance for a possible discount of 45 percent for a score of 1 (FEMA, 2018).

As of 2018 there were nearly 3.6 million flood insurance policies in approximately 1,450 communities.[4]

Finally, in the most pro-active reform, The Disaster Recovery Reform Act (DRRA) was signed into law October 5, 2018 as part of the Federal Aviation Administration Reauthorization Act of 2018. The Hazards Mitigation Grants Program provides funds to communities to mitigate future disaster risks. The DRRA modifies the Hazards Mitigation Grants Program with a focus on increasing mitigation and improving resilience to hurricanes, floods and wildfires. This program funds public infrastructure projects that increase community resilience before a disaster occurs. It allows applicants for flood claims to pursue other resilient options than simply rebuilding the same structure in the same place. One key feature is that under the DRRA 6 percent of the post-disaster assistance FEMA provides each year will be set aside for the FEMA's Pre-Disaster Mitigation fund. By providing more funding for pre-disaster mitigation, damage claims will be lower.

Flood insurance around the world

Flood insurance can differ by who "backs" the insurance (the government or the private sector) as well as whether or not the flood risk is bundled together with other risks. The possible combinations result in four types of insurance: bundled flood insurance backed by private markets; bundled flood insurance backed by the government; optional flood insurance backed by private markets; and optional flood insurance backed by the government.[5]

The United States follows the model in the last category; the National Flood Insurance Program is backed by the federal government. The flood risk is not bundled with any other risks (such as fire). As discussed previously, because of the numbers of policies in high risk areas, this program struggles to be financially viable.

Germany, Austria, and South Africa follow a similar model of unbundled flood insurance, but in these cases the insurance is backed by private markets. The opt-in (or optional) model suffers from the same issue as the NFIP with high numbers of policies in high risk areas. With private backers, however, prices fluctuate more and it is hard to keep prices low.

Insurance companies use the idea of pooled-risk in order to pay out claims for those experiencing damage from flooding events. Optional/non bundled insurance frequently causes a situation in which most policy holders experience damage since low risk policies are not bundled with high risk.

One solution to this problem is to bundle different risks together under one insurance policy thus spreading out the risk. If fewer policy holders are likely to make claims, financial viability is more likely. Maximizing the risk pool helps keep costs low especially if the insurance is backed by private markets which is the case in the United Kingdom, Hungary and China.

France and Spain also bundle risks for insurance, but use a model that is backed by the government. In France, for example, home and building insurance contracts are required by law to protect against natural disasters including floods. Private insurers are responsible for a certain amount and after that the government pays the remainder.

In many developing countries in Asia where flooding is a huge problem, most residents are unable to afford to pay for flood insurance. According to the Geneva Association, in 2014, "only 10 percent of losses from all types of natural disasters in Asia were insured compared with 60 percent in North America."[6]

Rethinking flood insurance

In the United States, take up rates are surprisingly low, despite mandates to purchase flood insurance for those that live in the mapped flood zones. Take-up rates are only about 49 percent (Kunreuther, 2018). Why is this the case? Kunreuther (2018) and Meyer and Kunreuther (2017) suggest that individuals tend to underprepare for disasters and other risks for 6 reasons.

1. **Myopia** – the tendency to focus on overly short future time horizons when appraising immediate costs and the potential benefits of protective investments
2. **Amnesia** – the tendency to forget too quickly the lessons of past disasters
3. **Optimism** – the tendency to underestimate the likelihood that losses will occur from future hazards
4. **Inertia** – the tendency to maintain the status quo or adopt a default option when there is uncertainty about the potential benefits of investing in alternative protective measures
5. **Simplification** – the tendency to selectively attend to only a subset of the relevant facts to consider when making choices involving risk
6. **Herding** – the tendency to base choices on the observed actions of others

Myopia refers to the idea while a safer home might be appealing, the upfront costs can be large and tend to overshadow the potential for reduced losses in the future. Homeowner amnesia arises, for example, when many homeowners who have voluntarily purchased flood insurance, tend not to renew that policy once they have experienced a few subsequent periods with no storms. People also tend to be *optimistic* and believe they will be immune from threats, especially those with a low probability of occurrence. *Inertia* or simple procrastination is easier than large changes and impacts the purchase of flood insurance. Flood probabilities are not easy to interpret and the tendency to *simplify* the risks may lead homeowners to underestimate them. Finally, many homeowners do what their neighbors do. Flood insurance purchases have been found to be less correlated with flood risk than with whether residents believed their neighbors purchased flood insurance! Can you think of other examples that fit these categories when you or others you know have underprepared or ignored risks? It isn't hard to find examples.

Flood insurance is one mechanism that can help individuals and communities be more resilient to flood risks, but there are certainly others. The National Flood Insurance Program typically requires that funds paid out in damage claims be used to rebuild a house in the same location. If that location is subject to frequent or increased flooding, homeowners are likely to be rebuilding again and again. Is there a better way? Preventing flood damages in the form of zoning changes and new building codes can save significant amounts of money. Is it worth the cost? What about for other disasters?

Given rising frequency of disaster events and the increasing costs of recovery from those disasters across the United States, strategies aimed at reducing those damages can be very beneficial. The strategies or mitigation actions prevent property loss and loss of life. As we saw in Chapter 4, Benefit-Cost Analysis is a powerful tool that can aid in decision making. The National Institute of Building Sciences produces an annual report that details the costs and benefits of meeting and exceeding building codes for flood, wind, fire and earthquake hazards. They also report the costs and benefits of select utility and transportation infrastructure mitigation and for federal hazard mitigation grants. The original study (2005) showed that every $1 spent on mitigation saves an average of $4 in future disaster costs. The most recent reports, due to the inclusion of additional data and analyses, show that the returns are actually higher.

Table 11.1 details the results by type of risk and adaptation strategy.

Table 11.1 Benefit-Cost Ratios for Each of the Four Adaptation Strategies for Each of Five Different Types of Hazards

National Benefit-Cost Ratio Per Peril *BCR numbers in this study have been rounded	Exceed common code requirements	Meet common code requirements	Utilities and transportation	Federally funded
Overall Hazard Benefit-Cost Ratio	4:1	11:1	4:1	6:1
Riverine Flood	5:1	6:1	8:1	7:1
Hurricane Surge	7:1	Not applicable	Not applicable	Too few grants
Wind	5:1	10:1	7:1	5:1
Earthquake	4:1	12:1	3:1	3:1
Wildland-Urban Interface Fire	4:1	Not applicable	Not applicable	3:1

These results find that on average for every $1 spent on federal grants, $6 in future disaster costs are prevented (a benefit-cost ratio of 6:1!). Assuring that current model building codes are met returns $11 for every $1 invested, while upgraded (stronger than current) codes would result in a 4:1 benefit/cost ratio. Finally upgrading the nation's utilities and transportation infrastructure would return $4 for every $1 spent on making them more resilient.

Notice that the highest payoffs vary by the type of risk. For riverine floods the biggest bang for the buck can be obtained from improving utilities and transportation infrastructure. For wind and hurricanes it is meeting the 2018 International Building Codes for new buildings. For hurricane surges and wildland-urban interface fires it involves enacting new, stronger codes.

What do these benefits include? The 2018 report quantifies benefits including future deaths, nonfatal injuries, repair costs for damaged buildings and contents, sheltering costs for displaced persons, loss of revenue to businesses due to interruption, loss of economic activity in the community, loss of services such as from hospitals and schools that are damaged, insurance costs and search and rescue costs. In particular, they find that just implementing the adoption of model codes and mitigating infrastructure would prevent 600 deaths, 1 million nonfatal injuries, and 4,000 cases of post-traumatic stress disorder (PTSD). They also find that designing buildings to exceed 2015 building codes would result in 87,000 new long-term jobs.

Clearly, these adaptation investment strategies that are designed to increase resilience increase efficiency. As the frequency (and intensity) of natural disasters increases, and increasing costs of disaster recovery, pre-event adaptation planning is key. Moving from re-active strategies (insurance and rebuilding) to more pro-active strategies can pay off.

Sea level rise and the role for adaptation

Flooding from increased intensity of storms is one of the impacts of climate change. Sea level rise is another. Projections for sea level rise vary by location and emissions scenario, but sea levels are rising and will continue to rise, likely at increasing rates.[7]

Sea level rise visualization tools provide some insight into what is at risk. For example, the NOAA Sea Level Rise Viewer[8] allows users to input different sea level rise scenarios and examine vulnerability and who and what is at risk. Billions of dollars of buildings and critical infrastructure is at risk. Critical infrastructure includes things like bridges, roads, wastewater treatment plants, levees, etc.

Exposure to the risks of sea level rise is high, both globally and in the Unites States. Presently about 40 percent of the world's population (2.4 billion people) lives within 100 kilometers of the coast.[9] In the United States, approximately 126 million people live on the coast. Annually, coastal countics produce more than $8.3 trillion in goods and services, employ 55.8 million people, and pay $3.4 trillion in wages (www.NOAA.gov).

Adaptation to higher sea levels and the increased flood risk that comes with those higher seas can take several forms: Hard infrastructure, soft infrastructure, green infrastructure and simply moving people and infrastructure away from the risks (managed retreat).

Does economics have anything to say about how best to protect that economic value? It turns out that the tools of economics can be very helpful in prioritizing among options.

Sea rise adaptation strategies include shoreline stabilization policies. Defensive structures harden the shoreline to prevent erosion from wave. These include bulkheads or seawalls. Offensive structures dissipate wave energy before it reaches the shoreline, like breakwaters. Living shorelines stabilize the shore through enhancement of natural habitat including sills and marshes (Stafford, 2018). These adaptation strategies all have different benefits and costs.

Defensive or hard structural barriers like sea walls or bulkheads are extremely expensive. They can also reduce access to the water and cause flooding at neighboring properties by diverting the water to nearby shoreline. They also interrupt the natural shoreline ecosystems. On the benefits side, they are durable and will stabilize the shoreline.

Offensive structures like breakwaters are more permeable and do less damage to the shoreline ecosystem. They allow access to the water. They can also maintain water quality and they allow runoff from the land back to the sea. They are also relatively expensive.

Living shorelines are becoming popular stabilization tools because they are the most natural. A living shoreline is a protected coastal barrier made of natural materials such as plants, sand or rock. Some living shorelines have been made of materials such as oyster bags. They serve to break waves and protect the marsh or land behind them. They are the most inexpensive as well, but they do require maintenance. They also take time to establish, but once established work well to prevent flooding.

Another alternative is beach renourishment, the subject of Example 11.2.

EXAMPLE 11.2

Shoreline stabilization and beach renourishment: buying time

Many cities and towns look to beach renourishment as a way to maintain the large economic value that beaches provide to recreationists, to business and property owners as well as protecting the ecosystem services value that beaches provide as nesting habitat for shorebirds and sea turtles.

Beach nourishment typically involves the dredging of sand from offshore and moving that sand to the shoreline to increase the height and/or width of the beach.

In the United States, beach renourishment projects have been implemented on approximately 350 miles of coastline, mostly on the Atlantic and Gulf Coasts at a cost of approximately $3 billion between 1950–2006 (Qui and Gopalakrishnan, 2018). Sea level rise augmented by storm surges causes erosion on many beaches, sand costs have increased making beach renourishment a costly, but many times necessary solution.

The northern barrier island that makes up part of the Outer Banks in North Carolina includes the towns of Duck, Kitty Hawk, Kill Devil Hills and Nags Head. In an interesting (unplanned) experiment, the town of Nags Head chose to replenish the sand on their outer beaches in 2011. This project was financed locally through a fund that included monies from increased occupancy and property taxes. Neighboring Kitty Hawk was not part of the beach renourishment area and hence could be considered a control on this experiment.

When Hurricane Sandy hit in 2012, the differences in damages between the two towns was stark. South Nags Head which had a history of damage from major storms, suffered no significant structural damage to buildings or infrastructure. Nags Heads experienced only about $250,000 in damages while the neighboring towns of Kill Devil Hills and Kitty Hawk recorded millions of dollars in damages.[10] The neighboring towns subsequently renourished their beaches.

Each time a beach is renourished it gets more expensive as sand is harder to find and even what is found is further from shore. There is not enough money, nor enough sand, for it to be anything but a short term adaptation strategy.

Beach renourishment also creates an interesting feedback loop. A renourished beach attracts development and raises property values. Higher property values (and the increased revenue from property taxes the municipalities earn create pressure to continue renourishment . Qui and Gopalakrishnan (2018) find that beach renourishment does, as expected, improve property values, but not surprisingly beachfront and nearshore property owners gain disproportionately more than others.

Short-term adaptations do buy time. As then Nags Head Mayor Bob Oakes, suggested after Hurricane Sandy, this one was successful in increasing the resilience of Nags Head.

> The comparison between the flooding, standing water and massive quantities of sand left on the road in Kitty Hawk and the relatively minor overwash in South Nags Head could not be any starker, and there is growing evidence that the beach nourishment Nags Head completed last year has performed as advertised. It's a really dramatic comparison between South Nags Head and Kitty Hawk.
>
> (*Northbeach Sun* November 2012)

Sources: Qiu, Y., & Gopalakrishnan, S. (2018). Shoreline defense against climate change and capitalized impact of beach nourishment. *Available at SSRN 3117979*; Tabb, Kip. (2012). "Thoughts on Hurricane Sandy." *North Beach Sun*. November 29. www.northbeachsun.com/outer-banks-thoughts-on-hurricane-sandy/ Adaptation can buy time, as with beach nourishment, or it can be a more permanent solution. with strategies such as managed retreat.

Managed retreat: buyouts

Another strategy involves not rebuilding on the vulnerable land. After Hurricane Ike hit Texas, FEMA bought back 756 damaged or destroyed homes. Those homes were then removed and the land converted to parkland (Meyer and Kunreuther, 2017). The buyout cost $103 Billion.

Buyouts typically do two important things. First, they move people away from a flood hazard zone, by purchasing the home and mandating that homeowners use the money to buy or build on higher ground. Second, the damaged homes are typically destroyed with the land becoming a park or allowed to revert back to some natural state. These open spaces serve as valuable flood control, being able to store water during flood events. Further, if these open spaces revert to marshlands, which have valuable flood control properties, they can also serve to protect other nearby properties.

Between 1989–2017, more than 40,000 homes have been bought out by FEMA. The program bought homes from eligible homeowners who opted in after Hurricane Sandy, including several Staten Island neighborhoods. Residents used the funds to move elsewhere.

After Hurricane Harvey, approximately 4,000 homeowners in the Houston area volunteered to have their homes purchased. Harris County Texas has a buyout program that relies on FEMA funds. The buyout program has moved slowly and only a few hundred homes had been purchased within the two years after Harvey hit.

Buying out homes after a disaster is partially reactive in that the homes were damaged by the storm, but proactive in that homeowners cannot rebuild in the same high-risk location. Most proactive, however, would be moving people away from the flood risk prior to a major flood event. This is starting to happen in several locations.

Prioritizing among adaptation options in the presence of ethical boundaries

The analytical tools that economists use to facilitate effective decision making are the primary tools used by agencies such as The World Bank to prioritize among the many adaptation policies available – benefit-cost analysis and cost-effectiveness analysis. As you may recall from Chapter 4, these decision-making tools can be very powerful for evaluating different choices. Benefit-cost analysis is widely known and frequently used, but can be challenging when it confronts basic questions of fairness or gender equity.

One emerging question deals with who gets to participate in government programs.[11] Buyouts, for example, which many times rely on benefit-cost analysis to identify which homes are eligible for buyouts, may only define homes in high valued neighborhoods as eligible. (Can you see why that might be the normal outcome?) Environmental justice considerations could in principle be included with the use of distributional benefit-cost analysis which considers the weights of the benefits and costs (or *who* is benefiting and *who* is paying), but using that form of analysis requires a conscious political decision to do so.

Cost effectiveness can be useful when benefits, but not the costs, are expressed in physical terms rather than monetary terms.

A third option, multi-criteria analysis, uses qualitative and quantitative data to prioritize options and is useful when it is not possible to quantify the costs and benefits. Challenges arise when different experts use different criteria to weigh the options.

Economics tools are very powerful aids for decision making, but need to be combined with location specific criteria and knowledge.

Information as an adaptive strategy

One strategy for dealing with risks of these sorts is to try to provide specific information to potential victims early enough for them to minimize their risks by taking such actions as leaving the area, or fortifying the area where they will take refuge. Generally, you may immediately feel, as we did, that more information earlier is obviously better. As Example 11.3 points out perhaps that intuition is less obvious than we thought.

EXAMPLE 11.3

What to expect when you are expecting a hurricane: hurricane exposure and birth outcomes

How many times have you watched with fascination or horror at the forecasted path of a hurricane? The cone-shaped anticipated path of a hurricane is reported based upon necessarily uncertain current forecasts. Because hurricanes do change paths, the earlier a forecast is released, the more uncertainty there is in the expected (and ultimate actual) landfall location. Thinking a hurricane will make landfall in the location you live, whether it eventually does or does not, causes stress for those who live there. Urgent preparations and, in some cases evacuation, may lead to unnecessary stress for those ultimately not at risk.

Do the benefits of early warning outweigh the costs? Hochard and Li (2019 working paper) address this question. As it turns out, these stressors induce negative birth outcomes for pregnant women. A large and growing literature addresses the health impacts of high stress events. In a recent paper by Almond et al., (2018), they note, "most economists now accept that disasters early in life are likely to have negative long-term effects on survivors, i.e., shocks that are extreme enough are likely to have persistent effects. Moreover, the fetal origins perspective will never be pivotal in a cost-benefit analysis of measures designed to forestall such disasters."

In statistical analysis, a Type I error is a false positive. Imagine if you receive a diagnosis for something you do not actually have, like being told by a doctor that you are pregnant and it turns out you are not. A Type II error, on the other hand, is a false negative. This would be the case of a doctor telling you that you are not pregnant when you actually are! A hurricane forecast center is set up to avoid Type II errors (the hurricane is coming, but you are told it is not), but not Type I errors.

The "cone of uncertainty" tracks the most likely hurricane path. It is likely you have watched the forecasts of the path of a hurricane and have noticed when it suddenly alters its path. Forecasts are getting better, but the data gets released very early and a week out, the data on which a forecast is based, are riddled with uncertainty.

When Hurricane Irene was headed for North Carolina (August 2011), nearly two-thirds of those who were preparing for direct impact ultimately received only mild wind and rain. In a study of about 90,000 births in the months surrounding Hurricane Irene, Hochard and Li find that birth outcomes were impaired in sites that did not end up in the path of the storm despite spending time in the "cone of uncertainty." In fact, for every additional 6 hours spent in the cone of uncertainty, birth weights drop by 4 grams. Low birth weights are linked to negative outcomes in adults such as increased susceptibility to diseases, lower aptitude, IQ and lower productivity and wages later in life. They compare a control group (babies born in the five-year window before Hurricane Irene)[12] to a treatment group (babies exposed *in utero* during Hurricane Irene). Using data from the North Carolina Department of Health and Human Services and National Oceanic and Atmospheric Administration's National Hurricane Center, they find that for each additional six hours spent in the cone of uncertainty, infants lost 4 grams of birthweight. Even though the western portion of the state was not hit by the hurricane, time spent in the cone of uncertainty led to impaired birth outcomes by women exposed, psychologically but not necessarily physically, to the storm. This is the cost of a Type I error. The authors conclude that actual storm damages depend on both predicted and actual storm paths. With the intensity and frequency of hurricanes expected to increase, forecasting agencies are likely to become increasingly risk averse. Risk aversion also comes at a cost though. Ultimately this begs the question: When is the ideal time to release a forecast?

Sources: Hochard, Jacob and Yuanhao Li. "Anticipating Mother Nature: Uncertain Hurricane Forecasts Impair Birth Outcomes" (2019 working paper.); Almond, Douglas, Janet Currie and Valentina Duque. (2018). "Childhood Circumstances and Adult Outcomes: Act II." *Journal of Economic Literature*, 56(4): 1360–1446.

Climate adaptation: managing water shortages

While climate change will increase the frequency of flooding at some times and in some areas, others will experience increased climate-induced water shortages. Impending water shortages can be dealt with by increasing water supplies (desalination of ocean water in coastal areas, for example,) or by learning to use less. The increasing need to conserve water during times of drought is giving rise to some novel adaptation mechanisms is in municipal water pricing.

Water scarcity is not a new topic by any means and economics has played a role in helping communities allocate water across multiple users. What we have learned from these experiences therefore may provide a foundation for developing particular strategies for dealing with impeding water scarcity. The task will not be easy. Many legal barriers inhibit the achievement of efficient water allocation, but municipalities have a variety of pricing structures to choose from that can be helpful for adaptation during either short-term or long-term water scarcity.

Municipal water pricing

Municipal water utilities must balance the competing goals of revenue stability, providing signals about water scarcity, reasonable prices for commercial users and equitable prices for homeowners.

Water utilities are typically regulated because they have a monopoly in the local area. One typical requirement for the rate structure of a regulated monopoly is that it earns only a "fair" rate of return. Excess profits are not permitted.

Due to high fixed costs these natural monopolies typically have falling average costs over a significant portion of their production. Water utilities have a variety of options to choose from when charging their customers for water knowing they need to balance pricing with revenue stability and water conservation during drought. Figure 11.5 illustrates the most common volume-based price structures. Some utilities still use a flat fee, which, from a scarcity point of view, is the worst possible form of pricing. Since a flat fee is not based on volume, the marginal cost of additional water consumption is zero. ZERO! Water use by individual customers is not even metered.

While more complicated versions of a flat-fee system are certainly possible, they do not solve the incentive-to-conserve problem. At least up until the late 1970s, Denver, Colorado, used eight different factors (including number of rooms, number of persons, and number of bathrooms) to calculate the monthly bill. Despite the complexity of this billing system, because the amount of the bill was unrelated to actual volume used (water use was not metered), the marginal cost of additional water consumed was still zero.

Volume-based price structures require metering. Some price structures include a fixed fee plus the consumption-based rate and some may include minimum consumption. Three common types of volume-based structures are uniform (or linear or flat) rates, declining block rates, and inverted (increasing) block rates (Figure 11.3).

Uniform or flat-rate pricing structures are extremely common due to their simplicity. Charging customers a flat marginal cost for all levels of consumption suggests that the marginal cost of providing

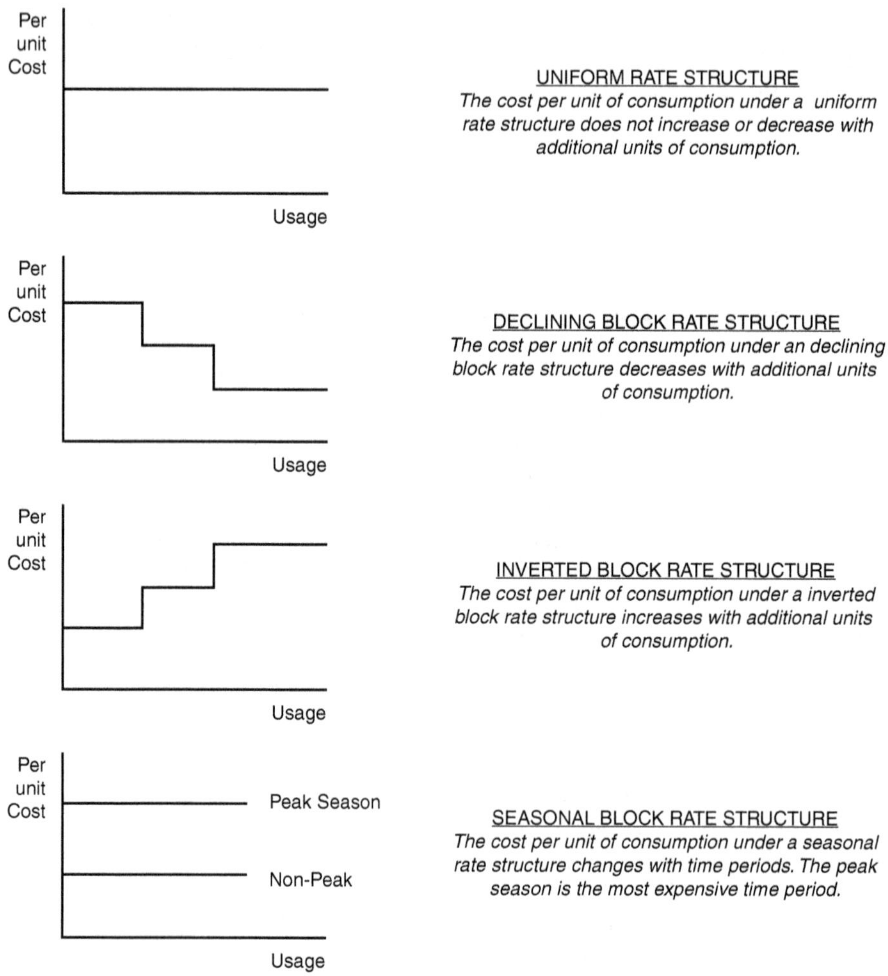

Figure 11.3 Overview of the Various Variable Charge Rate Structures

Source: Four examples of consumption charge models from water rate structures in Colorado: How Colorado cities compare in using this important water use efficiency tool, September 2004, p. 8 by Colorado Environmental Coalition, Western Colorado Congress, and Western Resource Advocates. Copyright © 2004 by Western Resource Advocates. Reprinted with permission.

water is constant. Although this rate does incorporate the fact that the marginal cost of water is not zero, it is still inefficient.

Declining-block-rate pricing has historically been much more prevalent than increasing block pricing. Declining block rates were popular in cities with excess capacities, especially in the eastern United States, because they encouraged higher consumption as a means of spreading the fixed costs more widely. Since utilities with excess capacity are typically natural monopolies with high fixed costs, decreasing block rates reflect the decreasing average and marginal costs of this industry structure. Additionally, municipalities attempting to attract business may find this rate appealing. However, as demand rises with population growth or increased use, costs will eventually rise, not fall, with increased use and this rate is inefficient.

By charging customers a higher marginal cost for low levels of water consumption and a lower marginal cost for higher levels, regulators are also placing an undue financial burden on low-income people who consume little water, and confronting high-income people with a marginal cost that is too low to provide adequate incentives to conserve. As such, many cities have moved away from a decreasing-block-rate structure (Tables 11.3 and 11.4).

One way that water utilities are attempting to respect the rate of return requirement while promoting water conservation is through the use of an inverted (increasing) block rate. Under this system, the price per unit of water consumed rises as the amount consumed rises.

Table 11.2 Pricing Structures for Public Water Systems in the United States (1982–2013)

	1982	*1987*	*1991*	*1998*	*2002*	*2004*	*2006*	*2008*	*2010*	*2012/13*
	%	%	%	%	%	%	%	%	%	%
Flat Fee	1	–	3	–	–	–	–	–	–	–
Uniform Volume Charge	35	32	35	34	37	39	40	32	31	30
Decreasing Block	60	51	45	35	31	25	24	28	19	18
Increasing Block	4	17	17	31	32	36	36	40	49	52
Total	100	100	100	100	100	100	100	100	100	100

Source: Raftelis Rate Survey, Raftelis Financial Consulting.

Table 11.3 World Cities and Rate Structures 2016

Rate Type	*Number of Cities*	*Percentage*
Fixed	4	1
Flat Rate or Linear	155	40.4
Increasing Block Rate	199	51.8
Declining Block Rate	11	2.8
Other	16	4.1
Total	385	100

Source: Global Water International, 2016 Tariff survey, www.globalwaterintel.com/tariff-survey/

This type of structure encourages conservation by ensuring that the marginal cost of consuming additional water is high. At the margin, where the consumer makes the decision of how much extra water to use, quite a bit of money can be saved by being frugal with water use. However, it also holds revenue down by charging a lower price for the first units consumed. This has the added virtue that those who need some water, but cannot afford the marginal price paid by more extravagant users, can have access to water without placing their budget in as much jeopardy as would be the case with a uniform price. For example, in Durban, South Africa, the first block is actually free (Loftus, 2005). Many utilities base the first block on average winter (indoor) use. As long as the quantity of the first block is not so large that all users remain in the first block, this rate will promote efficiency as well as send price signals about the scarcity of water.

How many U.S. utilities are using increasing block pricing? As Table 11.2 indicates, the number of water utilities using increasing block rates is on the rise, but the increase has been slow.

What about internationally? Global Water International's 2016 tariff survey suggests that worldwide the trend is moving toward increasing block rates (Table 11.3). Since their last survey in 2012, the number of increasing or inverted block rates increased (from 48 percent to about 52 percent), and is the leader in terms of pricing structures. Just about all the cities that reported have some sort of volumetric pricing, mostly flat and increasing block rates. Interestingly, nine of the 14 declining block rates are in U.S. cities.

Other aspects of the rate structure are important as well. Efficiency dictates that prices equal the marginal cost of provision (including marginal user cost when appropriate). Several practical corollaries follow from this theorem. First, prices during peak demand periods should exceed prices during off-peak periods. For water, peak demand is usually during the summer. It is peak use that strains the capacity of the system and therefore triggers the need for expansion. Therefore, seasonal users should pay the extra costs associated with the system expansion by being charged higher rates. Few current water pricing systems satisfy this condition in practice though some cities in the southwest United States are beginning to use seasonal rates. For example, Tucson, Arizona, has a seasonal rate for the months of May through September. Also, for municipalities using increasing block rates with the first block equal to average winter consumption, one could argue that this is essentially a seasonal rate for the average user. The average user is unlikely to be in the second or third blocks, except during summer months. The last graph in Figure 11.3 illustrates a seasonal uniform rate.

In times of drought, seasonal pricing makes sense, but is rarely politically feasible. Under extreme circumstances, such as severe drought, however, cities are more likely to be successful in passing large rate changes that are specifically designed to facilitate coping with that drought. During the period from 1987 to 1992, Santa Barbara, California, experienced one of the most severe droughts of the century. To deal with the crisis of excess demand, the city of Santa Barbara changed both its rates and rate structure 10 times between 1987 and 1995 (Loaiciga and Renehan, 1997). In 1987, Santa Barbara utilized a flat rate of $0.89 per ccf.[10] By late 1989, they had moved to an increasing block rate consisting of four blocks with the lowest block at $1.09 per ccf and the highest at $3.01 per ccf. Between March and October of 1990, the rate rose to $29.43 per ccf (748 gallons) in the highest block! Rates were subsequently lowered, but the higher rates were successful in causing water use to drop almost 50 percent. It seems that when a community is faced with severe drought and community support for using pricing to cope is apparent, major changes in price are indeed possible. As droughts become more frequent or more intense, these adaptations in pricing can ensure water availability.

In response to the more recent severe drought in California, Governor Jerry Brown mandated a 25 percent reduction in water use for residential customers. From a utility perspective, however, large reductions in consumer use can risk revenue stability and utilities may have trouble covering their (large) fixed costs. Recall, that water utilities are natural monopolies with very high fixed costs. Example 11.4 compares an alternative price structure focused on revenue stability with increasing block rates. In this case, revenue stability can be achieved, but at the expense of equitable pricing.

EXAMPLE 11.4

The cost of conservation: revenue stability versus equitable pricing

In January 2014, California Governor Jerry Brown proclaimed a drought state of emergency and asked all Californians to reduce water consumption by 20 percent. In April 2015, an executive order was issued that increased this to 25 percent. California was experiencing a severe drought and the state was running short of water. While these types of mandates do promote conservation of water, extreme reductions in water use can wreak havoc on water utility revenues since consumption-based rates help to cover utility costs.

As you have learned, natural monopolies, companies with very high fixed costs and hence declining average and marginal costs, must try to balance efficient pricing with covering their costs (including the fixed costs). Water utilities that charge consumption-based rates would suffer from revenue shortfalls when consumers conserve.

Spang et al. (2015) present a theoretical argument for a solution to the problem of revenue stability. They recommend a Consumption-Based Fixed Rate (CBFR) that divides a consumer's bill into three parts. Each part is based on a type of utility cost: fixed costs, fixed-variable costs (fixed costs that can rise with expansion, for example), and purely variable costs. Table 11.4 illustrates these types of costs.

The CBFR distributes fixed-fixed costs across all users while distributing the partial variable and variable costs more proportionally based on a percentage of total water consumed that month, that is, costs times (consumer's consumption/total water consumed system-wide).

Curious about whether or not the CBFR would work in practice, Bates College senior Amy Schmidt decided to try and find out. For her undergraduate senior thesis, Schmidt collected water utility data for two towns, one in California and one in Colorado, and found that the CBFR does indeed stabilize revenues, but at the expense of the low water users.

Table 11.4 Cost Definitions and Categorization

Fixed-Fixed Costs: Constant regardless of system use	Compliance costs, safety checks, office personnel, treatment plant energy use, etc.
Fixed-Variable Costs: Exist regardless of system use, but change in magnitude based on system demand	Piping infrastructure, chemicals, repairs and maintenance, etc.
Variable Costs: Depend directly upon consumption levels	Water purchases, energy for water pumping, etc.

Table 11.5 Estimated Consumer Bills as a Percentage of Actual under Simulated CBFR System, FY 2013–2014

	Lomita	*Longmont*
High-use consumers (50 hcf) % IBR System	CA 30%	CO 35%
Average-use (35 hcf) % IBR System	40%	171%
Low-use (15 hcf) % IBR System	63%	268%

Source: Adapted from Schmidt and Lewis (2017)

In other words, the CBFR solves the revenue problem, but creates inequities across individual water users. Low water users (usually lower income users) see large bill increases in some cases, while high water users benefit significantly with lower water bills.

Both towns – Lomita, California, and Longmont, Colorado – currently use increasing block rates. For both towns, the CBFR formula provides greater financial savings for high-use versus low-use consumers. This is due to the fact that high fixed costs are split evenly across all consumers. For Longmont, Colorado, medium- and low-users' bills actually increase significantly. For the low-use water consumers, water bills nearly triple (Table 11.5).

This result is due, in part, to how costs are categorized at this utility. For both towns, the CBFR clearly creates some inequities in pricing. While solving one problem, it creates another.

The results suggest caution with the CBFR method given the equity considerations. It could be useful, however during times of severe drought on a temporary basis to mitigate threats of revenue shortfalls.

Given these equity implications Schmidt and Lewis (2017) simulated a modified CBFR price structure with prices partially weighted by household income. Using this proportional pricing method or "Scaled Consumption-Based Fixed Rates," high-use consumers face increased water bills and low-use water consumers will pay approximately 30 percent less. They recommend consideration of such an alternative pricing model. The Scaled Consumption-Based Fixed Rate (SCBFR) appears to be a better option for ensuring revenue stability for the utility without jeopardizing affordability for low-income households.

Sources: Schmidt, A., & Lewis, L. (2017). The cost of stability: Consumption-based fixed rate billing for water utilities. *Journal of Contemporary Water Research and Education, 160*, 5–24; Spang, E. S., Miller, S., Williams, M., & Loge, E. J. (2015). Consumption-based fixed rates: Harmonizing water conservation and revenue stability. *American Water Works Association, 107*, 164–173.

Another corollary of the marginal-cost pricing theorem is that when it costs a water utility more to serve one class of customers than another, each class of customers should bear the costs associated with its respective service. Typically, this implies that those farther away from the source or at higher elevations (requiring more pumping) should pay higher rates. In practice, utility water rates make fewer distinctions among customer classes than would be efficient. As a result, higher-cost water users are in effect subsidized; they receive too little incentive to conserve and too little incentive to locate in parts of the city that can be served at lower cost.

Full cost recovery pricing

Another available pricing mechanism is to allow water utilities to earn more than a normal rate of return by charging a full cost recovery (FCR) price for water services. Full cost recovery includes both environmental and resource costs. Since allocative efficiency cannot be achieved without users receiving a clear signal regarding the value of water, FCR is a potential solution.

Full cost recovery is one of the pillars of the European Union's Directive on Water Policy. This Water Framework Directive states, "Member States shall ensure that water-pricing policies provide adequate incentives for water users to use water resources efficiently, and thereby contribute to the environmental objectives of this objective." What would implementing FCR pricing mean for member states?

Reynaud (2016) assesses the impact of full cost recovery pricing on European households in nine countries (Austria, Bulgaria, Czech Republic, Estonia, France, Greece, Italy, Portugal, and Spain). In particular, he was interested in the impacts of price changes on consumption and also on affordability and equity.

For the first measure, consumption, Reynaud estimates the required price increase resulting from implementing FCR pricing and estimates the price elasticity of demand (responsiveness to price). Not surprisingly, the results vary significantly by country. For Estonia and Italy, prices rise significantly and water consumption decreases by 21.2 percent and 33.8 percent respectively. For Italy, he measures the largest loss of consumer surplus at 81.2 euros per capita. This is likely due to the high price responsiveness of Italian households. The results are more moderate for Bulgaria, the Czech Republic, and Spain and there is very little effect for the others.

Water affordability is measured as the share of household income that is spent on water and a "water-poor" household is one that spends 3 percent or more of its income on water services. Of the nine countries examined, water affordability only becomes a problem in Bulgaria under FCR pricing since there households would then devote more than 3 percent of income on water services.

Clearly, FCR pricing must be evaluated on a case-by-case basis. Reynaud suggests that efficiency dictates that all households should pay the efficient price. Income redistribution schemes could then be utilized to address water affordability. In practice, however, such schemes might be difficult to implement. In the absence of such a scheme, subsidies or social pricing will be second best. Several European countries have implemented some form of social pricing.

Desalination and wastewater recycling

Changes in precipitation patterns due to climate change, combined with rising water demands are exacerbating existing water scarcity issues in some areas and creating them in others. According to the United Nations, more than two billion people live in countries experiencing "high water stress" (UN, 2018).[13] That number is expected to grow.

Solving water scarcity issues will become increasingly challenging, but desalination technologies, water reuse, and capturing (and storing) rainwater are all helping to make water supplies more reliable. Desalination provides only about 1 percent of drinking water worldwide, but that number is expected to grow.

Until recently, desalinized seawater has been prohibitively expensive and thus not a viable option outside of the Middle East. However, technological advances in reverse osmosis, nanofiltration, and ultrafiltration methods have reduced the price of desalinized water, making it a potential new source for water-scarce regions. Reverse osmosis works by pumping seawater at high pressure through permeable membranes. According to the Global Water Intelligence approximately 16,000 desalting plants were in operation in 2018. Desalination operations can be found in over 150 countries, though nearly half are in the Middle East and North Africa. Large numbers of facilities are also located in the United States, China and Australia. These plants produce about 25 billion gallons per day (Jones et al., 2019).

The current technology is energy intensive and hence very expensive. Costs vary considerably, but even the lowest cost projects ($750 per acre-foot) are more than double the cost of groundwater in most places (Katz, 2014).[14] Costs can be as high as $2,000 per acre-foot. Costs are expected to continue to fall by as much as 20 percent over the next five years. However, many projects are being built at extraordinary cost. Example 11.5 looks at the feasibility of desalination in northern China.

In the United States, Florida, California, Arizona, and Texas have the largest installed capacity. However, actual production has been mixed. In Tampa Bay, for example, a large desalination project was contracted in 1999 to provide drinking water. This project, while meant to be a low cost ($0.45/m^3) state-of-the-art project, was hampered by difficulties. Although the plant became fully operational at the end of 2007, projected costs were $0.67/m^3 (Gleick, 2006). In 1991, Santa Barbara, California, commissioned a desalination plant in response to the previously described drought that would supply water at a cost expected to be $1.22/m^3. Shortly after construction was completed, however, the drought ended and the plant was never operated. In 2000, the city sold the plant to a company in Saudi Arabia. It has been decommissioned, but remains available should current supplies run out.

In California, desalinated water from the new plant in San Diego costs approximately $2,000 per acre-foot, much more than the city currently pays for water diverted from the Colorado River and San Joaquin River Delta. In China, the choices between moving water or desalting it both prove to be exceptionally expensive (Example 11.5).

EXAMPLE 11.5

Moving rivers or desalting the sea? Costly remedies for water shortages

In most of northern China, freshwater is extremely scarce. China has been pursuing immense engineering projects in order to bring new water sources to this desperately dry, yet rapidly growing region. One three-phase project involves the diversion of water from the Yangzi River basin through hundreds of kilometers of canals and pipelines at extraordinary cost ($34 billion so far). The project is only partially complete. The other is a $4.1 billion power and desalination plant in the port city of Tianjin. The Beijing Power and Desalination Plant began operating in 2009. The capacity of the desalination plant will satisfy only a small portion of China's demand for water.

As of 2013, water from the plant cost 8 yuan per cubic meter (about $1.30) to produce. Diverted water from the Yangzi is expected to cost about 10 yuan. Both of these are at least 60 percent higher than what households currently pay, though water rates are rising. Even if higher water prices were imposed on consumers, prices would be unlikely to cover the true cost of either source. Desalination is very energy intensive. In China, that energy comes mainly from burning dirty coal. Diverting water is not without external costs either. Diverting water deprives southern China of the water needed to combat drought. Developing scarcity in a crucial resource like water can force some tough choices!

Source: Removing salt from seawater might help slake some of northern China's thirst, but it comes at a high price. *Economist*, February 9, 2013.

In early 2011, a large desalination project in Dubai and another in Israel were scrapped mid-construction due to lower-than-expected demand growth and cost, respectively. These two projects represented 10 percent of the desalination market.[11] Increased water scarcity and rising cost of alternative sources will eventually level the playing field for this technology-based adaptation strategy.

Roles for public and private institutions

Effective adaptation policies need to involve both the private and public sectors. One way to think about the optimal respective roles for the public and private sectors is to look closely at the role private decision makers – households and businesses – can be expected to play (and indeed have already played in response to climate threats that have already occurred). Will private agents adapt to a modified climate? Are those reactions likely to be both effective and sufficient or is there a role for the public sector to fill in gaps?

A review of economic research in this this area by Fankhauser (2016) makes it clear that the answer to the first question is a resounding "yes"! Private agents do adapt. One of the most studied sectors, agriculture, reveals clear differences in agricultural practices, such as crop choices, under different climate conditions. In the longer term, farmers also respond to weather fluctuations by adjusting the size of their farm or moving into non-farm activities.

Although few studies examine business investments in adaptation, the fact that households adjust their energy consumption to climatic factors is well documented. Both energy demand and the demand for associated products like air conditioning units are found (as expected) to vary both seasonally and across climate zones. Further these private responses have been found to produce substantial social benefits in terms of reduced mortality and enhanced well-being.

So while the literature does provide compelling evidence that private agents do adapt, it does not provide compelling evidence that these responses are either completely effective or sufficient. To start with, the number of adaptation investment situations that have been studied is very limited. Further, few of those that have been studied focus on adaptation to the kinds of major damages that are expected from a changing climate. More importantly, however, the literature documents a number of barriers that inhibit private actions, thereby reducing the effectiveness of a purely private adaptation strategy.

- Property rights matter. (Remember earlier discussion about the differences in energy efficiency investment incentives between renters and owners?) Because they would incur the losses caused by property damages, owners have higher incentives to invest in adaptation than renters. In general, ambiguous or compromised property rights can be a barrier to effective private action.

- Effective private action depends on good information on both the nature of risks and options for adapting to them. Much of this information about future risks is a public good, which means that it will be undersupplied unless the government supplies it or participates in its supply.
- Adaptation choices can also be limited by affordability, including how a low income diminishes the ability to borrow.
- Finally, much of the adaptation would involve public capital like roads or public transportation systems, and the effectiveness of many private adaptation responses would be affected by those public adaptation responses.

Even this brief list suggests a multi-faceted role for governments.

- It should identify circumstances that lead to adaptation market failures and adopt policies that correct or remove the distortions in incentives that lead to the failures.
- It should provide public information on the risks being posed by a changing climate.
- It should provide financial mechanisms for assisting populations facing affordability problems with adaptation.
- It should develop adaptation plans for publicly owned capital such as the transportation infrastructure.

Summary

Climate mitigation refers to interventions that reduce greenhouse gas emissions. Adaptation refers to actions that decrease vulnerability or increase resilience. Ultimately, we need both.

Climate change impacts from flooding, wildfires and drought are already being felt in many places. Regardless of what mitigation policies we pursue, adaptation strategies are also and will continue to be necessary. Adaptation to climate change is appropriately considered the more difficult problem. Adaptation strategies are very context and location specific. What works in one place, may not in another. Local considerations such as the amount of available financing are important. Distributional effects of costs and benefits must also be considered.

Fortunately, economic analysis of the climate change problem not only defines the need for action, but also sheds light on effective forms that action might take. Benefit-cost analysis and cost effectiveness analysis are powerful analytical methods that can aid in decision making when multiple options and time frames are being considered. Distributional benefit-cost analysis can help ensure that benefits and costs are most equitably distributed.

Policies can be reactive to the damages that actually occur (providing emergency shelters after every flood) or pro-active to reduce local vulnerability to the climate changes and, hence reduce the resulting damages (managed retreat). Clearly the latter is likely to be more cost-effective in the long run. Managed climate retreat can prevent an urgent climate refugee crisis, for example.

Adaptation is on-going and is very context and location specific. There is much work to be done in this rapidly growing area of environmental economics.

Discussion questions

1 What is your national, regional, or state government doing about climate change? Has your community participated in the CRS program? If so, how is it working out? What about buyouts? Is anyone working on an adaptation plan in your area? Do the basics of those approaches seem consistent with some of the characteristics of an efficient strategy discussed in this chapter? Why or why not?

2 *An ounce of prevention* is a common phrase in health care. It also seems to hold true for mitigation of storm and flood damages. How does benefit-cost analysis help with decision making on mitigation strategies?

Self-test exercises

1 a This chapter makes the point that normally a cost-effective climate change policy would involve both emissions mitigation and adaptation rather than choosing one approach or the other. Why?
b Under what conditions, if any, might it be cost-effective to use only emissions mitigation or adaptation, but not both?

Notes

1 Shalizi, Z., & F. Lecocq. (2010). To mitigate or to adapt: Is that the question? Observations on an appropriate response to the climate change challenge to development strategies. *The World Bank Research Observer,* 25(2) (August), 295–321, 295.
2 www.fema.gov/national-flood-insurance-program-community-rating-system
3 These adaptation activities are organized into four categories: provision of public information; mapping and regulations; flood damage reduction; and flood preparedness
4 www.fema.gov/national-flood-insurance-program-community-rating-system
5 www.naic.org/documents/cipr_study_1704_flood_risk.pdf?99
6 www.claimsjournal.com/news/international/2017/09/05/280336.htm
7 https://oceanservice.noaa.gov/facts/sealevel.html; https://sealevelrise.org/forecast/; www.globalchange.gov/browse/indicators/global-sea-level-rise
8 https://coast.noaa.gov/slr/
9 www.un.org/sustainabledevelopment/wp-content/uploads/2017/05/Ocean-fact-sheet-package.pdf
10 Personal communication, Andrew Keeler, Coastal Studies Institute, Eastern Carolina University, May, 2019.
11 Have there been buyouts in your city or town? You can search the FEMA database at this link. Available at: https://apps.npr.org/fema-table/ (Accessed July 2019).
12 The control group consisted of approximately 620,000 observations from earlier years involving pregnant women that did not experience a hurricane.
13 www.unwater.org/water-facts/scarcity/
14 An acre-foot of water is the amount of water it takes to cover one acre of land, 12 inches deep, or about the amount a family of five in the United States uses in a year.

Further reading

Colgan, C. S. (2016). The economics of adaptation to climate change in coasts and oceans: Literature review, policy implications and research agenda. *Journal of Ocean and Coastal Economics*, 3(2), 1.

Fankhauser, S. (2016). Adaptation to climate change. Grantham Research Institute on Climate Change and the Environment Working Paper No. 255. Available at: www.lse.ac.uk/GranthamInstitute/publication/adaptation-to-climate-change/. Last accessed on April 1, 2017. A survey of the economics of adaptation.

Fourth National Climate Assessment: Volume II: Impacts, Risks, and Adaptation in the United States. 2018. Available at:https://nca2018.globalchange.gov/

Meyer, R., & Kunreuther, H. (2017). *The Ostrich Paradox: Why We Underprepare for Disasters*. Wharton Digital Press, Philadelphia.

Stern, N. (2008). The economics of climate change. *American Economic Review*, 98(2), 1–37. As assessment by the former chief economist of the World Bank.

U.S. Environmental Protection Agency. (2016). *Climate Change Indicators in the United States*, 4th ed. EPA 430-R-16-004. Available at: www.epa.gov/climate-indicators. This report presents 37 indicators to help readers understand changes observed from long-term records related to the causes and effects of climate change, the significance of these changes, and their possible consequences for people, the environment, and society.

Additional references and other historically significant references are available on this book's eResource page: www.routledge.com/9781138587595

Chapter 12

Transportation

Managing congestion and local pollution

There are two things you shouldn't watch being made, sausage and law.

– Anonymous

Introduction

Mobility has two major impacts on policy. On the one hand, pollution is partly caused by the temporary location of the source – a case of being in the wrong place at the wrong time. This occurs, for example, during rush hour in metropolitan areas. Since the cars have to be where the people are, relocating them – as might be done with electric power plants – is not a viable strategy. On the other hand, it is more difficult to tailor vehicle emissions rates to local pollution patterns, since any particular vehicle may end up in many different urban and rural areas during the course of its useful life.

Mobile sources are also more numerous than stationary sources. In the United States, for example, while there are approximately 27,000 major stationary sources, well over 250 million motor vehicles have been registered, a number that has been growing steadily since the 1960s, when there were 74 million. Highway vehicle miles traveled (VMT) reached 3.1 million in 2015 after growing steadily since data started being collected in 1960 (U.S. Bureau of Transportation Statistics).[1]

Externalities from vehicle pollution is covered in Chapter 10. This chapter will focus on the other externalities that emerge from Transportation such as congestion externalities.

Subsidies and externalities

Vehicles emit an inefficiently high level of pollution because their owner-drivers are not bearing the full cost of that pollution. This inefficiently low cost, in turn, has two sources: (1) implicit subsidies for road transport and (2) a failure by drivers to internalize external costs.

Externalities

Road users also fail to bear the full cost of their choices because many of the costs associated with those choices are actually borne by others. For example:

- The social costs associated with accidents are a function of vehicle miles. The number of accidents rises as the number of miles driven rises. Generally the costs associated with these accidents are paid for by insurance, but the premiums for these insurance policies rarely reflect the mileage-accident relationship. As a result, the additional private cost of insurance for additional miles driven is typically zero, although the social cost is certainly not zero.
- Road congestion creates externalities by increasing the amount of time required to travel a given distance. Increased travel times also increase the amount of fuel used.
- The social costs associated with greenhouse gas emissions are also a function of vehicle miles. These costs are rarely borne by the driver of the vehicle.
- Recent studies have indicated high levels of pollution inside vehicles, caused mainly by the exhaust of cars in front.

Because the social costs of driving are not fully borne by motorists, the number of miles driven is inefficiently high.[2]

To elaborate on the congestion point, consider Figure 12.1. As traffic volumes get closer to the design capacity of the roadway, traffic flow decreases; it takes more time to travel between two points. At this point, the marginal private and social costs begin to diverge. The driver entering a congested roadway will certainly consider the extra time it will take her to travel that route, but she will not consider the extra time that her presence imposes on everyone else; it is an externality.

The efficient ratio of traffic volume to road capacity (V_e) occurs where the marginal benefits (as revealed by the demand curve) equal the marginal social cost. Because individual drivers do not internalize the external costs of their presence on this roadway, too many drivers will use the roadway and traffic volume will be too high (V_p). The resulting efficiency losses would be measured by the triangle *ACD* (the shaded area). One recent study estimates that highway congestion in 2014 caused 6.9 billion

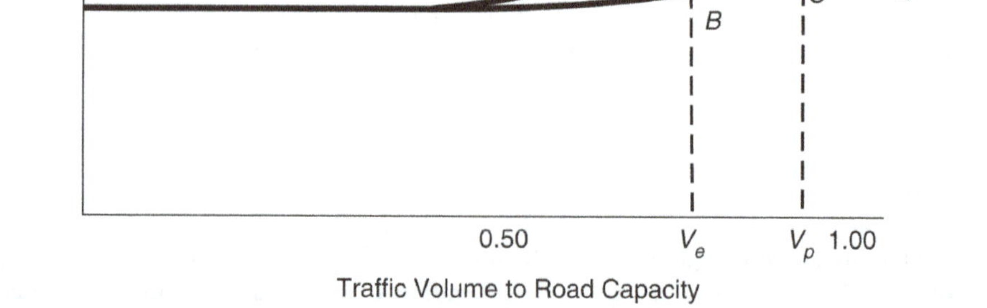

Figure 12.1 Congestion Inefficiency

hours of delay, 3.1 billion gallons of additional fuel to be used, resulting in a cost of $160 billion to highway users.

Consequences

Understated road transport costs create a number of perverse incentives. Too many roads are crowded. Too many miles are driven. Too many trips are taken. Transport energy use is too high. Pollution from transportation is excessive. Competitive modes, including mass transit, bicycles, and walking, suffer from an inefficiently low demand.

Perhaps the most pernicious effect of understated transport cost, however, is its effect on land use. Low transport cost encourages dispersed settlement patterns. Residences can be located far from work and shopping because the costs of travel are so low. Unfortunately, this pattern of dispersal creates a path dependence that is hard to reverse. Once settlement patterns are dispersed, it is difficult to justify high-volume transportation alternatives (such as trains or buses). Both need high-density travel corridors in order to generate the ridership necessary to pay the high fixed cost associated with building and running these systems. With dispersed settlement patterns, sufficiently high travel densities are difficult, if not impossible, to generate.

Policy toward mobile sources

European Union policy

Europe not only has much higher gasoline prices, but also it has developed strategies to make better use of transportation capital. Its intercity rail system is better developed than the one in the United States, and public transit ridership is typically higher within cities. Europe was also a pioneer in the use of car-sharing arrangements, an idea that the United States has now begun to mimic (see Example 12.1).

EXAMPLE 12.1

Car-sharing: better use of automotive capital?

One of the threats to sustainable development is the growing number of vehicles on the road. Though great progress has been made since the 1970s in limiting the pollution each vehicle emits per mile of travel, as the number of vehicles and the number of miles increase, the resulting increases in pollution offset much of the gains from the cleaner vehicles.

How to limit the number of vehicles? One strategy that started in Europe and has migrated to America is car-sharing. Car-sharing recognizes that the typical automobile sits idle most of the time, a classic case of excess capacity. (Studies in Germany suggest the average vehicle use per day is one hour.) Therefore the car-sharing strategy tries to spread ownership of a vehicle over several owners who share both the cost and the use.

Car sharing is now a major industry and there are car sharing programs in 30 countries on five continents.

The charges imposed by car-sharing clubs typically involve an upfront access fee plus fees based both on time of actual use and mileage. (Use during the peak periods usually costs more.) Some car-sharing clubs offer touch-tone automated booking, 24-hour dispatchers, and such amenities as child-safety seats, bike racks, and roof carriers.

Swiss and German clubs started in the late 1980s. As of 2013, 460,000 Germans belonged to car sharing clubs, up from 20,000 in 1997. An estimated 30 percent of customers sell their own cars after joining a car sharing program. The greatest concentrations of car-sharing vehicles in Europe are in the Netherlands, Austria, Germany, and Switzerland. The European idea of car-sharing was captured by some U.S. entrepreneurs who started Zipcar, a company that now boasts 400,000 members and fleets of car-sharing vehicles in 50 cities in North America and the United Kingdom. Similar car-sharing companies can now be found in hundreds of cities.

The University of California, Berkeley's Transportation Sustainability Research Center (TSRC) and Susan Shaheen have been tracking car-sharing developments worldwide since 1997. They report that as of January 1, 2014, 24 U.S. car-sharing programs claimed 1,228,573 members sharing 17,179 vehicles.

What could the contribution of car-sharing be to air pollution control in those areas where it catches on? It probably does lower the number of vehicles and the resulting congestion. Zipcar claims that each Zipcar takes 15–20 personally owned vehicles off the road. In addition, peak-hour pricing probably encourages use at the less polluted periods. On the other hand, it does not necessarily lower the number of miles driven, which is one of the keys to lowering pollution. The contribution of this particular innovation remains to be clarified by some solid empirical research.

Sources: Oliviera Jr., Pedro (2013). "Car sharing takes off in Germany," Available at: www.pri.org/stories/2013-10-04/car-sharing-takes-germany; (October 10, 2010). *The Economist*. "What do you do when you are green, broke and connected? You share." Retrieved from: www.economist.com/node/17249322?story_ id=17249322&fsrc=rss; www.zipcar.com; Shaheen, Susan, & Chan, Nelson. (March 2015). "Mobility and the sharing economy: Impacts synopsis - spring 2015." Available at: http://innovativemobility.org/?project=mobility-and-the-sharing-economy-impacts-synopsis-2.

Transportation pricing

The pricing of transportation falls into several categories: fuel taxes; congestion pricing; emissions pricing; pricing of accident externalities; pricing of roads; and pricing or subsidizing public transport. Some of examples of road pricing are highlighted later on.

Fuel taxes

As controls on manufacturers have become more common and vehicles have become cleaner, attention is increasingly turning to the user. Drivers have little incentive to drive or maintain their cars in a manner that minimizes emissions because the full social costs of road transport have not been internalized by current policy. How far from a full internalization of cost are we? Parry et al. (2007) compile estimates from the literature and find the sum of mileage-related external marginal costs to be approximately $2.10 per gallon.

Mileage-related externalities include local pollution, congestion, and accidents. Fuel external costs, such as oil dependency and climate change, are another $0.18 per gallon. Figure 12.2 illustrates current fuel taxes by country. These data suggest current fuel taxes would have to be much higher in many countries in order to internalize the full social cost of road transport.

But fuel taxes are not the only way to begin to internalize costs, and, by themselves, they would be a blunt instrument anyway because typically they would not take into account when and where the emissions occurred. One way to focus on these temporal and spatial concerns is through congestion pricing.

Congestion pricing

Congestion is influenced not only by how many vehicle miles are traveled, but also where and when the driving occurs. Congestion pricing addresses the spatial and temporal externalities by charging for driving on congested roads or at congested times. Four different types of congestion pricing mechanisms are in current use: (1) cordon (area or zonal) pricing, (2) facilities pricing (roads bridges tunnels), (3) pricing lanes, and (4) high occupancy toll (HOT) lanes.[3] Congestion pricing of roads or zones has recently been gaining considerable attention as a targeted remedy for these time- and space-specific pollutant concentrations. Anas and Lindsey (2011) note that truly efficient congestion pricing is challenging to implement because the toll not only varies over time, but also varies with lane width, travel speed, and the types of vehicles on the road. The amount of information necessary to implement fully efficient tolls may be unrealistically high.

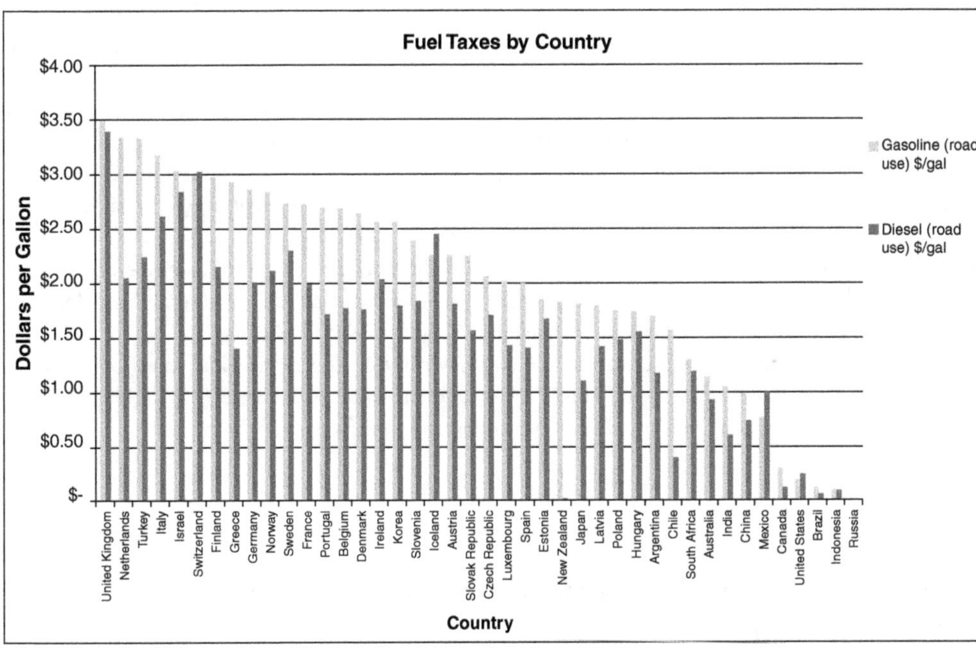

Figure 12.2 2019 Fuel Taxes in Selected Countries

Note: Tax rates are federal, with the exception of the United States and Canada, which include average state/provincial taxes.

Source: www.afdc.energy.gov/afdc/data/

Toll rings have existed for some time in Oslo, Norway, and Milan, Italy. In the United States, electronic toll collection systems are currently in place in many states. Express lanes for cars with electronic meters reduce congestion at toll booths. Reserved express bus lanes during peak hour periods are also common in the United States for congested urban highways. (Reserved lanes for express buses lower the relative travel time for bus commuters, thereby providing an incentive for passengers to switch from cars to buses.) High occupancy vehicle (HOV) lanes have also been established for some highways. During certain hours, vehicles traveling in the HOV lanes must have more than one passenger. Honolulu, Hawaii, has a high occupancy "zipper lane." The zipper lane is in the middle of the highway; in the morning commute hours the traffic travels toward Honolulu and by mid-afternoon the lane is literally zipped up on one side and unzipped on the other, creating an additional lane for the outgoing evening commute.

Several cities have also undertaken some innovative approaches to congestion charges including London, Stockholm, and Singapore. Perhaps the most far-reaching can be found in Singapore (Example 12.3). Bangkok also bars vehicles from transporting goods from certain parts of the metropolitan area during various peak hours, leaving the roads available to buses, cars, and motorized tricycles.

Beijing is currently evaluating a draft proposal to charge a congestion fee for commuters who enter certain parts of the city. In Beijing there are over 6 million vehicles, more than any other city in the world. Linn et al. (2015) find that the proposed fee will affect those who make discretionary trips rather than commuters. In part that is due to the nature of the affected commuters. The commuters most likely to be affected by the charge will be wealthier since they tend to live outside the congestion ring and typically drive to work, but they are likely to be less responsive than those with lower incomes would be.

Safirova et al. (2007) compare six different road-pricing instruments all aimed at internalizing the congestion externality. These include three types of cordon pricing schemes (area-based congestion taxes): a distance-based toll on highways, a distance-based toll on metro roads only, and a fuel tax. Examining the effectiveness of these instruments for the Washington, D.C., metropolitan area in 2000, they explicitly model how residential choice (and hence travel time) could be affected by the type of policy instrument employed. The question they ask is "But how do policies designed to address congestion alone fare, once the many other consequences associated with driving – traffic accidents, air pollution, oil dependency, urban sprawl, and noise, to name a few – are taken into account?"[4] They find that using "social-cost pricing" (incorporating the social costs of driving) instead of simple congestion pricing affects the outcome of instrument choice. Specifically, when the policy goal is solely to reduce congestion, variable time-of-day pricing on the entire road network is the most effective and efficient policy. However, when additional social costs are factored in, the vehicle miles traveled (VMT) tax is almost as efficient.

In general, for congestion charges to be efficient they must equal the marginal social cost of each trip and all vehicles should be charged. This is easier said than done as Example 12.2 highlights. New York City is the first city in the United States to impose congestion pricing.

EXAMPLE 12.2

New York City's congestion pricing plan: will it really reduce congestion?

In 2019 New York City passed a congestion pricing plan setting itself up to be the first US city to incorporate congestion pricing. The plan will be a form of "cordon pricing," in which motorists pay to enter a zone. For New York City, the zone will be Manhattan south of 60th Street and drivers of cars are expected to pay somewhere between $10-$15 to drive into the city. Truck drivers can expect to pay closer to $25. The tolls are expected to bring in $15 billion in revenue to be used to upgrade New York's aging subway system.

Congestion pricing is not a new idea. Nobel Laureate William Vickery first proposed a distance-based or time-based fare system for the New York City Subway in 1952. The goal of congestion pricing is, of course, to reduce congestion externalities by incentivizing commuters and other travelers entering a congested zone (usually a city center) to use alternative methods of transportation or to travel at less popular times. Will the NYC plan be successful? In other words, will it reduce congestion?

London may offer lessons for New York City. London has had a congestion pricing scheme since 2003 with the revenue dedicated to upgrading public transport. At the time of implementation, 300 additional city buses were introduced in order to facilitate the transition from cars to public transport. Has it worked? Yes. Traffic has been reduced 25 percent; private cars are down 39 percent. In the year following implementation, emissions were down 16 percent.

That does not mean the system is not without problems. London's congestion charge was implemented long before transportation network company (TNC) vehicles (Ubers, Lyfts, etc.) skyrocketed. Planners did not foresee those impacts. TNC registrations are up 75 percent over the last few years. Those vehicles are currently exempt from the congestion pricing! According to the Mayor of London's 2018 Transport Strategy, more than 18,000 different private TVC vehicles enter the congestion charging zone each day. These exempted vehicles are reducing the positive congestion impacts of the charge.

In NYC, Uber and Lyft and other TNC vehicles already pay a congestion charge of $2.75. Although this fee is small in comparison to a typical congestion charge, these drivers are clamoring for an exemption.

TNCs such as Uber and Lyft have changed the landscape of transportation. In New York City, bus ridership is down and subway use is stagnant. Clearly there is a need to get the charges right and recognize that exemptions can undermine the intended effects. Further using the revenue to create transportation alternatives can heighten the effects of the charge while providing a good low-cost substitute for those who need to enter the city and cannot afford the charge.

Revisiting the main questions: Will the NYC plan reduce congestion? It turns out that it depends on which vehicles get exemptions from the fee and what the fee revenue is used for.

Sources: "What is Better than Sitting in Traffic? Paying to Sit in NYC Traffic," www.wbur.org/onpoint/2019/04/04/new-york-congestion-pricing-traffic, April 4, 2019; "London Congestion Charge: what worked, what didn't, what next." The Conversation, March 2, 2018, http://theconversation.com/london-congestion-charge-what-worked-what-didnt-what-next-92478.

EXAMPLE 12.3

Zonal mobile-source pollution-control strategies: Singapore

Singapore has one of the most comprehensive strategies to control vehicle pollution in the world. In addition to imposing very high vehicle-registration fees, this approach also includes the following:

- Central Business District parking fees that are higher during normal business hours than during the evenings and on weekends.
- An area-licensing scheme that requires the display of an area-specific purchased vehicle license in order to gain entry to restricted downtown zones during restricted hours. These licenses are expensive and penalties for not displaying them when required are very steep.
- Electronic peak-hour pricing on roadways. These charges, which are deducted automatically using a "smart card" technology, vary by roadway and by time of day. Conditions are reviewed and charges are adjusted every three months.
- An option for people to purchase an "off-peak" car. Identified by a distinctive red license plate that is welded to the vehicle, these vehicles can only be used during off-peak periods. Owners of these vehicles pay much lower registration fees and road taxes.
- Limiting the number of new vehicles that can be registered each year. In order to ensure that they can register a new car, potential buyers must first secure one of the fixed number of licenses by submitting a winning financial bid.
- An excellent mass-transit system that provides a viable alternative to automobile travel.

Has the program been effective? Apparently, it has been quite effective in two rather different ways. First, it has provided a significant amount of revenue for the government, which the government can use to reduce more burdensome taxes. (The revenues go into the general treasury; they are not earmarked for the transport sector.) Second, it has caused a large reduction in traffic-related pollution in the affected areas. The overall levels of carbon monoxide, lead, sulfur dioxide, and nitrogen dioxide are now all within the human-health guidelines established by both the World Health Organization and the U.S. Environmental Protection Agency.

Source: Chia, N. C., & Phang, S.-Y. (2001). Motor vehicle taxes as an environmental management instrument: The case of Singapore. *Environmental Economics and Policy Studies*, 4(2), 67–93.

Private toll roads

New policies are also being considered to ensure that road users pay all the costs of maintaining the highways, rather than transferring that burden to taxpayers. One strategy, which has been implemented in Mexico and in Orange County, California, is to allow construction of new private toll roads. The tolls are set high enough to recover all construction and maintenance costs and, in some cases, may include congestion pricing.

Parking cash-outs

Providing parking spaces for employees costs employers money, yet most of them provide this benefit free of charge. This employer-financed subsidy reduces one significant cost of driving to work. Since this subsidy only benefits those who drive to work, it lowers the relative cost of driving vis-à-vis all other transport choices, such as walking, biking, and public transport. Most of those choices create much less air pollution; therefore, the resulting bias toward driving creates an inefficiently high level of pollution.

One way to rectify this bias is for employers to compensate employees who do not use a parking space with an equivalent increase in income. This would transfer the employer's savings in not having to provide a parking spot to the employee and remove the bias toward driving to work.

Bike sharing programs

Expensive and hard to find city parking and congestion helps incentivize consumers to find alternative means of transportation. Urban bike sharing programs have emerged in cities and are growing in popularity. Large cities such as Denver, Montreal, Minneapolis, New Orleans, and others have adopted these systems. New York City's Citibike program logs over 60,000 riders on some days (www.citibikenyc.com/system-data).

Common pricing for these bike share programs involves a membership fee plus pricing based on the rental time used. Typically, 30 minutes or less is free and over 30 minutes is priced at an increasing block rate. Data suggests that many riders who are approaching the 30-minute mark will return that bike to a stand and take out another. That new bike now has 30 minutes for "free." This behavior of docking a bicycle to keep trip length under a time limit is called "daisy-chaining." Daisy-chaining adds time to a commute since riders might need to go a short distance out of their way to dock the bike and take out another, but the cost savings can be significant depending on the marginal price of the next 30 minutes.

Pricing public transport

The common notion is that public transit reduces vehicle miles and hence reduces both emissions and energy use. That outcome, however, is not inevitable and the fares charged on public transit should reflect the actual situation.

In the absence of congestion, public transportation fees should equal the marginal cost of the service minus a subsidy that reflects the external benefits of taking public transportation (Anas and Lindsey, 2011). If the public transport actually turns out to increase congestion, however, fares should also include a congestion charge.

The level of the external benefits subsidy should also reflect the local situation. Although the subsidy may attract new riders to public transit, the source of these riders is important in structuring the fares. Did they actually come from personal vehicles? Or were they riders that would not otherwise have taken a trip? Subsidies may also attract riders that use public transport (such as light rail) as a complement, rather than a substitute, for driving. Subsidies that were designed by assuming that all public transit trips represent shifts from private vehicles will be excessively high to the extent these other trip sources are prevalent (Anas and Lindsey, 2011).

Feebates

Some research has found that consumers may undervalue fuel economy. One study found that consumers only consider the first three years of fuel savings when choosing a more fuel-efficient vehicle. This understates the value of fuel savings by up to 60 percent (NRC, 2002). To remedy this undervaluation bias among consumers purchasing new vehicles, feebates combine taxes on purchases of new high-emitting (or high-fuel-consumption) vehicles with subsidies for purchases of new low-emitting/low-fuel-consumption vehicles. By raising the relative cost of high-emitting vehicles, it encourages consumers to take the environmental effects of those vehicles into account. Feebate system structures are based on a boundary that separates vehicles charged a tax from those entitled to rebates. The simplest feebate structure uses a constant dollar rate per gallon of fuel consumed. The revenue from the taxes can serve as the financing for the subsidies, but previous experience indicates that policies such as this are rarely revenue-neutral; the subsidy payouts typically exceed the revenue from the fee. Feebates are not yet widely used, but Ontario, Canada, and Austria have implemented feebates. Greene et al. (2005) find that feebates achieve fuel economy increases that are two times higher than those achieved by either rebates or gas guzzler taxes alone.

Tax credits for electric vehicles

Tax credits subsidize the purchase of electric vehicles and can be as high as $7,500 per vehicle in the United States. Consumers who purchase electric vehicles not only receive a tax credit but also pay less for fuel and emit fewer greenhouse gases, both of which have external benefits. However, tax credits also have a downside – they lower tax revenue. The loss of revenue due to tax credits has been estimated to be $7.5 billion through 2019. Yet, since they help manufacturers reduce their miles per gallon average for new cars, the sales of electric vehicles help them to meet the CAFE standards.[5]

The availability of credits for any particular manufacturer's cars expires after that automaker sells 200,000 qualified vehicles. The theory behind this number is that it should be enough sales to produce sufficient economies of scale to make their unsubsidized price competitive.

Pay-as-You-Drive (PAYD) insurance

Another possibility for internalizing an environmental externality associated with automobile travel, thereby reducing both accidents and pollution, involves changing the way car insurance is financed. As Example 12.4 illustrates, small changes could potentially make a big difference.

EXAMPLE 12.4

Modifying car insurance as an environmental strategy

Although improvements in automobile technology (such as air bags and antilock brakes) have made driving much safer than in the past, the numbers of road deaths and injuries are still inefficiently high. Since people do not consider the full societal cost of accident risk when deciding how much and how often to drive, the number of vehicle miles traveled is excessive. Although drivers are very likely to consider the risk of injury to themselves and family members, other risks are likely to be externalized. They include the risk of injury their driving poses for other drivers and pedestrians, the costs of vehicular damage that is covered through insurance claims, and the costs to other motorists held up in traffic congestion caused by accidents. Externalizing these costs artificially lowers the marginal cost of driving, thereby inefficiently increasing the pollution from the resulting high number of vehicle miles.

Implementing PAYD insurance could reduce those inefficiencies. With PAYD insurance, existing rating factors (such as age, gender, and previous driving experience) would be used by insurance companies to determine a driver's per-mile rate, and this rate would be multiplied by annual miles driven to calculate the annual insurance premium. This approach has the effect of drastically increasing the marginal cost of driving an extra mile without raising the amount people spend annually on insurance. Estimates by Harrington and Parry (2004) suggest that calculating these insurance costs on a per-mile basis would have the same effect as raising the federal fuel tax from $0.184 to $1.50 per gallon for a vehicle that gets 20 miles per gallon. This is a substantial increase and could have a dramatic effect on people's transport choices (and, therefore, the pollution they emit) despite the fact that it imposes no additional financial burden on them.

Source: Harrington, W., & Parry, I. (2004). Pay-as-you-drive for car insurance. In R. Morgenstern & P. Portney (Eds.). *New Approaches on Energy and the Environment: Policy Advice for the President*. Washington, D.C.: Resources of the Future, 53–56.

Accelerated retirement strategies

A final reform possibility involves strategies to accelerate the retirement of older, polluting vehicles. This could be accomplished either by raising the cost of holding onto older vehicles (as with higher registration fees for vehicles that pollute more) or by providing a bounty of some sort to those retiring heavily polluting vehicles early.

Under one version of a bounty program, stationary sources were allowed to claim emissions reduction credits for heavily polluting vehicles that were removed from service. Heavily polluting vehicles were identified either by inspection and maintenance programs or remote sensing. Vehicle owners could bring their vehicle up to code, usually an expensive proposition, or they could sell it to the company running the retirement program. Purchased vehicles are usually disassembled for parts and the remainder is recycled. The number of emissions reduction credits earned by the company running the program depends on such factors as the remaining useful life of the car and the estimated number of miles it would be driven and is controlled so that the transaction results in a net increase in air quality.

Another accelerated retirement approach was undertaken in 2009 as a means to stimulate the economic recovery, while reducing emissions. Example 12.5 explores how well this Cash-for-Clunkers program worked.

We also have learned some things about what doesn't work very well. One increasingly common strategy involves limiting the days any particular vehicle can be used, as a means of limiting miles traveled. As Example 12.6 indicates, this strategy can backfire!

EXAMPLE 12.5

The Cash-for-Clunkers program: did it work?

On July 27, 2009, the Obama administration launched the car allowance rebate system (CARS), known popularly as "Cash for Clunkers." This federal program had two goals: to provide stimulus to the economy by increasing auto sales, and to improve the environment by replacing old, fuel-inefficient vehicles with new, fuel-efficient ones.

Under the CARS program, consumers received a $3,500 or $4,500 discount from a car dealer when they traded in their old vehicle and purchased or leased a new, qualifying vehicle. In order to be eligible for the program, the trade-in passenger vehicle had (1) to be manufactured less than 25 years before the date it was traded in, (2) to have a combined city/highway fuel economy of 18 miles per gallon or less, (3) to be in drivable condition, and (4) to have been continuously insured and registered to the same owner for the full year before the trade-in. The end date was set at November 1, 2009, or whenever the money ran out. Since the latter condition prevailed, the program terminated on August 25, 2009.

During the program's nearly one-month run, it generated 678,359 eligible transactions at a cost of $2.85 billion. Using Canada as the control group, one research group (Li et al., 2010) found that the program significantly shifted sales to July and August from other months.

In terms of environmental effects, this study found that the program resulted in a cost per ton ranging from $91 to $301, even including the benefits from reducing criteria pollutants. This is substantially higher than the per ton costs associated with other programs to reduce emissions, a finding that is consistent with other studies (Knittel, 2009; Gayer and Parker, 2013). In addition, the program was estimated to have created 3,676 job-years in the auto assembly and parts industries from June to December of 2009. That effect decreased to 2050 by May 2010.

In summary, this study found mixed results. An increase in sales did occur, but much of it was simply shifting sales that would have occurred either earlier or later into July and August. And while it did produce positive environmental benefits, the approach was not a cost-effective way to achieve those benefits. This case study illustrates a more general principle, namely that trying to achieve two policy objectives with a single policy instrument rarely results in a cost-effective outcome.

Sources: United States Government Accountability Office. (2010). Report to Congressional Committees: Lessons Learned from Cash for Clunkers Program Report # GAO-10–486; Li, S., Linn, J., & Spiller, E. (2010). *Evaluating 'Cash-for-Clunkers': Program Effect on Auto Sales, Jobs and the Environment*. Washington,

D.C.: Resources for the Future Discussion Paper 10–39; Knittel, C. R. (August 31, 2009). The implied cost of carbon dioxide under the cash for clunkers program. Retrieved from: http://ssrn.com/abstract=1630647; Gayer, T., & Parker, E. (2013). *Cash for Clunkers: An Evaluation of the Car Allowance Rebate System*. Washington, D.C.: Brookings Institution.

EXAMPLE 12.6

Counterproductive policy design

As one response to unacceptably high levels of traffic congestion and air pollution, the Mexico City administration imposed a regulation that banned each car from driving on a specific day of the week. The specific day when the car could not be driven was determined by the last digit of the license plate.

This approach appeared to offer the opportunity for considerable reductions in congestion and air pollution at a relatively low cost. In this case, however, the appearance was deceptive because of the way in which the population reacted to the ban.

An evaluation of the program by the World Bank found that in the short run the regulation was effective. Pollution and congestion were reduced. However, in the long run the regulation not only was ineffective; it was actually counterproductive (paradoxically it increased the level of congestion and pollution). This paradox occurred because a large number of residents reacted by buying an additional car (which would have a different banned day), and, once the additional cars became available, total driving actually increased. Policies that fail to anticipate and incorporate behavior reactions run the risk that actual and expected outcomes may diverge considerably.

Source: Eskeland, G. S., & Feyzioglu, T. (December 1995). Rationing can backfire: The "day without a car program" in Mexico City. World Bank Policy Research Working Paper 1554.

Summary

The current policy toward transportation externalities is wide ranging.

Local approaches, such as targeted inspection and maintenance strategies and accelerated retirement strategies, have had mixed success in redressing this imbalance. Since a relatively small number of vehicles are typically responsible for a disproportionately large share of the emissions, a growing reliance on remote sensing to identify the most polluting vehicles is allowing the policy to target resources where they will produce the largest net benefit.

The historic low cost of auto travel has led to a dispersed pattern of development. Dispersed patterns of development make mass transit a less-viable alternative, which causes a downward spiral of population dispersal and low mass-transit ridership. In the long run, part of the strategy for meeting ambient standards will necessarily involve changing land-use patterns to create the kind of high-density travel corridors that are compatible with effective mass-transit use. Though these conditions already exist in much of Europe, it is likely to evolve in the United States over a long period of time. Ensuring that the true social costs of transportation are borne by those making residential and mode-of-travel choices will start the process moving in the right direction.

Policies such as fuel-economy standards, fuel taxes, feebates, and sales quotas imposed on auto manufacturers for low-emitting vehicles are designed to accelerate their entry into the vehicle fleet.

The second new emphasis focuses on influencing driver choices. The range of available policies is impressive. One set of strategies focuses on bringing the private marginal cost of driving closer to the social marginal cost through such measures as congestion pricing and pay-as-you-drive auto insurance. Others, such as parking cash-outs, attempt to create a more level playing field for choices involving the mode of travel for the journey to work.

Complicating all of these strategies is the increased demand for cars in developing countries. In 2007, Tata Motors, the Indian automaker, introduced "the world's cheapest car," the Tata Nano. The Nano sells for about 100,000 rupees (US $2,500). Tata Motors expects to sell millions of these affordable, stripped-down vehicles. Fuel efficiency of these cars is quite good (over 50 miles per gallon), but the sheer number of vehicles implies sizable increases in the demand for fuel, congestion, and pollution emissions.

Affecting the choices facing drivers can only transpire if the economic incentives associated with those choices are structured correctly.

Discussion question

1 The NYC congestion pricing plan is proving to be quite controversial with different types of drivers clamoring to be exempted from the fee. Who should receive an exemption? How do you decide?

Self-test exercises

1 Suppose the nation wished to reduce fuel consumption not only to promote national security, but also to reduce the threats from climate change.

   a How effective is a strategy relying on the labeling of the fuel efficiency of new cars likely to be? What are some of the advantages or disadvantages of this kind of approach?
   b How effective would a strategy targeting the retirement of old, fuel-inefficient vehicles be? What are some of the advantages or disadvantages of this kind of approach?
   c Would it make any economic sense to combine either of these polices with pay-as-you-drive insurance? Why or why not?

2 a If a pay-as-you-drive insurance program is being implemented to cope with automobile-related externalities associated with driving, what factors should be considered in setting the premium?
   b Would you expect a private insurance company to take all these factors into account? Why or why not?

Notes

1 www.bts.gov/product/national-transportation-statistics
2 Data on vehicle miles traveled for the United States can be found at www.rita.dot.gov/bts/sites/rita.dot.gov.bts/files/publications/national_transportation_statistics/htl/table_01_35.html
3 Congressional Budget Office. (2009). *Using Pricing to Reduce Traffic Congestion.* Washington, DC: A CBO Study.
4 www.rff.org/rff/News/Releases/2008Releases/MarginalSocialCostTrafficCongestion.cfm
5 www.cbo.gov/publication/43633

Further reading

Anas, A., & Lindsey, R. (2011). Reducing urban road transportation externalities: Road pricing in theory and in practice. *Review of Environmental Economics and Policy*, 5(1), 66–88. A survey of the literature on road pricing and policy.

Harrington, W., & McConnell, V. (2003). Motor vehicles and the environment. In H. Folmer & T. Tietenberg (Eds.), *International Yearbook of Environmental and Resource Economics 2003/2004.* Cheltenham, UK: Edward Elgar, 190–268. A comprehensive survey of what we have learned from economic analysis about cost-effective ways to control pollution from motor vehicles.

Additional references and other historically significant references are available on this book's eResource page: www.routledge.com/9781138587595

Chapter 13

Water

Managing water quality for rivers, lakes, and oceans

Introduction

While various types of pollution share common attributes, important differences are apparent as well. These differences form the basis for the elements of policy unique to each pollutant. We have seen, for example, that although the types of pollutants emitted by mobile and stationary sources are often identical, the policy approaches differ considerably.

Water pollution control has its own unique characteristics as well. The following stand out as having particular relevance for policy:

1. Recreation benefits are much more important for water pollution control than for air pollution control.
2. Large economies of scale in treating sewage and other wastes create the possibility for large, centralized treatment plants as one control strategy, while for air pollution on-site control is the standard approach.
3. Many causes of water pollution are more difficult to trace to a particular source. Runoff from streets and agriculture, pharmaceutical waste discharged into waterways as well as atmospheric deposition of pollutants are major diffuse sources of water pollution. Control of these sources adds additional complexities for water pollution control.

These characteristics create a need for yet another policy approach. In this chapter we explore the problems and prospects for controlling this unique and important form of pollution.

Nature of water pollution problems

Types of waste-receiving water

Three primary types of water are susceptible to contamination. The first, *surface water*,consists of the rivers, lakes, and oceans covering most of the earth's surface. Historically, policy makers have focused almost exclusively on preventing and cleaning up lake and river water pollution.

Groundwater, once considered a pristine resource, has been shown to be subject to considerable contamination from toxic chemicals. *Groundwater* is water beneath the earth's surface in soils or rocks, or in geological formations that are fully saturated.

Oceans, the third type of water susceptible to contamination, has recently begun receiving much more attention.

While surface water serves as a significant source of drinking water, it has many other uses as well. Recreational benefits, such as swimming, fishing, and boating, are important determinants of surface water policy in areas where the water is not used for drinking. Groundwater is used primarily for irrigation and as a source of drinking water.

Sources of contamination

For pollution policy purposes, it is useful to distinguish between two sources of contamination – point and nonpoint – even though the distinction is not always crystal clear. *Point sources* generally discharge into surface waters at a specific location through a pipe, outfall, or ditch, while *nonpoint sources* usually affect the water in a more indirect and diffuse way. Examples of nonpoint source pollution include the runoff of fertilizers and pesticides from lawns and farms after rainstorms. From the policy point of view, nonpoint sources are more difficult to control because both the source and timing are hard to predict and, as such, they have received little legislative attention until recently. As a result of the gains made in controlling point sources, nonpoint sources now compose over half of the waste load borne by the nation's waters.

Contamination of groundwater occurs when polluting substances leach into a water- saturated region. Many potential contaminants are removed by filtration and adsorption as the water moves slowly through the layers of rock and soil. Toxic organic chemicals are one major example of a pollutant that may not be filtered out during migration. Once these substances enter groundwater, very little, if any, further cleansing takes place. Moreover, since the rate of replenishment for many groundwater sources, relative to the stock, is small, very little mixing and dilution of the contaminants occur.

Three primary sources of ocean pollution are oil spills, ocean dumping, and trash (primarily plastics) that ends up in the ocean. Oil spills from tankers have become less frequent and have (mostly) decreased in magnitude since 1970 (see Figure 13.1). Spills, however, are still not uncommon, as shown in Table 13.1. In 2018, the largest spill in 24 years was recorded after the MT Sanchi spilled 116,000 tons in the East China Sea. Offshore drilling has increased the risks, as the recent "BP spill" in the Gulf of Mexico illustrated. Various unwanted by-products of modern life have also been dumped into ocean waters based upon the mistaken belief that the vastness of the oceans allows them to absorb large quantities of waste without suffering noticeable damage. Dumped materials have included sewage and sewage sludge, unwanted chemicals, trace metals, and even radioactive materials. More recently, vast amounts of plastics have been found in the ocean. Much of this plastic gets ingested by sea life and kills thousands of marine birds and mammals each year.

Types of pollutants

For our purposes, the large number of water pollutants can be usefully classified by means of the taxonomy developed in Chapter 3.

Fund pollutants

Fund pollutants are those for which the environment has some assimilative capacity. If the absorptive capacity is high enough relative to the rate of discharge, they may not accumulate at all. One type of

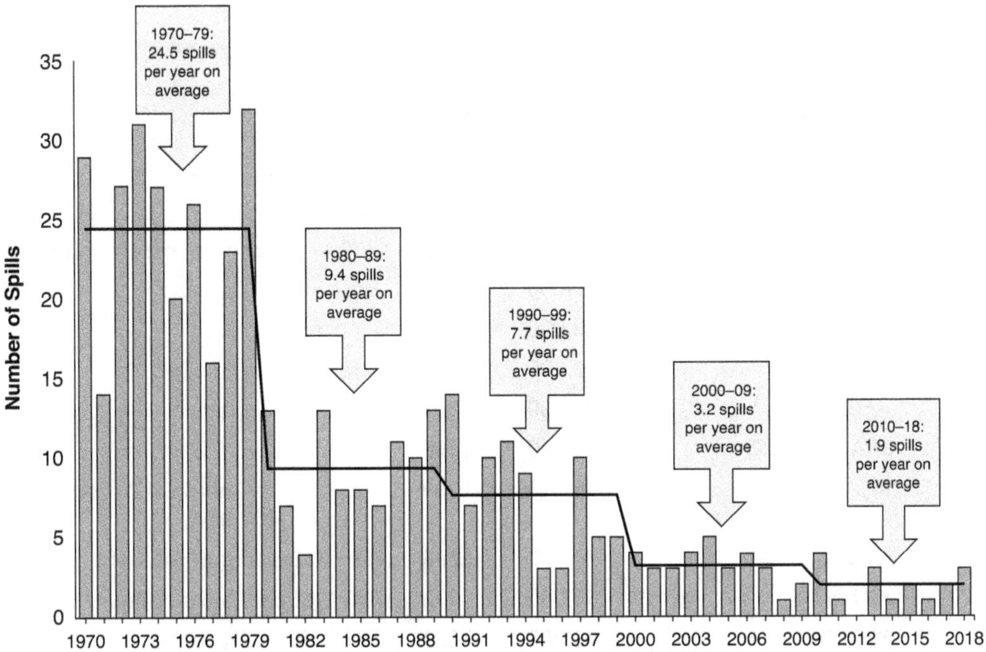

Figure 13.1 The Decreasing Frequency of Oil Spills from Tankers and Barges
Source: International Tanker Owners Pollution Federation Limited, www.itopf.com/informationservices/data-and-statistics/statistics/index.html

Table 13.1 Notable Oil Spills from Tankers

Rank	*Ship Name*	*Spill Size (tons)*	*Year*	*Location*
1	*ATLANTIC EMPRESS*	287,000	1979	Off Tobago, West Indies
2	*ABT SUMMER*	260,000	1991	700 nautical miles off Angola
3	*CASTILLO DE BELLVER*	252,000	1983	Off Saldanha Bay, South Africa
4	*AMOCO CADIZ*	223,000	1978	Off Brittany, France
5	*HAVEN*	144,000	1991	Genoa, Italy
6	*ODYSSEY*	132,000	1988	700 nautical miles off Nova Scotia, Canada
7	*TORREY CANYON*	119,000	1967	Scilly Isles, UK
8	*SEA STAR*	115,000	1972	Gulf of Oman
9	*SANCHI*	113,000	2018	Off Shanghai, China
10	*IRENES SERENADE*	100,000	1980	Navarino Bay, Greece

(*Continued*)

Table 13.1 Continued

Rank	Ship Name	Spill Size (tons)	Year	Location
11	*URQUIOLA*	100,000	1976	La Coruna, Spain
12	*HAWAIIAN PATRIOT*	95,000	1977	300 nautical miles off Honolulu
13	*INDEPENDENTA*	94,000	1979	Bosphorus, Turkey
14	*JAKOB MAERSK*	88,000	1975	Oporto, Portugal
15	*BRAER*	85,000	1993	Shetland Islands, UK
16	*AEGEAN SEA*	74,000	1992	La Coruna, Spain
17	*SEA EMPRESS*	72000	1996	Milford Haven, UK
18	*KHARK 5*	70,000	1989	120 nautical miles off Atlantic coast of Morocco
19	*NOVA*	70,000	1985	Off Kharg Island, Gulf of Iran
20	*KATINA P*	67,000	1992	Off Maputo, Mozambique
21	*PRESTIGE*	63,000	2002	Off Galicia, Spain
36	*EXXON VALDEZ*	37,000	1989	Prince William Sound, Alaska, USA
132	*HEBEI SPIRIT*	11,000	2007	South Korea

Source: International Tanker Owners Pollution Federation Limited, 2018, www.itopf.com/knowledge-resources/data-statistics/statistics/#major.

fund water pollutant is called *degradable* because it degrades, or breaks into its component parts, within the water. Degradable wastes are normally organic residuals that are attacked and broken down by bacteria in the stream.

The process by which organic wastes are broken down into component parts consumes oxygen. The amount of oxygen consumed depends upon the magnitude of the waste load. All of the higher life-forms in watercourses are *aerobic*; they require oxygen for survival. As a stream's oxygen levels fall, fish mortality increases, with the less tolerant fish becoming the first to succumb. The oxygen level can become low enough that even the aerobic bacteria die. When this happens, the stream becomes *anaerobic* and the ecology changes drastically. This is an extremely unpleasant circumstance because the stream takes on a dark hue, and the stream water stinks![1]

To control these waste loads, two different types of monitoring are needed: (1) monitoring the ambient conditions in the watercourse; and (2) monitoring the magnitude of emissions, or effluent as it is commonly labeled for water pollutants. One measure commonly used to keep track of ambient conditions for these conventional fund pollutants is *dissolved oxygen* (DO). The amount of dissolved oxygen in a body of water is a function of ambient conditions, such as temperature, stream flow, and the waste load. The measure of the oxygen demand placed on a stream by any particular volume of effluent is called the *biochemical oxygen demand* (BOD).

Using modeling techniques, effluent (measured as BOD) at a certain point can be translated into DO measures at various receptor locations along a stream. This step is necessary in order to implement an ambient permit system or an ambient emissions charge.

If we were to develop a profile of dissolved oxygen readings on a stream where organic effluent is being discharged, that profile would typically exhibit one or more minimum points called *oxygen sags*.

These oxygen sags represent locations along the stream where the dissolved oxygen content is lower than at other points. An ambient permit or ambient charge system would be designed to reach a desired DO level at those sag points, while a cap-and-trade or effluent charge system would simply try to hit a particular BOD reduction target. The former would take the location of the emitter into account, while the latter would not. Later in this chapter we examine studies that model these systems on particular watercourses.

A second type of fund pollutant, thermal pollution, is caused by the injection of heat into a watercourse. Typically, *thermal pollution* is caused when an industrial plant or electric utility uses surface water as a coolant, returning the heated water to the watercourse. This heat is dissipated in the receiving waters by evaporation. By raising the temperature of the water near the outfall, thermal pollution lowers the dissolved oxygen content and can result in dramatic ecological changes in that area.

Yet another example is provided by a class of pollutants, such as nitrogen and phosphorus, that are plant nutrients. These pollutants stimulate the growth of aquatic plant life, such as algae and water weeds. In excess, these plants can produce odor, taste, and aesthetic problems. A lake with an excessive supply of nutrients is called *eutrophic.*

The various types of fund pollutants could be ordered on a spectrum. On one end of the spectrum would be pollutants for which the environment has a very large absorptive capacity and on the other end pollutants for which the absorptive capacity is virtually nil. The limiting case, with no absorptive capacity, is stock pollutants.

Near the end of that spectrum is a class of inorganic synthetic chemicals called *persistent* pollutants. These substances are called persistent because their complex molecular structures are not effectively broken down in the stream. Some degradation takes place, but so slowly that these pollutants can travel long distances in water in a virtually unchanged form.

These persistent pollutants accumulate, not only in the watercourses, but also in the food chain. The concentration levels in the tissues of living organisms rise with the order of the species. Concentrations in lower life-forms such as plankton may be relatively small, but because small fish eat a lot of plankton and do not excrete the chemical, the concentrations in small fish would be higher. The magnification continues as large fish consume small fish; concentration levels in the larger fish would be even higher.

Because they accumulate in the food chains, persistent pollutants present an interesting monitoring challenge. The traditional approach would involve measurements of pollutant concentration in the water, but that is not the only variable of interest. The damage is related not only to its concentration in the water, but its concentration in the food chain as well. Although monitoring the environmental effects of these pollutants may be more compelling than for other pollutants, it is also more difficult.

Infectious organisms such as bacteria and viruses can be carried into surface water and groundwater by human and animal wastes and by wastes from such industries as tanning and meatpacking. These live organisms may either thrive and multiply in water or their population may decline over time, depending upon how hospitable or hostile the watercourse is for continued growth.

Most recently, medicinal waste has been found in watercourses and in fish tissue. In 2002, the USGS tested 139 rivers in 30 states and found that 80 percent of the streams sampled resulted in evidence of residuals from drugs such as birth-control pills and antidepressants. Residuals from soaps, perfumes, and caffeine were also found. A 2004–2009 USGS study found that pharmaceutical manufacturing facilities are also a significant source of contamination to the environment. They found that effluent at nearby wastewater treatment plants had 10 to 1000 times higher concentrations of pharmaceutical waste than a sample of 24 other wastewater treatment plants that do not receive the same type of waste. Antibiotics and drugs from animal-feeding operations are another source of pharmaceutical contaminants.[2]

While the magnitude of the damage that will ultimately be caused by these substances is not yet clear, it is certainly a challenge for water pollution control policy.

Stock pollutants

The most troublesome cases of pollution result from stock pollutants, which merely accumulate in the environment. No natural process removes or transforms stock pollutants; the watercourse cannot cleanse itself of them.

Inorganic chemicals and minerals comprise the main examples of stock pollutants. Perhaps the most notorious members of this group are the heavy metals, such as lead, cadmium, and mercury. Extreme examples of poisoning by these metals have occurred in Japan. One ocean-dumping case was responsible for *Minamata disease*, named for the location where it occurred. Some 52 people died and 150 others suffered serious brain and nerve damage. Scientists puzzled for years over the source of the ailments until tracing it to an organic form of mercury that had accumulated in the tissues of fish eaten three times a day by local residents.

In the United States, mercury contamination of fish has led to consumption advisories for many freshwater and migratory fish. Women of childbearing age and children especially are cautioned against eating large amounts of certain species. Debate 13.1 examines the effects of fish consumption advisories on consumer behavior.

In another case in Japan, known as the *itai itai* (literally, *ouch-ouch) disease*, scientists traced the source of a previously undiagnosed, extremely painful bone disease to the ingestion of cadmium. Nearby mines were the source of the cadmium, which apparently was ingested by eating contaminated rice and soybeans.

DEBATE 13.1

Toxics in fish tissue: do fish consumption advisories change behavior?

Since mercury persists and bioaccumulates, the concentrations of mercury rise as you move up the food chain. Ingested mercury has been linked to neurological disorders in infants and children. In January 2001, the Food and Drug Administration (FDA) released an advisory on methyl mercury in fish. An updated advisory was issued in 2004 and again in 2006. Part of that advisory reads as follows:

However, nearly all fish and shellfish contain traces of mercury. For most people, the risk from mercury by eating fish and shellfish is not a health concern. Yet, some fish and shellfish contain higher levels of mercury that may harm an unborn baby or young child's developing nervous system. The risks from mercury in fish and shellfish depend on the amount of fish and shellfish eaten and the levels of mercury in the fish and shellfish. Therefore, the Food and Drug Administration (FDA) and the Environmental Protection Agency (EPA) are advising women who may become pregnant, pregnant women, nursing mothers, and young children to avoid some types of fish and eat fish and shellfish that are lower in mercury

The FDA targeted women planning on becoming pregnant within six months, pregnant women, and nursing women to receive information about the new advisory on methyl mercury.

Using the Bureau of Labor Statistics' Consumer Expenditure Survey, Shimshack et al. (2007) examined the effectiveness of advisories in affecting consumer choices. In particular, they looked at the effects of the advisory on the consumption of canned fish during 1999–2002, a time period that includes two years before and two years after the advisory. They examined whether the groups targeted reduced their consumption of canned fish and what determined the responses.

Comparing target households (those with young children) to nontarget households, they found that targeted consumers significantly reduced their canned fish consumption as a result of the warning. College-educated consumers responded quite strongly. Additionally, they found that newspaper and magazine readership were significant in influencing the post-advisory reduction in fish consumption, but health consciousness was not. Interestingly, they also found evidence of spillover effects; nontargeted consumers also reduced their consumption of canned fish.

Access to information is clearly important to the success of a health advisory. At-risk consumers who were less educated and nonreaders did not significantly reduce consumption. The authors suggest that this particular group is also less likely to be able to withstand negative health shocks.

What is the best way to get information to different population groups? Unequal access to information creates unevenly distributed health risks and might be labeled an environmental justice issue.

Sources: Shimshack, J. P., Ward, M. B., and Beatty, T. K. M. (2007). Mercury advisories: Information, education and fish consumption. *Journal of Environmental Economics and Management*, *53*(2), 158–179; www.fda.gov;www.cfsan.fda.gov/~dms/admehg3.html.

As is typical with persistent pollutants, some of the stock pollutants are difficult to monitor. Those accumulated in the food chains give rise to the same problem as is presented by persistent pollutants. Ambient sampling must be supplemented by sampling tissues from members of the food chain. To further complicate matters, the heavy metals may sink rapidly to the bottom, remaining in the sediment. While these could be detected in sediment samples, merely drawing samples from the water itself would allow these pollutants to escape detection.

Traditional water pollution control policy

Water pollution control policies vary around the world. In this section we begin with a detailed discussion of U.S. policy, which provides a rich example of a typical legal approach to regulation. Later in the chapter we will look at the European approach, which has depended more heavily on economic incentives.

U.S. policy for water pollution control predates federal air pollution control. We might suppose that the policy for water pollution control would, therefore, be superior, since authorities have had more time to profit from early mistakes. Unfortunately, that is not the case.

The U.S. experience

Early legislation

The first federal legislation dealing with discharge into the nation's waterways occurred when Congress passed the 1899 Refuse Act. Designed primarily to protect navigation, this act focused on preventing any discharge that would interfere with using rivers as transport links. All discharges into a river were prohibited unless approved by a permit from the Chief of the U.S. Engineers. Most permits were issued to contractors dredging the rivers, and they dealt mainly with the disposal of the removed material. This act was virtually unenforced for other pollutants until 1970, when this permit program was rediscovered and used briefly (with little success) as the basis for federal enforcement actions.

The Water Pollution Control Act of 1948 represented the first attempt by the federal government to exercise some direct influence over what previously had been a state and local function. A hesitant move, since it reaffirmed that the primary responsibility for water pollution control rested with the states, it did initiate the authority of the federal government to conduct investigations, research, and surveys.

Early hints of the current approach are found in the amendments to the Water Pollution Control Act, which were passed in 1956. Two provisions of this Act were especially important: (1) federal financial support for the construction of waste treatment plants, and (2) direct federal regulation of waste discharges via a mechanism known as the *enforcement conference.*

The first of these provisions envisioned a control strategy based on subsidizing the construction of a particular control activity – waste water treatment plants. Municipalities could receive federal grants to cover up to 55 percent of the construction of municipal sewage treatment plants. This approach not only lowered the cost to the local governments of constructing these facilities, but also it lowered the cost to users. Since the federal government contribution was a grant, rather than a loan, the fees users were charged did not reflect the federally subsidized construction portion of the cost. The user fees were set at a lower rate that was high enough to cover merely the unsubsidized portion of construction cost, as well as operating and maintenance costs.

The 1956 amendments envisioned a relatively narrow federal role in the regulation of discharges. Initially, only polluters contributing to interstate pollution were included, but subsequent laws have broadened the coverage. By 1961, discharges into all navigable water were covered.

The mechanism created by the amendments of 1956 to enforce the regulation of discharges was the enforcement conference. Under this approach, the designated federal control authority could call for a conference to deal with any interstate water pollution problem, or it could be requested to do so by the governor of an affected state. The fact that this authority was discretionary and not mandatory and that the control authority had very few means of enforcing any decisions reached meant that the conferences simply did not achieve the intended results.

The Water Quality Act of 1965 attempted to improve the process by establishing ambient water quality standards for interstate watercourses and by requiring states to file implementation plans. This sounds like the approach currently being used in air pollution control, but there are important differences. The plans forthcoming from states in response to the 1965 Act were vague and did not attempt to link specific effluent standards on discharges to the ambient standards. They generally took the easy way out and called for secondary treatment, which removes 80–90 percent of BOD and 85 percent of suspended solids. The fact that these standards bore no particular relationship to ambient quality made them difficult to enforce in the courts, since the legal authority for them was based on this relationship.

Subsequent legislation

Point sources

The tone of the 1972 Amendments to the Water Pollution Control Act, now commonly called the Clean Water Act (CWA), is established immediately in the preamble, which calls for the achievement of two goals: (1) "that the discharge of pollutants into the navigable waters be eliminated by 1985" and (2) "that wherever attainable, an interim goal of water quality which provides for the protection and propagation of fish, shellfish, and wildlife and provides for recreation in and on the water be achieved by June 1, 1983." The stringency of these goals represented a major departure from previous policy.

This Act also introduced new procedures for implementing the law. Permits were required of all dischargers (replacing the 1899 Refuse Act, which, because of its navigation focus, was difficult to enforce). The permits would be granted only when the dischargers met certain technology-based effluent standards. The ambient standards were completely bypassed as these effluent standards were uniformly imposed and, hence, could not depend on local water conditions.[3]

According to the CWA, the effluent standards were to be implemented in two stages. By 1977, industrial dischargers, as a condition of their permit, were required to meet effluent limitations based on the "best practicable control technology currently available" (BPT). In setting these national standards, the EPA was required to consider the total costs of these technologies and their relation to the benefits received, but not to consider the conditions of the individual source or the particular waters into which it was discharged. In addition, all publicly owned treatment plants were to have achieved secondary treatment by 1977. By 1983, industrial discharges were required to meet effluent limitations based on the presumably more stringent "best available technology economically achievable" (BAT), while publicly owned treatment plants were required to meet effluent limitations that depended on the "best practicable waste treatment technology."

The 1977 amendments to the CWA continued this regulatory approach, but with some major modifications. This legislation drew a more careful distinction between conventional and toxic pollutants, with more stringent requirements placed on the latter, and it extended virtually all of the deadlines in the 1972 Act.

For conventional pollutants, a new treatment standard was created to replace the BAT standards. The effluent limitations for these pollutants were to be based on the "best conventional technology" In setting these standards, the EPA was required to consider whether the costs of adding the pollution control equipment were reasonable when compared with the improvement in water quality. For unconventional pollutants and toxics (any pollutant not specifically included on the list of conventional pollutants), the BAT requirement was retained but the deadline was shifted to 1984.

Municipal wastewater treatment subsidies

The program of subsidizing municipal water treatment plants, begun in 1956, was continued in a slightly modified form by the CWA. Whereas the 1965 Act allowed the federal government to subsidize up to 55 percent of the cost of construction of waste treatment plants, the 1972 Act raised the ceiling to 75 percent. The 1972 Act also increased the funds available for this program. In 1981, the federal share was returned to 55 percent. This program has run into problems as well, ranging from deficiencies in the allocation of the subsidies to the incentives created by the program.

The allocation of funds

Since the available funds were initially allocated on a first-come, first-served basis, it is not surprising that the funds were not spent in areas having the greatest impact. It was not uncommon, for example, for completed treatment plants to dump effluent that was significantly cleaner than the receiving water. Also, federal funds have traditionally been concentrated on smaller, largely suburban communities, rather than on the larger cities with the most serious pollution problems.

The 1977 CWA amendments attempted to deal with this problem by requiring states to set priorities for funding treatment works, while giving the EPA the right, after holding public hearings, to not only veto a state's priority list but also to request a revised list. This tendency to ensure that the funds are allocated to the highest-priority projects was reinforced with the passage of the Municipal Wastewater Treatment Construction Grant Amendments of 1981. Under this Act, states were required to establish project priorities for targeting funds to projects with the most significant water quality and public health consequences.

Operation and maintenance

This approach subsidized the *construction* of treatment facilities but provided no incentive to *operate* them effectively. The existence of a municipal wastewater treatment plant does not by itself guarantee cleaner water. The EPA's annual inspection surveys of operating plants in 1976 and 1977 found only about half of the plants performing satisfactorily. Later surveys found that the general level of wastewater treatment performance had remained substantially unchanged from previous years.

When sewage treatment plants chronically or critically malfunction, the EPA may take a city to court to force compliance with either a direct order or a fine. Because of various constitutional legal barriers, it is very difficult to force a city to pay a fine to the federal treasury. Without an effective and credible sanction, the EPA is in a difficult position to deal with municipalities. Therefore, the end of the treatment-plant malfunction problem cannot yet be pronounced with any assurance.

Capital costs

Due to the federal subsidies, local areas ended up paying only a fraction of the true cost of constructing these facilities. Since much of the money came from federal taxpayers, local communities had less incentive to hold construction costs down. The Congressional Budget Office (1985) estimated that substantially increasing the local share could reduce capital costs by as much as 30 percent. Local areas would be expected to be more careful with their own money.

Pretreatment standards

The final modification made by the 1977 amendments involved the introduction of pretreatment standards for waste being sent to a publicly owned treatment system. These standards were designed to prevent discharges that could inhibit the treatment process and to prevent the introduction of toxic pollutants that would not be treated by the waste treatment facility.

These standards suffer the same deficiencies as other effluent standards; they are not cost-effective. The control over wastewater flows into treatment plants provides one more aspect of environmental policy where economic incentive approaches offer yet another unclaimed opportunity to achieve equivalent results at a lower cost. They also do not cover emerging pollutants such as pharmaceuticals.

The Safe Drinking Water Act

The 1972 Act focused on achieving water quality sufficiently high for fishing and swimming. Because that quality is not high enough for drinking water, the Safe Drinking Water Act of 1974 issued more stringent standards for community water systems. The primary drinking water regulations set maximum allowable concentration levels for bacteria, turbidity (muddiness), and chemical-radiological contaminants. National secondary drinking water regulations were also established to protect "public welfare" from odor and aesthetic problems that may cause a substantial number of people to stop using the affected water system. The secondary standards are advisory for the states; they cannot be enforced by the EPA.

The 1986 Amendments to the Safe Drinking Water Act required the EPA to (1) issue primary standards within three years for 83 contaminants and by 1991 for at least 25 more, (2) set standards based on the BAT, and (3) monitor public water systems for both regulated and unregulated chemical contaminants. Approximately 60,000 public water systems are subject to these regulations. Civil and criminal penalties for any violations of the standards were also increased by the amendments.

More recent drinking water rules and standards cover MTBE, arsenic, radon, lead, microbials, and disinfection by-products. In 2007, the EPA issued a final ruling on lead and copper in drinking water, two contaminants that enter through plumbing materials. Many older homes have faucets or fittings of brass, which contain some lead, lead pipes, or copper pipes with solder.

The Clean Water Rule

The Clean Water Rule, also referred to as Waters of the United States (WOTUS), enacted by the Obama administration in 2017, was designed to take the existing federal protections on large water bodies and expand them to include the wetlands and small tributaries that flow into these larger waters. This rule closed loopholes that had left streams wetlands at risk for pollution.

In 2015, The EPA and the US Department of the Army issued a report examining the costs and benefits of expanding the definition of the "waters of the United States." Their estimate concluded that the water protections would indeed come at an economic cost – between $236 million and $465 million annually, *but* the report also concluded that the economic benefits of preventing water pollution would be much greater: between $555 million and $572 million. As we have seen throughout this book, estimating both the costs and the benefits informs decision making on environmental policy.

In early 2017, the President of the United States issued an Executive Order directing EPA and the Department of the Army to review and rescind or revise the 2015 Rule. In 2019, the EPA and the Department of the Army, under the Trump administration proposed to revise the definition of WOTUS to exclude some of those tributaries and wetlands suggesting that their value cannot be monetized. Their new analysis estimated the benefits at only $50 million per year (nearly 90 percent less) while the costs remained the same. Why the big difference? The EPA claimed that the nonmarket valuation studies that were used to evaluate the benefits were not recent enough and introduced uncertainty and thus assigned a value of $0 to the ecological benefits that were assigned a value of over $400 million under a different administration (Boyle and Kotchen, 2019). Is a value of $0 reasonable? Unlikely. As you recall from Chapter 5, there are well established methods to evaluate the benefits. And as you also know now from earlier chapters, making policy based solely on costs without a full evaluation of benefits is flawed policy indeed.

The TMDL program

In 1999, recognizing the problems with both the technology-based national effluent standards and the growing importance of nonpoint pollution control, the U.S. EPA proposed new rules designed to breathe fresh life into the previously unenforced *Total Maximum Daily Load (TMDL) program* of the Clean Water Act. A TMDL is a calculation of the maximum amount of a pollutant that a water body can receive and still meet water quality standards as well as an allocation of that amount to the pollutant's sources. The calculation must include a margin of safety to ensure that the water body can be used for its designated purpose. The calculation must also account for seasonable variation in water quality.

The TMDL program moves water pollution control toward the ambient standard approach long used to control air pollution. Under this program, water quality standards are promulgated by states, territories, and/or tribes. The promulgated standards are tailored to the designated uses for each water body (such as drinking water supply or recreational uses such as swimming and/or fishing). The states must then undertake strategies for achieving the standards, including significantly bringing nonpoint source pollutants under control.

Nonpoint source pollution

Nonpoint sources

In contrast to the control of point sources, the EPA was given no specific authority to regulate nonpoint sources. This type of pollution was seen by Congress as a state responsibility.

Section 208 of the CWA authorized federal grants for state-initiated planning that would provide implementable plans for area-wide waste-treatment management. Section 208 further specified that this area-wide plan must identify significant non-point sources of pollution, as well as procedures and methods for controlling them. The reauthorization of the Clean Water Act, passed over President Reagan's veto during February 1987, authorized an additional $400 million for a new program to help states control runoff, but it still left the chief responsibility for controlling nonpoint sources to the states.

The main federal role for controlling nonpoint sources has been the Conservation Reserve Program run by the U.S. Department of Agriculture rather than the EPA. Designed to remove some 40–45 million acres of highly erodible land from cultivation, this act provides subsidies to farmers for planting grass or trees. These subsidies are designed to result in reduced erosion and to reduce loadings of nitrogen, phosphorus, and total suspended solids.

Since the late 1980s, efforts focused on nonpoint sources have increased dramatically. Voluntary programs and cost-sharing programs with landowners have been the most common tools. Section 319 of the Clean Water Act specifies guidelines for state implementation of nonpoint source-management plans. Another recent role for municipalities has been the separation of storm water and sewer drains so that sewage treatment plants do not overflow during rainstorms. Federal subsidies have also assisted with these projects.

Nonpoint source pollution has become, in many areas, a significant part of the total problem. In some ways, the government has tried to compensate for this uneven coverage by placing more intensive controls on point sources. Is this emphasis efficient?

It could conceivably be justified on two grounds. If the marginal damages caused by nonpoint sources are significantly smaller than those of point sources, then a lower level of control could well be justified. Since in many cases, nonpoint source pollutants are not the same as point source pollutants, this is a logical possibility.

Or, if the costs of controlling nonpoint sources even to a small degree are very high, this could justify benign neglect as well. Are either of these conditions met in practice?

Costs

The research on economic incentives for nonpoint source pollution control is relatively thin as cost information is relatively scarce. Some of the case-specific studies available, however, can give us a sense of the economic analysis. Most of the available studies focus on nonpoint source pollution from agriculture.

McCann and Easter (1999) measured the size of transaction costs associated with various agricultural nonpoint source pollution control policies. Transaction costs (the administrative costs associated with implementing a policy) are an important consideration for nonpoint source pollution control because monitoring costs tend to be much higher than for point sources. The net gain from implementing a policy is the abatement cost savings minus the transaction costs; if the transaction costs are too high, they can offset all or a major part of the abatement cost gains from implementing the policy.

McCann and Easter looked specifically at the Minnesota River, where severe water quality problems made the river "unswimmable, unfishable and uncanoeable" near the Twin Cities. Four policies aimed at reducing agricultural sources of phosphorus were considered: education about best management practices, a conservation tillage requirement, expansion of a program that obtained permanent development rights, and a tax on phosphorus fertilizers. They found that a tax on phosphorus fertilizers had the lowest transaction costs ($0.94 million). Educational programs had the second-lowest transaction costs at $3.11 million. Conservation tillage and expansion of the conservation easement program had the highest transaction costs at $7.85 million and $9.37 million, respectively. In terms of transaction costs, their results suggest a comparative advantage for input taxes relative to the other approaches. However, since the price elasticity of demand for phosphorus fertilizers is low (it has been estimated at between –0.25 and –0.29), a considerable tax increase would be needed to guarantee the desired level of water-quality improvements.

Schwabe (2001) examines various policy options for nonpoint source pollution control for the Neuse River in North Carolina. He compares cost-effectiveness of both the initial and final proposed rules considered by the State of North Carolina. In 1998, nutrient loads in the Neuse River basin were so high that the basin received a *nutrient sensitive waters* classification.[4] In the two years prior to his study, two large swine waste spills caused major algal blooms and killed 11 million fish. The state of North Carolina initially proposed a rule requiring all farms with land adjacent to a stream to install vegetative filter strips. This was compared to a uniform rollback that measured loadings by county with the objective of a 30 percent reduction in total nitrogen loadings. Using a least-cost mathematical programming model, Schwabe finds that the uniform rollback is the more cost-effective strategy, especially since the 30 percent reduction target would be unlikely to be met using the vegetative strips. However, the author notes that the dominance of the uniform strategy is specific to this particular setting and should not be taken as a general proposition.

Despite this evidence, the regulatory reform movement that played such an important role for air pollution control has been much slower to emerge for water pollution control. An early attempt at trading was implemented for the Fox River in Wisconsin, but only one trade was completed in the first ten years after implementation.

Watershed-based trading

More recently, watershed-based trading programs have been gaining attention. In 1996, the EPA began exploring trading programs for the Tar-Pamlico River in North Carolina, Long Island Sound, Chesapeake Bay, and the Snake and Lower Boise rivers in Idaho. Dozens more followed. Worldwide, 57 trading programs are now in various stages of operation; 26 active, 21 under development, and ten inactive. All but six of these are in the United States. (Selman et al., 2009). Trading for water pollution control typically involves point source polluters meeting water quality standards by purchasing reductions from other sources (point or nonpoint sources) that have lower marginal costs of abatement.

Most of the markets currently in place focus on either nitrogen or phosphorus trading and most are too new to evaluate, but at least 23 U.S. water trading programs have carried out at least one trade (for some examples see Table 13.2). The six trading programs outside of the United States include four in Australia (three of which are active and one under development), one in Canada, and one in New Zealand (Selman et al., 2009).

Table 13.2 Summary of NPDES Trading Programs That Have Traded at Least Once as of June 2007

Point–Point Trades	*Pollutant(s) Traded*	*Point–Nonpoint Trades*	*Pollutant(s) Traded*
Long Island Sound, CT	Total Nitrogen	Wayland Center, MA	Total Phosphorus
Bear Creek, CO	Total Phosphorus	Croton Watershed, NY	Total Phosphorus
Neuse River, NC	Total Nitrogen	Pinnacle, DE	Total Nitrogen, Total Phosphorus
Charlotte Mecklenburg, NC	Total Phosphorus	Rahr Malting, MN	Offset Biological Oxygen Demand with Total Phosphorus
Cobb County, GA	Total Phosphorus	Southern MN Beetsugar Cooperative, MN	Total Phosphorus
City of Newman, GA	Total Phosphorus	Red Cedar River, WI	Total Phosphorus
MN General Permit	Total Phosphorus	Great Miami River, OH	Total Nitrogen, Total Phosphorus
Las Vegas Wash, NV	Total Ammonia, Total Phosphorus	Taos Ski Valley, NM	Total Nitrogen
		Carlota Copper, AZ	Copper
		Clean Water Services, OR	Temperature
		Cherry Creek, CO	Total Phosphorus
		Chatfield Res, CO	Total Phosphorus
		Lake Dillon, CO	Total Phosphorus

Source: Table from Summary of NPDES Trading Programs that Have Traded at Least Once as of June 2007. Retrieved from www.ecosystemmarketplace.com/pages/dynamic/article.page.php?page_id=5335&section=home&eod=1. Reprinted with permission of Ecosystem Marketplace.

EXAMPLE 13.1

Effluent trading for nitrogen in Long Island Sound

Long Island Sound experiences severe hypoxia (low levels of dissolved oxygen) during the summer months. This *eutrophication* is caused primarily by excess nitrogen discharges from municipal sewage-treatment plants. As discussed earlier in this chapter, most past policies for water pollution control focused on technology standards to control discharges. Economic theory suggests that lower costs can be achieved by providing flexibility to the plants via a permit-trading program. In the late 1990s, Connecticut, New York, and the U.S. EPA began exploring this possibility for sewage-treatment plants with discharges reaching Long Island Sound. The plan targeted trading to certain management zones. The overall goal of this management plan was a 58.5 percent reduction in nitrogen over 15 years, beginning in 1999.

Bennett et al. (2000) estimate the costs associated with the proposed scheme, whereby trading is restricted to the 11 management zones designated by the *Long Island Sound Study*. They then estimate the cost savings of alternative programs that expand the zone of trading to (1) trading among sources and across zones, but within state boundaries, and (2) trading across all sources. For each trading scenario, polluting sources are grouped into trading "bubbles" that are based on geographic location. Trading is allowed to take place within each bubble, but not among bubbles.

Bennett et al. find what economic theory would predict – that cost savings rise (and rise substantially) as the scope of trading expands (meaning, fewer bubbles). Expanding trading across the two state bubbles could save up to 20 percent or $156 million, based on their estimates. The following table is reproduced from their results.

Table 13.3 Effluent Trading in Long Island Sound: Cost Savings Estimates from Expanding the Scope

Number of Trading Bubbles	*Present Value of Total Costs ($ million)*	*Cost Savings Relative to 11 Bubbles ($ million)*	*Percentage Savings*
11	781.44	—	—
2	740.55	40.89	5.23
1	625.14	156.30	20.00

Not all discharges have the same impact. In fact, discharges from zones in the eastern portion of Long Island Sound and the northern parts of Connecticut do not have as detrimental effects as those closer to New York City. Despite differences in abatement cost, the proposed management plan recommends that each management zone be responsible for an equal percentage of nitrogen reduction.

While marginal abatement costs vary widely across management zones (suggesting that trades could reduce costs), the marginal contributions to damages also vary widely, thus ruling out a simple system of ton-for-ton effluent trades. (More complicated ambient, or location based trading ratios would be required to achieve cost-effectiveness for this nonuniformly mixed pollutant.) Currently, in recognition of this complexity, trading is not being considered across the boundaries of the 11 management zones despite the apparent potential cost savings.

Between 2002 and 2004, Connecticut's Long Island Sound program reduced more total nitrogen via trading than was needed to meet the TMDL requirement. Between 2002 and 2009, 15.5 million nitrogen credits were exchanged at a total value of $45.9 million. Cost savings through trading are estimated at $300 to $400 million. The credit price in 2002 was $1.65 and rose to $4.54 in 2009. As it turns out, however, the price is set by the state and trades go through the nitrogen credit exchange, so potential gains from trade resulting from allowance price fluctuations are not captured.

Sources: Bennett, L. L., Thorpe, S. G., & Guse, A. J. (December 2000). Cost-effective control of nitrogen loadings in Long Island Sound. *Water Resources Research*, 36(12), 3711–3720; Kibler, V., & Kasturi, K. (2007). Status of water quality trading programs today. Katoomba Group's Ecosystem Marketplace. Retrieved from www.ecosystemmarketplace.com; Connecticut Department of Environmental Protection. (2010). Retrieved from www.ct.gov/deep/cwp/view.asp?a=2719&q=325572&deepNav_GID=1635%20

Ex ante studies, however, suggest that the economic benefits can be large. Example 13.1 illustrates the potential for tradable effluent cost savings for treating hypoxic (low levels of dissolved oxygen) conditions in Long Island Sound. Allowing firms the flexibility to exploit economies of scale in pollution-control technology can provide for large savings. This point-point trading program has resulted in cheaper *and* faster cleanup.

The EPA supports market-based programs for certain pollutants if they can help meet Clean Water Act goals. In 2008, the EPA issued a Water Quality Trading Evaluation and found significant cost savings and nutrient (nitrogen and phosphorus) reductions for the trading programs they evaluated. Comparing across programs is somewhat challenging, however, since they do not all rely on the same trading mechanism. Some trades are case-by-case, while others are open-market trades. Some rely on a broker, while others operate through direct negotiations. And some are not based on market mechanisms at all.[5] Watershed-based trading is complicated by the difficulties of accounting for spatial distribution of pollutants, thus requiring complicated trading ratios (Olmstead, 2010). A trading ratio ensures that the reduction in pollution after a trade is equal to the required reduction. Important features of the trading ratio are the location of the sources, the distance between buyers and sellers, uncertainty if nonpoint source pollutants are involved and whether or not the pollutant is equivalent after discharge. Complicated trading ratios may be one barrier to trade. Using the Upper Ohio River Basin as a case study, Farrow et al. (2005) demonstrate that social costs can be minimized if trading ratios are based on relative damages between sources. Of course, calculating the damages remains a challenge.

Water quality trading is frequently complicated by measurement and enforcement challenges (especially for nonpoint sources), abatement cost differentials, sufficient trading volumes, and trading flexibility (Fisher-Vanden and Olmstead, 2013). Where markets are thin (few traders) or when cost differentials are slight, there will be very few feasible trades. Large differences in marginal abatement costs can result in the largest gains from trade; the most significant gains are likely to come from point – nonpoint source trades. Lack of flexibility in trading over time and space has also inhibited water quality trading (Fisher-Vanden and Olmstead, 2013).

The fact that point and nonpoint sources have received such different treatment from the EPA, however, suggests the possibility that costs could be lowered by a more careful balancing of these control options. Point sources have received the most attention and have cleaned up considerably. Nonpoint sources have received very little attention. This suggests that perhaps the marginal cost of additional abatement for point sources is now sufficiently high that it justifies moving control toward nonpoint sources. Figure 13.2 portrays the current situation. The marginal cost of abatement of point sources (MC_{PS}) is everywhere lower than the marginal cost of abatement of nonpoint sources (MC_{NPS}). However, with policy focus on the point source, the point source has cleaned up, meaning that source is on a higher portion of its marginal cost curve. Without policy addressing the nonpoint source, the nonpoint source is still at zero cleanup. Now, comparing the two at their different cleanup levels, the nonpoint source has a *lower* marginal cost of abatement! Consider a scenario in which point sources have already cleaned up 50 percent of their discharges (point d in Figure 13.2) and the nonpoint source has cleaned up none. Suppose the regulatory agency is seeking additional cleanup of 10 percent. Can you see how the total cost of this additional abatement would be less for the nonpoint source than the point source? The point source could clean up 10 percent at a total cost of the area defined by the points labeled defg. Or the nonpoint source could clean up the same amount for the smaller cost of area 0abc. In other words, the total cost for the point source of additional cleanup (or area defg) is more than the total cost for the same amount of cleanup from the nonpoint source (0abc). These two sources can reduce total cost by trading until marginal cost is equalized at the dotted line. After that point, all gains from trade would be eliminated.

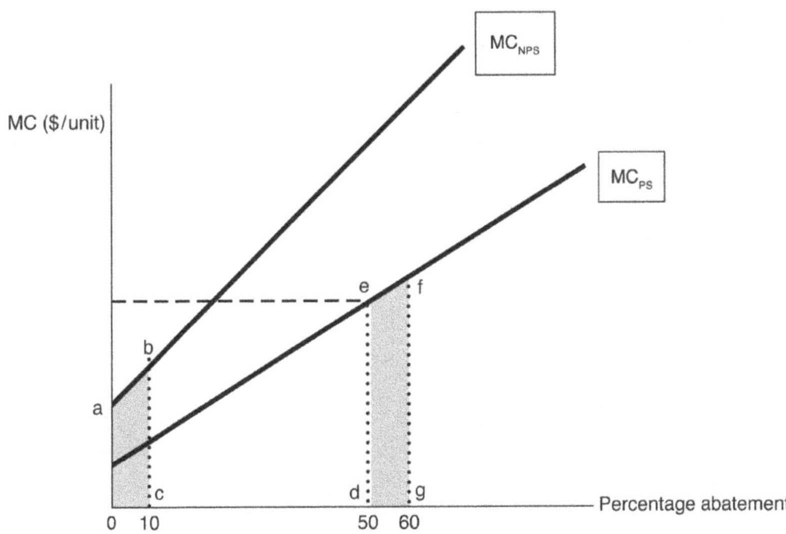

Figure 13.2 Potential Cost Savings with Trading across Point and Nonpoint Sources

Such a scenario also offers an incentive for point source – nonpoint source trading. One situation like this happened in Colorado. An Industrial Economics, Inc. (1984) study of phosphorus control in the Dillon reservoir in Colorado provides empirical support that such point-nonpoint trading could be more cost-effective.

In this reservoir, four municipalities constitute the only point sources of phosphorus, while numerous uncontrolled nonpoint sources are in the area. The combined phosphorus load on the reservoir from point and nonpoint sources was projected to exceed its assimilative capacity.

The traditional way to rescue the projected phosphorus load would be to impose even more stringent controls on the point sources. The study found, however, that by following a balanced program controlling both point and nonpoint sources, the desired phosphorus target could be achieved at a cost of approximately $1 million a year less than would be spent if only point sources were controlled more stringently. The more general point to be carried away from this study is that as point sources are controlled to higher and higher degrees, rising marginal control costs will begin to make controlling nonpoint sources increasingly attractive. As the list of 13 point-nonpoint trades in Table 13.2 demonstrates, we have apparently already reached that point.

Trades can sometimes achieve greater effluent reductions in addition to cost savings. Kibler and Kasturi (2007) describe one case for which reductions have actually been much greater than anticipated. When the Southern Minnesota Sugar Beet Industry needed to offset 6,500 pounds of total phosphorus per year, they actually achieved 15,767 pounds per year reductions by trading. Does your state have a water pollutant trading program?

Atmospheric deposition of pollution

An additional complexity comes in the form of the nonpoint source pollution from the atmosphere that ends up in water bodies. Airborne pollutants, such as sulfur dioxide, mercury, and nitrogen, eventually find their way to rivers and lakes via atmospheric deposition. *Wet deposition* refers to pollutants that travel to the ground with rainfall. *Dry deposition* occurs when pollutants become too heavy and fall to the ground even in the absence of precipitation.

Debate 13.1 highlighted some of the issues surrounding one approach to dealing with airborne deposition – fish consumption advisories due to mercury levels found in many fish. A quite different complication for water pollution control stems from a lack of coordination with air quality regulations. Simply put, they may or may not take into consideration the impacts of the air quality regulation on the soil (or in the water). The external benefits from air quality improvements are likely to be quite large. What does this suggest about the optimal level of air quality and the fact that air and water quality are controlled by separate offices within EPA?

The European experience

European water legislation originated in the 1970s with standards for drinking water and set targets for fish and shellfish, bathing and groundwater. In 1988, a second phase of water legislation began with the adoption of the Urban Waste Water Treatment Directive, a Nitrates Directive and a revised Drinking Water Objective. In 1996, a Directive for Integrated Pollution and Prevention Control (IPPC) was adopted to address pollution from large industrial installations.[6]

Economic incentives have been important in water pollution control in Europe, where effluent charges play a prominent role in a number of countries. These charge systems have taken a number of forms. One common approach, illustrated by the former Republic of Czechoslovakia, used charges to achieve predetermined ambient standards. Others, such as the former West Germany, used charges mainly to encourage firms to control more than their legal requirements. A third group, illustrated by Hungary and the former East Germany, combined charge systems with effluent standards.

The former Republic of Czechoslovakia used effluent charges to maintain water quality at predetermined levels for several decades. A basic charge was placed on BOD and suspended solids and complemented by a surcharge ranging from 10 to 100 percent, depending upon the contribution of the individual discharge to ambient pollutant concentrations. The basic rates could be adjusted to reflect the quality of the receiving water. This system is conceptually very close to the ambient emissions charge system known to be cost-effective.

The charge system in the former West Germany was announced in 1976 and implemented in 1981. The level of charge was related to the degree of compliance with the standards. Firms failing to meet their required standards paid a charge on all actual emissions. If, according to the issued permit, federal emissions standards (which are separately defined for each industrial sector) were met, the charge was lowered to 50 percent of the base rate and was applied to the level of discharge implied by the minimum standard. If the discharge was lower than 75 percent of minimum standards, one-half of the base rate was applied to the (lower) actual discharge level. The charge was waived for three years prior to the installation of new pollution control equipment promising further reductions of at least 20 percent. Revenues from the charges could be used by the administering authorities for administrative costs and financial assistance to public and private pollution abatement activities.

The approach used in Hungary and the former East Germany combined effluent charges with effluent standards. The charges are levied on discharges in excess of fixed effluent limits. In the Hungarian system, the level of the charge is based on the condition of the receiving waters, among other factors. Initially the Hungarian charges had little effect, but when the charge levels were raised, a flurry of wastewater treatment activity resulted. France charges an effluent tax that is proportional to the quantity of the pollution. The revenues are then used for subsidizing wastewater treatment.

Though these European approaches differ from one another and are not all cost-effective, their existence suggests that a variety of effluent charge systems are possible and practical. The German Council of Experts on Environmental Questions estimated the German effluent charge policy to be about one-third cheaper for the polluters as a group than an otherwise comparable uniform treatment policy. Furthermore, it encouraged firms to go beyond the uniform standards when it was cost-justified.

In a very different approach, Bystrom (1998) examines reducing nonpoint source nitrogen pollution by constructing wetlands in Sweden, where reducing nitrogen loads to the Baltic Sea is an important policy goal. Although it is well known that wetlands can help reduce nitrogen concentrations through the uptake of biomass, how cost-effective is this approach when it is compared to alternative, more traditional methods of control?

To answer this question, Bystrom estimates nonpoint source abatement costs for constructed wetlands and compares them to the costs of reducing nitrogen by means of land-use changes, such as the planting of fuel woods. This study finds that marginal abatement costs for wetlands are lower than transitioning to different crops, but still higher than the marginal costs of simply reducing the use of nitrogen fertilizer.

The European Water Framework Directive (WFD) was adopted in October of 2000 with a goal of achieving "'good status' for all ground and surface waters (rivers, lakes, transitional waters, and coastal waters) in the EU by 2015."

Ek and Persson (2016) evaluate the implementation of the WFD in Sweden and find that cost-effectiveness is challenged by the complexities of water management. While the directive emphasizes the role of economic tools, the goals are not based on economic efficiency. The absolute targets make designing an effective economic instrument challenging at best. The existing system in Sweden is also based primarily on command and control. In the Netherlands and in France, charges have been used for heavy metals and other discharges with revenues going toward water infrastructure (Olmstead, 2010).

Effluent is not the only water pollution problem. Plastics are a growing source of pollution, much of which ends up in the ocean. Ireland was the first country to tax the use of plastic bags. Example 13.2 examines the effect of the Irish bag levy.

EXAMPLE 13.2

The Irish bag levy

Rapid economic growth in Ireland in the 1990s was marked by a significant increase in the amount of solid waste per capita. The lack of adequate landfill sites resulted in escalating costs of waste disposal, which in turn led to more illegal dumping and littering. It was feared that tourism, one of Ireland's largest industries, would be negatively affected as a consequence of the degradation of the environment. The food industry, which based a significant amount of its marketing strategies on a healthy, wholesome reputation, also suffered as a result of the public perception of its role in the increased litter.

The most visible element of litter was plastic bags, so in 2002 the government introduced the Plastic Bag Environmental Levy on all plastic shopping bags (the "PlasTax"), with a few exceptions that were sanctioned for health and safety reasons. Retailers were charged a fee of 15 cents per plastic bag, which they were obliged, by the government, to pass on to the consumer. This levy was designed to alter consumer behavior by creating financial incentives for consumers to choose more environmentally friendly alternatives to plastic, such as "bags-for-life." (Bags-for-life are heavy-duty, reusable cloth or woven bags, which were made available in all supermarkets, at an average cost of €1.27.)

Expectations that this levy would bring about a 50 percent reduction in the number of plastic bags used were exceeded when the estimated actual reduction turned out to be 95 percent! In a single year, Irish consumers reduced their consumption of plastic bags from 1.26 billion to 120,000, while concurrently raising approximately €10 million in revenue for the government. Placed in the Environmental Fund, this revenue finances environmental initiatives such as recycling, waste management, and, most importantly, anti-litter campaigns.

This levy has been viewed as a major success by the government and environmental groups alike. It has also been enthusiastically embraced by Irish consumers, thanks to an intensive environmental-awareness campaign that was launched in conjunction with the levy. Irish retailers, although skeptical in the beginning, have also recognized the huge benefits of this levy. Estimates suggest that their costs were offset by the savings from no longer providing disposable bags to customers free of charge, as well as the profit margin earned on the sale of "bags-for-life," whose sales have increased by 600–700 percent since the introduction of the levy.

The amount of plastic being sent to Irish landfills has been dramatically reduced, bringing about a clear visual improvement. The success of this case has promoted the diffusion of this idea. For example, in 2008 China banned super-thin plastic bags and imposed a fee on other plastic bags.

Source: Dungan, L. What were the effects of the plastic bag environmental levy on the litter problem in Ireland? Retrieved from http://personal.colby.edu/personal/t/thtieten/litter.htm

Developing country experience

The move from command-and-control regulations to economic incentives for water pollution control has not seen as rapid a transition in developing countries. Several attempts to use discharge fees and marketable permits have failed. This may be due to lack of regulatory capacity – for example, lack of technical, political, and financial means to set up and monitor a fee or permit program effectively. Noncompliance and lack of infrastructure have hampered many programs. Example 13.3 explores Colombia's experience with a discharge fee program – one case deemed successful.

For developing countries, water pollution control is further complicated by poverty, lack of enforcement, and lack of technology. Deaths from waterborne diseases are much more frequent in developing countries. Of the 1.6 million deaths in 2003 attributed to water and sanitation, 90 percent were children under 5 and most were from developing countries. In 2004, 2331 deaths from cholera occurred in Africa. No deaths from cholera were recorded in the Americas. According to the World Health Organization, improved water supply reduces diarrhea morbidity by 6–25 percent, and improved sanitation reduces diarrhea morbidity by 32 percent.

EXAMPLE 13.3

Economic incentives for water pollution control: the case of Colombia

In 1997, Colombia experimented with a new nationwide program of pollution discharge fees. Polluters would be charged per unit of pollution emitted. Colombia has 33 regional environmental authorities (CARs), some of which had discharge fees in place for 30 years. This was the first nationwide program.

This new program mandated that CARs would first collect and map out data on all discharging facilities that generated biological oxygen demand (BOD) and total suspended solids (TSS). They were then to set five-year reduction goals for aggregate discharge in each basin and charge a fee per unit of BOD and TSS. The ministry set a minimum fee, but CARs could adjust this fee upward every six months if reduction targets were not being met.

The program ran into several problems, including uneven levels of implementation across CARs, incomplete coverage of dischargers, and widespread noncompliance by municipal sewage authorities. Between the start of the program in 1997 and 2003, municipal sewage authorities were assessed over 30 percent of all discharge fees, but only paid 40 percent of what they were charged. Given that some CARs were raising fees based on meeting reduction targets, noncompliance by one group of dischargers was responsible for large rate hikes for others.

Was the Colombia program thus unsuccessful? Surprisingly, evidence actually suggests it was successful! In a number of basins, discharges dropped significantly between 1997 and 2003. BOD discharge from point sources in the program dropped by 27 percent and TSS discharges fell by 45 percent.

One suggested reason for the apparent success of the program is that previously lacking enforcement had to be improved simply to set up a discharge program. Collecting information on discharge amounts and locations is also a necessary component for successful implementation. Increased transparency over command-and-control programs contributed to the program's success.

The author of this study suggests that one of the most important components of a successful program is adequate infrastructure.

Source: Blackman, A. (Spring 2006). Economic incentives to control water pollution in developing countries: How well has Colombia's wastewater discharge fee program worked and why? *Resources,* 20–23.

A study on the costs and benefits of meeting the United Nations Millennium Development Goal of halving the proportion of people without sustainable access to improved water supply and sanitation determined it would:

> definitely bring economic benefits, ranging from US$3 to US$34 per US dollar invested, depending on the region. Additional improvement of drinking water quality, such as point-of-use disinfection, in addition to access to improved water and sanitation would lead to benefits ranging from US$5 to US$60 per US dollar invested.
>
> (Hutton and Haller, 2004)

China has implemented a different approach to enforcement than the type of sanction commonly used in the United States and Canada. China imposes a graduated pollution levy where the per-unit fine rises with the level of noncompliance (Wang & Wheeler, 2005). China also relies on self-reporting. Wang and Wheeler examine data from 3,000 Chinese factories and estimate a model that incorporates the joint determination of levy and emissions. They show that progressive penalties, combined with self-reporting, are a significant deterrent. Regional variation in local enforcement, however, is a factor and inhibits universal compliance.

Ocean pollution

Oil spills

The Clean Water Act prohibits discharges of "harmful quantities" of oil into navigable waters. Since the EPA regulations define "harmful" to include all discharges that "violate applicable water quality standards or cause a film or sheen upon the surface of the water," virtually all discharges are prohibited.

Industry responsibilities include complying with Coast Guard regulations (which deal with contingency planning in case of a spill and various accident avoidance requirements) and assuming the financial liability for any accident. If a spill does occur, it must be immediately reported to the Coast Guard or the EPA. Failure to report a spill can result in a fine up to $10,000 and/or imprisonment for up to one year.

In addition to giving notice, the discharger must either contain the spill or pay the cost of cleanup by a responsible government agency. The discharger's liability for the government's actual removal cost is limited to $50 million unless willful negligence or willful misconduct can be proved. Successful proof of willful negligence or willful misconduct eliminates the liability limit. In addition to cleanup costs, removal costs also include compensation for damages to natural resources. (Natural resource damages are defined as "any costs or expenses incurred by the federal government or any state government in the restoration or replacement of natural resources damaged or destroyed as a result of a discharge of oil.") Example 13.4, later in this chapter, presents damage estimates for the Deepwater Horizon oil spill.

Ocean dumping

Except for oil spills, which are covered by the Clean Water Act and the Oil Pollution Act of 1990, discharges to the ocean are covered by the Marine Protection Research and Sanctuaries Act of 1972. This act governs all discharges of wastes to ocean waters within U.S. territorial limits and discharges of wastes in ocean waters by U.S. vessels or persons regardless of where the dumping occurs. With only a few exceptions, no ocean dumping of industrial wastes or sewer sludge is now permitted. Radiological, chemical, and biological warfare agents and high-level radioactive wastes are specifically prohibited by the statute. Under the amended statute, the only ocean-dumping activities permitted are the disposal of dredged soil, fish wastes, human remains, and submerged vessels. This dumping is subject to specific regulations and is approved on a case-by-case basis.

Ocean trash

Similar to nonpoint source pollution, floating trash found in the ocean comes from a variety of sources and is almost impossible to attribute to a particular location. Marine debris, in particular plastics, are harmful to marine life that frequently mistakes plastics for food. Ingesting the plastic objects, many of which contain toxics, kills thousands of sea birds and other sea life each year. Sea turtles and albatross have both been known to mistake the plastics for food and feed pieces to their young.

The "Great Pacific Garbage Patch" also known as the Pacific Trash Vortex is a giant floating mass of marine garbage located in the North Pacific Ocean. Scientists are not sure of its exact size, but all of the estimates are enormous.

Few laws govern ocean trash except for explicit dumping. Some states and countries have bans or fees for the use of plastic bags in grocery stores. Several states have statewide bans on plastic bags, though they difficult to enforce and may have unintended consequences.[4] Debate Box 13.2 considers an example.

DEBATE 13.2

To ban or not to ban: the unintended consequences of plastic bag policies

The plastic materials filling our landfills and oceans has motivated many cities and towns to implement policies to reduce plastic use. One easy target is the disposable plastic bags that have become norm in many places for packing groceries. Polices in place are wide ranging: from a fee per bag, to a refund for using a reusable bag or to simply banning plastic bags altogether. Unfortunately, many well-intended policies can have unintended consequences. Taylor (2019) examines such consequences by measuring the impacts regulations on some bags can have on the consumption of substitute bags.

The evaluation of environmental policies can be challenged if there is "leakage" or other unintended downstream effects of the policy. Leakages occur when the pollution is removed from one location (or source) only to surface in another. Leakage in this context refers to consumers simply buying more new trash bags when plastic grocery bags are banned.

In the U.S, 242 local government implemented disposable carryout bag (DCB) policies between 2007 and 2016). At the same time, other types of plastic bags were unregulated. Since DCBs can also be reused, this begs the question of what the impact of DCB policies has on unregulated bans. Taylor (2019), examines this question using data from California. 139 California municipalities implemented DCB policies between 2007 and 2015. Ultimately, California voters approved a state-wide ban on DCBs in November 2016. Using an empirical strategy called an event-study, Taylor is able to examine the impacts across space and time since different municipalities have different implementation dates.

Using retail scanner data collected by Nielson, Taylor examines sales data for different size trash bags, 4 gallons, 8 gallons, 13 gallons and 30 gallon bags as well as data collected on the type of carry out bag used at the final sale. The results suggest a rather large "substitution effect" from DCBs to other small trash bags. Figure 13.3 shows the jump in sales of 4- and 8-gallon bags. Consumers are "willing to pay for the trash bag services that gained from 'free' plastic carryout bags."[7]

Ultimately, these bans succeeded in reducing disposable carryout bag use leading to 40 million fewer pounds of trash each year (Rosalsky, 2019). However, much of this reduction is offset by increased new bag use. New bags are thicker and use more plastic, "So about 30 percent of the plastic that was eliminated by the ban comes back in the form of thicker garbage bags," Taylor said in an interview with NPR (Rosalsky, 2019).

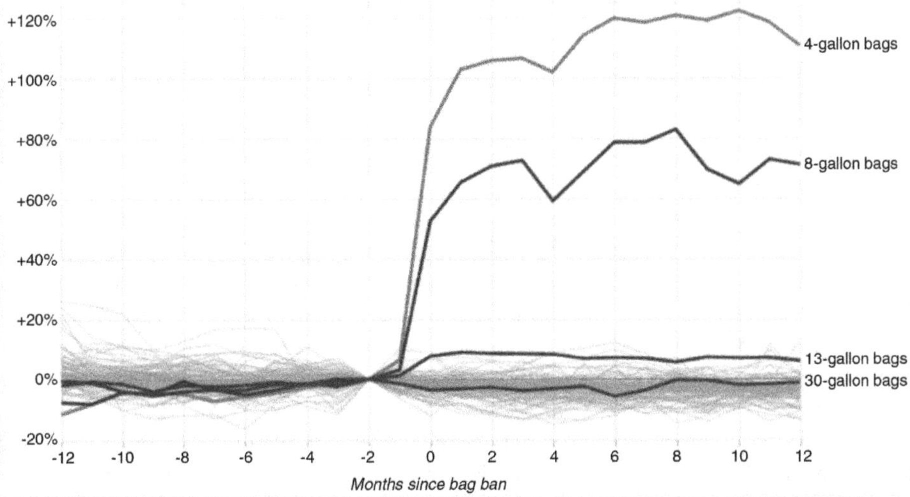

Figure 13.3 Trash Bag Sales Before and After Bag Ban Policy Implementation

Source: Original data reprinted from the *Journal of Environmental Economics and Management*, Volume 93, Taylor, 'Bag leakage: The effect of disposable carryout bag regulations on unregulated bags', Pages 254–271, Copyright 2019, with permission from Elsevier. Reproduced in Rosalsky (2019) www.npr.org/sections/money/2019/04/09/711181385/are-plastic-bag-bans-garbage

To make matters worse, cities with bag bans also increased use of paper bags. Taylor estimates these bags resulted in about 80 million pounds of extra paper trash per year. The production of both paper bags and cloth bags result in negative externalities as well including greenhouse gas emissions and water use.

Is there something better than a ban? It turns out that a small fee, according another study by Taylor, is just as effective as a ban, raises revenue and offers consumers the flexibility should they want to reuse those disposable carryout bags. Ultimately, the message here is that policy analysis should incorporate measures of leakage and unintended consequences.

Sources: Taylor, R. (2019. "Bag leakage: The effect of disposable carryout bag regulations on unregulated bags." *Journal of Environmental Economics and Management:* 93: 254–271; https://doi.org/10.1016/j.jeem.2019.01.001; Rosalsky, G. (2019). "Are plastic bag bans garbage?" NPR Planet Money, April 9. www.npr.org/sections/money/2019/04/09/711181385/are-plastic-bag-bans-garbage.

Oil spills – tankers and offshore drilling

One of the chief characteristics of the current approach to oil spills is that it depends heavily on the ability of the legal system to internalize the costs of a spill through liability law. In principle, the approach is straightforward. Consider how liability for spills might affect the incentives for a tanker fleet. Forcing the owner of a vessel to pay for the costs of cleaning up the spill, including compensation for natural resource damages, creates a powerful incentive to exercise care. But is the outcome likely to be efficient in practice?

One problem with legal remedies is their high administrative cost; assigning the appropriate penalties is no trivial matter. Even if the court were able to act expeditiously, the doctrines it imposes are not necessarily efficient since the financial liability for cleaning up spills is limited by statute. This point is demonstrated in Figure 13.4, which depicts the incentives of a vessel owner to take precautions. The owner will minimize costs by choosing the level of precaution that equates the marginal cost of additional precaution, with the resulting reduction in the marginal expected penalty. The marginal reduction in expected penalty is a function of two factors: the likelihood of a spill and the magnitude of financial obligation it would trigger. This function slopes downward because larger amounts of precaution are presumed to yield smaller marginal reductions in both the likelihood and magnitude of resulting accidents.

The vessel owner's cost-minimizing choice with unlimited liability is shown as Q ★. As long as the imposed penalty equaled the actual damage and the probability of having to pay the damage once an accident occurred was 1.0, this outcome would normally be efficient. The external costs would be internalized. The owner's private costs would be minimized by taking all possible cost-justified precaution measures to reduce both the likelihood and the seriousness of any resulting spill; taking precautions would simply be cheaper than paying for the cleanup.

Limited liability, however, produces a different outcome. With limited liability, the expected penalty function rotates inward for levels of precaution lower than that level that would produce an accident resulting in damages exactly equal to the limit.[8] Lower levels of precaution imply damages that exceed the limit, but the vessel owner would not have to pay anything above the limit. (The only benefit to the vessel owner faced with limited liability of increasing precaution at lower levels of precaution is the reduction in the likelihood of a spill; in this range, increasing precaution does not reduce the magnitude of the financial payment should a spill occur.) The deviation in the magnitude of the limited expected penalty function from the normal expected penalty function is greatest at lower levels of precaution; it declines to zero at that precaution level where the expected magnitude of an accident is equal to the liability limit.

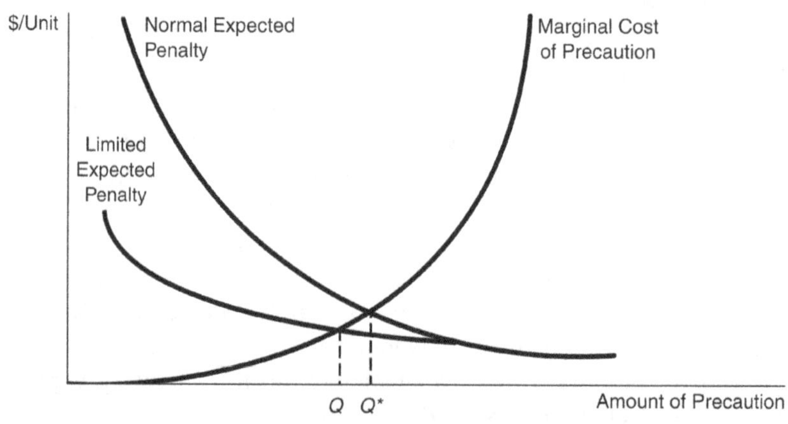

Figure 13.4 Oil Spill Liability

What is the effect of limited liability on the vessel owner's choice of precaution levels? As long as the liability limit is binding (which appears to routinely be the case with recent spills), the owner will choose too little precaution. (The owner's choice is shown as Q in Figure 13.3.) Both the number and magnitude of resulting spills would be inefficiently large.[9]

Garza-Gil et al. (2006) estimate the economic losses from the *Prestige* oil spill off the Spanish city of Galicia. Ultimately 63,000 tons were spilled (Table 13.1) and the tanker sank. This spill was considered one of the worst tanker spills due not only to the size of the spill but also to the "black tides" caused by the spill in valuable tourist regions of northern Spain and southern France. Garza-Gil et al. consider short-term (immediately following the spill) damages to the fishing industry and the tourism sector and find losses of almost 200 million euros. Including cleanup and restoration costs brings the total to 762 million euros. They were not able to include lost recreation opportunities or passive use-value losses. The current international liability framework does not allow for the inclusion of these values. (Recall the importance of these for the *Exxon Valdez* damage estimates discussed in Chapter 4.) What effect would omitting these values be expected to have on the incentives for risk-aversion by tanker owners?

While the frequency of spills from tankers has diminished significantly, offshore drilling has been increasing the risk of spills. In 2010, the Deepwater Horizon, a rig operated by British Petroleum (BP), exploded in the Gulf of Mexico, spewing 134 million gallons of oil, the largest spill on record in the United States. Example 13.4 examines the economic damages from this spill. Increasing interest in offshore drilling, especially in the Arctic waters, raises the risk of more spills like this one.

An overall assessment

Although the benefit estimates from water pollution control are subject to much uncertainty, they do exist.

One early study concluded that the net benefits from water pollution control policy were positive but were likely to become negative as costs escalate in the future. Relying on benefits estimates derived from contingent valuation, Carson and Mitchell (1993) estimated that aggregate benefits from water pollution control in 1990 exceeded aggregate costs by $6.4 billion. They also found, however, that projected aggregate costs would exceed projected aggregate benefits because of the high marginal costs and the low marginal benefits associated with bringing the remaining bodies of water up to swimmable quality.

EXAMPLE 13.4

Deepwater Horizon BP oil spill – estimating the damages

In the spring of 2010, the Deepwater Horizon, a rig operated by British Petroleum (BP) in the Gulf of Mexico, exploded and began spewing oil. By the time the leaking well was capped in August 2010, an estimated 134 million gallons had been spread through the Gulf of Mexico, almost 20 times greater than the *Exxon Valdez* spill, and the largest maritime spill in U.S. history.

In 2016, after a six-year study of the impacts, economists estimated the damages to the natural resources from the spill at $17.2 billion. This number represents the "benefits to the public to protect against damages that could result from a future oil spill in the Gulf of a similar magnitude."[10]

Using the first nationally represented, stated preference survey (recall from Chapter 4), Bishop et al. (2017) estimated the monetary value of natural resource damages from the spill. They interviewed a random sample of American adults. Respondents were told about the state of the Gulf prior to the spill, and about the accident – causes and injuries.

They were then told about a proposed program for preventing a similar accident. Respondents were asked how much their household would be willing to pay for a onetime tax based on their income to prevent future spills. The money would be used to pay for a second pipe safety feature intended to prevent a spill like this. There were two versions of the survey. Version A described the harm to three items: birds (brown pelicans, northern gannets, and royal terns), marshes, and recreation. Version B described harm to more animals and plants including snails, sea turtles, and bottlenose dolphins.[11]

Using state-of-the-art survey design techniques, they used a combined approach of both mail surveys and face-to-face interviews. They specifically tried to reduce bias including social desirability bias. Social desirability bias occurs when respondents try to present themselves in a favorable light, the common example being voters claiming to have voted when they did not. Survey administrators were concerned that respondents might over exaggerate their willingness to pay given the scenario. The alternative was that they might underestimate (or protest) their willingness to pay given that taxation for Americans is frequently seen as socially *undesirable*. They did not receive a large number of protest votes even though the payment vehicle was increased taxes.

The Oil Pollution Act of 1990 specifies that both use and nonuse values be included in natural resource damage assessments and these assessments can inform settlements. It also allows for damages to be assessed for the losses experienced by the entire U.S. population.

The calculation of total economic loss is conducted by multiplying the estimated population lower bound marginal willingness to pay (MWTP) by the appropriate number of households. For Version A the point estimate of economic losses is $15,332,412,434 (112,647,215 households multiplied by $136.11). For Version B, the point estimate of economic losses is $17,236,150,367 (112,647,215 households multiplied by $153.01).

The case was settled in 2016 for $20.8 billion, of which $8.8 billion was for natural resource damages. This amount is in addition to the approximately $30 billion already spent on cleanup.

Sources: www.fws.gov/doiddata/dwh-ar-documents/980/DWH-AR0290376a.pdf; www.fws.gov/doiddata/dwh-ar-documents/980/DWH-AR0290122a.pdf; www.fws.gov/doiddata/dwh-ar-documents/980/DWH-AR0302133.pdf; Bishop, R. C. et al. (2017). Putting a value on injuries to natural assets: The BP oil spill. *Science,* 356(6335), 253–254.

Griffiths and Wheeler (2005) summarize the costs and benefits of the most economically significant[12] water quality rules that are subject to benefit-cost analysis. For the five rules that relate to surface water, they find that two of them do not pass a benefit-cost analysis and for the other three the range of benefits estimates bounds the costs. They point out that policies do not necessarily have to pass a benefit-cost test to be adopted; benefit-cost calculations are simply one source of information for the decision-making process.

Using cost-effective policies rather than the current approach, it would be possible to reduce costs substantially, without affecting the benefits. Cost-effectiveness would require the development of better strategies for point source control and for achieving a better balance between point and nonpoint source control. The resulting reduction in costs probably would allow net benefits to remain positive even with the more stringent control levels envisioned for the future. Even positive net benefits would not necessarily make the policy efficient, however, because the level of control might still be too high or too low (meaning the present value of net benefits would not have been maximized). Unfortunately, the evidence is not rich enough to prove whether the overall level of control maximizes the net benefit.

In addition to promoting current cost-effectiveness, economic incentive approaches would stimulate and facilitate change better than a system of rigid, technology-based standards. Russell (1981) assessed the importance of the facilitating role by simulating the effects on the allocation of pollution-control responsibility in response to regional economic growth, changing technology, and changing product mix. Focusing on the steel, paper, and petroleum-refining industries in the 11-county Delaware Estuary Region, his study estimated the change in permit use for three water pollutants (BOD, total suspended solids, and ammonia) that would have resulted if a marketable permit system had been in place over the 1940–1978 period. The calculations assume that the plants existing in 1940 would have been allocated permits to legitimize their emissions at that time, that new sources would have had to purchase permits, and that plant shutdowns or contractions would free up permits for others to purchase.

This study found that for almost every decade and pollutant a substantial number of permits would have been made available by plant closing, capacity contractions, product-mix changes, and/or by the availability of new technologies. In the absence of a marketable permit program, a control authority would not only have to keep abreast of all technological developments so emissions standards could be adjusted accordingly, but it would also have to ensure an overall balance between effluent increases and decreases so as to preserve water quality. This tough assignment is handled completely by the market in a tradable permit system, thereby facilitating the evolution of the economy by responding flexibly and predictably to change.

Tradable effluent permits encourage, as well as facilitate, this evolution. Since permits have value, in order to minimize costs firms must continually be looking for new opportunities to control emissions at lower cost. This search eventually results in the adoption of new technologies and in the initiation of changes in the product mix that result in lower amounts of emissions. The pressure on sources to continually search for better ways to control pollution is a distinct advantage that economic incentive systems have over bureaucratically defined standards.

Summary

Historically, policies for controlling water pollution have been concerned with conventional pollutants discharged into surface waters. More recently, concerns have shifted toward toxic pollutants, which apparently are more prevalent than previously believed; toward groundwater, which traditionally was thought to be an invulnerable pristine resource; and toward the oceans, which were mistakenly considered immune from most pollution problems because of their vast size.

Early attempts at controlling water pollution followed a path similar to that of air pollution control. Legislation prior to the 1970s had little impact on the problem. Frustration then led to the enactment of a tough federal law that was so ambitious and unrealistic that little progress resulted.

There the similarity ends. Whereas in air pollution a wave of recent reforms have improved the process by making it more cost-effective, little parallel exists for control of water pollution. Policy toward cleaning up rivers and lakes was based upon the subsidization of municipal waste-treatment facilities and national effluent standards imposed on industrial sources.

The former approach was hampered by delays, by problems in allocating funds, and by the fact that about half of the constructed plants were not performing satisfactorily. The latter approach gave rise to delays and to the need to define the standards in a series of court suits. In addition, effluent standards have assigned the control responsibility among point sources in a way that excessively raises cost. Non-point pollution sources have, until recently, been virtually ignored. Technological progress is inhibited, rather than stimulated, by the current approach.

This lack of progress could have been avoided. It did not result from a lack of toughness. Rather, it has resulted from a reliance on direct regulation, rather than on emissions charges or tradable effluent permits, which are more flexible and cost-effective in both the dynamic and static sense. Recognizing this deficiency, watershed-based new trading programs are now gaining attention. The European Water Framework Directive, by contrast, has focused on economic tools, but not necessarily economic efficiency.

It is largely the court system that controls oil spills, in that it ensures that those responsible for the spills assume the financial liability for cleaning up the site and compensating for any resulting damages to natural resources. While in principle this approach can be efficient, in practice it has been hampered by liability limitations and the huge administrative burden an oil spill trial entails.

Discussion questions

1 "The only permanent solution to water pollution control will occur when all production by-products are routinely recycled. The zero-discharge goal recognizes this reality and forces all dischargers to work steadily toward this solution. Less stringent policies are at best temporary palliatives." Discuss.

2 "In exercising its responsibility to protect the nation's drinking water, the government needs to intervene only in the case of public-water supplies. Private-water supplies will be adequately protected without any government intervention." Discuss.

3 The Deepwater Horizon "BP" oil spill in the Gulf of Mexico was the largest spill in U.S. history. How do natural resource damage assessments such as the one presented in Example 13.4 help decision makers who may be grappling with increased well-permitting requests? Do the benefits outweigh the risks?

Self-test exercises

1 Suppose you have three production facilities that are polluting a river. Each emits ten units of pollution. Their marginal cost functions for reducing emissions are, respectively, $MC_1 = \$3$, $MC_2 = \$4$, and $MC_3 = \$5$.

   a If the objective is to cut emissions in half (to 15) cost-effectively, how much reduction should be assigned to each firm?

   b What would be the total variable cost of controlling these emissions?

c What would be the total variable cost that would result from forcing each facility to control one-half of its emissions? Is this different from the cost associated with the cost-effective allocation? Why or why not?

Notes

1 The danger of anaerobic conditions is highest in the late summer and early fall, when temperatures are high and the stream flow is low.
2 www.usgs.gov/special-topic/water-science-school/science/pharmaceuticals-water?qt-science_center_objects=0#qt-science_center_objects
3 Actually, the ambient standards were not completely bypassed. If the uniform controls were not sufficient to meet the desired standard, the effluent limitation would have to be tightened accordingly.
4 Nutrient sensitive waters are defined as waters subject to excessive plant growth and requiring limitations on nutrient inputs.
5 U.S. EPA Water Quality Trading page: www.epa.gov/npdes/water-quality-trading
6 http://ec.europa.eu/environment/water/water-framework/info/intro_en.htm
7 Taylor (2019) p. x
8 To avoid confusion, note that the marginal expected penalty for additional precaution when the damage would exceed the liability limit is not zero. While further precaution does not lower the ultimate penalty in this range, it does lower the likelihood of an accident and, hence, the expected penalty.
9 Suppose, at the efficient level of precaution, the magnitude of a resulting spill was less than the liability limit. How would this be depicted graphically? Would you expect the vessel owner's choice to be efficient?
10 www.sciencedaily.com/releases/2017/04/170420141825.htm
11 www.fws.gov/doiddata/dwh-ar-documents/980/DWH-AR0290122a.pdf
12 Defined as rules with an economic impact of more than $100 million.

Further reading

Boyle, K. J., & Kotchen, M. J. (2019). The need for more (not less) external review of economic analysis at the U.S. EPA. *Review of Environmental Economics and Policy*, rez006. https://doi.org/10.1093/reep/rez006

Brouwer, R., & Pearce, E. (Eds.). (2005). *Cost Benefit Analysis and Water Resources Management.* Cheltenham, UK: Edward Elgar. A collection of benefit/cost analysis case studies for water pollution control projects, flood control, and water allocation. Most of the cases occurred in Europe.

Fisher-Vanden, K., & Olmstead, S. (Winter 2013). Moving pollution trading from air to water: Potential problems and prognosis. *Journal of Economic Perspectives*, 27(1), 147–172. An analysis of water quality trading programs to date and the challenges that remain to implementing water quality trading.

Olmstead, S. M. (Winter 2010). The economics of water quality trading. *Review of Environmental Economics and Policy*, 4(1), 44–62. A thorough review of the literature on the economics of water quality.

Selman, M., Greenhalgh, S., Branosky, E., Jones, C., & Guiling, J. (March 2009). Water quality trading programs: An international overview. *WRI Issue Brief*, 1. WRI (World Resources Institute). An overview and analysis of 57 water quality trading programs worldwide.

Additional references and other historically significant references are available on this book's eResource page: www.routledge.com/9781138587595

Chapter 14

Toxics policy and environmental justice

Introduction

In one of the ironies of history, the place that focused public attention in the United States on toxic substances is called the Love Canal. *Love* is not a word any impartial observer would choose to describe the relationships among the parties to that incident.

The Love Canal typifies in many ways the dilemma posed by toxic substances. Until 1953, Hooker Electrochemical (subsequently Hooker Chemical, a subsidiary of Occidental Petroleum Corporation) dumped waste chemicals into an old abandoned waterway known as the Love Canal, near Niagara Falls, New York. (Hooker was acquired by Occidental in 1968.) At the time it seemed a reasonable solution, since the chemicals were buried in what was then considered to be impermeable clay.

In 1953, Hooker deeded the Love Canal property for $1 to the Niagara Falls Board of Education, which then built an elementary school on the site. The deed specifically excused Hooker from any damages that might be caused by the chemicals. Residential development of the area around the school soon followed.

The site became the center of controversy when, in 1978, residents complained of chemicals leaking to the surface. News reports emanating from the area included stories of spontaneous fires and vapors in basements. Medical reports suggested that the residents had experienced abnormally high rates of miscarriage, birth defects, and liver disease.

Similar contamination experiences befell Europe and Asia. In 1976, an accident at an F. Hoffmann-La Roche & Co. plant in Sevesco spewed dioxin over the Italian countryside. Subsequently, explosions in a Union Carbide plant in Bhopal, India, spread deadly gases over nearby residential neighborhoods with significant loss of life, and water used to quell a warehouse fire at a Sandoz warehouse near Basel, Switzerland, carried an estimated 30 tons of toxic chemicals into the Rhine River, a source of drinking water for several towns in Germany. In 2010, an explosion and fire at the BP/Deepwater Horizon drilling rig off Louisiana's coast in the Gulf of Mexico killed 11 people and ruptured an underwater pipe that caused a massive oil spill.

In previous chapters, we touched on a few of the policy instruments used to combat toxic substance problems. Emissions standards govern the types and amounts of substances that can be injected into the air. Effluent standards regulate what can be discharged directly into water sources, and pretreatment standards control the flow of toxics into wastewater treatment plants. Bans have been imposed on those substances that are simply too dangerous for the public to be exposed to. Maximum concentration levels have been established for many substances in drinking water.

This impressive array of policies is not sufficient to resolve the Love Canal problem or others having similar characteristics. As Flint, Michigan's water contamination disaster demonstrated in 2015, for example, by the time violations of the standards for drinking water are detected, the water is already contaminated. Specifying maximum contaminant levels helps to identify when a problem exists, but it does nothing to prevent or contain the problem. The various standards for air and water emissions that do protect against *point* sources do little to prevent contamination by *nonpoint* sources. Furthermore, most waterborne toxic pollutants are stock pollutants, not fund pollutants; they cannot be absorbed by the receiving waters. Therefore, temporally constant controls on emissions (a traditional method used for fund pollutants) are inappropriate for these toxic substances since they would allow a steady rise in the concentration over time. Finally controlling accidental discharges may require a rather different set of policies. Some additional form of control is necessary.

In this chapter, we describe and evaluate the main policies that deal specifically with the creation, use, transportation, and disposal of toxic substances and how those policies affect environmental justice. Many dimensions will be considered: what are appropriate ways to dispose of toxic substances? How can the government ensure that all waste is appropriately disposed of in a way that does not disproportionately disadvantage some socioeconomic groups? How do we prevent surreptitious dumping? Who should clean up old sites and how should the cleanup be financed? Should victims be compensated for damages caused by toxic substances under the control of someone else? If so, by whom? What are the appropriate roles for the legislature and the judiciary in creating the proper set of incentives?

Nature of toxic substance pollution

A main objective of the current legal system for controlling toxic substances is to protect human health, although protecting other forms of life is a secondary objective. The potential health danger depends upon the toxicity of a substance to humans and their exposure to the substance. *Toxicity* occurs when a living organism experiences detrimental effects following exposure to a substance. In normal concentrations, most chemicals are not toxic. Others, such as pesticides, are toxic by design. Yet, in excess concentrations, even a benign substance such as table salt can be toxic.

While a degree of risk is involved when using any chemical substance, there are benefits as well. The task for public policy is to define an acceptable risk by balancing the costs and benefits of controlling the use of chemical substances.

Health effects

Two main health concerns associated with toxic substances are risk of cancer and effects on reproduction.

Cancer

While many suspect the mortality rate for cancer may be related to increased exposure to carcinogens, proving or disproving this link is very difficult due to the latency of the disease. *Latency* refers to the state of being concealed during the period between exposure to the carcinogen and the detection of cancer. Latency periods for cancer run from 15 to 40 years, and have been known to run as long as 75 years.

In the United States, part of the increase in cancer has been convincingly linked to smoking, particularly among women. As the proportion of women who smoke has increased, the incidence of lung cancer has increased as well. Smoking does not account for all of the increase in cancer, however.

Although it is not entirely clear what other agents may be responsible, one suggested cause is the rise in the manufacture and use of synthetic chemicals since World War II. A number of these chemicals have been shown in the laboratory to be carcinogenic. That evidence is not necessarily sufficient to implicate them in the rise of cancer, however, because it does not take exposure into account. The laboratory can reveal, through animal tests, the relationship between dosage and resulting effects. To track down the significance of any chemical in causing cancer in the general population would require an estimate of how many people were exposed to specific doses. Currently, our data are not extensive enough to allow these kinds of calculations to be done with any confidence.

Reproductive effects

Tracing the influence of environmental effects on human reproduction is still a new science. A growing body of scientific evidence, however, suggests that exposure to smoking, alcohol, and chemicals known as endocrine disruptors may contribute to infertility, may affect the viability of the fetus and the health of the infant after birth, and may cause genetic defects that can be passed on for generations.

Problems exist for both men and women. In men, exposure to toxic substances has resulted in lower sperm counts, malformed sperm, and genetic damage. In women, exposure can also result in sterility or birth defects in their children.

These are not the only health concerns, however, since exposure to toxic substances can have much more pervasive effects. Muir and Zegarac (2001) found, for example, that at least 10 percent, and up to 50 percent of the cumulative costs in Canada and the United States associated with four specific health problems – diabetes, Parkinson's disease (PD), neurodevelopmental effects and hypothyroidism, and deficits in intelligence quotient (IQ) – are environmentally induced.[1]

Policy issues

Many aspects of the toxic substance problem make it difficult to resolve. Three important aspects that add to this difficulty are the number of substances involved, latency, and uncertainty.

Number of substances

Of the tens of millions of known chemical compounds, approximately 100,000 are actively used in commerce. Many exhibit little or no toxicity, and even a very toxic substance represents little risk as long as it is isolated. The trick is to identify problem substances and to design appropriate policies as responses. The massive number of substances involved makes that a difficult assignment.

Latency

The period of latency exhibited by many of these relationships compounds the problem. Two kinds of toxicity are exhibited: acute and chronic. *Acute toxicity* is present when a short-term exposure to the substance produces a detrimental effect on the exposed organisms. *Chronic toxicity* is present when the detrimental effect arises from exposure of a continued or prolonged nature. One size does not fit all.

The process of screening chemicals as potentially serious causes of chronic illness is even more complicated than that of screening for acute illness. The traditional technique for determining acute toxicity is the lethal-dose determination, a relatively quick test performed on animals that calculates the dose that results in the death of 50 percent of the animal population. This test is less well suited for screening substances that exhibit chronic toxicity.

The appropriate tests for discovering chronic toxicity typically have involved subjecting animal populations to sustained low-level doses of the substance over an extended period of time. These tests are very expensive and time consuming. If the EPA were to perform these tests, given its limited resources, it could only test a few of the estimated 700 new chemicals introduced each year. If the industries were to do the tests, the expense could preclude the introduction of many potentially valuable new chemicals that have limited, specialized markets.

Uncertainty

Another dilemma inhibiting policy makers is the uncertainty surrounding the scientific evidence on which regulation is based. Effects uncovered by laboratory studies on animals are not perfectly correlated with effects on humans. Large doses administered over a three-year period may not produce the same effects as an equivalent amount spread over a 20-year period. Some of the effects are *synergistic* – that is, their effects are intensified or diminished by the presence of other variable factors. (Asbestos workers who smoke are 30 times more likely than their nonsmoking fellow workers to get lung cancer, for example.) Once cancer is detected, in most cases it does not bear the imprint of a particular source. Policy makers have to act in the face of limited information.

From an economic point of view, how the policy process reacts to this dilemma should depend on how well the market handles toxic substance problems. To the extent that the market generates the correct information and provides the appropriate incentives, policy may not be needed. On the other hand, when the government can best generate information or create the appropriate incentive, intervention may be called for. As the following sections demonstrate, the nature and the form of the most appropriate policy response may depend crucially on how the toxic source and the affected party or parties are related.

Market allocations and toxic substances

Toxic substance contamination can arise in a variety of settings. In order to define the efficient policy response, we must examine what responses would be forthcoming in the normal operation of the market. Let's look at three possible relationships between the source of the contamination and the victim: employer-employee, producer-consumer, and producer-third party. The first two involve normal contractual relations among the parties, while the latter involves noncontracting parties, whose connection is defined solely by the contamination.

Occupational hazards

Many occupations involve risk, including, for some people, exposure to toxic substances. Do employers and employees have sufficient incentives to act in concert toward achieving safety in the workplace?

The caricature of the market used by the most ardent proponents of regulation suggests not. In this view, the employer's desire to maximize profits precludes spending enough money on safety. Sick workers can simply be replaced. Therefore, the workers are powerless to do anything about it; if they complain, they are fired and replaced with others who are less vocal.

The most ardent opponents of regulation respond that this caricature overlooks or purposefully ignores significant market pressures, such as employee incentives and the feedback effects of those incentives on employers. When the full story that includes these pressures is considered, regulation may be unnecessary or even counterproductive.

According to this market incentives worldview, employees will only accept work in a potentially hazardous environment if appropriately compensated for taking that risk. Riskier occupations should call forth higher wages. The increase in wages should be sufficient to compensate them for the increased risk, otherwise they will work elsewhere. These higher wages represent a real cost of the hazardous situation to the employer. They also produce an incentive to create a safer work environment, since greater safety would result in a lower risk premium and, hence, lower wages. One cost could be balanced against the other. What was spent on safety could be recovered in lower wages (see Figure 14.1).

The first type of cost, the marginal increase in wages, is drawn to reflect the fact that the lower the level of precaution, the higher the wage bill. Two such curves are drawn to reflect high-exposure and low-exposure situations. The high-exposure case assumes larger numbers of workers are exposed than in the low-exposure case. The low-exposure cost curve rises more slowly because the situation is less dangerous at the margin.

The second type of curve, the marginal cost of providing precaution, reflects an increasing marginal cost. The two different curves depict different production situations. A firm with a few expensive

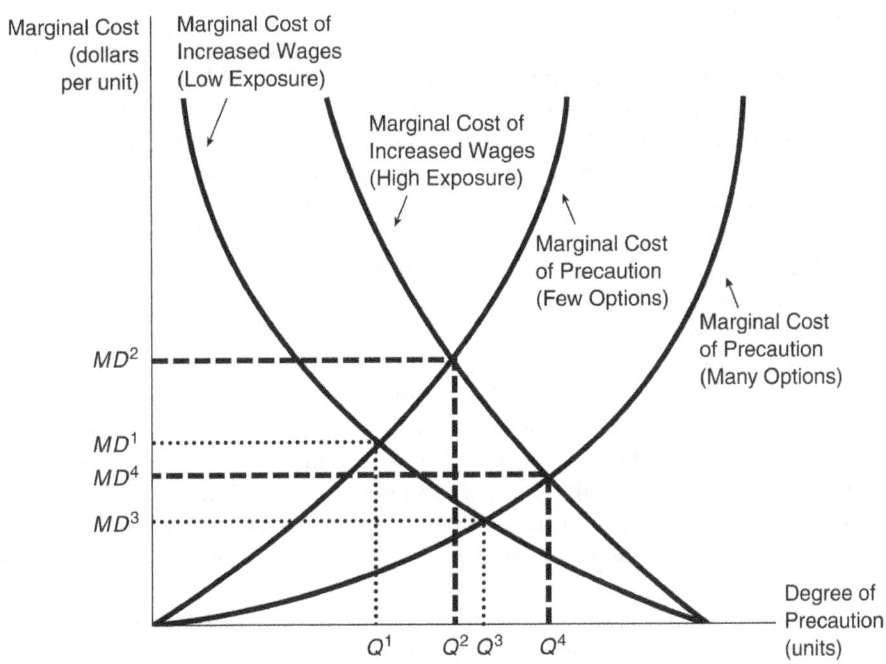

Figure 14.1 Market Provision of Occupational Safety

precautionary options will face a steeply sloped marginal cost curve, while a firm with many cheaper options will face a lower marginal cost at every comparable degree of precaution chosen.

The graph depicts four possible outcomes – one for each possible combination of these four marginal cost curves. Note that very different choices will be made, depending on the circumstances. Also note that the level of risk chosen (as indicated by the marginal damage, labeled *MD*) and the degree of precaution are not perfectly correlated. The highest marginal risk is MD^2, but the associated level of precaution (Q^2) is not the largest. The reason, of course, is that the cost of taking precautions matters, and sometimes it is cheaper to accept the risk and compensate for it than it is to prevent it.

Because the marginal increased wages curve accurately reflects marginal damages (since the higher wages are demanded by workers to compensate them for damages), these market equilibria are also efficient. Thus, the efficient resolution of the occupational hazards problem varies not only from substance to substance, but also from plant to plant. As long as this stylized view of the world is correct, the market will tailor the appropriate degree of precaution to the situation.

Proponents of this view point out that this allocation would also allow more choices for workers than would, for example, a system requiring all workplaces to be equally safe. With varying occupational risk, those occupations with more risk (such as working to clean up toxic spills) would attract people who were less averse to risk. These workers would receive higher- than-average wages (to compensate them for the increased risk), but paying these higher wages would be cheaper to the firm (and, hence, consumers) than requiring every workplace to meet the same risk standard. The risk-averse workers would be free to choose less risky occupations.

Do wages actually reflect risk? Existing empirical studies make clear that wages in risky occupations in countries like the United States do contain a risk premium (Viscusi and Aldy, 2003). Two conclusions about these risk premiums seem clear from these studies: (1) the willingness to pay for apparently similar risk reductions varies significantly across individuals, and (2) the revealed willingness to pay for risk reduction is substantial.

In those cases where wages accurately reflect risk is there any appropriate role for the government in controlling contamination in the workplace? Perhaps. The efficient solution may not always be considered the most ethical solution, a point that has been addressed in the courts. For example, if the employee is a pregnant woman and the occupational hazard involves potential damage to the fetus, does the expectant mother have the right to risk the unborn child, or is some added protection for the fetus needed? Furthermore, if the lowest-cost solution is to ban pregnant, or even fertile, women from a workplace that poses a risk to a fetus, is that an acceptable solution, or is it unfair discrimination against women? As Example 14.1 suggests, these are not idle concerns.

Ethical concerns are not the only challenges for market solutions. Wages may not reflect the actual risk. The ability of the worker to respond to a hazardous situation depends on his or her knowledge of the seriousness of the danger. With toxic substances, that knowledge is likely to be incomplete in general, but completely inadequate in settings such as developing countries. Consequently, the marginal increased wages function may be artificially rotated toward the origin. In this case, the employer would choose too little precaution and the market will not provide sufficient pressure to rectify this worker hazard. By having access to the health records of all employees, the employer could potentially be in the best position to assess the degree of risk posed, but the employer also has an incentive to suppress that information since publicizing the risk would mean demands for higher compensatory wages and possible lawsuits.

Information on the dangers posed by exposure to a particular toxic substance is a public good to employees; each employee has an incentive to be a free rider on the discoveries of others. Individual employees do not have an incentive to bear the cost of doing the necessary research to uncover the degree of risk. Thus, it seems neither employers nor employees can be expected to produce the efficient amount of information on the magnitude of risk.[2]

EXAMPLE 14.1

Susceptible populations in the hazardous workplace: an historical example

Some employees are especially susceptible to occupational hazards. Pregnant women and women in the childbearing years are particularly vulnerable. When an employer attempts to manage a work situation that poses a hazardous threat, either the susceptible population can be separated from the hazard or the hazard can be controlled to a sufficient level that its risk is acceptable to even the most susceptible employees.

The economic aspects of this choice are easily deduced from Figure 14.1. Suppose that the firm has few control options and is on the uppermost of the two marginal cost of precaution curves. By removing the susceptible population, it could face the low- exposure curve. Removal of the susceptible population results in lower marginal risk to the workers, lower costs to the firm, and less precaution taken. But is it fair to those who are removed from their jobs?

This issue came to a head in 1978 when American Cyanamid decided to respond to an occupational risk by banning all fertile women from jobs in the section manufacturing lead chromate pigment at Willow Island, West Virginia. After reviewing the decision, the Occupational Safety and Health Administration (OSHA) cited the company under the general duty clause of the Occupational Safety and Health Act, which requires an employer to provide a workplace free of hazards, and fined it $10,000. That was not the end of the story. In early 1980, the Oil, Chemical, and Atomic Workers Union sued the company under the 1964 Civil Rights Act on the grounds that the company had discriminated unfairly against women. In March 1991, the Supreme Court ruled that banning fertile women from any workplace posing a risk to a fetus was not an acceptable way to control risk. The workplace must be made safe for all.

Source: International Union v. Johnson Controls, 499 U.S. 187 (1991).

As a result, the government may play a substantial role in setting the boundaries on ethical responses, in stimulating research on the nature of hazards, and in providing for the dissemination of information to affected parties. It does not necessarily follow, however, that the government should be responsible for determining the level of safety in the workplace once this information is available and the ethical boundaries are determined. For situations that are sufficiently dangerous that no rational worker would voluntarily choose to work there, the role of the government would be to set and enforce a safety threshold.

This analysis suggesting that the market is not likely to provide an efficient level of information on occupational risk is consistent with the enactment of "right-to-know" laws in several states. These laws require businesses to disclose to their employees and to the public any potential health hazards associated with toxic substances used on the job. Generally employers are required to (1) label toxic substance containers, (2) inventory all toxic substances used in the workplace, and (3) provide adequate training on the handling of these substances to all affected employees. Significantly, proponents of these laws suggest that the targets are not the large chemical companies, which generally have excellent disclosure programs, but the smaller, largely nonunion plants.

Product safety

Exposure to a hazardous or potentially hazardous substance can also occur as a result of using a product, as when eating food containing chemical additives. Does the market efficiently supply safe products?

One view holds that the market pressures on both parties (consumers and producers) are sufficient to yield an efficient level of safety. Safer products are generally more expensive to produce and carry a higher price tag. If consumers feel that the additional safety justifies the cost, they will purchase the safer product. Otherwise they won't. Producers supplying excessively risky products will find their market drying up, because consumers will switch to competing brands that are safer, despite their higher price. Similarly, producers selling excessively safe products (meaning they eliminate, at great cost, risks consumers are perfectly willing to take in return for a lower purchase price) find their markets drying up as well. Consumers will choose the cheaper, riskier product.

This theory also suggests that the market will not (and should not) yield a uniform level of safety for all products. Different consumers will have different degrees of risk aversion. While some consumers might purchase riskier, but cheaper, products, others might prefer safer, but more expensive, products.[3]

Under this worldview it would be common to find products with various safety levels supplied simultaneously, reflecting and satisfying different consumer preferences for risk. Forcing all similar products to conform to a single level of risk would not be efficient. Uniform product safety is no more efficient than uniform occupational safety.

If this view of the market were completely accurate, government intervention to protect consumers would not be necessary to ensure the efficient level of risk. By the force of their collective buying habits, consumers would protect themselves.

The problem with the market's ability to provide such self-regulation is, once again, the availability of information on product safety. The consumer generally acquires his or her information about a product either from personal experience or from labels and warnings. With toxic substances the latency period may be so long as to preclude any effective market reaction arising from personal experience. Even when some damage results several years later, it is difficult for the consumer to associate it with a particular source. While an examination of the relationships between purchasing patterns of a large number of consumers and their subsequent health might well reveal some suggestive correlations, it would be difficult for any individual consumer to deduce this correlation. Furthermore, it may be that the risk is so large that no knowledgeable consumer would accept that risk so that banning the product is the appropriate remedy. (Note that banning was the choice of several states in managing the risk from BPA, as described in Example 3.1.)

In situations where adequate information is available on the risks, consumers should have a substantial role in choosing the acceptable level of risk through their purchases, but varying levels of access to information can make this problematic.

Third parties

The final case involves *third parties*, victims who have no contractual relationship to the source. Oil spills are one example. Another occurs when groundwater is contaminated by a neighboring wastewater treatment facility, by surreptitious dumping of toxic wastes, or by a neighbor's improper application of a pesticide. In all of these examples the victims are third parties. Since in third-party situations the affected party cannot bring any direct market pressure to bear on the source, the case for additional government intervention is stronger.

This does not necessarily imply, however, that executive or legislative remedies are appropriate. The most appropriate response may come from simply requiring better information on the risk or from using the judicial system to impose liability.

Liability law provides one judicial avenue for internalizing the external costs in third-party situations. If the court finds (1) that damage occurred, (2) that it was caused by a toxic substance, and (3) that a particular source was responsible for the presence of the substance, the source can be forced to compensate the victim for the damages caused. Unlike regulations that are uniformly (and, hence, inefficiently) applied, a court decision can be tailored to the exact circumstances involved in the suit. Furthermore, the impact of any particular liability assignment can go well beyond the parties to that case. A decision for one plaintiff can remind other sources that they should take the efficient level of precaution now to avoid paying damages later.

In principle, liability law can force potential sources of toxic discharges, including nonpoint sources, to choose efficient levels of precaution. Unlike regulation, liability law can provide compensation to the victims. Bringing suit to recover damages, however, is a costly process so these administrative costs must be balanced against the potential gains in efficiency when choosing the appropriate remedy for any particular situation.

Using liability law to resolve toxic situations can also take a long time. In the famous case of Flint, Michigan, decisions made as early as 2007 resulted in lead contamination of the city's water supply. A flurry of lawsuits followed, but it wasn't until March 2017 that a federal judge approved a $97 million settlement.

The incidence of hazardous waste siting decisions

Flint, Michigan's population is 56.6 percent African American and 41 percent of the population live below the poverty line. Did the fact that this was largely a poor, minority community play any role in what happened and how long it took to resolve the problem?

For some historical context for thinking about the possible linkages between race and exposure to toxic substances, it may be instructive to review what we know about the role of race in the siting of toxic waste facilitates.

History

In 1979, Robert Bullard, then a sociologist at Texas Southern University, completed a report describing a futile attempt by an affluent African American neighborhood in Houston, Texas, to block the location of a hazardous waste site within their community. His analysis suggested that race, not just income status, was a probable factor in this local land use decision.

Environmental justice, as revealed though the siting of hazardous waste plants, became a national issue in 1982 when some 500 demonstrators protested against the location of a proposed PCB landfill in a predominantly low-income community in North Carolina. On returning from the protests, Walter Fauntroy, the District of Columbia congressional delegate, asked the General Accounting Office (GAO) to study the characteristics of hazardous waste sites in the EPA's Region 4 (Georgia, Florida, Mississippi, Alabama, Kentucky, Tennessee, North Carolina, and South Carolina). The 1983 study found that three out of four commercial hazardous waste facilities were in predominantly African American communities, and the fourth was in a low-income community.

In 1987, the United Church of Christ Commission for Racial Justice examined the issue of hazardous waste siting for the nation as a whole. According to their statistical analysis of communities with commercial hazardous waste facilities, they determined that:

> Race proved to be the most significant among the variables tested in association with the location of commercial hazardous waste facilities. This represented a consistent national pattern.

In 1994, the Center for Policy Alternatives issued "Toxic Wastes and Race Revisited: An Update of the 1987 Report." That study found that commercial toxic waste facilities were even more likely to be located in minority communities at that time than in 1980, despite growing national attention to the issue.

Not all studies have reached this conclusion, but in a detailed review of the literature, Hamilton (2003) found that, for most U.S. studies, low-income and minority residents do indeed face higher risks from hazardous waste facilities. Less detailed information exists on the exposure of these populations to hazardous waste risks in other industrialized countries.

Environmental justice research and the emerging role of GIS

The application of geographic information systems (GIS) technology has allowed studies of the distributional inequities with respect to either pollution or hazardous waste site location to become more sophisticated. GIS technology also allows analyses to be conducted at the facility level, the city level, or another geographical area. Most regional offices of the EPA, for example, now use demographic data from the U.S. Census Bureau, combined with GIS mapping. This technique allows for the overlay of census data onto concentric rings around a hazardous waste facility or a Superfund site, for example, in order to discover who lives in close proximity to the site. The distribution of risks can also be estimated by combining assumptions about the radius of the externalities around a facility with data from epidemiological studies (Hamilton, 2006).

What have these studies found? The results from these studies are quite varied, but they demonstrate that using only one measure of equity, such as low income, could prove misleading. Hamilton and Viscusi (1999), for example, consider multiple measures of equity, including racial distribution, mean household income, and potential cancer risks, and their work demonstrates how sensitive the results are to the specific measure that is used.

Other studies have utilized the EPA's Toxic Release Inventory (TRI) data. This data set contains self-reported information on toxic releases from all plants that are required to report. Studies using these data have found that demographic groups most likely to face the threat of exposure to toxic air emissions include minorities, renters, people with incomes below the poverty line, and individuals with fewer years of schooling. Studies have also found significant negative effects of pollution on house values and incomes in New England states (Example 14.2).

What explains these findings? What do these findings imply for policy?

The economics of site location

One point of departure is to understand the dynamics of hazardous waste treatment site location and how both income and race might play a role. Our analysis begins by recognizing that hazardous waste facilities are generally unpopular neighbors. Even if the treatment of hazardous waste makes sense for society as a whole, all potential recipient communities must face the NIMBY (Not in My Backyard) opposition.

EXAMPLE 14.2

Do new polluting facilities affect housing values and incomes? Evidence from New England

Combining census data for New England for 1980 and 1990 with Toxics Release Inventory (TRI) data for manufacturing firms that began operations during that period, Hanna (2007) explores the effect of polluting facilities on the surrounding neighborhoods. The study looks specifically at how prices, wages, pollution, and incomes vary among census tracts in the New England states.

Hanna uses data on new plants with an index of pollution exposure calculated as a weighted sum of the distance between the census tract and the pollution source times the TRI-reported releases for that pollution source. Some 167 New England sites were in the TRI data. Ten percent of the new plant emissions were of dichloromethane, an airborne contaminant classified as a probable human carcinogen. Significant negative effects of pollution on house values and incomes were found. These estimates suggest that a house located one mile closer to a polluting manufacturing plant has its value reduced by 1.9 percent.

Source: Hanna, B. G. (2007). House values, incomes, and industrial pollution. *Journal of Environmental Economics and Management, 54*, 100–112.

Understanding the economics of site location requires consideration of the incentives facing both the owners of the proposed facility and the incentives of the host community. Since the owners want to maximize profits, they will look for a site that can process the wastes at a low cost. Being located near the sources of the waste would be attractive as a means of holding down transport costs. Lower land costs would also be attractive since these facilities are frequently land-intensive. Finally, the site should pose as few liability risks as possible in order to limit future payouts.

The host community has its own agenda in order to ensure that it reaps benefits that outweigh costs. They would want to ensure, insofar as possible, that the site was safe for both employees and the inhabitants of the surrounding community. They would also want adequate compensation for assuming the risk of being near these sites. This compensation could take many forms (for example, employment, enhanced tax revenues, or new public services).

What does efficiency suggest about the characteristics of host communities? Low-income communities become attractive as disposal sites not only because land prices are relatively low in those communities, but also because those communities will typically require less compensation in order to accept the risk. Targeting low-income communities would be the expected, not the exceptional, outcome. Furthermore, once hazardous waste facilities are located in a community, the composition of that community is likely to become even poorer due to migration and the negative effects on surrounding property values. Assuming that the willingness to pay for risk-avoidance is higher for higher-income families, more lower-income families may be attracted by the unusually low land prices (or rents), while higher- income families may depart for less risky neighborhoods. Even if the community were not low income at the time of the siting, it is likely to become more so over time.

While even an efficient siting process might target a disproportionate share of these facilities in low-income communities, it is much more difficult to develop a clear economic rationale for why race is a more important predictor than income. Explaining that finding requires greater attention to market failures.

Efficient location requires both full information and adequate enforcement of agreements. In the absence of full information, host communities can fail to fully understand the risk and therefore are likely to undervalue it. One hypothesis explains the importance of race by noting that minority communities have less access to full information than comparably situated white communities. This would imply they are more likely to be unwittingly subject to flawed agreements that are biased against them. Another hypothesis is that they lack the power to enforce community will, perhaps because of under-representation on governing boards. This hypothesis implies that even potentially efficient agreements may be inefficiently implemented (Bullard, 1990). Taken as a whole, this evidence on the prominence of race as an independent predictor variable (over and above income) suggests not only that the current siting process may be discriminatory, but also that it is not efficient. Until such time as recipient communities can be guaranteed both full information and the capability to enforce the community's will, the hazardous waste siting process will remain seriously flawed.

EXAMPLE 14.3

Which came first – the toxic facility or the minority neighborhood?

Pastor et al. (2001) explore "which came first" in Los Angeles County. Using data from 1970 to 1990, they explore whether toxic storage and disposal facilities (TSDFs) moved into a minority neighborhood or whether the TSDF was there first. Using geo-coded site locations and GIS, they were able to identify affected census tracts. By mapping the facility location and creating circular buffers of one-quarter mile and one mile, they were able to determine the potentially affected residents. Their data set contains 83 TSDFs, 39 of which are high capacity and handle most of the waste. Some 55 census tracts were within one-quarter mile of these facilities and 245 tracts were within one mile.

They find that areas receiving TSDFs during this time period were indeed low-income, minority areas with a disproportionate number of renters. After the TDSFs were in place, however, increases in minority residents occurred, but were not disproportionate to the rest of the "move-ins." In other words, prior to any siting decision, neighborhoods with below-average incomes and above-average percentages of Latinos and African Americans were more likely to receive a TSDF. After the siting decision, little evidence suggests disproportionate in-migration along racial or ethnic lines.

The authors acknowledge two limitations of this study. One is that any analysis at the neighborhood level does not capture individual exposure rates, which may vary within the neighborhood. A second limitation arises from the fact that the perceived risks of living near a site are not certain. Some evidence suggests that people are more worried about hazards to which they have been exposed involuntarily.

Source: Pastor, Jr., M., Sadd, J., & Hipp, J. (2001). Which came first? Toxic facilities, minority move-in and environmental justice. *Journal of Urban Affairs, 23*, 1–21.

One lingering issue of debate has to do with the direction of causality. Consider two quite different possibilities. In the first case these population groups could face higher exposures because a hazardous facility was attracted by low land prices. In the other case, attracted by lower land and/or housing prices, people could have moved in after the hazardous waste site located in that community. This chicken-and-egg question has been explored in a few studies.[4] Example 14.3 illustrates one such study in Los Angeles.

The policy response

Environmental justice and hazardous waste sites

In recognition of the problems associated with locating hazardous waste sites, the Office of Environmental Equity was officially established within the U.S. Environmental Protection Agency on November 6, 1992. Its mandate is to deal with environmental impacts affecting people of color and low- income communities. Although the issue that precipitated the creation of this office was largely focused on the siting of hazardous waste facilities, the concerns of this office go well beyond that. Initial efforts are focused on gathering more information about the problem and strengthening enforcement inspections and compliance monitoring in impacted communities.

In 1994, President Clinton issued Executive Order 12898, "Federal Action to Address Environmental Justice in Minority Populations and Low-Income Populations." The goal of this order was to make sure that minority groups and low-income populations are not subjected to an unequal or disproportionately high level of environmental risks.

How effective has the order been? In 2004, the EPA issued an evaluation report of this Executive Order and did not award a good grade. In fact, the report suggests that Executive Order 12898 has not been fully implemented and that the EPA has "not consistently integrated environmental justice into its day-to-day operations." The report also states that the "EPA has not . . . identified populations addressed in the Executive Order, and has neither defined nor developed criteria for determining the disproportionately impacted."[5]

In 2014, Dr. Robert Bullard summed up his sense of what had been the result of Executive Order 12898 on the twentieth anniversary of its enactment:

> After decades of hard work, struggle, and some victories along the way, the quest for environmental justice for all communities has yet to be achieved. Even in 2014, the most potent predictor of health is zip code. Race and poverty are also powerful predictors of students who attend schools near polluting facilities, the location of polluted neighborhoods that pose the greatest threat to human health, hazardous waste facilities, urban heat islands, and access to healthy foods, parks, and tree cover.[6]

Simultaneous exposures to various types of risk make discerning the causal relationships even more complex. Those with lower incomes may live close to a plant with high emissions, but lower incomes are also associated with a poorer diet and less access to health care, both of which can also be associated with increased levels of illness (Hamilton, 2006).

Environmental justice in Canada and Europe

The number of empirical studies outside the United States is rather limited, but some case studies have been conducted, particularly in Canada and Europe. These case studies are useful in helping to discern what kinds of strategies can be effective in the quest to achieve environmental justice in the siting of hazardous waste facilities.

Public participation has been cited as an important factor in the successful siting of hazardous waste facilities in the Canadian provinces of Alberta and Manitoba. ("Successful" in this case means not only that the facility was able to find a home, but also that no environmental justice concerns have arisen after the fact in the host communities.) The siting process in these provinces is not only voluntary, but it also provides multiple stages at which the community can exercise veto power over the project.

Interestingly, the resulting locations are not always in low-income neighborhoods. In fact, one such location, the town of Swan Hills, has an average household income significantly higher than the average in the province and one of the lowest levels of unemployment.

Why would any community accept such a facility? Potential jobs at the facilities are apparently one large factor, as is the property tax revenue that might accrue.

One corollary of the jobs hypothesis might be that we would expect the presence of local high unemployment to increase the likelihood a community would accept a hazardous waste facility. That commonly seems to be the case. In a survey of successful sitings in France, Hungary, Italy, the Netherlands, and Spain, for example, Dente et al. (1998) found that areas with higher unemployment are, as expected, more likely to accept facilities. They also found, however, that communities are more likely to accept waste if it is seen as "local" since, in that case, the residents of the host community will also be reaping the benefits from employment in the plants generating the waste.

The role of risk perception

The NIMBY (Not In My Back Yard) attitude has been explored in both the economics and cognitive psychology literatures. Delving into the psychology of risk perception, Messer et al. (2006) summarize the results of a study that evaluated the benefits of hazardous waste cleanup under the Comprehensive Environmental Response, Compensation, and Liability Act (CERCLA), more commonly known as Superfund. Although this legislation was passed in 1980, legal complexities in the Act have delayed the cleanup of many Superfund sites. These authors wanted to know if the length of delay affected the ultimate recovery of property values after the cleanup.

The authors examined four Superfund sites: Operating Industries, a landfill in Los Angeles; Montclair, West Orange, and Glen Ridge Townships in New Jersey, formerly the site of US Radium Corporation; Industri-plex and Water Wells G&H in Woburn, Massachusetts; and Eagle Mine in Colorado. Cleanup was significantly delayed and/or hampered at all of these sites.

They found that the designation of the site as a Superfund site, the cleanup itself, and the associated news items all negatively affected the property values. Media announcements were found to affect public perceptions of risk so profoundly that a "shunning" of the property may result. Current owners may not be willing to stay in their homes if their perceived costs of remaining are greater than the value of their homes and potential buyers are likely to be few and far between. In this study, property values continued to fall over time as cleanup was delayed. If cleanup were delayed for 20 years, for example, they found that the benefits of cleanup (measured by the recovery of property values) would be negligible in present value economic terms, since it would take another five to ten years for property values to recover.

Compensation as a policy instrument

One policy device for attempting to achieve environmental justice is paying compensation or host fees to communities accepting hazardous waste facilities. In principle, this would serve to make sure that benefits, not merely costs, accrue to the local community. Additionally, paying the compensation would internalize the cost of the environmental risk as that cost was passed on to those whose waste was being treated.

While compensation frequently is an effective device for finding common ground, as Debate 14.1 suggests, that is not always the case!

DEBATE 14.1

Does offering compensation for accepting an environmental risk always increase the willingness to accept the risk?

One week before a referendum in Switzerland on the siting of a nuclear-waste repository, a survey was conducted in the community where the repository was to be located. Researchers found that an offer of compensation to accept the facility *reduced* willingness to accept it! Specifically, Frey and Oberholzer-Gee (1997) and Frey et al. (1996) found that when asked whether they would accept a nuclear-waste repository without compensation, 50.8 percent of the respondents said "yes." This rate dropped to 24.6 percent when compensation was offered! The researchers suggest that acceptance rates drop with compensation because offering the compensation crowds out a feeling of civic duty. If respondents feel that accepting a facility is part of his or her civic duty, he or she will be less likely to feel this sense of responsibility once a payment is introduced. In this context, the authors believe that the compensation was viewed as a morally unacceptable bribe and, hence, should be rejected.

An alternative explanation might suggest that compensation could play a signaling role. Perhaps the risks are perceived as being small until such time as compensation is offered. At that moment, introducing compensation into the mix might be taken by the community as a signal that the risks are much higher than previously thought – indeed, so high that compensation must be paid!

How common is this outcome? In a very different setting (Japan), Lesbirel (1998) examined the siting of energy plants. In this context, the author found that compensation did, as expected, actually facilitate the siting of these plants. He interprets his findings as consistent with the belief that in Japan, institutional structures facilitate participatory negotiations on risk management strategies that result in productive bargaining between the plants and host communities. This process effectively removes the moral stigma and eliminates the signaling role of compensation. Whether this characterization of the Japanese process continues to be valid following the Fukushima nuclear accident remains to be seen.

What is the moral of the story? This evidence suggests that compensation does not automatically increase the likelihood of a community accepting a hazardous facility, but it might. The context matters.

Sources: Frey, B. S., & Oberholzer-Gee, F. (1997). The cost of price incentives: An empirical analysis of motivation crowding out. *American Economic Review, 87*(4), 746–755; Frey, B. S, Oberholzer-Gee, F., & Eichenberger, R. (1996). The old lady visits your backyard: A tale of morals and markets. *Journal of Political Economy, 104*(6),

International agreements

One of the issues erupting during the 1990s concerned the efficiency and morality of exporting hazardous waste to areas that are willing to accept it in return for suitably large compensation. A number of areas, particularly poor countries, appear ready to accept hazardous waste under the "right conditions." The right conditions usually involve alleviating safety concerns and providing adequate compensation (in employment opportunities, money, and public services) so as to make acceptance of the wastes desirable from the receiving community's point of view. Generally, the compensation required is less than the costs of dealing in other ways with the hazardous waste, so the exporting nations find these agreements attractive as well.

A strong backlash against these arrangements arose when opponents argued that communities receiving hazardous waste were poorly informed about the risks they faced and were not equipped to handle the volumes of material that could be expected to cross international boundaries safely. In extreme cases, the communities were completely uninformed as sites were secretly located by individuals, with no public participation in the process at all.

The Basel Convention on the Control of Transboundary Movements of Hazardous Wastes and Their Disposal was developed in 1989 to provide a satisfactory response to these concerns. Under this convention, the 24 nations that belong to the Organisation for Economic Co-operation and Development (OECD) were required to obtain written permission from the government of any developing country before exporting toxic waste there for disposal or recycling. This was followed, in 1994, by an additional agreement on the part of most, but not all, industrialized nations to completely prohibit the export of toxic wastes from any OECD country to any non-OECD country.

With the huge growth in sales of electronic devices and the valuable materials in the postconsumer e-waste resulting from these sales, enforcement of laws on exporting toxic materials in e-waste is getting more difficult.

Some used electronic goods exported to developing countries become electronic waste (e-waste) that is usually disassembled in those developing countries. The concern is that the recovery process can be dangerous to the health of the disassemblers, particularly if it is done without the proper safeguards. E-waste often contains toxic substances such as lead, mercury, cadmium, and flame retardants.

Kinnaman and Yokoo (2011) report on studies that have found the following:

- Ambient dioxin and furan concentrations in the air around an e-waste dismantling site in China are the highest in the world. As a result, blood lead levels in children within proximity to this Chinese dismantling site significantly exceed the Chinese mean.
- Concentrations of lead, dioxins, and furans in e-waste dismantling sites in India also exceed World Health Organization guidelines.

A bill titled the Responsible Electronics Recycling Act, which would have banned U.S. exports of electronic waste, was introduced in Congress in 2011, but not enacted.

Summary

The potential for contamination of the environmental asset by toxic substances is one of the most complex environmental problems. The number of substances that are potentially toxic is in the millions. Some 100,000 of these are in active use.

Although it is not always sufficient to provide an efficient outcome, the market provides a considerable amount of pressure toward resolving toxic substance problems as they affect employees and consumers. With reliable information at their disposal, all parties have an incentive to reduce hazards to acceptable levels. This pressure is absent, however, in cases involving third parties. Here, the problem frequently takes the form of an external cost imposed on innocent bystanders.

The efficient role of government can range from ensuring the provision of sufficient information (so that participants in the market can make informed choices) to setting exposure limits on hazardous substances. Unfortunately, the scientific basis for decision making is weak. Only limited information on the effects of these substances is available, and the cost of acquiring complete information is prohibitive. Therefore, priorities must be established and tests developed to screen substances so that efforts can be concentrated on those substances that seem most dangerous.

In contrast to air and water pollution, the toxic substance problem is one in which the courts may play a particularly important role. Liability law not only creates a market pressure for more and better information on potential damages associated with chemical substances, but also it provides some incentives to manufacturers of substances, the generators of waste, the transporters of waste, and those who dispose of it to exercise precaution. Judicial remedies also allow the level of precaution to vary with the occupational circumstances and provide a means of compensating victims.

Judicial remedies, however, are insufficient. They are expensive and ill-suited for dealing with problems affecting large numbers of people. The burden of proof under the current American system is difficult to surmount, although in Japan some radical new approaches have been developed to deal with this problem. Furthermore, court cases may take a considerable amount of time to resolve.

Is the burden posed by environmental risks and the policies used to reduce them distributed fairly? Apparently not. The siting of hazardous waste facilities seems to have resulted in a distribution of risks that disproportionately burdens low-income populations, and minority communities. This outcome suggests that current siting policies are neither efficient nor fair. The responsibility for this policy failure seems to lie mainly with the failure to ensure informed consent of residents in recipient communities and very uneven enforcement of existing legal protections.

The theologian Reinhold Niebuhr once said, "Democracy is finding proximate solutions to insoluble problems." That seems an apt description of the institutional response to the toxic substance problem. Our political institutions have created a staggering array of legislative and judicial responses to this problem that are neither efficient nor complete. They do, however, represent a positive first step in what must be an evolutionary process.

Discussion questions

1 Did the courts resolve the dilemma posed in Example 14.2 correctly in your opinion? Why or why not?
2 Over the last several decades in product liability law, there has been a movement in the court system from *caveat emptor* ("buyer beware") to *caveat venditor* ("seller beware"). The liability for using and consuming risky products has been shifted from buyers to sellers. Does this shift represent a movement toward or away from an efficient allocation of risk? Why?
3 Would the export of hazardous waste to developing countries be efficient? Sometimes? Always? Never? Would it be moral? Sometimes? Always? Never? Make clear the specific reasons for your judgments.
4 How should the public sector handle a toxic gas, such as radon, that occurs naturally and seeps into some houses through the basement or the water supply? Is this a case of an externality? Does the homeowner have the appropriate incentives to take an efficient level of precaution?

Self-test exercises

1 Firms whose economic activity might pose an environmental risk are sometimes required to post performance bonds before the activity is allowed to commence. The amount of the required bond would be equal to the present value of anticipated damages. Any restoration of the site resulting from a hazardous waste leak could be funded directly and immediately from the accumulated funds. Any unused proceeds would be redeemable at specified dates if the environmental costs turned out to be lower than anticipated.

What is the difference in practice between an approach relying on performance bonds and one imposing strict liability for cleanup costs on any firm for a toxic substance spill?

2 Is informing the consumer about any toxic substances used in the manufacture of a product sufficient to produce an efficient level of toxic substance use for that product? Why or why not?

Notes

1 Muir, T., & M. Zegarac. (2001). Societal costs of exposure to toxic substances: Economic and health costs of four case studies that are candidates for environmental causation. *Environmental Health Perspectives*, 109(Suppl 6), 885–903.

2 Unions would be expected to produce more efficient information flows since they represent many workers and can take advantage of economies of scale in the collection, interpretation, and dissemination of risk information. Available evidence suggests that the preponderance of wage premiums for risk has been derived from data involving unionized workers.

3 A classic example is provided by the manner in which Americans choose their automobiles. It is quite clear that some larger cars are safer and more expensive than smaller, cheaper ones, at least to their owners. Some consumers are willing to pay for this additional level of safety, and others are not.

4 Boyce, J.K. (2007) *Power Inequalities and the Political Economy of Environmental Protection,* Available at: http://tuvalu.santafe.edu/files/gems/sustainability/sustain12.pdf.

5 Report of the Office of the Inspector General, March 1, 2004.

6 Bullard, Robert. (2014). *New Report Tracks Environmental Justice Movement over Five Decades*. Available at: www.nrdc.org/experts/albert-huang/20th-anniversary-president-clintons-executive-order-12898-environmental-justice (Accessed December 7, 2016).

Further reading

Banzhaf, S., Ma, L., & Timmins, C. (2019). Environmental justice: The economics of race, place, and pollution. *Journal of Economic Perspectives*, 33(1), 185–208. This paper reviews the environmental justice literature, especially where it intersects with work by economists.

Jenkins, R. R., Klemicky, H., Kopitsz, E., & Marten, A. (2012). Policy monitor: U.S. emergency response and removal: Superfund's overlooked cleanup program. *Review of Environmental Economics and Policy*, 6(2), 278–297. Describes and evaluates a key component of the nation's response capability regulations to respond to actual and threatened hazardous releases, including deliberate releases by terrorists: The Superfund Emergency Response and Removal (ERR) Program.

Mendelsohn, R., & Olmstead, S. (2009). The economic valuation of environmental amenities and disamenities: Methods and applications. *Annual Review of Environment and Resources*, 34, 325–347.

Reviews the evolution of our ability to estimate the economic value of environmental amenities and disamenities over the last four decades.

Sigman, H., & Stafford, S. (2011). Management of hazardous waste and contaminated land. *Annual Review of Resource Economics*, 3. A review of the hazardous-waste management from an economic perspective.

Additional references and other historically significant references are available on this book's eResource page: www.routledge.com/9781138587595

Chapter 15

Meeting the challenges

The role of economics

Introduction

We have now come full circle. We began our study with questions about efficient environmental management strategies including those targeting some looming challenges facing our society in the future. Of particular interest is the role that economics can play and has played in understanding and improving those responses.

During our investigations of several specific environmental contexts, we examined both the existing and the possible novel responses to present and future effective management challenges. Our examinations uncovered a host of useful insights about the determinants of effective management in these individual situations. Now it is time to step back and coalesce those context-specific insights into a systematic assessment of the role that the government policy and the market economy can play, both individually and in concert, in helping to craft effective, equitable responses to the challenges that environmental policy faces.

Addressing the issues

We opened with a close examination of a view held by some on one side of the partisan divide, namely that the market could handle these challenges without interference of the government. We found that while the market certainly has some useful aspects that can help in finding solutions to these management challenges, in many environmental situations market responses, by themselves, are not sufficient.

While markets do succeed in some circumstances, in others they fail to provide equitable and/or efficient strategies for managing the balance between human activities and the environment. The main circumstances that lead to failure, of course, is that environmental issues frequently involve significant externalities. The costs that result from pollution, for example, frequently are not born by the polluters; rather they are born by others. Those that actually do bear the external costs include those who are exposed to either the human-health impacts of air or water pollution, or to the damages imposed by a modified climate. Because these costs are externalized, they are insufficiently considered by those who actually make the decisions about how much pollution to control. As a result market decisions are biased; they result in less pollution control than would be efficient. In the climate case, for example, an inefficiently low level of both fuel switching and energy efficiency investments would result from relying exclusively on market decisions compared to more efficient choices. This bias is exacerbated when the external costs are born by people in other countries; due to their location on a different side of the border from the pollution sources they have little or no political access to corrective measures on those sources.

Another set of circumstances that lead to inefficient market behavior is when resources are extracted from a free-access commons such as some fisheries. The incentives created by a free-access commons promote excessive exploitation of the extracted resources, even to the extent that the stock of resources, even renewable biological resources, can be harvested to extinction; in this circumstance by itself the market does not provide a means of preventing overharvesting even when the resources are quite valuable. An understanding of these perverse incentives goes a long way toward explaining why so many ecological services can be degraded despite their social value.

While these situations explain why we cannot count exclusively on unregulated markets to produce efficient outcomes, a different set of problems arise when the outcomes are not equitable. Markets respond very well to demand. The magnitude of demand for a particular product or activity results not only from the strength of consumer preferences for them, but also the amount of money that buyers can afford to spend to fulfill those preferences. In markets money does talk; the preferences of low-income consumers will not receive the same attention as preferences that are backed with more spending power.

It is important *not* to interpret these examples as demonstrating a stronger conclusion, namely that markets are never efficient, equitable or capable of playing an important role in the transition to a sustainable future. As we have seen markets have many desirable attributes that, when used appropriately, can contribute to better environmental management. They are flexible and can respond to changes relatively rapidly. They are innovative and are constantly bringing newer, better products to market (see Example 15.1). They can also be equitable when the products needed by low-income consumers can be supplied at a profit. Remember how entrepreneurs were able to provide electricity services to off-the-grid consumers in Kenya.

How about governments? Can an exclusive reliance on governmental mandates consistently produce efficient and equitable outcomes?

In theory governments are there to protect the public interests of the people they serve and much of the time they do precisely that. However, governments have weaknesses as well. As the amount of money in politics has risen, donor expectations as to what they will get for that money have risen as well. The sheer cost of running for office has increased so much that politicians have to spend an inordinate amount of time with donors fund-raising. Private interests may use *rent-seeking* to enhance either their individual or corporate interests or both. For example while some Presidents use this strategy more than others, most Presidents fill at least some of the nation's ambassadorships with their big donors.

Sometimes rent-seeking involves *regulatory capture*, where a regulatory agency becomes controlled by the very interests it has been created to regulate. When this happens, the public interest become subservient to those private interests. If you think that is a far-fetched concept in modern America, you might be interested to know that some suggest that it is going on right now in the approach to environmental management in the U.S. federal government.[1]

EXAMPLE 15.1

Private incentives for sustainable development: can adopting sustainable practices be profitable?

Motivated by what it perceived to be great inefficiencies associated with its industry, the Interface Corporation, a carpet manufacturer founded by Ray Anderson, totally transformed the nature of its business. How it managed this transformation is instructive.

First, the company recognized that unworn carpet, usually under furniture, did not need to be replaced. In response, the company switched from selling traditional wall-to-wall carpet to selling a carpet tile system. Whereas, in traditional practice, wear in any part of the carpet meant that the entire carpet had to be replaced; with carpet tiles only those specific tiles showing wear are replaced. As an added benefit, the reduction in carpet replacement simultaneously reduces the amount of potentially harmful glue fumes being released into the indoor air.

Next, Interface totally changed its relationship with its customers. Rather than selling carpet, Interface leased it. In effect, it became a seller of carpet services rather than a seller of carpets. Carpet tiles can be easily replaced overnight by Interface employees, eliminating the loss of productivity that could occur from halting company activities during the day. The cost to consumers is substantially lower not only because less carpet is replaced but also because leasing allows tax advantages. Leased carpet is treated by the tax code as an expense, not an asset, and, hence, lowers taxes.

The environment also benefited. In traditional industry practice, most used carpet was transported to landfill. Much of the rest was remanufactured into much-lower-valued uses. Seeing that as a waste of resources, Interface created an entirely new product that, when recycled at the end of its useful life, could be remanufactured back into carpet. Not only was this production process less wasteful in terms of its drain on energy and raw materials, the product was also reportedly highly stain-resistant, four times as durable as regular carpet material, and easily cleaned with water.

These moves toward more sustainable manufacturing did not result from government mandates. Rather, an innovative company found that it could benefit itself and the environment at the same time.

The Interface story is a compelling one. Fifteen years after Anderson's initiative, Interface had:

- Cut greenhouse gas emissions by 94 percent
- Cut fossil fuel consumption by 60 percent
- Cut waste by 80 percent

- Cut water use by 80 percent
- Invented and patented new machines, materials, and manufacturing processes
- Increased sales by 66 percent, doubled earnings, and raised profit margins.

Sources: Hawken, P., Lovins, A., & Lovins, L. H. (1999). Natural Capitalism: Creating the Next Industrial Revolution. Boston, MA: Little, Brown and Company; Anderson, Ray, with Robin White. (2011). Business Lessons from a Radical Industrialist. New York: St. Martin's Griffin.

Since many of the problems, such as climate change, are global in scope, the solutions must be global as well. Unfortunately creating and enforcing international agreements for these types of problems are very difficult. Because national emissions reduction to reduce the risk from a modified climate are *public goods*, nations who do less than their fair share of emission reductions can become *free-riders* on the efforts of those countries who do undertake efficient steps to reduce their pollution; free riders benefit from the reduction whether or not they contribute to it. This causes an inefficiently low level of pollution control internationally.

This conceptual difficulty is confirmed in practice by the major international agreements dealing with climate change; they have not been strong enough to reduce emissions sufficiently as to satisfy the specified international reduction goals.

We also saw that governments do not have a particularly solid track record when it comes to implementing policies that produce efficient outcomes. Traditional regulatory mandates typically do not produce cost-effective outcomes since they do not result in equal marginal costs. Additionally, since the compliance possibilities are frequently so numerous and depend upon local circumstances, regulatory agencies typically do not have as good a knowledge of the compliance choices as the regulated businesses do. One size does not usually fit all and yet regulators tend to avoid differentiating the regulations with respect to local conditions because creating differentiated policies complicates instrument design considerably.

We have also seen, especially in the location of hazardous waste treatment facilities (Chapter 14), where government decisions may not protect the interests of those who are in the minority. Majority rule certainly does not automatically protect the minority.

Our review of the evidence suggests a more promising organizational design for efficient and equitable environmental management – combining the strongest aspects of government policy with market implementation in a joint program of government-market partnerships. Consider, for example, allowing government to produce policy targets that eliminate the externality or free-access common property biases and enforcing the responses to those choices. The market could be allowed via market-based policy instruments to choose the specific responses that both encourage innovation and are cost-effective as a means of flexibly meeting those targets. Specific examples we have discussed in the text include carbon pricing, fishing quotas and congestion pricing in large cities.

As we have seen, carbon pricing can produce a cost-effective allocation of the emission control responsibility and it can use revenue rebates to make sure that the cost burden is fairly distributed. Consider one additional example. California's cap-and-trade program is designed to reduce greenhouse gas emissions to 40 percent below 1990 levels by 2030. It generates revenue while it works to reduce emissions. California law directs that 35 percent of greenhouse gas auction proceeds should be used for the benefit of low-income neighborhoods and disadvantaged communities. Some 2,007 designated disadvantaged communities have benefitted from cap-and-trade investments.[2]

Congestion pricing can be designed to reduce traffic flow to efficient levels without forcing the government to decide who gets to travel during congested period and who does not; those decisions would be made by the individual travelers who are in the best position to know at this time and in this place what the best choice is for them, given that toll structure. Making sure that the toll revenue can at least in part be used to assure adequate alternative *public* modes of transport (buses, subways, etc.) that are available for all at a reasonable cost goes a long way to assuring that the burdens of reducing congestion are shared fairly.

We have also seen circumstances in which market incentive structures would not inherently lead to biased decisions as long as market participants had full information about the choices facing them. In those circumstances where market participants do not have the requisite information, the government can supply it. Using government policies to assure that all parties have complete information on risks posed by toxic substances, for example, can be an important component of the over-all strategy. Better information can unleash private incentives for efficient and equitable risk management that would otherwise be silences by ignorance. Recall, for example, the experience with Proposition 65 in California where this information disclosure regulation actually outperformed more traditional approaches to controlling lead in drinking water (see Example 3.3).

The government functions we have discussed so far are those found in the executive and legislative branches. How about the judiciary branch?

Placing monetary values on environmental assets is one important contribution economics can contribute to management strategies based upon judicial decisions. Historically in many contexts environmental resources were in principle recognized as being important, but in practice were taken for granted. Supplied by nature rather than human activity, the services they provided were not routinely monetized.

Frequently damage to these resources is managed by suing the parties responsible for the damage under liability law. A normal remedy in liability law involves requiring the party responsible for the damage to pay not only for restoration, but also to compensate the victims for the damage they suffered. Implementing this remedy requires a monetized measure of the damages. Economic valuation can supply, and has supplied, that value for the courts.

Consider, for example, an oil spill into an abundant marine area. One effect might be to kill fish and to lower the harvest, perhaps for a considerable time. Because the fish are marketed, the prices they fetch are known, so using these prices to calculate the loses accruing from lower harvest levels in commercial fisheries is relatively easy.

How about the other forms of damage, however? What about injured birds and the entire marine ecosystem that sustain the commercial fisheries? Monetary values for these are harder to produce simply because these species are typically not marketed. Fortunately modern valuation techniques for nonmarketed resources have become much more sophisticated and can fill this void. They also can also incorporate deeper social values that previously were ignored. While the importance of these deeper values was recognized in a spiritual sense, we did not, until relatively recently, have the metrics to monetize them.

This enhanced ability to measure damages from oil spills more comprehensively matters to efficient environmental management. Each successful liability suit that requires those responsible for the oil spill to pay the damages they caused creates incentives not only for the plaintiff in this suit, but also by setting a precedent for all those companies that might experience an oil spill in the future. If the damage awards are inefficiently low, the companies will be tempted to spend less on taking precaution against an oil spill in the future. That not only means that future damages will be higher than efficient as well. In addition the prices for those products that used that oil in their production would also be too low.

Valuation of environmental resources is also useful to Federal agencies as they try to direct funding to those projects that will realize the biggest bang for public expenditures, given limited budgets. Valuation is currently being used to designate critical habitat under the Endangered Species Act (U.S. Fish and Wildlife Service), to evaluate dam relicensing applications (The Federal Energy Regulatory Commission) and to estimate the costs and benefits of the Clean Air Act and the Clean Water Act.

Valuation can also be useful in demonstrating the economic worth of ecosystem services The Costa Rican PSA program, for example, protects purification and recharge services provided by upstream forests to downstream private water users. Payments from the downstream beneficiaries are now used to protect the forests that provide these services. Economic valuation of these services is the basis for setting an appropriate price. (Chapters 5 and 6)

The different analytical foundations of economics support many different forms of evidence that can be brought to bear to inform and improve environmental management.

- Econometrics uses statistical techniques as the basis for providing a number of useful services. As examples in earlier chapters have demonstrated it can be used to discover the effects of an implemented policy (see Example 12.5) and to forecast future outcomes based upon historical experience (see Chapter 10).
- Before and after comparisons of operating program involving similar resource contexts but differential policy treatments, allow for isolating the effect of the policy differences (see Example 7.2).
- Experimental economics provides a way to examine decision making in a highly controlled lab environment. This setting has the advantage of limiting the possible contaminating influences of factors other than the influences of interest (see Example 1.1).
- Behavioral economics draws from psychology to add a new dimension for instrument design that can tailor the approach to the specific cognitive process that people use to make decisions in that circumstance (see Example 3.5).
- The evolution of Geographic Information Systems (GIS) has allowed richer (geo-coded) data sets for evaluating the spatial dimensions of valuation (see Example 5.4).

The sustainable development challenge

Historically, increases in inputs and technological progress have been important sources of economic growth in the industrialized nations. In the future the development of new technologies such as self-driving cars and robots will act as labor substitutes and, hence, will reduce the drag that would have otherwise be occurred due to lower population growth rates. On the other hand limits to technological progress imposed by the second law of thermodynamics imply that the growth process must culminate in a steady or stationary state where growth ultimately, but inevitably, diminishes to zero.

The economy is currently being transformed. It is not business as usual. The increasing corporate focus on sustainability is playing a role. Additionally as citizens become better informed about the consequences of their choices, they are beginning to use their power as consumers, employees, shareholders, and voters to let companies know that they support business behavior that is compatible with sustainable outcomes.

Recognizing that conventional measures of economic growth shed little light on the question, some crude attempts have been made to estimate whether or not growth in the industrialized countries has historically made the citizens of those countries better off. Results of some of these studies suggest that because growth has ultimately generated more leisure, longer life expectancy, and more goods and services, it has, on balance, been beneficial. Yet other measures, such as the ecological footprint, convey a more cautionary story. They remind us that our inability to measure precisely the earth's carrying capacity for supporting human activity in no way diminishes the existence and importance of those potentially existential limits.

The evidence suggests that the notion that all of the world's people are automatically benefited by economic growth is naïve. Economic growth has demonstrably benefited large numbers of people, but that outcome is certainly not inevitable for all people in all settings. Expanding pollution and diminishing access to crucial resources such as water or land can offset or even exceed the gains for at least some subset of the population. New sustainable forms of development are possible and desirable, but they will not automatically be adopted in either the high-income or the low-income nations.

The economic incentives approach to environmental regulation has become a significant component of environmental policy. Instead of mandating prescribed actions, such as requiring the installation of a particular piece of pollution control equipment, this approach achieves environmental objectives by changing the economic incentives of those doing the polluting. When their incentives are modified appropriately, consumers and producers can be encouraged to select the best means of meeting their needs in a sustainable manner. When it is in the interest of individuals to change to new forms of development, the transformation can be amazingly rapid.

Public policy and sustainable development must proceed in a mutually supportive relationship. In some cases that relationship takes the form of public – private partnerships that involve explicit agreements between government and the private sector regarding the provision of public services or infrastructure (see Example 15.2). In other cases, it involves government regulatory action to ensure that the market is sending the right signals to all participants so that the sustainable outcome is compatible with other business objectives. Economic-incentive approaches are a means of establishing that kind of compatibility. The experience with the various versions of this approach used in the United States, Europe, and Asia suggests that allowing business great flexibility within a regulatory framework that harmonizes private and social costs in general is both feasible and effective.

How about global environmental problems? Economic-incentives approaches could be helpful here as well. Pollution pricing facilitates cost sharing among participants while ensuring cost-effective responses to the need for additional control. By separating the question of what control is undertaken from the question of who ultimately pays for it, the government significantly widens the control possibilities and lowers compliance costs.

EXAMPLE 15.2

Public–private partnerships: the Kalundborg experience

Located on an island 75 miles off the coast of Copenhagen, the city of Kalundborg has achieved a remarkable symbiosis among the various industries that provide the employment base for the city. The four main industries, along with small businesses and the municipal government, began developing cooperative relationships in the 1970s designed to lower disposal costs, attain less expensive input materials, and receive income from their waste products.

A coal-fired power plant (Asnaes) transports its residual steam to a refinery (Statoil). In exchange, Statoil gives Asnaes refinery gas that Asnaes burns to generate electricity. Asnaes sells excess steam to a local fish farm, to a heating system for the city, and to a pharmaceuticals and enzyme producer (Novo Nordisk). Continuing the cycle, the fish farm and Novo Nordisk send their sludge to farms to be used as fertilizer. Produced fly ash is sold to a cement plant and gypsum produced by its desulfurization process is sold to a wallboard manufacturer. Statoil, the refinery, sells the sulfur removed from its natural gas to a sulfuric acid manufacturer, Kemira.

This entire process resulted not from centralized planning, but simply because it was in the individual best interests of the public and private entities involved. Although the motives were purely financial, this synergetic situation has clear environmental benefits. It is therefore likely to be economically, as well as environmentally, sustainable.

Sources: Desroches, P. Eco-industrial parks: The case for private planning, *Report # RS 00–1*. Political Economy Research Center, Bozeman, MT 59718; Kalundborg Symbiosis: www.symbiosis.dk/en (accessed December 23, 2016)

The good news is that many countries around the world now have implemented pricing strategies to control greenhouse gases and other global pollutants. These environmental policies trigger a search for possible ways to reduce the damage, including changing inputs, changing the production process, transforming the residuals to less-harmful substances, and recycling by-products. As illustrated about rapidly falling solar (photovoltaic) prices, some of these transitions can occur quite rapidly.

Fees and auctioned allowances also raise revenue. Successful development, particularly sustainable development, requires a symbiotic partnership between the public and private sectors. To function as an equal partner, the public sector must be adequately funded. If it fails to raise adequate revenue, the public sector becomes a drag on the transformation process, but if it raises revenue in ways that distort incentives, that, too, can impede the transition to sustainability. Effluent or emissions charges and auctioned allowances offer the realistic opportunity to raise revenue for the public sector, while reducing the drag from more distortionary taxes.

Whereas other types of taxation discourage growth by penalizing legitimate development incentives (such as taxing wages), emissions or effluent charges provide both incentives and revenue to support sustainable development. Some work from the United States suggests that the drag on development avoided by substituting carbon pricing for more traditional revenue-raising mechanisms, such as capital gains, income, and sales taxes, could be significant.

The bad news, as we have seen in Chapter 8, concerns the inherent challenges of achieving a coordinated international action on global problems. International agreements must confront serious free-rider problems that undermine incentives of individual countries to join and comply with agreements that are strong enough to solve the problem. With respect to climate change so far these difficulties have impeded action that is sufficient to meet the established international temperature targets. World Bank studies make it clear that the prices in existing carbon pricing programs are generally too low to achieve the international targets. While the solutions path of stipulated emissions reductions is clear, as of 2019 (when this is being written) the collective political will to do what is necessary is not there.

Economics studies have pointed out that action on reducing greenhouse emissions is cheaper than inaction, that delay increases the cost of the necessary action over time, and that appropriate carbon pricing strategies can be effective, efficient and fair. However none of that has been enough to generate an efficient sustainable response.

What are the consequences? At a minimum economic analysis makes it clear that this shortfall of collective political will has raised, and will continue to raise as long as responses are delayed further, the costs of solving this threat. The fact that emissions are now higher than required by the efficient solutions path means that damages will be higher, possibly much higher, than they would have with earlier control. Additionally, expensive adaptation strategies will necessarily become a more significant of the part of the solutions package as the delay means that there will be more risks to try to mediate. This will also add to the cost.

Finally the fact that economics incentives CAN be an important part of an efficient, equitable and sustainable solutions package does not mean that they will in practice. The details matter. Economic incentives can be misapplied as well as appropriately applied (Example 12.6). Incentive approaches must be used with care.

A concluding comment

Our society is evolving. When a complementary relationship among the economic system, the court system, and the legislative and executive branches of government can be maintained, we can make progress. As the high degree of partisanship in the United States illustrates, however, we are not yet out of the woods. Significantly, not only must politicians learn to work together to produce bipartisan or nonpartisan solutions to our most pressing problems, but we the public must learn that part of the responsibility is ours. Solutions are unlikely to prevail without our significant participation and support.

Not all behavior can be regulated. It costs too much to catch every offender. Our law enforcement system works because most people obey the law, whether anyone is watching or not. A high degree of voluntary compliance is essential for the system to work smoothly.

The best resolution of the toxic substance problem, for example, is undoubtedly for all makers of potentially toxic substances to be genuinely concerned about the safety of their products and to bite the bullet whenever their research raises questions. The ultimate responsibility for developing an acceptable level of risk must rest on the integrity of those who make, use, transport, and dispose of the substances. The government can assist by penalizing and controlling those few who fail to exhibit this integrity, but regulation can never completely substitute for integrity. We cannot and should not depend purely upon altruism to solve these problems, but we should not underestimate its importance either.

We also need to recognize that markets serve our preferences as consumers. Making sure our purchases and investments reflect environmental values will help markets move in the right direction. Zero-emission automobiles will enter the market much faster if many consumers demand them. Sustainably harvested fisheries will proliferate once consumers shun fish from those fisheries that are managed unsustainably. It is easy to see large corporations as villains, but it is tougher to notice the villains in our mirrors.

The notion that we are at the end of an era may well be true. But we are also at the beginning of a new one. With foresight the decline of civilization can be avoided, but success will require its transformation. The road may be strewn with obstacles and our social institutions may deal with those obstacles with less grace and less finesse than we might have hoped, but we can make progress.

Discussion questions

1 Are you optimistic or pessimistic about the future? Why?
2 In thinking about the appropriate balance between the market and the government in achieving sustainability, do you think the government needs to take a stronger role or would you favor reducing government influence over the market? Why?

Notes

1 Whitehouse, Senator Sheldon. *Legal Responses to Regulatory Capture* (November 9, 2018) From a blog that is available on the web at: www.acslaw.org/acsblog/blog-post-for-the-american-constitution-society-legal-responses-to-regulatory-capture/

2 Brown, Patricia Leigh. (2018). Green upgrade: How California is pioneering 'energy justice'. *Yale E360.* Available at: https://e360.yale.edu/features/green-upgrade-how-california-is-pioneering-renewable-energy-justice-cap-and-trade

Further reading

Anderson, T., & Leal, D. (Eds.). (2015). *Free Market Environmentalism for the Next Generation.* London: Palgrave Macmillan. This book provides a free-market vision for environmentalism's future, based on the success of environmental entrepreneurs around the world. It explores the next generation of environmental market ideas.

Hawken, P. (2010). *The Ecology of Commerce Revised Edition: A Declaration of Sustainability.* New York: Harper Collins. A classic in the field, this book makes the case for why business success and sustainable environmental practices need not – and, for the sake of our planet, must not – be mutually exclusive any longer.

Speth, J. G. (2012). *America the Possible: Manifesto for a New Economy.* New Haven, CT: Yale University Press. Speth presents a vison of the future from the progressive point of view. He finds that we have let conditions of life in America deteriorate across a broad front and are headed straight to a place we would not want for our children and grandchildren. He presents a vison of how we could chart a better course.

Answers to self-test exercises

Chapter 1

1 A shortage would promote higher prices, thereby lowering demand until it equaled the new smaller supply. This response acts to reduce rather than intensify the shortage.

If consumers anticipate these higher prices, however, thereby buying and hoarding extra amounts before the prices rise, this intensifies the shortage.

Chapter 2

1 a Set $MC = P$, so $80 - 1q = 1q$. Solving for q finds that $q = 40$ and $P = 40$.

b Consumer surplus = \$800. Producer surplus = \$800. Consumer surplus plus producer surplus = \$1,600 = economic surplus.

c The marginal revenue curve has twice the slope of the demand curve, so $MR = 80 - 2q$. Setting $MR = MC$, yields $q = 80/3$ and $P = 160/3$. Using Figure 2.8, producer surplus is the area under the price line *(FE)* and over the marginal-cost line *(DH)*. This can be computed as the sum of a rectangle (formed by *FED* and a horizontal line drawn from *D* to the vertical axis) and a triangle (formed by *DH* and the point created by the intersection of the horizontal line drawn from *D* with the vertical axis).

The area of any rectangle is base × height. The base = 80/3 and the

$$\text{Height} = P - MC = \frac{160}{3} - \frac{80}{3} = \frac{80}{3}.$$

Therefore, the area of the rectangle is 6400/9. The area of the right triangle is

$$\frac{1}{2} \times \frac{80}{3} \times \frac{80}{3} = \frac{3,200}{9}.$$

$$\begin{aligned}\text{Producer surplus} &= \frac{3,200}{9} + \frac{6,400}{9} \\ &= \frac{\$9,600}{9}\end{aligned}$$

$$\begin{aligned}\text{Consumer surplus} &= \frac{1}{2} \times \frac{80}{3} \times \frac{80}{3} \\ &= \frac{\$3,200}{9}\end{aligned}$$

1 $\frac{\$9{,}600}{9} > \$800$

2 $\frac{\$3{,}200}{9} < \$800$

3 $\frac{\$12{,}800}{9} < \$1{,}600$

2 a Descriptive. It is possible to estimate this linkage empirically.
b Normative. A descriptive analysis could estimate the impacts of expenditures on endangered species, but moving from that analysis to a conclusion that expenditures would be wasted requires injecting values into the analysis.
c Normative. A descriptive analysis could compare the effects of privatized and nonprivatized fisheries, but moving from these results to a conclusion that the fisheries must be privatized to survive normally requires an injection of values. If the data revealed that all privatized fisheries survived and none of the others did, the move to "must" would have a very strong descriptive underpinning.
d Descriptive. This linkage could be estimated empirically directly from the data.
e Normative. This statement could be descriptive if it was stated as "birth control programs actually contribute to a rise in population" since this is an empirical relationship that could be investigated.

However, as stated, it allows a much wider scope of aspects to enter the debate and weighing the importance of those aspects will normally require value judgments.

3 a A pod of whales is a common-pool resource to whale hunters. It is characterized by nonexclusivity and divisibility.
b A pod of whales is a public good to whale watchers since it is characterized by both nondivisibility and nonexclusivity.
c The benefits from reductions of greenhouse gas emissions are public goods because they are both nondivisible and nonexclusive.
d For residents, a town water supply is a common-pool resource because it is both divisible and nonexclusive to town residents. It is not a common-pool resource for nonresidents since they can be excluded.
e Bottled water is neither; it is both divisible and exclusive. In fact it is a private good.

Chapter 3

1 a Set $MC = P$, so $80 - 1q = 1q$. Solving for q finds that $q = 40$ and $P = 40$.
b Consumer surplus = \$800. Producer surplus = \$800. Consumer surplus plus producer surplus = \$1,600 = economic surplus.
c The marginal revenue curve has twice the slope of the demand curve, so $MR = 80 - 2q$. Setting $MR = MC$, yields $q = 80/3$ and $P = 160/3$. Using Figure 2.8, producer surplus is the area under the price line (*FE*) and over the marginal-cost line (*DH*). This can be computed as the sum of a rectangle (formed by *FED* and a horizontal line drawn from *D* to the vertical axis) and a triangle (formed by *DH* and the point created by the intersection of the horizontal line drawn from *D* with the vertical axis).

The area of any rectangle is base × height. The base = 80/3 and the

$$\text{Height} = P - MC = \frac{160}{3} - \frac{80}{3} = \frac{80}{3}.$$

Therefore, the area of the rectangle is 6400/9. The area of the right triangle is

$$\frac{1}{2}\times\frac{80}{3}\times\frac{80}{3}=\frac{3,200}{9}.$$

$$\text{Producer surplus}=\frac{3,200}{9}+\frac{6,400}{9}$$
$$=\frac{\$9,600}{9}$$
$$\text{Consumer surplus}=\frac{1}{2}\times\frac{80}{3}\times\frac{80}{3}$$
$$=\frac{\$3,200}{9}$$

1 $\frac{\$9,600}{9}>\$800$

2 $\frac{\$3,200}{9}<\$800$

3 $\frac{\$12,800}{9}<\$1,600$

2 The policy would not be consistent with efficiency. As the firm considers measures to reduce the magnitude of any spill, it would compare the marginal costs of those measures with the expected marginal reduction in its liability from reducing the magnitude of the spill. Yet the expected marginal reduction in liability from a smaller spill would be zero. Firms would pay $X regardless of the size of the spill. Since the amount paid cannot be reduced by controlling the size of the spill, the incentive to take precautions that reduce the size of the spill will be inefficiently low.

3 If "better" means efficient, this common belief is not necessarily true. Damage awards are efficient when they equal the damage caused. Ensuring that the award reflects the actual damage will appropriately internalize the external cost. Larger damage awards are more efficient only to the extent that they more closely approximate the actual damage. Whenever they promote an excessive level of precaution that cannot be justified by the damages, awards that exceed actual cost are inefficient. Bigger is not always better.

Chapter 4

1 With risk-neutrality, the policy should be pursued because the expected net benefits (0.85 × $4,000,000 + 0.10 ×$1,000,000 + 0.05 ×–$10,000,000 = $3,000,000) are positive. Related Discussion Question: Looking at these numbers, do you think risk-neutrality is how you would actually think about this situation? Or would you be more risk averse and weigh the third outcome more heavily than its expected likelihood?

2 a Cost-effectiveness in this case (according to the second equimarginal principle) requires that that target be met (ten fish removed) and the marginal costs of each method be equal. We know that $q_1 + q_2 + q_3 = 10$ and that $MC_1 = MC_2 = MC_3$. The key is to reduce this to one equation with one unknown. Since $MC_1 = MC_2$ we know that $\$10q_1$ will equal $\$5q_2$, or $q_1 = .5q_2$. Similarly, $MC_2 = MC_3$, so $\$5q_2 = \$2.5q_3$ or $_3 = 2q_2$. Substituting these values into the first equation yields $5q_2 + 1q_2 + 2q_2 = 10$. So $q_2 = 10/3.5 = 2.86$ (to two decimal places). That means $q_1 = 1.43$ and $q_3 = 5.72$. (The fact that this adds to 10.01 rather than 10.00 is due to rounding.)

b All three of these methods have a marginal cost that increases with the amount removed. Thus the cost of removing the first fish for each is cheaper than removing the second fish with that method, and so on. Consider the marginal cost of removing the last fish if all fish are removed by method three. In that case the marginal cost would be $2.5 × 10 or $25. Notice that the cost-effective allocation, the cost of removing the last fish when the marginal costs are equal (using q_1 for the calculation) is $10 × $1.43 = $14.30. In the case of increasing marginal costs using a combination is much cheaper.

c In this case you would only use method three because the marginal cost of removing each fish would be $2.5. This is lower than the *MC* for method 1 ($10) and lower than the *MC* for method 2 ($5). Note that the marginal costs only have to be equal for the methods that are actually used. The marginal costs for unused methods will be higher.

3 Since the benefit cost test requires that the present value of benefits be greater than the present value of the costs, we can find the maximum allowable current cost by calculating the present value of the benefits. This can be calculated as $\$500{,}000{,}000{,}000/(1 + r)^{50}$ where *r* is either 0.10 or 0.02. Whereas with a 10 percent discount rate the present value is approximately $4.3 billion, with a 2 percent discount rate it is approximately $185.8 billion. Clearly the size of the discount rate matters a lot in determining efficient current expenditures to resolve a long-range problem.

Chapter 5

1 In order to maximize net benefits, Coast Guard oil-spill prevention enforcement activity should be increased until the marginal benefit of the last unit equals the marginal cost of providing that unit. Efficiency requires that the level of the activity be chosen so as to equate marginal benefit with marginal cost. When marginal benefits exceed marginal cost (as in this example), the activity should be expanded.

2 a According to the figures given, the per-life cost of the standard for unvented space heaters lies well under the implied value of life estimates given in the chapter, while per-life cost implied by the proposed standard for formaldehyde lies well over those estimates. In benefit-cost terms, the allocation of resources to fixing unvented space heaters should be increased, while the formaldehyde standard should be relaxed somewhat to bring the costs back into line with the benefits.

b Efficiency requires that the marginal benefit of a life saved in government programs (as determined by the implied value of a human life in that context) should be equal to the marginal cost of saving that life. Marginal costs should be equal only if the marginal benefits are equal and, as we saw in the chapter, risk valuations (and hence the implied value of human life) depend on the risk context, so it is unlikely they are equal across all government programs.

3 a The total willingness to pay for this risk reduction is $200 million ($50 per person × 4 million exposed people.) The expected number of lives saved would be 40 (1/100,000 risk of premature death × 4,000,000 exposed population). The implied value of a statistical life would be $5,000,000 ($200,000,000 total willingness to pay/40 lives saved).

b The program is expected to save 160 lives ((6/100,000 – 2/100,000) × 4,000,000). According to the value of a statistical life in (a), the program will have more benefits than costs as long as it costs no more than $800,000,000 ($5,000,000 value per life × 160 lives saved).

Chapter 6

1 a Carbon reduction credits are generally created in developing countries that do not have a cap on their emissions. Since their purpose is to be used as one means of complying with emissions limits imposed by a cap, they have no value in the country of origin. Making them transferable

across national boundaries allows them to be sold to the highest bidder. This transferability provides incentives for the credit supplier to create the credits and to sell them to the highest bidders. They buyers who acquire the credits are likely to have the most to gain from their acquisition. Efficiency is enhanced because both buyer and seller gain from the transaction and so net benefits are increased.

b Conservation banking allows landowners to fulfill their conservation obligations on one site by acquiring the requisite conservation entitlements from a much larger project on another site. If these entitlements were not transferable from one site to another, the original owner would have to fulfill the obligation on her own land. Because that approach would likely be smaller in scale, typically would involve less suitable, fragmented habitat, and would be more expensive, transferability allows the obligation to be met with lower cost and at a better (less fragmented) scale, while making more appropriate habitat available to the endangered species.

2 With a rise in demand in the recreational fishery its members are likely to want to increase their catch shares. In the absence of inter-sector transferability this is likely to occur only if an administrative process changes the historical catch shares to allocate more to the recreational fishery and less to the commercial fishery. Any such change is likely to be opposed by the commercial fishery members since each share transferred represents a monetary loss for them. With inter-sector transferability, however, the recreational fishery members would have to buy the additional shares. They would do this by offering a higher price for catch shares, resulting in a shift in some shares from the commercial to a recreational fishery. Transferability reduces conflict because the transactions are voluntary and in this case the sellers gain, not lose.

Chapter 7

1 a The maximum sustainable yield is obtained when the marginal benefit of an additional reduction in the population size is zero: $20P - 400 = 0$ or $P = 20{,}000$ tons. The maximum sustainable yield can then be calculated using the g equation: $g = 4(20) - 0.1(20)^2 = 40$ tons.

b The efficient sustained yield can be found by setting marginal cost equal to marginal benefit: $20P - 400 - 2(160 - P)$; therefore, $P = 32.7$, which is a larger population than the one that would produce the maximum sustainable yield.

2 a No, despite the fact that this approach yields the efficient sustainable yield, this would not be an efficient solution. Net benefits would not be maximized because costs would be too high. Everyone would have an incentive to capture as large a share of the quota for him- or herself as quickly as possible. This would lead to excessively large boats and would not guarantee that the fishermen who could catch the fish most cheaply would do the harvesting. The net benefits would be smaller than possible.

b Yes, this would be efficient. This quota system creates exclusive property rights and, therefore, eliminates the need to catch as much as possible and as soon as possible. Each fisherman can proceed on the most individually appropriate schedule because his or her share of the catch is guaranteed. Since the need to rush harvesting is eliminated, the need for excessively large boats is also eliminated. Fishermen with high harvesting costs would find it in their interest to sell their quotas to fishermen with low harvesting costs in order to maximize their return from their quota. These transfers guarantee that the fish are caught by those with the lowest harvesting costs, so net benefits are maximized.

3 The increase in the license fee is represented as a parallel upward shift of the total cost line, whereas the per-unit tax on effort is represented as a leftward rotation of the total cost curve around the zero-effort point. The latter increases the marginal cost of fishing effort, while the former has no effect on the marginal cost.

In the private-property fishery, the license fee will have no effect on effort (unless it is so high as to make fishing unprofitable, in which case the effort will drop to zero), while the tax on effort will unambiguously reduce effort.

In the free-access fishery, both will reduce effort by exactly the same amount. (Remember, in the free-access fishery the equilibrium occurs where total cost equals total benefit. Since these two policy instruments raise the same revenue, both affect total cost by the same amount.)

4 When trying to reduce the degree of inefficiency from an open-access fishery, a regulation that increases the marginal cost of fishing effort by banning certain types of gear would be less efficient than a tax on effort. Although they both rotate the total cost of effort upward, the tax imposes a transfer cost, which is compatible with efficiency because it does not waste net benefits, and the gear restriction is incompatible with efficiency because in this case the net benefits are simply lost, not merely transferred.

5 a In answering this question remember that the benefits are defined as price times the quantity of fish harvested. A fall in the price of fish would be reflected as a movement inward of that benefit curve.

In the typical economic model of an efficient fishery, a fall in the price of fish would generally result in a smaller sustainable harvest. The efficient level of effort is determined where $MB = MC$. A fall in the price of fish lowers MB but leaves MC unchanged. The only way to reestablish $MB = MC$ is by increasing MB by lowering effort, which, because the efficient point is to the left of the maximum sustained yield, would lower the sustainable harvest.

b If the fishery allows free access, the effect is a bit more complex. Remember that for a free-access fishery the equilibrium level of effort occurs where $TB = TC$. In this case, because the TB curve has shifted downward, the effort level is reduced. That effect is the same as in (a). However, in this case, because the free-access equilibrium is normally to the right of the maximum sustained yield effort level, lowering the effort level means a higher sustained harvest. In essence, in this case, taking the pressure off the fish population allows that population to experience more sustained growth, which means that more fish can be caught with less effort.

6 a This change is such that the after curve has a flatter slope but a higher intercept with the Y-axis. For the static efficient level of effort, where $MB = MC$, the MC would have fallen. Reestablishing $MB = MC$ would be accomplished by expanding effort (thereby, lowering MB – remember MB is the tangent to [or slope of] the TB curve) until it once again equaled MC. Increasing effort on this side of the maximum sustained yield point would necessarily *increase* the size of the sustained harvest.

b In a free-access fishery, since the total cost is lower after the change, effort would expand. However, since this level of effort is to the right of the maximum sustained yield point, this increased effort would result in a smaller sustained yield.

Chapter 8

1 Although the cooperative outcome would be collectively preferred, it is not the most likely outcome due to the free-rider effect. Although collectively nations would be better off if everyone cooperated, individual nations can well be better off if they choose not to join the agreement. This paradox about the divergence between individual and collective incentives can arise because non-joiners can still obtain any of the benefits of the agreement and avoid the abatement cost obligations that accrue to those who join.

Chapter 9

1 The paper company. The high-cost energy is appropriately assigned to the five paper machines because that is the energy cost that would be eliminated if the machines were shut down. The company would not shut down all energy sources in proportion; it would shut down the most expensive sources. In making a shutdown decision, therefore, it is essential that the machines in question cover the cost of the energy that would be saved if the machines were shut down; otherwise, the company is losing money.

2 Peaking plants run only a small percentage of the time, so the capital expenditures remain unused most of the time. Operating costs are incurred only when they are needed. It makes sense, therefore, for utilities to design peaking plants so as to keep capital costs as low as possible, even if it means incurring higher operating cost. Base-load plants, on the other hand, run almost continuously, so the capital costs are prorated over a very large number of kilowatt-hours and therefore are less of a burden.

3 The existence of a renewable energy credit market would lower the compliance costs associated with meeting a renewable portfolio standard by providing more flexibility to compliance units. For example, without such a market utilities would have to ensure that they supplied the requisite amount of renewable power within their market area regardless of whether that market area was suitable for that renewable power or not. With a renewable energy credit market, producers can create the renewable power in those areas that are most suitable (e.g., have the requisite wind flow, water flow, or solar flux) and sell any excess to jurisdictions that could only generate their own renewable power at a much higher cost. Substituting this more efficiently produced (and hence lower-cost) power for the more inefficiently produced (and hence higher-cost) power allows the standard to be met at a lower cost.

4 Incorporating national security concerns, but ignoring climate change impact means that domestic production is determined by the intersection of S_{d1} with P_{w2} and total consumption is determined by the intersection of P_{w2} with domestic demand. Note that this results in a lower price level (P_{w2} *rather than* P_{w3}), more domestic production (since domestic producers are ignoring the climate-change impact), and more domestic consumption (due to the lower price).

5 a When comparing two bulbs that give the same amount of light, you would need to specify: (1) the planning horizon (how many years will be covered by the analysis), (2) the cost of each type of bulb, (3) how much the bulbs can be expected to be used on average per year, (4) how long the bulbs will last before they need to be replaced, (5) how much electricity is used by each type of bulb, and (6) the per kilowatt-hour cost of the electricity. The planning horizon would be no longer than the useful life of an LED bulb. Each year in the planning horizon would be a column and each row would be either one of the data items used in the calculation or the results of the calculations for that year – two rows would contain the amount spent on the purchase of bulbs each year for each type of bulb, another two rows would contain the amount spent on electricity to run each bulb during the periods of use and the two primary rows would contain the present value of cost of each bulb for that year. The present value of cost for each bulb would be found by summing the individual year present value results over all the years of the planning horizon. The most cost- effective bulb would be the one that has the lowest present value of cost over that planning horizon.

b It depends crucially on which component is changed. Changing the monthly charge would affect both bulb calculations the same and hence not change the difference between them. Changing the kilowatt-hour charge, however, would hit the incandescent bulb much harder since that type of bulb consumes more electricity. Therefore an increase in the kilowatt-hour charge would relatively discourage incandescent bulbs and encourage LED bulbs.

6 Yes, you would expect the magnitude of interest rates to affect the decision, especially for those who borrow the money to finance the purchase. Not only does it increase the financing cost of purchasing the heat pump, but this interest rate would typically be used as the discount rate in calculating the cost-effectiveness of the purchase. A higher discount rate lowers the relative importance of the energy savings in the decision (since they are spread out over the future years, whereas the cost of the purchase occurs in the first year).

Chapter 10

1 The emissions charge equalizes marginal cost, a required condition for cost-effectiveness. The subsidies induce utilities to choose options with a higher marginal cost. By equalizing their after-subsidy marginal costs, utilities will minimize their outlays. This will not minimize total costs of control, since a greater reliance on carbon-capture technologies will result than would be cost-effective.

2 High revenues in this context arise from a combination of high charges and large amounts of uncontrolled emissions. This circumstance arises when the marginal cost of control function rises steeply at relatively low levels of control. Since the charge is equal to the marginal cost of control, high marginal control costs imply a high charge rate. Furthermore, if the function rises steeply at relatively low levels of control, then there are large amounts of emissions to which this high rate of charge is applied. Multiplying a high charge times a large amount of uncontrolled emissions yields high revenues.

3 a *Uncertain.* Although in most circumstances being discussed this would be true (since a tax would internalize the external costs associated with the damages caused by greenhouse gases), it does depend on the level of the tax. It is possible to set a tax rate so high as to force the benefits from its imposition to be lower than the costs.

b *True.* Regional systems control only emitters in their jurisdictions, so unless all possible regions have control systems in place some emitters will remain uncontrolled. Leakage results from the flow of business from controlled entities to uncontrolled entities (because they can produce at lower cost and, hence, charge lower prices). This flow of business from controlled to uncontrolled emitters results in an increase in emissions that at least partially offsets the reductions achieved within the region. A truly global system that included all emitters in the same emissions trading system or facing the same greenhouse gas emissions tax would exempt no one and hence eliminate the problem of leakage.

4 a Since $P_A = MC_A$ and $P_B = MC_B$ at the level of reduction where each domestic cap is met, the price would be \$10 in Country A and \$40 in Country B. Each country would be reducing 40 tons.

b In the linked case $P = MC_A = MC_B$ because allowance can flow from one market to the other until the prices are equalized. Because Country A can abate at a fixed marginal cost of \$10, that will be the *MC* and the price for both markets. (Can you see why?) Achieving the desired 60 tons overall reduction implies that Country B will abate 10 tons ($MC_B = \$1 \times 10 = \$10$) and Country A will abate 50 ($MC_A = \$10$) tons. Thus Country A would use 20 tons of its 50 ton abatement to satisfy its cap and export the remaining 30 tons of allowances to Country B. Country B would apply its 10 ton reduction to its cap and import 30 tons of abatement allowances from Country A.

Chapter 11

1 a The chapter notes that both approaches involve upward sloping supply curves. The cost-effective mix requires marginal control costs to be equal. If you want to think of this graphically go back to Figure 3.1 and assume that the two curves in that figure reflect the marginal cost

curve for mitigation activity (from the left-hand axis) and the marginal cost curve for adaptation activity (drawn from the right-hand axis). Note that the cost-effective allocation where the two curves are equal) is the point where the two curves cross. This point normally would involve some of both activities.

b The only time the curves would not cross is when the marginals costs of one of these approaches is uniformly lower *for all levels of activity* than the marginal cost of *any* activity of the other approach. In that admittedly unusual case it would make sense to only use the activity that always has the uniformly lower marginal costs.

Chapter 12

1 a Labeling has the virtue that it seems to be politically feasible, and it can encourage a more fuel-efficient new vehicle fleet. However, it only affects new cars and it has no effect on how many miles the cars are driven. Furthermore, as we have noted in earlier chapters, labeling works best when it affects attributes that directly affect consumers. Saving energy certainly directly affects consumers, but some of the benefits of this approach, particularly those relating to national security and climate change, are externalities and are therefore probably not likely to be completely internalized by prospective purchasers. These disadvantages would compromise its effectiveness.

b Older fuel-inefficient vehicles do typically disproportionately contribute to the problem, and therefore they are a useful target of opportunity, but they are still only part of the problem. By itself, this strategy does not internalize the large number of other externalities associated with the purchase of new automobiles or reducing emissions from the fleet of automobiles that are not old enough to be affected by this program. Furthermore, many of these older automobiles are owned by lower-income households. Depending on how these vehicles are retired (not compensating owners, for example), taking away their transportation could impose a considerable burden on the poor (particularly the rural poor who have no mass transit option).

c Pay-as-you-drive insurance *could* probably be a useful complement because, unlike the others, it focuses on internalizing some of the externalities associated with miles driven. Thus it addresses a component that would not otherwise be addressed.

2 a From a social point of view, efficiency would require that the marginal premium per mile driven include all costs that are specifically related to miles driven. These would include potential accident damage, contributions to climate change (greenhouse gas emissions), and national security damages (stemming from import dependence).

b A private company would be concerned about recovering the costs related to the claims it will have to pay out – accident damages, not the others. Internalizing the other damages would require the participation of the government.

Chapter 13

1 a With these *constant* marginal cost functions, cost-effectiveness is achieved by securing as much reduction as possible from the facility or facilities with the lowest marginal cost. In this case, that means securing the first 10 units of reduction from the first facility and the next 5 from the second facility.

b The total variable cost in this case is simply the sum of the marginal costs for each unit of reduction. Therefore, the cost from reducing at the first facility would be \$30 (10 units × \$3) and the cost of the reductions at the second unit would be \$20 (5 units × \$4), so the total variable cost would be \$50.

c The total variable cost if all 3 facilities were forced to reduce *5* units would be $15 (5 units × $3) + $20 (5 units × $4) + $25 (5 units × $5) = $60. The extra $10 over the cost-effective allocation results from the fact that this allocation of responsibility substitutes *5* units at $*5* for the 5 units at $3. The extra $20 per unit reduced accounts for the additional $10.

Chapter 14

1 One main difference in practice between an approach relying on performance bonds and one imposing strict liability for cleanup costs on any firm for a toxic substance spill is that the former requires money to be deposited in an escrow account before the operation commences. For the firm, the performance bond ties up capital for the period the bond is in effect, a cost it does not incur with strict liability. For the government, a performance bond assures the availability of funds to clean up the toxic substance immediately should the need arise. This availability can make a significant difference if the firm responsible for the spill turns out to not have sufficient funds to be able to fund the cleanup (this is known as the "judgment-proof firm" problem). In that case imposing strict liability would have little effect since the firm would be unable to fulfill its legal obligations.

2 Informing the consumer about any toxic substances used in the manufacture of a product is likely to represent a move toward efficiency for those risks actually borne by consumers. However, risks borne by the workers making the product or the workers recycling or disposing of the product after its useful life are externalities to the consumer, and informing the consumer is not likely to internalize those risks sufficiently to produce an efficient outcome.

Glossary

Absorptive Capacity – The ability of the environment to absorb pollutants without incurring damage.

Acute Toxicity – The degree of harm caused to living organisms as a result of short-term exposure to a substance.

Aerobic – Water containing sufficient dissolved oxygen concentrations to sustain organisms requiring oxygen.

Agglomeration Bonus – A voluntary incentive mechanism that is designed to protect endangered species and biodiversity by reuniting fragmented habitat across private land in a manner that minimizes landowner resistance.

Alternative Fuels – Unconventional fuels such as ethanol and methanol.

Ambient Standards – Legal ceilings placed on the concentration level of specific pollutants in the air, soil, or water.

Anaerobic – Water containing insufficient dissolved oxygen concentrations to sustain life.

Anthropocentric – Human-centered.

Asset – An entity that has value and forms part of the wealth of the owner.

Asymmetric Information – A source of market failure that can arise when all of the economic agents involved in a transaction do not have the same level of information.

Automobile Certification Program – The testing of automobiles at the factory for conformity to federal emissions standards.

Average-Cost Pricing – When prices charged for resource use are based on average costs. (Sometimes used by regulatory agencies to ensure that regulated firms make zero economic profits, but it is not normally efficient.)

Base-Load Plants – Electric generators that produce virtually all the time. (They generally have high fixed costs, but low variable costs.)

Benefit-Cost Analysis – An analysis of the quantified gains (benefits) and losses (costs) of an action.

Benefit Transfer – Transferring benefits estimates developed in one context to another context as a substitute for developing entirely new estimates.

Best Available Technology Economically Achievable (BAT) – A more stringent effluent standard than best practicable control technology, which has been defined by the EPA as "the very best control and treatment measures that have been or are capable of being achieved."

Biochemical Oxygen Demand (BOD) – The measure of the oxygen demand placed on a stream by any particular volume of effluent.

Block Pricing – A form of pricing in which the charge per unit consumption is held fixed until a threshold is reached where a new per-unit charge is imposed for all consumption beyond the threshold. For increasing block pricing, the per-unit charge after the threshold is higher.

Cap-and-Trade System – A form of emissions trading where the government specifies a cap on emissions and allocates allowances to emission sources, either by gifting or auctioning, based upon this cap. These allowances are freely transferable among sources.

Carbon Budget – the amount of additional CO_2e emissions that could be injected into the atmosphere without causing the temperature increase to exceed the international target level (2° or 1½°C).

Carbon Tax – A policy that would control climate modification by placing a per-unit emissions tax on the carbon content of carbon-emitting sources.

Cartel – A collusive agreement among producers to restrict production and raise prices. In this case the group tends to act like a monopolist and to share the gains from collusive behavior.

Chapter 11 – A provision in the North American Free Trade Agreement that protects investors from government regulations that decrease the value of their investments.

Chronic Toxicity – The degree of harm caused to living organisms as a result of continued or prolonged exposure to a substance.

Clean Development Mechanism – An emissions trading mechanism set up under the Kyoto Protocol that allows industrialized countries to invest in greenhouse-gas-reducing strategies in developing countries and to use the resulting certified reductions to meet their assigned amount obligations.

Coase Theorem – A remarkable proposition, named after Nobel Laureate Ronald Coase, that suggests that in the absence of transaction costs, an efficient allocation will result regardless of the property rule chosen by the court.

Command and Control – Controlling pollution via a system of government-mandated legal restrictions. Under this approach the government has the responsibility not only for setting the environmental targets, but also for allocating the source-specific responsibilities for meeting those targets.

Common-Pool Resource – A resource that is shared among several users.

Common-Property Regimes – A property rights system in which resources are managed collectively by a group.

Comparative Advantage – In trade theory a comparative advantage prevails for products that have the lowest opportunity cost of production.

Compensating Variation – A method for evaluating the welfare effects of a price increase. It is the increase in income it would take to make the consumer as well off as he or she was before the price increase.

Competitive Equilibrium – The resource allocation at which supply and demand are equal when all agents are price takers.

Composite Asset – An asset made up of many interrelated parts.

Composition of Demand Effect – Shifts in demand brought about by changes in the relative cost of inputs. (For example, rising costs of ores coupled with stable prices for recycled inputs could make the products of firms relying more heavily on recycled inputs relatively less expensive and hence more attractive to consumers.)

Congestion Externalities – Higher costs imposed on others resulting from an attempt to use resources at a higher-than-optimal capacity. Commonly used with reference to traffic flows.

Congestion Pricing – Charging higher tolls during peak hours to discourage vehicle traffic (and the resulting air pollution) and encourage public transit ridership.

Conjoint Analysis – A survey-based technique that derives willingness to pay by having respondents choose between alternate states of the world where each state of the world has a specified set of attributes and a price.

Conjunctive Use – The combined management of surface and groundwater to optimize their joint use and to minimize the adverse effects of excessive reliance on a single source.

Constant Dollar – Output measures that have been purged of increases due to price rises.

Consumer Surplus – The value of a good or service to consumers above the price they have to pay for it. Calculated as the area under the demand curve that lies above the price.

Consumption – The amount of goods and services consumed by households.

Consumptive Use – In water law this refers to water that is removed from the source without any return.

Contingent Ranking – A valuation technique that asks respondents to rank alternative situations involving different levels of environmental amenity (or risk). These rankings can then be used to establish trade-offs between more of the environmental amenity (or risk) and less (or more) of other goods that can be expressed in monetary terms.

Contingent Valuation – A survey method used to ascertain willingness to pay for services or environmental amenities.

Conventional Pollutants – Relatively common substances found in most parts of the country, and presumed to be dangerous only in high concentrations.

Corporate Average Fuel Economy (CAFE) Standards – Minimum average miles-per-gallon standards imposed on each auto manufacturer for new vehicles sold in a specific vehicle class. Autos are in one class and SUVs and light trucks in another.

Criteria Pollutants – Conventional air pollutants with ambient standards set by the Environmental Protection Agency (includes sulfur oxides, particulate matter, carbon monoxide, ozone, nitrogen dioxide, and lead).

Degradable – Pollutants that are capable of being decomposed chemically or biologically.

Demand Curve – A function that relates the quantity of a commodity or service consumers wish to purchase to the price of that commodity.

Differentiated Regulation – Imposing more stringent regulations on one class of sources (such as new vehicles) than on others (such as used vehicles).

Discount Rate – The rate used to convert a stream of benefits and/or costs into its present value.

Dissolved Oxygen – Oxygen that naturally occurs in water and is usable by living organisms.

Divisible Consumption – One person's consumption of a good diminishes the amount available for others. (For example, if I use some timber to build my house, you receive no benefits from that timber.)

Double Dividend – A second welfare advantage that accrues to revenue-raising pollution control policy instruments (over and above the welfare gain due to pollution reduction) when the revenue is used to reduce distortionary taxes (thereby reducing the welfare losses associated with those taxes).

Dynamic Efficiency – The chief normative economic criterion for choosing among various allocations occurring at different points in time. An allocation satisfies the dynamic efficiency criterion if it maximizes the present value of net benefits that could be received from all possible ways of allocating those resources over time.

Economies of Scale – The percentage increase in output exceeds the percentage increase in all inputs. Equivalently, average cost falls as output expands.

Ecosystem Services – Services supplied by nature that directly benefit at least one person.

Ecotourism – A form of tourism that appeals to ecologically minded travelers. It can serve as a source of revenue to protect the local ecosystem.

Efficient Pricing – A system of prices that supports an efficient allocation of resources. Generally, efficient pricing is achieved when prices are equal to private and social marginal cost.

Emission Charge – A charge levied on emitters for each unit of a pollutant emitted into the air or water.

Emission Standard – A legal limit placed on the amount of a pollutant an individual source may emit.

Emissions Allowance System – A type of transferable permit system in which the permits are defined in terms of the right to emit a stipulated amount of emissions. This design can be used to achieve a cost-effective allocation of control responsibility for uniformly mixed pollutants.

Emissions Banking – Firms are allowed to store emissions reduction credits or allowances for subsequent use or sale.

Emissions Reduction Credit (ERC) – Part of a transferable permits system. Any source reducing emissions beyond required levels can receive a credit for excess reductions. These can be banked for future use or sold to other sources.

Emissions Trading – An economic incentive-based alternative to the command-and-control approach to pollution control. Under emissions trading, a regulatory agency specifies an allowable level of pollution that will be tolerated and allocates emission authorizations among sources of pollution. Total emissions authorized by these allowances cannot exceed the allowable level. Pollution sources are free to buy, sell, or otherwise trade allowances.

Energy Efficiency Investment – An investment that is designed to reduce the amount of energy input required to supply a given amount of useful energy services such as lighting or heating.

Enforceability – Property rights should be secure from involuntary seizure or encroachment from others.

Entropy – Amount of energy not available for work.

Environmental Sustainability – This definition of sustainability is fulfilled if the physical stocks of designated resources do not decline over time.

Equivalent Variation – A method for evaluating the welfare effects of a price increase. It is the reduction in income that would leave a consumer indifferent between accepting the income reduction or accepting the price increase.

Eutrophic – A body of water containing an excess of nutrients.

Exclusivity – All benefits and costs accrued as a result of owning and using the resources should accrue to the owner, and only the owner, either directly or indirectly by sale to others.

Expected Present Value of Net Benefits – The sum over possible outcomes of the present value of net benefits for a policy, where each future outcome is weighted by its probability of occurrence.

Expected Value – In situations where the value of a resource depends on which of several outcomes might prevail, the expected value of a resource is the sum over all outcomes of the likelihood of each outcome multiplied by the value that would prevail in that outcome.

External Diseconomy – The affected party is damaged by an externality. (For example, my well is polluted by chemicals from a factory next door.)

External Economy – The affected party is benefited by an externality. (For example, my neighbor decides not to develop a wetland that serves as a recharge area for my water supply.)

Externality – The welfare of some agent, either a firm or household, depends on the activities of some other agent. The externality can take the form of either an external economy or external diseconomy.

Feebates – A system that combines taxes on purchases of new high-emitting vehicles with subsidies for new purchases of low-emitting vehicles. The revenue from the taxes is supposed to serve as the primary source of funding for the subsidies.

First Law of Thermodynamics – Neither energy nor matter can be created or destroyed.

Fixed Cost – Costs that do not vary with output.

Fleet Average Standard – Used in the Corporate Average Fuel Economy Standards, this standard is imposed on the sales weighted average of vehicles sold rather than forcing every vehicle to meet it.

Free-Rider Effect – When a good exhibits both the consumptive indivisibility and nonexcludability properties, consumers may enjoy the benefits of goods purchased by others without paying anything themselves. (For example, countries that decide not to take any steps to control global warming can "free ride" on the steps taken by others.)

Fuel-Economy Standards – A government program that mandates how many miles per gallon a manufacturer's new cars must achieve by specific deadlines.

Full-Cost Pricing – In water management this pricing system seeks to recover not only all of the costs of providing water and sewer services but also the cost of replacing the depreciated capital in older water systems.

Global Environmental Facility – An international organization, loosely connected to the World Bank, that provides loans and grants to developing countries to facilitate projects that contribute to solving such global problems as protecting the oceans, preserving biodiversity, protecting the ozone layer, and controlling climate modification. The fund uses the "marginal external cost" rule to allocate funds.

Government Failure – An inefficiency produced by some government action.

Greenhouse Gases – Global pollutants that contribute to climate modification by absorbing the long-wave (infrared) radiation, thereby trapping heat that would otherwise radiate into space. (Includes carbon dioxide, methane, and chlorofluorocarbons, among others.)

Green Paradox – An effect that occurs when a program which is designed to reduce emissions, paradoxically either speeds up the flow of emissions or increases the total amount of emissions.

Groundwater – Subsurface water that occurs beneath a water table in soils, rocks, or fully saturated geological formations.

Groundwater Contamination – Pollution that leaches into a water-saturated region.

Health Threshold – A standard to be defined with a margin of safety sufficiently high that no adverse health effects would be suffered by any member of the population as long as the pollutant concentration is no higher than the standard.

Hedonic Property Values – The values of environmental amenities (or risks) that are determined from differences in the values of property exposed to different levels of the amenities (or risks).

Hedonic Wage Studies – A valuation technique that allows the value of an environmental amenity (or risk) to be determined from differences in the values of wages paid to workers exposed to different levels of the amenity (or risk).

Hypothetical Bias – Ill-considered responses that may arise in surveys based on contrived rather than actual situations or choices.

Impact Analysis – An analysis that attempts to make explicit, to the extent possible, the consequences of proposed actions. May mix quantitative with qualitative information and monetized with nonmonetized information.

Income Elasticity – Measures the percentage change in demand for commodities or services in response to a 1 percent change in income.

Individual Transferable Quotas (ITQs) – A means of protecting a fishery and the income derived from it by limiting the number of fish caught. Individual fishermen are allocated quotas that entitle them to portions of the authorized total allowable catch. These quotas can be transferred to other fishermen or used to legalize their harvest.

Indivisible Consumption – One person's consumption of a good does not diminish the amount available for others. (For example, the benefits I receive from controlling greenhouse gases do not diminish the benefits you receive.)

Information Bias – Arises when contingent valuation survey respondents are forced to value attributes with which they have little or no experience.

Intangible Benefits – Benefits that cannot be easily assigned a monetary value.

Interactive Resources – The size of the resource stock is determined jointly by biological considerations and actions taken by humans.

Isoquant – A curve showing possible combinations of two inputs that produce the same output level.

Junior Claims – Used in water management, this class of rights for specified amounts of water is subordinate to senior claims. In times of water scarcity, these rights become valid once the senior claims have been fulfilled.

Kyoto Protocol – An international agreement to control greenhouse gases that went into effect in February 2005.

Law of Comparative Advantage – A country or region should specialize in the production of those commodities for which it has a comparative advantage.

Law of Diminishing Marginal Productivity – In the presence of a fixed factor, successively larger additions of variable factors will eventually lead to a decline in the marginal productivity of the variable factors.

Law of Diminishing Returns – The relationship between inputs and outputs when some inputs are increased and others are fixed, eventually leading to the decreased productivity of the variable inputs.

Lead Phaseout Program – A transferable permit program designed to lower the costs of phasing out lead in gasoline as well as to eliminate lead earlier than otherwise would have been possible. It allocated transferable rights to use lead in refining gasoline to refiners. The number of rights declined over time until at the end of the program they expired.

Liability Rules – Rules used in courts that award monetary compensation from an injurer to an injured party after damage has occurred.

Low-Emission Vehicles – A class of vehicles that emit fewer emissions per mile driven than conventional vehicles.

Marginal-Cost Pricing – Basing the prices charged for resource use upon marginal costs. (This pricing scheme is generally consistent with efficiency.)

Marginal Opportunity Cost – The additional cost of providing the last unit of a good as measured by what is given up.

Marginal User Cost – Present value of forgone future opportunity costs at the margin.

Marginal Willingness to Pay – The amount of money an individual is willing to pay for the last unit of a good or service.

Market Economy – An economic system in which resource allocation decisions are guided by prices that result from the voluntary production and purchasing decisions by private consumers and producers.

Market Failure – An inefficient allocation produced by a market economy.

Microgrid – A group of interconnected electrical loads and distributed energy resources with clearly defined boundaries that acts as a single controllable entity. Depending on the situation microgrids may be either connected to a larger electrical grid or operate completely independently.

Model – Formal or informal framework for analysis that highlights some areas of the problem in order to better understand complex relationships.

Monopoly – A situation in which the seller side of the market is dominated by a single producer.

Montreal Protocol – An international agreement to control ozone-depleting gases.

Multilateral Fund – A fund set up by the parties to the Montreal Protocol to help developing countries meet the phaseout requirements for ozone-depleting gases.

Myopia – Nearsightedness; excessive concern for the present.

Natural Capital – The endowment of environmental and natural resources.

Negligence – A doctrine in tort law suggesting that the party responsible for a tortious act owes a duty to the affected party to exercise due care. Failure to fulfill that duty can lead to a requirement for the injurer to pay compensation to the victim.

Net Benefit – The excess of benefits over costs resulting from some allocation.

Noncompliance Penalty – A charge used to reduce the profitability of noncompliance with pollution control requirements. It is designed to eliminate all the economic advantage gained from noncompliance.

Nonconsumptive Use – In water law this refers to a use that does not involve diverting the water from the source or that does not diminish its availability. (Swimming, for example.)

Nonexcludability – No individual or group can be excluded from enjoying the benefits a resource may confer, whether they contribute to its provision or not.

Nonpoint Sources – Diffuse water sources such as runoff from agricultural or developed land.

Nonrenewable Resources – Resources that cannot be reproduced during a human timescale, so their supply is considered finite and limited.

Nonuse (Passive-Use) Values – Resource values that arise from motivations other than personal use.

Normative Economics – The branch of economics that is concerned with evaluating the desirability of alternative resource allocations. It is concerned with "what ought to be."

Nutrient Sensitive Waters – Water bodies that have excessive levels of nutrients causing algal blooms, low oxygen levels, and increased fish kills.

Open-Access Resources – Common-pool resources with unrestricted access.

Opportunity Cost – The net benefit forgone because the resource providing the service can no longer be used in its next-most-beneficial use.

Optimal – Best or most favorable option.

Optimization Procedure – A systematic method for finding the optimal means of accomplishing an objective.

Option Value – The value people place on having the option to use a resource in the future.

Overallocation – More than the optimal level of a resource is dedicated to a given use or time period.

Oxygen Sag – A point of low dissolved oxygen concentration generally located around effluent injection points.

Ozone-Depleting Gases – Global pollutants that destroy the stratospheric ozone layer. (Includes chlorofluorocarbons and halons, among others.)

Pareto Optimality – An allocation such that no reallocation of resources could benefit any person without lowering the net benefits for at least one other person. (Named after economist Vilfredo Pareto.)

Pay-as-You-Drive (PAYD) Insurance – A system in which an individual's annual premium for automobile insurance is calculated by multiplying a rating factor times the number of miles driven. It is designed to reduce inefficiency by internalizing those costs of accidents that are related to the amount of driving.

Peaking Units – Those electricity-producing facilities used only during peak periods. (They generally have low fixed costs, but high variable costs.)

Peak-Load Pricing – Charging resource users during the peak period the higher cost of supplying resources during that period. The surcharge during the peak period is designed to cover the cost of expansion since the need to expand is triggered by increased demands during the peak period.

Peak Periods – Times of especially high electricity demand. (For example, the demand for electricity during the hottest part of the summer when air-conditioning is in heavy use.)

Pecuniary Externalities – External effects that are transmitted through higher prices. (For example, the value of my land increases because surrounding employers expand their operations, thereby creating a scarcity of housing in the immediate area.) Unlike most externalities, pecuniary externalities do not generally result in inefficient allocations.

Persistent Pollutants – Inorganic synthetic pollutants with complex molecular structures that are not effectively broken down in water.

Planning Horizon – The time period over which the benefits and costs are considered in time-related decisions. For a specific investment such as a power plant, for example, the planning horizon might correspond to the useful life of the project. For forestry, it could either correspond to the age of the stand of trees when harvested (the finite planning horizon) or extend forever (the infinite planning horizon).

Point Sources – Sources of pollution that discharge effluent through a readily identifiable emission point such as an outfall or discharge pipe. (Most industrial and municipal sources are point sources.)

Positive Economics – The branch of economics that is concerned with describing alternative resource allocations without forming a judgment as to their desirability. Concerned with "what is."

Present Value – The current discounted value of a stream of benefits and/or costs over time.

Present Value Criterion – Resources should be allocated to those uses that maximize the present value of the net benefits received from all possible uses of those resources.

Price Controls – The establishment of maximum or minimum prices by the government.

Primary Effects – The direct, measurable effects of an action.

Prior Appropriation Doctrine – Entitlements for water are allocated to the agent who diverts and first puts water to a beneficial use.

Private Marginal Cost – The cost of producing an additional unit of the resource that is borne by the producer.

Producer Surplus – The value of a good or service to producers above the cost to them of producing it. Calculated as the area below the demand curve that is above marginal cost.

Product Charges – A charge imposed on a product that is associated with emissions (such as a gasoline tax). This indirect form of controlling emissions is used when placing the charge directly on emissions proves difficult.

Property Rights – A bundle of entitlements defining the owner's rights, privileges, and limitations for use of the resource.

Property Rules – Legal rules that govern the initial allocation of entitlements. Valuation of the entitlements is left to the market.

Proposition 65 – A California law that requires companies producing, using, or transporting one or more of the specified substances in amounts over the "safe harbor" threshold to notify those who are potentially impacted.

Public Good – A resource characterized by nonexclusivity and indivisibility.

Real Resource Costs – As opposed to transfer costs, these are costs borne by both private parties and society as a whole because they involve the loss of net benefits, not merely their transfer.

Rebound Effect – An increase in consumption that results from an energy efficiency investment (i.e., lowers the amount of input energy necessary to product a given level of useful energy services). Examples including driving more miles after acquiring a fuel-efficient car or turning up the target temperature after making your house more energy efficient.

Regional Pollutants – Pollutants that can cause damage some distance from the emission source. (Examples include the precursors for acid rain and tropospheric ozone.)

Regressive Distribution – Net benefits from a policy received by various income groups represent a larger portion of the income of the rich than of the poor.

Regulatory Capture – When the actions of a regulatory agency become controlled by the private sector being regulated._

Renewable Energy Credit – An official record granted to producers of qualified renewable energy that can be sold separately from the energy to allow the recovery of the extra costs associated with renewable power. It can be used to prove compliance with a renewable portfolio standard.

Renewable Portfolio Standards – These standards specify enforceable targets and deadlines for producing specific proportions of electricity from renewable resources.

Renewable Resources – Resources that can be naturally regenerated over time on a human timescale.

Rent Seeking – The use of resources in lobbying and other activities directed at securing increased profits through protective regulation or legislation.

***Res Nullius* Regime** – A property rights system in which no one owns or exercises control over resources. Resources covered by this regime can usually be exploited on a first-come, first- served basis.

Return Flow – A term used in water management that refers to the unconsumed portion from an upstream user's water allocation that will eventually return to the watercourse (and, hence, be available to a downstream user).

Revenue-Neutral Tax or Fee – A government charge that does not add to the total government revenue. This can be achieved by such means as rebating the revenue back to households or lowering the rates on existing charges such that the decrease in revenue from those sources equals the increase in revenue from the revenue-neutral source, leaving total revenue unchanged.

Riparian Rights – Allocates the right to use water to the owner of the land adjacent to the water, as long as no adverse effects are imposed on other rights holders.

Risk-Free Cost of Capital – Rate of return earned on an investment when the risk of earning more or less than expected returns is zero.

Risk-Neutrality – An agent who has no preference between options that produce the same expected value.

Risk Premium – Additional rate of return required to compensate the owners of the capital when the expected and actual returns may differ. It represents compensation for a willingness to undertake some risk.

Scale Effects – How the size of an operation affects average costs.

Second Law of Thermodynamics – Entropy, the energy not available for work, increases.

Senior Claims – Used in water management, this class of claims entitles the holder to a priority for specified amounts of water. These rights have a higher priority in times of low water availability than junior claims.

Social Cost of Carbon – The additional economic damage that would accrue from emitting one more ton of CO_2 or CO_2e into the atmosphere.

Socialist Economy – A centrally planned economy where the means of production are controlled by the government.

Social Marginal Cost – The cost of producing an additional unit of the resource that is borne by society at large. Generally includes private marginal costs plus external marginal costs.

Starting-Point Bias – Arises when a contingent valuation survey respondent is asked to check off his or her answer from a predetermined range of possibilities and the answers depend on the range specified by the survey instrument.

Static Efficiency – The chief normative economic criterion for choosing among various allocations when time is not an important consideration. An allocation satisfies the static efficiency criterion if it maximizes the net benefits from all possible uses of the resource.

Stationary Source – An immobile pollution source. (Factories, for example, as opposed to automobiles.)

Statistically Significant – Observed differences are unlikely to result from pure chance.

Strategic Bias – A respondent provides a biased answer to a contingent valuation survey in order to influence a particular outcome.

Strategic Petroleum Reserve – A petroleum stockpile established by an importing nation to minimize the damage that could be done by an embargo imposed by a foreign supplier. It would serve as an alternative source of supply for a short period.

Stratosphere – The atmosphere that lies above the troposphere. It extends to about 31 miles above the earth's surface.

Suboptimal Allocation – An allocation that could be rearranged so that one or more people could be made better off while no one was made worse off. (Also called an inefficient allocation.)

Subsidies – Payments or tax breaks from the government that make the cost to the buyer lower than the marginal cost of production.

Substitution – Replacing one resource with another. May occur, for example, when the original resource is no longer cost-effective or is diminishing in quantity or quality.

Sulfur Allowance Program – A transferable permit program targeted at electric utilities that was designed to reduce sulfur emissions from 1980 levels by 10 million tons. Involves an auction and an emissions cap.

Surface Water – The freshwater in rivers, lakes, and reservoirs that collects and flows on the earth's surface.

Sustainability Criterion – A criterion for judging the fairness of allocations of resources among generations. Generally requires that resource use by any generation should not exceed a level that would prevent future generations from achieving a level of well-being at least as great.

Sustainable Yield – Harvest levels of biological resources (e.g., fish or forests) that can be maintained indefinitely, achieved by setting the annual harvest equal to the annual net growth of the population.
Tangible Benefits – Benefits that can reasonably be assigned a monetary value.
Technological Progress – An innovation in process or technique that allows more output or services to be derived from a given set of inputs.
Thermal Pollution – Pollution caused by the injection of heat into a watercourse.
Third Parties – Victims who have no contractual relationship to a pollution source. (They are neither consumers of the product produced by the source nor employed by the source.)
Total Cost – The sum of fixed and variable costs.
Toxicity – The degree of harm caused to living organisms as a result of exposure to the substance.
Toxic Release Inventory – A system for reporting toxic emissions releases from individual facilities in the United States. By making the data public, it was designed to warn communities of the risks they face and to encourage reductions prior to regulation.
Transaction Costs – Costs incurred in attempting to complete transactions.
Transferability – Property rights can be exchanged among owners on a voluntary basis.
Transfer Cost – A cost to a private party that is not a cost to society as a whole, because it involves a transfer of net benefits from one private party to another.
Troposphere – The atmosphere that is closest to the earth. Its depth ranges from about ten miles over the equator to about five miles over the poles.
Two-Part Charge – As used in water management, this type of charge combines volume pricing with a monthly fee that doesn't vary with the amount used. The monthly fee is designed to help cover fixed costs.
Underallocation – Less-than-optimal levels of a resource are dedicated to a given use or time period.
Uniform Emission Charge – A charge on effluent that applies the same per-unit rate to all sources regardless of their size or location.
Usufruct Right – Holders of this right may use a resource (normally subject to restrictions), but do not have full ownership rights, such as the privilege of being able to sell it to someone else.
Variable Cost – Production costs that vary with output.
Volume Pricing – Making the cost of the service a function of the volume used. Used in both trash disposal and water distribution.
Welfare Measure – A measure that reflects whether economic activity increases or decreases society's well-being.
Zero Discharge – No emissions of the targeted pollutant are allowed.
Zero Emission Vehicle – Automobiles that directly emit no air pollutants. (Examples include vehicles powered by solar energy and fuel cells.)
Zoned Effluent Charge – A charge on effluent that applies different per-unit rates to sources depending on their location. Generally sources closer to, and upstream from, locations with more serious pollution problems face higher rates.

Index

Note: Page numbers in *italic* indicate a figure and page numbers in **bold** indicate a table on the corresponding page.

For Product Safety Concerns and Information please contact our EU
representative GPSR@taylorandfrancis.com
Taylor & Francis Verlag GmbH, Kaufingerstraße 24, 80331 München, Germany

www.ingramcontent.com/pod-product-compliance
Lightning Source LLC
LaVergne TN
LVHW061921140725
816116LV00005B/215